¡SATIRISTAS!

Billy Connolly Robi
Paul Krassner Step
te Randy Newma
ers Brothers Conan
g Stanhope Rosean
Judd Apatow Mike
n Jay Leno Janeane
Matt Stone Ver
Novello Michael M

!t
itbooks
AN IMPRINT OF HARPERCOLLINS PUBLISHERS

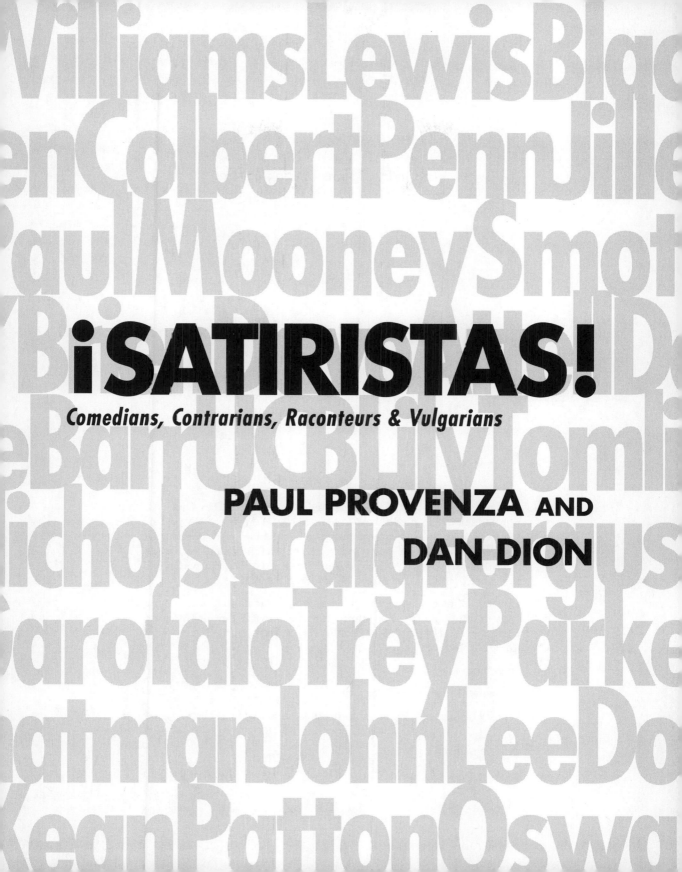

¡SATIRISTAS!

Comedians, Contrarians, Raconteurs & Vulgarians

PAUL PROVENZA AND
DAN DION

For George Denis Patrick Carlin

HarperCollins books may be purchased for educational, business, or sales promotional use. For information please write: Special Markets Department, HarperCollins Publishers, 10 East 53rd Street, New York, NY 10022.

FIRST EDITION

Designed by Paula Russell Szafranski

Library of Congress Cataloging-in-Publication Data has been applied for.

ISBN 978-0-06-185934-2

10 11 12 13 14 ov/wc 10 9 8 7 6 5 4 3 2 1

CONTENTS

Chase, Ackroyd, Belushi and Michaels in Elaine's kitchen, NYC. © Jonathan Becker 1976— *Saturday Night Live.*

Mike Meehan

Bob Rubin

PHOTOGRAPHER'S PREFACE

I've always respected the disrespectful. When I was a child, the hilarious impudence of Bugs Bunny, *Mad* magazine, and Hawkeye Pierce whet my appetite for the greater blasphemies of George Carlin and Lenny Bruce. When San Francisco became the flashpoint of the comedy boom of the eighties, I dove into the local scene with a zeal that most of my teenage peers had for music. But I wasn't interested in what was simply silly, derogatory, or observant. I wanted insight and bite, with savage wit and a scowl at authority and convention. Stand-up became my punk rock.

Twenty-five years after I saw my first live stand-up show at thirteen, seventeen years after I joined the staff of the Holy City Zoo comedy club at twenty-one, and after I've been its most prolific portrait artist for about ten years, this book is my love-letter to comedy.

A headshot differs from a portrait in that a good portrait captures the stature and spirit of its subject as a testament of who he or she is in the world. A headshot is a desperate cry for attention. It's an image designed to mask the subject's need for work and love with an attitude, gesture, or look that might be marketable.

MARC MARON

Many years after I started photographing comics, Marc Maron summed up the philosophy I'd never quite put into words. I came to recognize that my aesthetic was created in reaction against the world of hack headshots, and was forged by the ubiquitous black-and-white eight-by-tens of open-mouthed muggers that encircled most comedy clubs. Their banality made me all the more drawn to the engaged honesty of August Sander and the elegant composition of Arnold Newman.

I began to wed my two passions, comedy and photography, while on staff at the Holy City Zoo comedy club. I took two photos that changed the course of my career, and neither were portraits: Mike Meehan onstage, and Bob Rubin off. In the supposedly jovial world of comedy, both revealed a dark and brutal vision. Meehan said it was his favorite photo of himself, and Rubin said his hungover, daylight agony during a morning radio broadcast said all that needed to be said about stand-up.

I was inspired by their support, and recognized that there were other levels to these performers, which were rarely shown. I set out to create work that elevates the subject, and I think my portraits represent how I feel about comics: respectful, enamored, appreciative. I'm not asking the monkey to dance.

Jonathan Becker's portrait of young Lorne Michaels, Dan Aykroyd, Chevy Chase, and John Belushi from 1976, just as the country was hipping to their genius, served as a kind of high bar for me, and still does.

I will admit to not being a very "conceptual" photographer. While working with comedians would seem to be fertile ground for that kind of thing, I don't very often create gag photos, though there are some exceptions. I never want to make my subjects uncomfortable. Greg Proops told me that in his last shoot the photographer wanted to put him in giant shoes. I could feel his disdain, and knew that my smoky noir shot would certainly suit him better. Comics, by definition, need approval from the audience, but I want approval from *them*—the world's greatest critics.

In general, stand-up comics hate to do photo shoots, while sketch performers pose at the sound of the camera bag unzipping. Sometimes the challenge is to draw out their true character, or sometimes it's to tame the spaz. I don't think portraits necessarily need to have something *happening* in them. I'm more interested in showing who someone is than in a concept or joke. Famous comedians in particular are used to photographers wanting them to "just do something crazy!"—which is especially annoying to comics who view themselves as social commentators rather than clowns. When my subjects ask me, "What am I supposed to be doing?" I reply, "Nothing. Just be here." It manifests a stillness and re-

laxation, and I get to feel all Zen and shit.

I've often been told that I capture the "essence" of comics, which is a great compliment, and I've tried to break down why. My intimacy with the comedy world allows me to pick locations that are appropriate, but it is most influential in the edit, when I get to choose just one frame to encapsulate a comic mind. The great music photographer Jim Marshall taught me very early that the key to the guarded door of celebrity photography is trust. Without it, you don't get in. Betray it, and the drawbridge is raised and you are thrown to the alligators. I can honestly state that I have never taken a celebrity or performer's photo offstage without their cooperation (and I have a feverish contempt for paparazzi). The other main factor is my shooting style itself, which is built for both comfort and speed. By far the most common comment I get after a shoot is "That was painless," which is something I've come to pride myself on.

My luxury is that the portraits are the purpose. With this work, I'm not shooting for casting directors, magazine editors, or managers, but for exhibitions, this book, and the artists themselves.

• • •

I met Paul Provenza on my first night at a comedy festival in Sydney. In a dodgy King's Cross pub, over many pints and smokes, we bonded over our admiration of Dana Gould and Maria Bamford. Over the next week, I came to know the irreverent intersection of intellectual and scatological that is also known as Provenz. I've never met anyone who knows as much about comedy as Paul, who floats freely between the rarefied air of network late-night, down to the New York club scene, to the subterranean stages of Edinburgh. And he doesn't give a fuck if you like what he says or not.

At the time I was on my seemingly continuous quest to find a publisher for a book of my comedian portraits. I soon realized that Paul, as comedy's insider inquisitor, would be the perfect person to interview the people in the book. He was game, but we needed a bit more focus rather than just comedy in general.

When we narrowed the scope to satirists, the preferred comic subset for both of us, we were able to quickly make a master wish-list of those we wanted to include; we got probably 90 percent of them, and many others along the way. While some of my favorite comics, like Stephen Wright, had to be excluded, the wide world of satirists is populated with a unique and dynamic sort.

Over the years I've had some incredible privileges with comedy legends: drinking wine with Tommy Smothers on his vineyard; doing Cheech & Chong's first portrait session in twenty-five years; exploring the multiple airport hangars of Jay Leno's car collection;

being invited to shoot inside the homes of Tom Lehrer, Fred Willard, and Jello Biafra; and shooting both Conan O'Brien and Stephen Colbert in their offices (on the same day). I've had the exalted rock awesomeness of hanging backstage with Spinal Tap and Tenacious D, and drank many after-show beers with reprobate geniuses like Dave Attell, Greg Giraldo, and Doug Stanhope. I had the bittersweet honor of having George Carlin say my photo was the one he wanted to be remembered by, three weeks before dying.

Logistically, we unfortunately weren't able to interview everyone pictured here, and some painful decisions were made to cut some interviews and portraits for space and design.

While getting some of these people required hoops and a ridiculous number of phone calls, e-mails, and scratched appointments, the vast majority were incredibly cooperative and permissive. None of these portraits were done in a photo studio. There were only two people who asked for approval of the image before publishing. Only on about four of the shoots did I have an assistant, and a makeup artist only on three of the women (and one dude).

These pages hold some of the world's greatest comic minds for you to connect with, and I hope my images help.

Thank you. Tip your wait staff.

Dan Dion
San Francisco, 2009

Dick Gregory

INTRODUCTION

¡SATIRISTAS!

"Number 1 Moustache Brother Par Par Lay is taken away. He in the slammer. Up the river. In the clink. He jail bird!"

That's how Lu Maw starts the Moustache Brothers' shows now. Five members of the Burmese special branch showed up at Par Par Lay's house one day and led him away, because he told a joke. He said, "In the past, thieves were called thieves. Now they are known as government workers."

For that, they gave Par Par Lay seven years in prison, hard labor.

Walid Hassan was famous for his comedy series on Iraqi TV, called *Caricature*. He mocked coalition forces and insurgents, and poked fun at the poor security, long gas lines, electricity blackouts, and the chaos of Iraqi government since the U.S.-led invasion.

For that, someone gave Walid Hassan a bullet through the head.

Stephen Colbert performed at a black-tie dinner in Washington, DC, before America's press and media, five-star generals, senators, congressmen, members of the Supreme Court, and the most powerful government leader in the world.

To the media, he said, "Fox News gives you both sides of every story: the president's side and the vice president's side." And, "Over the past five years, you journalists were so good about tax cuts, about WMD intelligence, about the effects of global warming. We Americans didn't want to know, and you had the courtesy not to try to find out."

Only feet away from the president, he said, "You always know where this president stands. He believes the same thing Wednesday that he believed on Monday, no matter what happened Tuesday. Events can change, but this man's beliefs never will."

For that, they gave Stephen Colbert a big, fat paycheck.

That's the kind of country America is. There always have been and always will be people who object and try to silence it, and people will write letters of complaint, boycott advertisers' products, and cancel magazine and newspaper subscriptions over it, but overwhelmingly, America loves to criticize itself. If a nation can be said to have a DNA, that fact is in America's.

Our Founding Fathers impregnated this country with it, and it doesn't take a paternity test to prove it. When it comes to criticizing America, some of us look more like the Founding Fathers than Prince Harry looks like Major James Hewitt.

It's no secret that one of the architects of

both the Declaration of Independence and the Constitution of these United States of America, Benjamin Franklin, was himself a satirist. And a damn good one, too. He created lots of biting satire and confrontational humor about the things he felt needed a good going-over in this country, and he printed up his own pamphlets loaded with the stuff, because newspapers couldn't be bothered. Yes, even back then, on the still-blistered heels of founding a new nation and a "great experiment" in freedom and self-government, a lot of the press was pretty content to leave well enough alone and avoid controversy.

To criticize America is to love it. It's part of the eternal vigilance that freedom demands. To criticize America is as American as apple pie purchased at Walmart that you really shouldn't eat 'cause you're lookin' like you could really stand to lose a few pounds there, my fellow American.

You'd never know it from the shrill din of so many self-righteous moralists, religious charlatans, loud-mouthed pundits, and opportunistic, power-hungry politicians, but there was a time when it was taken for granted that criticizing what's wrong with America was the most patriotic thing a person could do, short of taking to arms and overthrowing an oppressive, imperialistic government that violates the civil rights of its people. I'm just sayin'.

Criticizing their government is what made this nation's very first heroes heroes. For criticizing their country, they got big-ass monuments and had cities named after them. We put their pictures on our money, and we love those guys so much we just have to have as many pictures of them as we can get. Some of us have been collecting them all and not trading them with our friends.

But as brilliant, visionary, and fearless as they were, with the notable exception of the aforementioned Dr. Franklin, our Founding Fathers weren't nearly as funny as the people in this book. And those guys had all those goofy clothes and dopey wigs, so there's really no excuse for that.

But our Founding Fathers did sow their seeds of freedom, individual rights, and a government "of the people, by the people and for the people" with vigorous and determined promiscuity. Seeds of the ideas that all men are created equal and with inalienable rights, and that free speech is at the top of that list. Seeds of the ideas that privacy is a right, that a separation of church and state is crucial, that the government's powers should be kept in check, and "that whenever any form of government becomes destructive to these ends, it is the right of the people to alter or to abolish it."

It is their direct descendants that are represented in this book, all of whom are demanding their rightful inheritance, the treasure that is each and every one of those ideas.

And to many people in this country, some of whom are running it, that seems to be a revolutionary idea.

We have called the artists in this book *¡Satiristas!* first, because it's kinda funny, but also because, like the theme of this book, it's satire. Kinda, sorta. And as kinda, sorta satire goes, it's not bad. It's not great, but it's not too shabby. It *is* self-mocking. I mean, we're talking about people who want to have fun and make us all laugh, but *¡Satiristas!* brings to mind Ché Guevara, back before he got into the T-shirt business. It conjures a scrappy band of freedom fighters gathered in the wooded hills overlooking La Palazio del Governmento Muy Malo or something, furtively exchanging information and strategically planning their revolution.

But the *¡Satiristas!* approach to revolution is nothing like that. First of all, it's decidedly nonviolent. It harms no one's person or property. And these revolutionaries couldn't agree on any strategy if their lives depended on it. There's a reason there has never been a Comedians' Union. They couldn't agree on where the goddamn apostrophe goes in "Comedian's." I couldn't even agree on it, and I'm writing this by myself.

No, the *¡Satiristas!* approach to revolution is pretty much just a whole lot of fun. They're not throwing Molotov cocktails in some banana republic; they're slinging jokes 'cause they're going bananas over the state of our republic.

"Why," you may ask, "should we be interested in what a bunch of comedians have to say about anything? They're comedians. Why should we take anything they have to say seriously?"

Well, first of all, to a person, everyone in this book is brilliant. They just are. To be honest, most comedians are smarter than the average bear. It's just a fact. They have to be, or they can't be doing comedy. In comedy, you have to be at least a notch or two above your audience, and their audience is the average American. I rest my case.

They see the absurdity in everything, everywhere, all the time. They can't help it; it's a curse. And when you see enough of that, you start to get pretty skeptical about things.

So, they are thinkers. And a lot of them only work nights, so their days are free. That's a dangerous combination, there: a tendency to think and some time to do it.

And to read. They read a *lot*. They have to write material all the time, and a lot of information has to keep going in for the jokes to keep coming out. I guarantee you that most of the people in this book read a lot more than you do, and you're reading this, so I know you're someone who reads. There's a lot of time spent in airports and on planes for these people. Trust me, I know.

Now, I know that all of the above would immediately disqualify someone from holding elected office in this country, because it's "elitist," and this country feels the most important quality for leading the most powerful military in history is that the leader is someone they could sit and have a beer with and relate to. Call me crazy, I prefer whoever's running things to be way out of my league and to relate more to the president of China than to me, but apparently I'm not a core voter for anybody.

But guess what? You can sit and have a

beer with anybody in this book! Except the ones who went through rehab, but that's okay, they'll just have a soda or something. They are not power brokers or politicians, they're regular people. Some of them are rich, but they got rich because America loved their comedy and, guess what, related to them. So don't let their intelligence or the fact that they're well-read and they think a lot stop you from listening to what they have to say. Try and look past all that.

Comedians connect with audiences in a way that is revealing. The dark and very funny British comedian Jimmy Carr describes connecting with someone's sense of humor as being like a sexual attraction: everybody's got their own thing; if something turns you on, it turns you on and there's no accounting for it, and when it's right, it's right, and when it's not, it's not.

I take Jimmy's analogy just a bit further: the laugh is the orgasm. And let's be honest, when you can make someone come, you kinda know everything you really need to know about them. You know their most intimate, honest, unguarded self. You get who they are, what's underneath their mask, and whatever their particular kink may be. Comedians travel around the country and meet people from all walks of life—every race, creed, and color, rich and poor, gay and straight—by the hundreds or thousands at a time, and give them all simultaneous multiple orgasms every night.

Suffice it to say that the people in this book have learned a thing or two about the people in this country.

And what is that now, two jizz jokes? Well, we're talking to people who speak freely here, and that kinda thing comes with the territory.

And that makes three. Comedy usually comes in threes.

Shit, I blew it.

Fuck, I said "blew."

That's right; you'd better get used to it, 'cause we're talking to comics here, so there's a lot more where that . . . Well, you know.

Comedians just might know more about the cross section of the American people and what's going on "on the ground," as they say, than anyone else possibly could. Because in order to survive, they must have an instinct and an understanding of all varieties of Americans. In order to make them laugh in groups, you have to know what they think and why they think it, all the time. A joke works because it's a surprise. You have to know what they expect and what they don't expect before you can surprise them with the unexpected. You've got to know what the perceived truth is before you can subvert it. You have to have a feel for what they believe, why they believe it, and what they don't believe before you can question their beliefs.

You can't do your job if you don't know all of that every time you get up on a stage. A comedian spends his or her entire career learning about every conceivable way that someone in their audience could be looking at the world. They develop an instinct for that kind of thing, and they know more about the tenor of this country than any president or pundit ever will.

And I will make this absolute statement with 100 percent certainty: Not one single person who is in charge of any government, military, religious, or pseudo-religious organization or any power structure whatsoever—not one of them in the entire world—has the courage to get up on stage every night to learn as much about humankind as the people in this book understand.

It's a big statement, I know, and I stand by it. Because to really learn what comedians intuitively and instinctively understand about people, you have to be truthful with them yourself. Audiences may not know that

Mort Sahl

it matters to them, but we know it does. The laughs just aren't as big when we're faking it, and believe me, we pay close attention to the laughs. When the heart isn't there, when the fearlessness that comes from honesty isn't there, when you don't really believe what you're saying yourself, the audience isn't falling for it. It's a little frustrating, frankly, that we can't get any damn slack on that, but it's a frightening truth that half of this country will accept a lie that sends their loved ones to war quicker than they'll take insincerity from a comedian. Comedians who work artfully—which includes all of them in this book—are held to a higher standard when it comes to being real.

You have to say what you truly believe, you have to be able to be as wrong as you are right, and you have to be honest about what you feel and who you are. Night after night, with stranger after stranger, until you learn enough about each and every one of them to make them all laugh together at precisely the moment you want them to. There's not a public opinion poll in the world with such a small margin of error or as great a degree of accuracy.

And they play a lot of the same games as the powers they criticize do, so they know how the game works in politics and media. But they use their powers for good, not evil. They will trick you, but only into thinking about things you may not want to. They will surprise you, but with realizations. They may lure you into

ideological territories you didn't expect to be in, and trap you in conundrums. They may lie to their audience, but not to hide anything. If they lie, it is to reveal some greater truth about us all and the world we live in.

Comedians, more than anybody except maybe George Orwell and Karl Rove, know all about groupthink. They can smell it. They feel it. They know how to create it, and they know how to destroy it. If you don't think you're susceptible to groupthink, well then you have never seen a really good comedian. From the moment they step on the stage, groupthink is their medium. Comedy is just one small, beautiful genre of groupthink. So when it comes to criticizing America, these people know what they're talking about.

And they have no hidden agenda. Their agenda is transparent at every moment: to make you laugh. That's it. Making you laugh is how they consolidate control and grab power. And once they have it, they give it right back over to you to fight whatever power you may need to.

So all the people in this book are worth listening to. They may not be right about everything, and even if they are, you may not agree with them. But they're talking about things so many others are afraid to talk about, and they tell you the truth as they see it. That alone is a rare commodity, and maybe you should give it a listen, if only just to see what it's like.

And, of course, they're funny. Damned

funny. Every one of them was asked to be in this book because they are funny, first and foremost. But these particular comedy artists are all also social critics, and there's something else that comes along with the funny. These are some people who supersize your laugh.

Don't think for a second that comedians who only serve up the funny are somehow lesser, or aren't absolutely worth a possible second volume of this book. Anyone who makes you laugh is always doing more than just that, and we can't wait to get into some of that, too. We hope that we can spend some time with a bunch of other comedy artists, who work differently, but no less artfully, as well. If you buy another couple of copies of this one for some friends—it does make a great gift, doesn't it?—you can help make our dreams come true. But I digress.

In this book, we've chosen to present to you, even more intimately than they do in their own work, comedy artists who have things to say that resonate particularly in these times in which we live. This collection is not intended to be definitive, nor could it. But we have gathered some of the most important names in satire and socially critical comedy working today, and some of the most best-known ones as well. We've included some you've never heard of, and some who fall slightly outside the comedy fold but fit comfortably within it. There are some comedy veterans who've left a significant legacy, and some who are new to the game and picking up the legacy, showing great promise to become voices of a new generation in comedy. We've included some who work exclusively in the realm of stand-up comedy, and some who only write for others. There are some who are flourishing primarily on the Internet. There are a few Brits who've got an outsider's perspective.

And there is also George Carlin. He needs to be in a class of his own, and I interviewed him extensively only a week before he died.

If you think maybe I should have said something more like "only a week before his passing," one of his many great pieces was about just those kinds of euphemisms and how much he detested them. "Before he fuckin' up and died" is how he would really prefer I said it.

And that right there is one aspect of some of the work these artists do. They don't always care about being polite; politeness is sometimes only obfuscation and manipulation. They've got stuff to say, and we're all adults, and we all know what everyone really means when they're being polite anyway, so let's just cut to the chase and get real.

They don't care about offending you. They'd prefer it didn't go down that way, but maybe the fact that it offended you is part of the point they're trying to make. Maybe you're offended because they're right and you're wrong and you know it but you really don't want to admit it.

They don't care if you disagree. They're doing it anyway, so just hang in there; it'll be

Jon Stewart

funny. They're up for the fight if you wanna have it, but really, it's all just in good fun, so sit down and enjoy it or get up and leave, it ain't gonna make any difference either way.

Some of them use vulgar language. Big fuckin' deal.

Some of them work very gently and sweetly, too. And they may be the most subversive of all, as they seduce you into a comfort zone,

make their point, and then on the way home you go, "Say . . ."

Well, you wouldn't go, "Say . . ." unless you were driving home to around 1935, but you get my point.

Some of them make their points in song. Some of them make their points as characters.

They opened up to me as a fellow comedian, speaking freely about many things, so each conversation follows its own path with no roadmap. There are some things lots of people talk about, and some things specific to one or another. Ideas carry through in agreement and disagreement; in concert and in contrast. Most are very funny; some bounce between very funny and very serious. Some are mostly personal; some dwell more on political issues and larger social concerns.

They talk about themselves, each other, and the audiences they play. Some are high-profile enough to play to their fans, who will go with any idea they give them. Some are working club performers who say things some audiences don't expect or particularly want to hear. Their experiences are the same, and they are vastly different.

We wanted to balance out political ideologies, and began looking at the artists through a Right-wing/Left-wing perspective. We soon found that it was a waste of time. Very few of them have an outright political party affiliation. With a few exceptions, Right/Left is irrelevant. Most of them see politics in general as worthy of rage and mockery. I think they stole that from Mark Twain. Who stole it from Jonathan Swift. Who stole it from Aristophanes.

What they are trying to do is speak "truth to power." Whatever side of the political spectrum that may be gets taken to task. They are iconoclasts and they are individualists and they are humanists. What they care about is rarely the minutia of policy. They expose and fight against a lack of compassion toward those without the power. They care about class divisions, civil rights, and freedom.

They care about fear mongering and the hysterical, irrational responses to it; they see the results of it in their audiences with every joke that defies it. They care about information and who is controlling it; they know what their audiences believe and what they need to know but is not quite getting to them. They care about the myths that are being created for us and how the narratives are being driven; they see the groupthink as they try to unravel it in their audiences. They care about what their audience is focused on and why they're all focused in the same direction; they know how much great material they have to throw away because the audience has no idea what the hell they're talking about. They care about the distractions and who is blowing them out of proportion and for what reason. They care about our wars, they care about the lies and deceit that got us there, and they care about the fact that the people who decided we needed these wars profit from them financially, politically, and otherwise.

They care about people who are suffering and why, and the people and institutions that are responsible for it. They care about nationalism, and how perilously close it is to fascism. They care about who has the power, whom it is affecting, and to what end. They care about greed. They care about corporate influence over our government that is supposed to be of, by, and for all of us. They talk about our common humanity and how it is all too often lost; they see the audience struggling from it. They care about suffering, powerlessness, indignity, and perhaps, most of all, complacency. That really gets in the way of everyone having a good time, and they won't stand for it.

They'd like things to be different, but have few, if any, practical alternatives to offer. These people couldn't run anything in the country, and except for a couple of them who actually considered giving it a shot, they wouldn't want to if they could. But they can sure as hell tell you what's wrong with whomever is running things and how it's being run. They can't tell you how to fix the leaks, but they have an uncanny ability to smell the gas and tell you where it's coming from. It's up to someone else to do the fixing. Hey, a person can only do so much, and there are a lot of leaks in the pipe.

There's also some discussion about just what the hell "satire" really is. It's an art form, so there's bound to be some fuzziness around the edges. When is modern art "post," you know? And the meaning has changed a bit from its origins, so it depends on whom you ask anyway.

In the strictest, ancient-Greek-rules-of-drama-and-poetry sense of the word, it's defined as—and I'm paraphrasing here, because it's all really ancient Greek to me—mocking a point of view by embracing it so fully as to allow its absurdity to become self-evident. The clearest modern examples of this, I think, are Stephen Colbert and Sacha Baron Cohen's Borat. A little further back, Jonathan Swift and Mark Twain are at the top of the list. Their writing and speaking

come from a serious commitment to the very idea they want to mock. A little exaggeration later, and it's hilarious.

But the more generally accepted definition is broader than that:

SATIRE (n):

- The use of humor, irony, exaggeration, or ridicule to expose people's stupidity or vices, particularly in the context of contemporary politics and other topical issues.
- A literary work holding up human vices or follies to ridicule or scorn.
- Trenchant wit, irony, or sarcasm used to expose and discredit vice or folly.

There's a little dancing on the head of a pin about that kind of thing here or there, but, hey, that's the kind of thing some comics like to do. Most really couldn't be bothered, so it's kept to a minimum. In fact, this book isn't really about satire itself at all. But we had a cool title, so we're goin' with it anyway.

Really, though, talking with comedians about stuff like the accurate definition of "satire" is like talking about sound waves and frequencies with jazz cats. It's just not very relevant to what they do.

And it's important to remember that what you read here is not their work. This is off-stage and personal. They go into some heavy stuff here, but in their work, the last thing they want to do is preach. They know that no one stays awake in church, and they really want you to stay awake and alert. They have all the talent, skill, and craft it takes to communicate tough ideas in a way that'll have you asking for more. They make you laugh when you hear them and the more you laugh, the more you will hear.

So ultimately, no matter how passionate they are in these pages about the important things they care so deeply about, when they are doing comedy, none of it matters in the least.

It's ironic, I think, but because they want you to listen and pay attention, because they want you to relate, because they want you to think, because they want you to get angry, because they want you to know that you're not alone, because they want you to wake up, because they want you to learn, because they want you to understand them, because they want you to understand yourself, because they want us to understand each other, because they want you to be skeptical, because they want you to feel passion, because they want you to be empowered, because they

want you to be free, because the truth will set you free, because they want to tell the truth, because they want us to discover the truth, because truth is absolute, because everyone's truth is different, because, as William Shakespeare said, "Jesters do oft prove prophets," because as Dario Fo said, "With comedy I can search for the profound," because as Molière said, "The duty of comedy is to correct men by amusing them," because as Mark Twain said, "Against the assault of laughter, nothing can stand," because as George Orwell said, "Whatever is funny is subversive," because as Edmund Burke said, "The only thing necessary for the triumph of evil is for good men to do nothing," and because we all know what happens if someone doesn't stand up and say, "Stop drinking the Kool-Aid!," the only thing that matters is the laugh.

That's the one thing that everyone in comedy does agree on.

Paul Provenza

BILLY CONNOLLY

FROM A DARK, abusive childhood in a Glaswegian tenement was born the unlikeliest of comic heroes. Billy Connolly's path from welder to folksinger to Britain's most popular stand-up is at once revelatory, inspiring, and hilarious. While his oft-indecipherable brogue held him back from worldwide stardom, icons such as John Cleese and Elton John were pulling him into the spotlight. His storytelling punch-line-shy style blazed trails for countless U.K. successors, and his maniacal laugh surrounds important truths—not the least of which is humor's ability to triumph over anything.

BILLY CONNOLLY: I don't know much about comedy, I just like to be there when it's happening. I don't analyze it, but I know when it's in the fucking room. I know when it's in *me*.

Nobody even knows what laughter is. Nobody knows why your body expels air, makes that noise; the actual physical act isn't understood. They understand yawning to a degree, research has been done on sneezing, crying we understand a bit instinctively—but laughing? Your head pitches backward, your legs slide down, you're lying on the ground unable to get up from laughing, and we don't even know why our bodies do it. It's just . . . a physical expression of happiness, of *joy*.

Good hearty laughter is the next best thing to orgasm, isn't it? It's just the most extraordinary thing you can do for your fellow human being. What a gift to give a total stranger!

I think the biggest duty and asset of comedy is to instill *optimism* in people. And when used sensibly, comedy carries immense power. It can prove that the little man can destroy the big man. You can belittle *Hitler* with comedy. People in jodhpurs and jackboots storming into rooms, frightening the shit out of you . . . Give me a *microphone*. You can expose with a fucking searchlight the banality of dictatorship—just fucking *nail* it. One good line heard by enough people can destroy bastards' lives forever.

It can be very harmful, too, and destroy somebody you quite like. A good, liberal politician in Britain—a nice, honest man named David Steel—was very young, running against a much older politician. *Spitting Image* was a political satire show on telly then that portrayed politicians with big, exaggerated puppets, and Steel's puppet was this wee little boy. It was such well-done comedy that people could only think of him as a child and never took him seriously again. It destroyed his political career.

PAUL PROVENZA: Are you interested in making that kind of impact, or teaching anyone anything?

BILLY CONNOLLY: I don't want to teach anybody anything. I don't see comedians to be *taught* stuff, I go to *laugh*.

PAUL PROVENZA: But haven't you ever learned anything watching a comedian?

BILLY CONNOLLY: Oh, all the time—but that was never their *intention*. The comedians I know—even politically driven ones—don't want to change anybody; it's *art for art's sake*. You do it for *you*, not for them. It's a bonus if they like it, just as with painting and sculpture.

If you're doing it really well, you *should* be doing it for you; you should have your *own* standards you go by. You're not a service industry; you're not a *waiter*, to be sent back and come out with something different. You give your best, do what you can for them to enjoy what *your* best is, then you go home.

But when people are really good at something—whether it's a great comedian, guitarist, sitar player, someone doing sonatas on the piano—they bring this atmosphere with them that makes you *think* great. You find yourself wandering off in your brain. Sensually, it wakens you up. You're half asleep most of the time just waiting to be fed little bits of information, but this is different. This is *manna*—total nutrition.

There are painters who do it, musicians who do it . . . I don't know what it is. Just people who are *good at what they do.*

PAUL PROVENZA: Is it talent or intellect? Their love of what they do? Dedication to skill and craft?

BILLY CONNOLLY: *All* of those things. It's their *desire* to be good at it. And it's vocational; it's not come to on the spur of the moment. Every comedian I like does comedy because they *couldn't* do anything else; they were *driven.* They didn't particularly know why, didn't particularly want to do it, but were driven and couldn't *not* do it. Like a "calling."

And I don't think you're born with it. I think a set of circumstances come together—some darker than others. Having to overcome unhappiness gives you a desire to manifest happiness just to get above your own darkness—even if it means involving people you don't know.

That was my case, I think. I had a kind of darkness in my childhood—I won't go into it—but from being messed around sexually and physically, a broken family, unhappy household, all that crap. You have to get above it somehow. You have to get above *yourself,* so you start trying to make your friends, "the guys," laugh.

The only trouble is, it makes you attractive *to guys*!

PAUL PROVENZA: But all those polls in *Cosmo* and such say women think a sense of humor is the sexiest thing in a man.

BILLY CONNOLLY: Comedy's the *least* sexy thing in show business! Playing bass badly gets you more women than doing comedy *well* does. It's just one of those rotten things.

I've made bad choices as far as things that would get me laid. Playing banjo? Never in your life will you hear, "She's fucking the banjo player."

It just isn't in the lexicon. People who play banjo just *love* banjo; no one chooses it to get laid, believe me. They just love the noise of a banjo; couldn't resist it. Same thing with comedy—we're just *driven* in that direction.

People play *guitar* to get laid. They play piano because they're the youngest in the family and *somebody* had to play this piece of furniture; people play violin 'cause their mother made them, that social-climbing bitch; they play bass usually because they're the most boring guy in the band and, "You'll fucking play bass or you're out of the band, 'cause *anybody* can play bass."

People play drums because . . . Well, drummers . . . they're not well. They don't get laid much either, actually, 'cause nobody even knows they're in the band hiding behind all that shit.

But comedy? You only get laid when you're successful—and then you get laid for being successful, not for being in comedy. It's kinda weird.

PAUL PROVENZA: Your show is always different. I've seen you be completely silly; I've seen you do political material, or talk about religion, social issues—

BILLY CONNOLLY: You have to take what I've

got on the night; whatever comes in. And it's made of anger, adrenaline, and coffee. I have one coffee a day, about fifteen minutes before I go onstage. I have a coffee, go "Whoo-hooo!" and get up there.

The guitarist Paco Peña once said to me, "Don't you drink before you go on?"

I said, "No. Never, ever."

He said, "Well, you *behave* like a drunk man." Because it's about anger and shouting and bawling with me.

Peña always has one whiskey before going on, to take the edge off for playing—but I *want* that edge. I want to be jumpy, not smooth and ready. Smooth and ready is Vegas lounge: "Hello, ladies and gentlemen . . . Hey! Some kinda town!"

Fuck that; I want to see a guy who's thinking, whose *eyes* are thinking—so that's the level I go for in myself.

PAUL PROVENZA: When you do choose to do social commentary, isn't it to make some kind of statement?

BILLY CONNOLLY: No, most of it's a question, I find. I told my kids early in their lives, "Watch out for people who know the answer and avoid them. Try to keep the company of people who generally are trying to understand the question."

That's what I've done my whole life: tried to make sense of what's the question. If there's an answer, what's the *question*? I'm interested in the question.

I've always been intrigued by the fact that there are questions whose job is just to be a question, not to have an answer. People think questions should have answers, but some questions are complete on their own. Like when your mother says to you, "Where have you been till this time of night?"

The last thing on earth she wants you to do is *tell* her. It doesn't require an answer; the question's a statement. I kinda like just a question.

Most of the time I'm talking about things that baffle or intrigue me. Sometimes I'll tell the audience, "If you've never seen me before, I should tell you that you may feel a wee bit uncomfortable sometimes. Because sometimes I'll tell you stuff I find interesting and it's not particularly funny, so you won't know what to do 'cause there's no punch line. But I'll tell them to you anyway and you won't know what to do when I'm finished, but neither will I, so we'll stand just looking at each other for a while. But I'm sure we'll find a way out of it."

Because sometimes I *do* just tell them something where maybe the punch line's at the beginning—but you have to finish the story anyway to make any sense of what you just said even though there's no punch line at the *end*. Guys like me, you—modern guys—we're into a more rambling, non-punch-line-y style. The punch is all over the place. There are highlights and lowlights, but we've kind of got out of the way of punch lines and gimmicks and catch phrases. And it's a very happy place to be, because people don't know quite what to expect of you—and *you* don't know what to expect either.

A lot of comedians are more like salesmen: "Lemme *sell* you this bit here." That's where all the little bits of gimmickry come in—nods and winks and nudges and punch lines that sound exactly like punch lines.

Treating it as art, you do it for *you*. You're not thinking about the effect it's having on everybody, you're saying it because *you* believe it to be funny, you're thinking fast, speaking fast, and it kind of overtakes you. You're not sure what it is, but you're glad it's there beside you on this evening. I know you've had nights where you're just flying along and you think, "Oh, God . . . Don't end! *Wheeee!*" That's what I aim for.

People think, "Well, don't you listen to your audience?" What a stupid question! Of course we *listen* to them. I don't know what they're saying—I get it in some kind of code I don't really understand—but when I'm not getting it I'm deeply unhappy. When I can't hear them it's not fun, and when I can hear them again, I'm flying again. I hear them the way football players hear their audience: just a big noise, like a wave. And I'm a surfer.

I have to step onto this wave of noise they're making and *it* carries *me—Whooossshhh!* I step on at a certain point in the laughter, then more blah blah blah and *I'm* in charge again.

Watch Conan O'Brien; you see he has no idea what that is. I've said this to him personally, so I can say it publicly, too. He speaks at the wrong time and misses the wave. He'll be the first to tell you that he came to his show as a writer, not as a performer, so he doesn't have faith in performance and tries to create something rather than *feel* it.

I've told Conan, "You're not riding the wave.

You leave it too late to speak, until they're absolutely silent. When they go, 'Haaaaah!,' step *onto* it, become *part* of it, then you'll *conduct* it."

Letterman's a genius at it and probably doesn't even know how he does it or how to explain it; he just does it and always has. Leno and Ferguson too, 'cause they've done *lots* of live stand-up. They *know* that noise and how to surf it.

PAUL PROVENZA: I believe that you can learn anything you want to know about someone from what they do or don't do in their act.

BILLY CONNOLLY: Without question. Pete Townsend once said in an interview, "If you don't want anyone to know anything about you, don't write *anything*." Because your personality will come through; you'll always show exactly who you are.

PAUL PROVENZA: So what does your work say about you?

BILLY CONNOLLY: That I'm alone. I'm fucking *alone*. Everything I do is about making all these other people laugh, but if you listen to my stuff, you'll find there's this wee—not *lonely* guy, but *alone* guy.

Most comedians, I think, are. You'd think we're gregarious, but actually we're kind of loners. That comes from a lifetime of one-nighters. You're alone *all the time*.

There's nothing that's not "alone." People sometimes think "lonely," but they've got it wrong. I'm not *lonely* up there, but I am *alone*—and there's a certain power that comes with being alone up there.

You're born to be a loner when you're a comedian. That's what kind of molds you, and that's what makes you an original thinker.

PAUL PROVENZA: Being alone allows you to find a unique, individual perspective?

BILLY CONNOLLY: Aye. Eventually you're just telling people your life—exaggerated, but you basically single out your solitary self and put a light on it.

Barry Humphries—he's Dame Edna—said the loveliest thing about this: "Sometimes I'm surrounded by people, doing press conferences, dealing with people in the business . . . and then I walk onto the stage in front of three thousand people and think, 'Ahhh . . . Alone at last.'"

PAUL PROVENZA: Oh . . . That is *breathtaking.*

BILLY CONNOLLY: Doesn't that just hit home?

PAUL PROVENZA: Speaking of original thinking, when I discovered George Carlin in the seventies, he was for me what the Sex Pistols were for other people my age. His art inspired me to reject assumptions, question authority, and to feel that having a different view of things is not necessarily "wrong." He gave me "permission" to think differently.

BILLY CONNOLLY: Richard Pryor did that as well. It's making you into something, letting you be who you're gonna be.

The biggest favor we do for people is to release them. Society, culture, puts them in jail—and we let them out. The rule-makers, whoever they are, decided a box you're going to live in. We need to be reminded that you can step out of the box—and you can go right back in again if you want, too.

See, when you laugh about something,

something in it *must* be true. It got to you somehow; it hit something in you somewhere. *That's* the way change comes. You *reaffirm* in people's minds what they felt in the first place. Maybe you wake it up, but they have to feel it themselves to begin with. You can re-interest them in something; get people who are open to it to think differently as a result of your having been there. People who've never thought about something until you say it may continue thinking about it, and thereby change in some way.

But that's change starting from nowhere; I don't think you can change people who already think a certain way. I don't think change comes that way. I don't think the intellect even *works* that way. Even most people who read philosophy aren't trying to get *new* ideas, they're trying to reaffirm what they already think themselves. Most people go through life trying to find proof for what they already think.

But thinking too much about all that gets you into all sorts of trouble in comedy. Sometimes you should just go with the belly and the gut, with what you feel. Sometimes it's cruel, but not always. Sometimes you're so wrong *that's* funny. Sometimes your naiveté is funny; sometimes your accuracy is what's funny . . . But ours is not to reason why, I think. Ours is to just fucking get on with it.

And here's the toughest thing—and also the loveliest thing—about comedy: a comedian can't *nearly* win. You can't *nearly* get them. Even boxers can win if they *nearly* get somebody.

But not comedians.

ROBIN WILLIAMS LONG ago made the transition from manic, unpredictable stand-up to A-list actor— Oscar-winning and family-friendly. But he never abandoned the stand-up stage, and never strayed far from his stand-up roots. Unlike so many who move on to expansive careers in film or television, Robin still identifies as a stand-up comedian first and foremost. It's his default setting, and he's the perfect illustration of how you can take the comic out of stand-up, but you can't take the stand-up out of a comic. After entertaining our troops in Iraq and Afghanistan, he returned with a wider worldview and more finely honed sense of what humor can do and why it's more important now than ever.

ROBIN WILLIAMS: You just can't get better audiences than our troops overseas. They're glad as hell to see you, because, well . . . you know. They're like, "We *have* to, but *you?*"

They appreciate that you come there, but also that while you're there, you'll try to learn some of the discrepancies in what we're told—that everything is going well. The troops *want* the real truth to be told.

PAUL PROVENZA: How does political material work with the troops in the midst of it all?

ROBIN WILLIAMS: Back when the Hummers still hadn't been sufficiently armored yet, I said they should strap Dick Cheney to the front of a Humvee like that character "Lord Humungus" in *Road Warrior*. Strap him right to the front: "*Now* they're sufficiently armored!"

The troops were pretty into that kind of thing. When Rumsfeld commented publicly on the troops not having the equipment and armor they really needed, he said, "You fight a war with what you've got."

I said, "Yeah, but . . . eleventh-century Norman armor?"

They *loved* that stuff. Ripping on Bush with them was an easy shot, too—because they fucking *knew* how insane Bush was.

PAUL PROVENZA: In the comedy clubs, if you criticized the war or said *maybe* it was a bad idea—even now people *still* go, "No! We gotta *support the troops!*" But when there's military in the crowd, they *always* take my side of the argument.

ROBIN WILLIAMS: *Big* time. Especially if they've been over there. The troops realize more than anyone the insanity of what the fuck they've been put into. You talk to those guys, they'll tell you that questioning the government is *not* being unpatriotic, it's the *ultimate* patriotism!

If patriotism means "Don't question authority," we'd still be English: "Oh dear yes, things are going quite well, I think, really. Tea?"

Plus a lot of the troops are *way* beyond their tours of duty. They're stretched way beyond normal capabilities—and people are still actually floating the idea of going into *Iran??* The Army and Marines already lowered their standards to take in people with criminal records. If we need even more troops, they'll have to lower their standards to where they'll have the "Very Special Forces": *"Da Ahmy said dey have pudding evvy day! I in da Ahmy cause I love pudding in da Ahmy!"*

PAUL PROVENZA: Do you ever get flak for any material?

ROBIN WILLIAMS: Occasionally you'll get the born-again Christian who'll come at you hard. The Christian Reich—sorry, "Right." And you think, "When the Rapture comes and all you guys leave . . . the place will be *so* much quieter."

That idea that in the Rapture they'll go to the front of the line and get to heaven? Muslims have the same thing about them going to the front of the line, orthodox Jews have *their* own thing about that, and, you know . . . *Hmmm.*

The orthodox Jews—hard-core Lubavitch—they'll be occupying the West Bank, yet they won't be in the military, but they'll tell other Jews, "You're not *real* Jews!" "Oh.

Well, okay, let me put down my Uzi and we'll talk theology."

It's all that, "a Mormon's not *really* a Christian," and a Shiite's not really a Muslim, and a Sunni's not really a Muslim to Shiites . . . It's *all* these different people saying, "I'm the chosen one, you're not. You're *next* in line. We're in front. Nyah, nyah, nyah, nyah, nyah, nyah."

Even Scientologists—and they're the most litigious of all. If you make fun of them, they'll contact you and your lawyers *immediately*. I made a joke about "Profitology" with *N. Ron* Hubbard —which was really an Enron joke— but right away I was contacted by a celebrity who shall remain nameless saying, "You know, if you wouldn't do that, that would really be great."

PAUL PROVENZA: How'd you respond to *that?*

ROBIN WILLIAMS: Well, he called as a *friend*, so I tried to deal with it. I said, "It's not really a joke about Scientology, it's about Enron." And he said, "No, but, really . . . We'd appreciate it if you wouldn't." I said, "I'll try and be respectful of that."

And then I did a bit about the "Church of Gynecology." Just to go through those curtains would be wonderful. A *lot* of people would join.

But they were the *only* people that ever contacted me about anything like that. I never heard from the Catholic church when I talked about the "Divine Witness Protection Program" for pedophilic priests. But Scientology? They were right *on* me.

Anti-abortion people are pretty touchy, too. I'd said that if you actually brought them their very own crack baby, they might not be so into their own idea. Just show up at their homes, "You're anti-abortion, would you mind raising just this one child? The one screaming nonstop from the moment it was born? That would be really helpful." And I got hideous, horrifying letters wishing plagues upon me, attacking my family . . . So there's the love and compassion *there*, right?

But you take it in stride. It comes with the territory of saying what you believe and speaking your mind. I did some event and made fun of Sylvester Stallone, and Billy Crystal's going, "Stallone is *here!*" But if you can't do it right in front of them, then you have to ask yourself, "Just how brave *am* I?" Like when Joan Rivers actually wondered aloud why Elizabeth Taylor was angry at her. "Because you said she has more chins than a Chinese phone book. What do you fuckin' think!?"

If you can't take responsibility for it then you just have to admit you're *chicken shit*.

PAUL PROVENZA: I think we sometimes get conflicts with political material because we ask people to stop thinking just in terms of white hat/black hat or good vs. evil, and people don't want to deal with that—intellectually *or* emotionally.

ROBIN WILLIAMS: The point is you have to *make* them deal with it, or eventually they'll be dealing with it in far *worse* ways.

The Russian government used to say the Russian people are this big, powerful bear, but if you have them worried about balancing on a ball, they won't get off it and kill you. "Balancing on a ball" means *FEAR!* You make people too afraid of losing their balance to worry about anything else.

I think more people realize this now, but the only way to break through is to consistently stay on people, man. The big lie only breaks down when you hit 'em with the big truth. And you don't give up. You don't go, "Oh, well . . . Whatever." That's what the powers that be want—they *hope* you'll just go, "Oh, well."

PAUL PROVENZA: Are you more politicized now than you used to be?

ROBIN WILLIAMS: I'm finding myself all of a sudden waking up. After rehab, life changed. I realized I don't want to medicate myself in *any* form. I want to be awake and *aware*. There's a lot to be thankful for, and there's a lot to fight for. This country is such a mess, there's a lot to stand up about and go, "Hey!" And the fact is that we comics, *we can do that*. In other countries we'd be jailed or dead. A famous Iraqi comic, a big TV star over there, named Walid Hassan was killed a couple of years ago in Baghdad. *That's* a bad place to be a comic.

True story: In Germany, I was on this very dry German talk show with a woman hosting it, and at one point she said, "Vy do you zink zere's not so much comedy in Germany? Ve have some, but not a lot."

And I said, "Did you ever think it's because you tried to kill all the funny people?"

And here's the frightening part: She took a moment and then went, "No."

I thought, "Oh, *fuck*. There it is. That's it right there."

You know, if you go back in history to the fool—who was usually a dwarf or a deformed person, by the way—the fool's *purpose* was to point out to the king himself all the king's foibles and weaknesses, and as best he could, make the king go "Ha, ha" about them. His job was to remind the king, "You are *not* a god."

In *The Name of the Rose*, Umberto Eco talks about the comedies and Plato's theories. Comedy's job was to point out that even the pope *farts*. To give us a common humanity, to say, "These are our weaknesses; they come along with our strengths." When someone denies the weaknesses and lives in only righteousness, you have to say, "You've lost track of who we are. You've lost track of *humanity*."

There was a tradition at Jewish weddings of the "badchen," kind of like a wedding *tummler* who'd make fun of the bride and groom, kind of "roast" them before the wedding, almost as if to say, "This is how you're gonna survive together, because if you take yourselves or each other too seriously, you're gonna *kill* each other. This is the way—with humor—that you might make it a little longer."

That's our *purpose* as comedians.

Remember that Mormon Year for Zion group on that Texas compound, where they had multiple wives and children being raised communally and all that? They went in and rescued—well some people say "took away from their parents"—these kids who'd been raised in that severe religious environment, where one of the caveats was "No laughter." That *horrified* me! Children were not allowed to laugh—at *anything!* A life without laughter? How brutal would that be? Even in the most brutal situation there's *some* humor—and it's a kind of survival mechanism, when you come down to it.

PAUL PROVENZA: Do you think comedy can make any difference *politically?*

ROBIN WILLIAMS: I actually *thought* so for a while. Before Bush's reelection, I really thought, "Hell, we can *do* this! *Look* at this idiot." For comics, he was a gift. Just the sheer visual of him, looking possessed, like some low-rent antichrist: Two sixes and a five.

Margaret Cho had one of the best lines: "Bush is no Hitler—but if he *applied* himself . . ."

Patton Oswalt talked about Bush believing his legacy will be great and history will prove him right—like suddenly he thinks he's the Velvet Underground: "Yeah, everyone tortures their citizens and pees on the Constitution, but I did it when it wasn't *cool.*"

I mean, we had *brilliant* people making *hard-core* fun for all those years . . . and what did it do in the end? He got elected *again*! It's the ultimate *bad* punch line! I was like, "We have to find whatever medication this country is on, whatever they're hypnotizing us with . . . 'Wake *up*, Dorothy! Wake up before you start speaking Chinese, Dorothy!'"

If you tried to *write* those eight years and pitch it as a movie . . .

"OK, there's a complete idiot running the country, right? And people *don't even notice!* They just laugh, see?"

"Are you for real with this?"

"Listen, listen . . . So we're going into this war, right? *Everyone* in the world says, 'No, *don't* do it!' but he says, 'We're doin' it anyway!'"

"All right, cut it out. This is crazy."

"And then—"

"Wait, don't tell me. He gets elected again?"

"Yes! He gets elected *again!*"

"Ah, fuck you. That's a ridiculous story. No one will buy that."

So we made serious, no-holds-barred fun of this guy for four years, only to have four *more* of 'em!

And the most incredible *political* comedy performance—or of *any* kind of comedy for that matter—was Stephen Colbert at the White House Press Correspondents' Dinner a few years back. *That* was *brilliant!* By the time he said, "A lot of people say this administration is sinking like the *Titanic*; I say, no, it soars like the *Hindenburg,*" you realized that *they* finally realize he's fucking with them—and *right inside in the lion's den!* You could see Bush get visibly upset that this guy was allowed into his domain, into the inner sanctum, to make fun of the pope. And he's laying it down *hard.* That, to me, was like, "Wow!"

The only reason I can think that they hired him was that they thought he really *was* a Republican, but a funny one. They *must* have thought, "He's really with us," 'cause they *didn't* get the joke, I guess. Someone must have just taken him at face value . . . which is *really* stupid.

PAUL PROVENZA: It's not hard for me to believe they actually thought he was one of them because, really, I don't know if there's all that much difference between Colbert's *character* and say, Ann Coulter.

ROBIN WILLIAMS: The difference is that he's *funny*, and she's just *vicious*. I think they're actually using her pap smears as antivenom now.

But you're right, in a sense. Maybe it's perception. Maybe a lot of Republicans think Coulter's funny as shit. She's doing *something* well, because she gets $50,000 a speaking engagement and kicks *ass*. She plays to hard-core Republican crowds, who *love* her. But then other people want to kill her, you know, so . . .

Maybe *that's* the difference: Colbert can play to pretty much anyone because it's *really* good satire. He's kind of a political Andy Kaufman—or is he?—what *is* he? He's so fucking *original*!

But I don't know what changes this culture or what it takes to get people motivated. But we *have* to keep on talking, saying all the shit they don't want anyone to hear. Because we *can*.

We're like the Resistance, just listening to the BBC, waiting for the code word. "The fight shall continue."

Performing again and hanging out in clubs with Bobcat Goldthwait, watching comedians like Patton Oswalt, Dana Gould . . . It gives me such *hope*. And Rick Overton—so funny, so smart, and going so *deep*. A lot of people are keeping the spirit of Pryor and Carlin alive—it's out there, man.

It takes *balls*. Bravery. And a lot of the brave people get waled on, as we know. The other side will go after you, and try to disembowel you. But as a comic, you have to *keep* talking about everything, *keep* doing what you do, wherever you can. Talk about it in every way you know possible.

And then occasionally throw in a good dick joke.

LEWIS BLACK

LEWIS BLACK IS a man for his time: a walking, talking embodiment of frustration, rage, and finger-pointing disbelief. On *The Daily Show*, his apoplectic rants reached millions, giving solace to those sharing his befuddlement. His solo career takes him even further in defining and expanding his voice, attracting a widening audience dying for him to vent its collective spleen. With his unmitigated bluster, Black explains why people respond so viscerally to his point of view, how he learned he could do what he does, and why wealth keeps him hating the wealthy.

LEWIS BLACK: If I was as good at writing dick jokes as writing what I do, don't think for a second I wouldn't be doing *that*. Outrage and political humor is just what I think I'm best at, but I'm not Gandhi. You get lost if you think like that.

If I have any place where I want to make a difference—and I've rarely admitted it—it's with college kids. As you get older you just get stupid, but kids still have possibilities. The thing I punch them on is, "You're at college for four years. It's the greatest time in your life; the time when you get to experiment. So to say you're a Republican or a Democrat . . . what's the matter with you? Can't you go beyond that? *Especially* if you say you're a Republican. There's no such thing as a conservative *kid*. To be honest, it means maybe something's wrong with you because as you grow older you grow *more* conservative, and where do you have left to go? What are you gonna become, a Nazi?"

PAUL PROVENZA: Do you think comedy *can* teach or enlighten, even if just younger people?

LEWIS BLACK: Absolutely. I do this dopey joke that kind of demonstrates that fact: I read this article where this woman almost bites off her husband's penis while he's cooking pancakes. She's blowing him, I presume; he accidentally spills burning oil down her back, she bites down on his penis, and he brings the frying pan down hard on her head. This story should be in a physics textbook and given to ten-year-olds. I know we have a real fear of sex in this country, but I *guarantee* you, read that

story to a ten-year-old child and he'll *never* forget that for every action there's an equal and opposite reaction.

So there ya' go, Provenz. Comedy *can* teach.

PAUL PROVENZA: Clearly you underestimate your gift for dick jokes. But by not *just* doing dick jokes, you've become prominent in political stand-up and satire. Does that freak you out a little?

LEWIS BLACK: That's called, "If you stick around long enough and yell loud enough . . ."

I always feel like a lot of it has to do with the fact that I yell and scream. The kind of hook with what I do that allows people to hear it or deal with it is the fact that I've created a guy who's nuts onstage. I'm the most insane person in the room, so I can basically spout any kind of nonsense.

I'm also conscious of the fact that I get just as upset about things like the weather. There's the same level of insanity there for me, no matter how appropriate or inappropriate it may be: "That cocksucker Al Roker's fucking making five million a year? He's reading a *scroll*! You gotta be fucking kidding me!" The weather can make me just as nuts as the Christian Right and their hoo-ha about gay marriage does.

I think that helps people realize that for me it's not Democrat or Republican or red or blue state—it's *everything*.

PAUL PROVENZA: Your character also enables you to experience genuine emotion rather than just tell us about it, so the audience can connect with you emotionally, not just intellectually.

LEWIS BLACK: Yeah, it does. It's also partly that there's an anger that they have, too. They take abuse on a daily level that's just grown—especially the middle class. If the federal government has cheeks and an anus, it's sitting on their faces and shitting in their mouths, so they relate to a guy yelling like a lunatic about things.

PAUL PROVENZA: Did you find your voice straightaway when you started doing comedy?

LEWIS BLACK: I had it in terms of the writing. The writing was strong, but the performance was hideous at best. Nightmarish. Sad. But I felt I had a sense of the writing. I wrote plays, which is how I started, in part. I wrote plays because other people would have to perform them, and got into comedy basically because I couldn't get anybody else to do my stuff so I had to stand up and do it myself.

It was later that I started to get serious about it. I was initially doing that "What, are you kidding me?" point of view, but I also did a lot about my sex life. That was my strong suit; I had a very funny sex life, and all these great stories—and to me that was key. That's the key to comedy in a lot of ways. I think it's where the initial impetus of comedy comes from, and I think the best comics are ones who, in the end, tell a story. On whatever level, you're basically telling a story, whatever it is. "This is what I saw today; this is what I heard today." It's what we'd do in college or high school when everyone sits down and talks. Nobody starts out, "My aunt cut off her foot." You generally start, "You won't believe this . . ." and then bring them on a journey that *ends* with " . . . and then I got a hand job."

Generally that's the way we relate, and for me that's the impetus that kind of drove me onto the stage.

PAUL PROVENZA: Does it destroy your "common man" cred, being rich and successful and now one of the "have a lots" instead of the "have nots"?

LEWIS BLACK: As a matter of fact, it's reinforced everything I've ever thought about rich assholes. I've learned *firsthand* that everything I believed about people with money and the way they're all protecting it is true. I really don't think I've lost *that* perspective at all.

Because I've been very fortunate, I now have a corporation and I see the way business managers and accountants do things. I look at my own business guys like, "What kind of *scam* are you running? At the end of the year, my company's broke on paper so it doesn't pay any taxes? What the fuck *is* that? How can that be *right*?"

I *want* to put my taxes in, and it's like I'm some kind of nut job to them. I go, "I've waited my whole *life* to pay taxes! I don't *care* if they're not using it as well as they should be; they'll use it *better* at some point. I've waited my whole life to *have* money so I can *give* money!"

I *do* like that I've given people jobs and I generate income for people, and there's a fellowship in my brother's name that I've been helping generate money for, for the last five years. I can *shovel* money to them—because the pricks that watch my money aren't directing it *anywhere*! They're just, "We can get you a shelf built out of a giant Courvoisier bottle made in the 1700s" or some stupid shit. Those *fucks*.

PAUL PROVENZA: I'm guessing it makes sense to you, but a shelf made out of a giant Courvoisier bottle is just surreal to me.

LEWIS BLACK: It is. I don't know what the fuck that was about. That happens sometimes.

PAUL PROVENZA: Just checking. I'm curious what you make of the Pew Research Center study that says *The Daily Show* is a primary source of news for so many people.

LEWIS BLACK: Well, the news—I call it "news" by default—stopped giving us information; they just editorialize. If some ninety-two-year-old dies, it's "The sad departure of so-and-so . . ." They're even editorializing on *that* level, you know? *I'll* decide if it's a sad departure, you prick.

Once the *New York Times* apologized for not giving us information on Iraq—for not *doing their job*—because of *The Daily Show*, Colbert, and others, all of a sudden comedy in essence became a place where information actually became disseminated at least as well, if not better. Even Keith Olbermann is pretty satirical sometimes; he says a lot of things in a very funny way.

PAUL PROVENZA: A lot of comedians appear on *Hardball*-type shows now and then, but you *never* do.

LEWIS BLACK: I don't want to be a pundit; I don't want to be in that position. I watched Janeane Garofalo get blindsided; they used her like a punching bag and I thought it was disgusting.

You can't put me on with Arianna Huffington and Pat Buchanan and Stinky Valdez and Hoopy Poopa and have me sit there and come out with a few comic lines while everyone just looks at me. Comedy has to be in a context where people *know* you're being funny, otherwise they'll take your jokes at face value. I was on some FOX show, of all things, some money show with Buddy Bing or whoever, and Ben Stein was on via remote. They come around to me with some question about Arnold Schwarzenegger and I said, "This thing about him running for president is insane. And being Jewish, my hair stands on end whenever I hear an Austrian accent."

They're looking at me, like, "What is *wrong* with you?"

Then Ben Stein goes, "Excuse me, but Arnold has given millions of dollars to a variety of Jewish organizations."

And I go, "Thanks for ruining the joke, Ben. Thank you, you *putz*."

Then the host goes, "We'll be right back with Lewis Black, who obviously doesn't like Austrians."

It's just a totally different skill set. It's like the skill you needed as the wiseass in junior high when you had to learn to pull your punches to work within the context of the classroom and not get your ass kicked by the teacher.

PAUL PROVENZA: Do you ever see some amazing piece of work that's so funny and so rich and think, "I'm a total charlatan. I'm not fearless at all; I'm playing it safe. I'm not doing anything that would make my own head explode."

LEWIS BLACK: Yeah, I get that. I watch some of the writing on *The Daily Show,* and just go, "Wow!" Will Durst does stuff that's so good, I'm, like, "You gotta be *kidding* me. How'd he *do* that?"

Not long ago Andy Borowitz did this thing about reality shows, and said the one he'd really like to see would be *Trading Meds,* where someone with ADD trades their Ritalin with the meds of some paranoid schizophrenic, and I just thought, "Goddammit! Fuck *me.*"

Stephen Colbert, of course, has done something just astonishing. Truly *astonishing.* It's the most major step of comedy of our generation of comics. I watched it evolve on *The Daily Show,* where he'd do it, then he'd do it some more, and then he just kind of fell into it and *became* it. I watch him just to go, "What more could he *possibly* do with this?" It's that improv skill he's got, that commitment to character. "Commitment" is really the key word. From the very beginning he made me laugh, but I was always, like, "How long can he keep doing this??" But he just gets stronger and stronger with it.

PAUL PROVENZA: In your book, you mention reading Paul Krassner's story "The Parts Left Out of the Kennedy Book" as a kid, and that it inspired you and made you think about comedy in a whole different way. I had a similar reaction when I came across it as a kid, and I've since learned it was pretty influential for a *lot* of people in comedy.

LEWIS BLACK: I must've been fourteen or fifteen when I started getting Krassner's *The Realist,* and I was the *only* one I knew who was getting it. It arrived once a month, and *man*! He had references to Lenny Bruce, one issue had this poster of a Disney character sex orgy—and up until that point in my life, Disney was an icon, so it was like somebody went, "The emperor has no clothes!"

It just flipped my world over. When I was growing up in the suburbs, it was all of the good and wonderful, but there was also this sense of, "This is way too idyllic. It's . . . *weird.*" It's great and safe, but you're always kinda looking over your shoulder, and the stuff in *The Realist* suddenly made me feel comfortable. Like, "So this *is* bullshit. These people *are* actually nuts."

The really big one was the one you're asking about. It was about *The Death of the President* book, which is considered *the* important tome on the Kennedy assassination—about what really happened from the moment he was shot in Dallas right up until his burial—all the details everyone's still arguing about to this day, fifty years later. The book was a big deal when it came out, and in *The Realist,* Krassner claimed to have gotten hold of the parts that had been edited out of it. He had written them himself, of course—and each one was more shocking than the last.

The thing I remember most was when they're flying the president's body back from Dallas, and Jacqueline Kennedy goes to the back of Air Force One where Lyndon Johnson is standing over the open coffin. She thought Johnson was performing—I'll never forget this—some "ancient Indian rite he might have learned in his Texas boyhood," but she was stunned to find that Johnson was actually fucking the bullet hole in JFK's neck!

It was like somebody gave me a drug. My head *exploded*. The Kennedy assassination had been the single most important event that happened in my life and in the collective life of the *country* up to that point, and just two or three years after the fact, Krassner had taken it and said, *"Fuck you!"*—you know? "Enough already! Sixteen thousand other things are happening, and we've *got* to move on."

I showed it to my friends and they went nuts over it, too. They started writing these cartoons, kind of in that vein, about some kid in our school who'd committed suicide. The rumor was that he'd done the autoerotic-asphyxiation thing, and that was the first time I'd ever heard of it, so it was pretty bizarre—and pretty fuckin' funny if you didn't know the kid, which we didn't. My friends wrote this cartoon that was just *wrong*—but it was *seriously* funny.

So that Krassner story had a huge impact on all of us. After reading it, I realized I could think things that were shocking, and that other people were thinking things that were shocking, too, and that they could be *funny*. And that it was okay to be *wrong*, as long as it was *funny*.

PAUL KRASSNER

PAUL KRASSNER WAS a close friend, colleague, and kindred revolutionary comedic spirit of the legendary Lenny Bruce, and edited the groundbreaking comedian's autobiography. In the 1960s, Krassner, Abbie Hoffman, and Jerry Rubin cofounded the antiauthoritarian Youth International Party—the YIPPIES!—engaging in political and cultural agitprop that provoked and energized the entire counterculture of that chaotic, explosive era. He founded and edited the underground magazine *The Real-* *ist*, a cultural landmark that, like the Velvet Underground's first album, had influence far beyond its modest range and distribution. One of its most notorious satires was an ersatz excerpt from William Manchester's *The Death of a President*. In it, Krassner exploded the boundaries of what was possible in satire, influencing and expanding the terrain for countless artists to follow. He recounts the origins of that epochal moment, and how comedy and political activism can become one and the same.

PAUL KRASSNER: "The Parts Left Out of the Kennedy Book" is my favorite thing I've ever written. I was relatively jaded already, so if it blew *my* mind, I assumed it would blow the readers' minds. Over forty years later, people still refer to that piece.

Let me give you context: In 1967, *The Death of a President* by William Manchester came out. This was *the* book about the assassination, *authorized* by the Kennedy family. There were all these news stories that Jacqueline Kennedy and Bobby Kennedy had problems with certain parts of it and the book had been bowdlerized to satisfy them. There was a lot of speculation about what they forced Manchester to delete.

Through my publishing contacts, I tried to get a copy of the original manuscript before the cuts, but I was not successful, so . . . I was forced to write them myself, in Manchester's style, as if he had written them, and I said these were the parts that got cut out.

I wrote it as a seduction for the reader. I started with true, known facts. One was that during the 1960 presidential primary Lyndon Johnson said publicly that JFK's father, former U.S. ambassador to England, Joseph P. Kennedy, was a "Nazi sympathizer." There'd been a story in the *New York Times*, and it was on the record that indeed, Joseph Kennedy *had* made such statements—something to the effect of how he had admired Hitler. So I started with those true, credible facts; everything in my story was authentic at that point.

Then I added some stuff about John F. Kennedy's affair with Marilyn Monroe—*also* true. Journalists knew it to be true, but it was a taboo then, so no one wrote about it, but it was *known* to be true.

There had also been story after story about Jackie being upset about a cover story in *Photoplay*, a movie celebrity magazine: "Jacqueline Kennedy: Is It Too Soon for Her to Start Dating?" I used that *true* story about Jackie being upset about that, and had her asking very William Manchester–like things like, "What will they ask next, do I use a diaphragm or take the Pill? Do I keep it in a drawer or in the medicine cabinet?"

All of it could very well have been in Manchester's original manuscript, so the piece built up verisimilitude and credibility right up until the climactic scene. It was all true or extensions of what was known to be true, and I kept peeling layers off this onion of truth until I got to the totally fictional core, a scene of—well, "Presidential Neck-rophilia."

The climax was Jackie Kennedy accompanying the president's body from Dallas to the hospital in Bethesda, Maryland. She describes her state of shock when she went into the part of Air Force One where JFK's body was and saw Lyndon Johnson leaning over the casket, "making strange motions with his body." She says she thought he might be performing some traditional Indian rite, because Johnson had taught Native American kids in Texas at one point in his life—also true, by the way; he had—so that's how she first rationalized what she was seeing. Then I had her say, "But no, I realized that he was, and there is no other way to put it, *fucking my husband in his throat wound*."

Then she says, "I just froze." Now, everyone at the time knew this iconic photo of Jackie on Air Force One "frozen" in a state of shock, Johnson standing nearby. The implication was that this incident was what happened right before that picture was taken, capturing her reaction to it.

I even included notes and citations in the article, which I attributed to the Warren Commission, referring to a semen analysis and suggestions that Johnson's fucking the throat wound might have been functional, possibly to make an entry wound coming from the "grassy knoll" look like an exit wound from shots coming from behind, where Oswald was.

That issue of *The Realist* had a circulation of 100,000, but an estimated couple million in passed-on readership—if your mind is blown, you want to share it with other people, you know? Ken Kesey told me Neal Cassady did exactly that on the bus; he read it and went, "Kesey! Take a look at *this*."

PAUL PROVENZA: Younger people may not realize how the country was affected by Kennedy's assassination, but even *four years later*, publishing *that* was like doing hard-core 9/11 jokes on 9/15—and really *vile*, disgusting ones.

PAUL KRASSNER: The printer who always did *The Realist* refused to print it! I had to search for one that would; even the printer of the *Communist Daily Worker* wouldn't do it. I finally found this small printer in Brooklyn who would.

Even my radicalized readership had its threshold, and I got so many threats and subscription cancellations. The radical Lefty editors of *Ramparts* magazine said it was a mistake to publish it and would hurt my credibility for other articles I was doing, particularly this serious piece by a respected investigative journalist about the Malcolm X assassination. So even within the ranks everyone saw it through their own eyes, but almost everyone said, "You'll get killed; you'll get sued for libel . . ."

I didn't want to hear that stuff, because you can't help but absorb other people's paranoia, and the only other choice was to *not* do it. That issue was already two months late because of the printer problem, so it made me realize my commitment. I went ahead with it, and I accepted that this was no longer a *career;* it was now *a way of life*.

I felt exhilarated. I went to a store in the Village that carried *The Realist,* and saw a kid holding a copy looking *dazed*. We talked a bit and he said, "It doesn't make any difference if this is true or not. Because *it is*."

That was my first review!

Someone told me that a young woman recently told him my story as being *true*. She'd never heard of me or *The Realist,* and with all the conspiracy theories and Bohemian Grove stories and that kind of stuff we've been hearing for decades, it didn't seem at all far-fetched to her. But English professors have told me students sometimes believe Jonathan Swift's "A Modest Proposal" was investigative journalism, actually exposing the *truth* about England solving Irish overpopulation by eating Irish babies, so. . .

It happens. I was performing once during a period when a bunch of new drugs had begun showing up on the streets, and I joked that the latest one was called "FDA," which I always thought *sounded* like a drug. It ended up in *Time* magazine: "A new hallucinogenic on the streets known as 'FDA' . . ." How great is *that*?

But the Kennedy piece *seemed* real, because I played on real character. Johnson *was* crude. He'd talk about Vietnam with cabinet members while sitting on the toilet taking a dump with the door open. On his yacht once, with some reporters, he took out his penis, put it on the railing, and yelled, "Watch it touch bottom, boys!" I just extended his actual, known persona as far as I could, and his real personality suggested maybe he really *was* a little "off." Maybe all that odd stuff was his unconscious poking through and he really *was* a madman.

That was the challenge: to write something incredible, but nurture it in the credible so people would say, "I believed it—*just for a moment*." *In* that moment, it revealed that they could find it *conceivable*. And if it was *conceivable*, the president may actually *be* insane.

I also went on all these radio shows and would *not* cop to a hoax—partly to see the fury of the interviewers, but also with that old idea that if a politician says his opponent's a pig-fucker, it puts his opponent in the position of having to say, "I'm not a pig-fucker!"

Well, Albert Merriman Smith of UPI wrote, "Terrible, terrible things written about President Johnson are being scooped up at newsstands across the city, and though I can't say in a family newspaper what it is, it's not true; it never happened."

Which of course sounded to me like, "Lyndon Johnson is not only not a *pig*-fucker, he's not a *corpse*-fucker!"

That was success to me. There was no separation between my work and play. It was pure *art*. Of course, other people said, "This is filth you find on bathroom walls!" so "art" is subjective. As is humor, and as is "obscenity."

PAUL PROVENZA: *National Lampoon* did satire and subversive humor, but *The Realist* was as much about legitimate journalism and commentary along with comic, satirical pieces, and each gave different context to the other.

PAUL KRASSNER: That was conscious. I launched it in 1958 with entertainment and the First Amendment as two sides of the same coin in mind; it was not either/or. I wanted a by-product of what I published to be examining what mainstream media pass along as news with a bit more healthy skepticism.

Maybe 50 percent of it was critiquing organized religion and politics, and I wanted to phase some of that out, intending it to be *all* satire, but stories kept coming to me that weren't satirical; serious investigative journalism stories that had been rejected by other magazines not because they were undocumented or inaccurate but because they were too controversial or violated taste or made publishers fear lawsuits. I felt privileged to have an outlet for those kinds of stories, so it became a mixture.

Sometimes a journalistic story seemed so outrageous that people thought it was a satire, and sometimes a satire was so believable people thought it was pure reportage—and I never labeled any of them as one or the other.

PAUL PROVENZA: Yourself along with Abbie Hoffman, Jerry Rubin, the Yippies!, the Diggers—so many of the 1960s protest movement—engaged in genuine protest and community organizing through comic agit-prop and humor. It was serious activism for civil rights, to end the war in Vietnam . . . And many of you were imprisoned or beaten, in some cases killed, and you were all under government surveillance. It was very serious business, but so much of that activism was *genuinely funny*. Arguments about whether the protests of the 1960s did any good notwithstanding, it had *impact*. That's a real inspiration, and a serious indication of what is possible through comedy.

PAUL KRASSNER: What *all* the people I've been fortunate enough to hang around and become good friends with had in common—Lenny Bruce, Abbie Hoffman, all of them—was a sense of *playfulness*. There was a certain irony intertwined with the politics and you couldn't separate them.

Abbie was a master at it. He played pool with the cops who arrested him. When the Yippies! were going to scatter dollar bills over the floor of the stock exchange, security wouldn't let this group of hippies in for the free tour, and Abbie said, "You know, we're all

Jewish. You don't want to be accused of anti-Semitism do you?" So they let him in! To toss out dollar bills and create total havoc.

The spirit of the Yippies! came from something Phil Ochs said, "A demonstration should turn you on, not turn you off." A lot of the Left didn't like the Yippies! because they thought we weren't being serious about serious matters. Like Steve Allen said, "A lot of wars are fought between the good guys and the good guys."

But we showed them you didn't have to be serious, and could still get the message across. People don't like being lectured to, and if you make them laugh at any moment, they're all agreeing on the truth that the humor's revealing.

PAUL PROVENZA: Are you impressed by any satire and political comedy you see today?

PAUL KRASSNER: There's *lots* of good stuff on the Internet, and a lot of good people doing it live. *The Daily Show* is terrific; really valuable, and genuine. But there's also a lot of what passes for satire, but is really just name-calling. How many people just did jokes about Bush being dumb rather than getting to the real core of what you're supposed to be exposing?

There are so many comedians who are great at their craft, but choose to go with the flow instead of being on the crest of any wave. I respect Jay Leno and David Letterman immensely and think they're *terrific* comedians, but they just joined in on all the demonizing of Saddam Hussein in the run-up to the war, and only when public opinion shifted did they start to really go after Bush. They *follow* opinion; they don't really care to *lead* it.

PAUL PROVENZA: Do you see a difference in the *state* of satire today as opposed to in the past?

PAUL KRASSNER: In a lot of ways. One big aspect is that the pace of everything has accelerated and the rate of acceleration is accelerating, so there are *instant* deadlines now.

Another is language. People like Lenny, Carlin, and Pryor were leaders of a movement breaking down *barriers* to free speech rather than just proudly exercising it as comedians do now. Perhaps the biggest difference is that what they did was truly *courageous*. Lenny went to jail for things he said; Carlin went to the Supreme Court to *defend* his free speech. Because of what *they* went through, that fear doesn't even exist now. To say things then took a real kind of courage that it just doesn't take now, so there's a huge difference in the *spirit* of satire now. It's not as courageous.

Except for Stephen Colbert at the White House Correspondents' Dinner. My jaw dropped watching that. *That* was courage. *That* was brave.

STEPHEN COLBERT

WHEN COMEDY CENTRAL debuted *The Colbert Report* in 2005, it was widely lauded as one of the most important innovations in satire since the invention of the word "satire" itself. Among comedians and comedy writers, the degree of difficulty in what Stephen Colbert does is, frankly, astonishing. Like Chuck Yeager breaking the sound barrier, no one was even sure he could survive it until he did. When Colbert appeared at the White House Press Correspondents' Dinner eviscerating President Bush and saying to the man's face what half the country wished for years someone would, he was hailed as a conquering hero. It was a moment that gave everyone in comedy pause, and made them question their own timidity. But while the comedy community—and many Americans—view Colbert as fearless, important, and uncompromisingly ballsy, the man himself has a more measured view of what he does and the impact it has.

STEPHEN COLBERT: I don't consider what I did at the White House Correspondents' Dinner brave. Antiauthoritarian maybe, but I think there's a difference between that and bravery, because I *enjoyed* myself. I was not afraid of the people in the room. I think "bravery" is action in the face of what you consider reasonable fear. But I wasn't afraid; I was so *excited*. It's like, if there was this chasm to go over and my jokes were my bridge, I had confidence in the construction. I was so happy to go and do it.

PAUL PROVENZA: I couldn't help but wonder if they had any idea they were letting a fox into the Republican henhouse. If so, someone there has a real subversive streak and I can't believe they didn't end up in Guantanamo.

STEPHEN COLBERT: I have to say that afterward, I wrote to the Correspondents' Association people who had asked me to do it and said, "I had a wonderful time, I certainly hope I didn't make any trouble for you." Because I *didn't* want to; they were very nice to me, and I'm not an *assassin*. I really like doing my work and my jokes, but I really didn't want to fuck this guy who booked me. But he said, "We *loved* it! Thank you. We're thrilled."

PAUL PROVENZA: You faced some apparent disdain from Bush and others on the dais, and as I watched it I couldn't help thinking, "His tax returns for the past ten years had better be *impeccable*." Yet you never wavered, never backed down, never bailed. Those of us who know what it's like dealing with that in front of any audience, let alone in front of the actual subject of your mockery who just happens to be *the President of the United States* and *the Most Powerful Man in the World,* see that as unbelievable courage and fearlessness. Do you think your performance had a greater weight in that context?

STEPHEN COLBERT: He's *eight feet* away from me! How could it not?

PAUL PROVENZA: More than just *his* reaction, do you think it was perceived as something more than comedy? That it was a real confrontation with the powers that be?

STEPHEN COLBERT: Oh, I don't know if it was seen like that. I know that afterward there was a lot of talk in the press and the blogosphere about it, and much was made of whether there was any significance to the evening, but I purposely haven't read that stuff, and in the room, nobody talked to me so I have no idea.

PAUL PROVENZA: Spoiler alert: a lot of people *did* see it that way. So you're in what seems to me a very odd position: you're an actor, a comedian, and a comedy writer, but you and your show are quoted in op-ed pages, studies say you're considered by many to be an actual news source—or at least an alternative to distrusted news sources—and you, your jokes, and this comic character are part of the narrative of American politics and the national discourse. Is that disconcerting?

STEPHEN COLBERT: I don't know whether I accept that, Mr. Provenza. What I mean is I don't accept that responsibility, because I don't accept *any* responsibility for anything I do, but I also don't know if I accept that premise. I don't necessarily think that my work is all that informative or all that influential. I think that it *is* influential in this regard: that I can make people feel better at times about something that otherwise might make them feel *sick*. But I don't know if that's the same thing as changing their minds.

PAUL PROVENZA: Does any of this make any difference or are we really just entertainers, and nothing more?

STEPHEN COLBERT: Surely someone's given you the Peter Cook quote about satirists. When asked, "Does satire have a political effect?" he said something to the effect of, "Absolutely. All that great satire of the Weimar Cabaret, look how they stopped Hitler."

I think when we do the show well, or when I do my job well, on some level it reflects honest, passionately held beliefs. Now, could those influence people? They could. But I'm not doing it to do so, and I'm not expecting it to. I don't feel it's a failure if it doesn't. If somebody tells me that I influenced them, it's not for me to say they're wrong, but that's not my goal and it's not the definition of my success. I'm out for laughs. When people came up to me after the Correspondents' Dinner and said, "Fuck those people, man. What does it matter if they laugh?"

I was, like, "No, it kind of *matters* to me."

PAUL PROVENZA: Many people who do satire feel the same way you do: they're not sure they have any effect and doubt that they can change people's minds. But at the same time, many feel that Bill O'Reilly, Rush Limbaugh, and Right-wing talk shows *do* have an effect and *do* influence politics.

STEPHEN COLBERT: I'd say the *aggregate* of them has an effect. Whether or not Bill O'Reilly himself does, if you've got a Bill O'Reilly and flip the channel and somebody else is parroting those same points, the entire news cycle gets hijacked by a particular take.

PAUL PROVENZA: So as satirists, by picking up and commenting on what's already churning in media, are we not then allowing ourselves to be "hijacked" the way the news cycle is? Should we be the ones to dig deeper to find some other take than what's already gained traction? Or finding out what is *not* already in the discourse—but maybe *should* be—and presenting that instead?

STEPHEN COLBERT: I agree, and I think I do it. The danger, for example, is that I've got to do a show tonight, and today, the scripts aren't ready. Generally, we have scripts in pretty good shape twenty-four hours ahead of time, but we're doing a soup-to-nuts rewrite today. Sometimes you get pressed by that clock into a point of view that you don't necessarily believe is the best, but that you know will be *comedically* successful. That is a danger, but we try to continually name that danger. If we don't do it *half* the time, I feel great.

I can understand getting hijacked by a particular take, because on *The Colbert Report* we're constantly going, "Do we really want to say that, or are we just parodying what other people are saying?" We ask, "Is that really what the story is about?" all the time. I'm sure *actual* news [people] ask themselves that question all the time. But then there's the hungry beast of the clock, which goes, "Come on, we know Blitzer's going to be out there in *The*

Situation Room in five minutes. What's the story?"

And they go, "Well, *this* is just being reported."

"Okay, let's just go with *that*." I'm as human as they are. But the real crime here is laziness. Lazy thought and willful ignorance. After the first time we ever did *The Colbert Report,* I said, "If this show works and goes on and on for years, it won't matter who's in office, what the political landscape is or what the story of the day is, because what we're talking about is willful ignorance of *facts* over what *feels* like news to you, what *feels* like the story, what *feels* like the truth." I said, "*That* will *never* go away."

One of the great sins in modern news is that the facts really don't matter. Those nighttime shows are the most popular shows and they are all about *feeling*. That is not a sin specifically of the guys that I parody, that is a sin—and "sin" is a strong word, but I'm a Catholic—of laziness and fear: laziness about getting a different take on a subject, and fear that you won't serve the beast of the clock on the wall. In my opinion. I could be wrong—I'm a comedian.

PAUL PROVENZA: On *The Colbert Report,* you're actually satirizing a form and type of media personality more than satirizing newsmakers and actual events of the day.

STEPHEN COLBERT: We do both. I may be stealing this definition of satire from somebody, but "Satire is *parody with a point*." Presently, I am parodying willful ignorance. But I have to say the medium is a lot of my message.

PAUL PROVENZA: And as a comedian, I think what you're doing is completely unique in comedy. Can you point to any influences that got you to this fully formed character and comic idea?

STEPHEN COLBERT: Well, one for sure was Don Novello's *The Lazlo Letters.* I read the covers off those things. I loved Novello's stuff so much I wanted to ape it, and actually started writing letters like that myself when I was in college. As the phenomenon of the Young Republicans started—college-aged Republicans—I and a friend of mine, Rich Ferris, started an organization called "Us Young Republicans," and we would write to people, the way Novello did.

I love Novello's character of Lazlo Toth, and there's some of that DNA in what I do, for sure. I frequently think of Lazlo Toth when I think about my character's emotional ignorance.

PAUL PROVENZA: Do you meet people who don't get it? Who don't see your character as a character?

STEPHEN COLBERT: People who care to know me generally get it. I'm not saying people never get it wrong, but I myself have only encountered that once: when I was still at *The Daily Show*, I did a piece about how diverse the population of delegates was at the National Democratic Convention: African-Americans, Native-Americans, Jews, environmentalists—or "tree huggers," as I'd call them—homosexual rights lobbyists, union workers, "Gandhi Indians"—as I called them, as opposed to "Sitting Bull Indians"—that kind of thing.

I got them all together on a panel, and tried to get them to agree on things. Of course I picked very divisive topics, and it ended up being a cacophony that I just walked out of, like I couldn't wait to get to the Republican Convention where they all spoke with one voice.

Then I went to do a piece at the Republican Convention. It had been kind of a *dull* night. Madison Square Garden was empty, but I'm sitting in the bleachers, thinking, "How am I going to cut this together into something?" and a guy comes over in one of those "here's your cowboy hat for being at the convention" cowboy hats and he says, "I'm from Bush Headquarters in Dallas, and I gotta tell you, I *love* that piece you did on the Democrats and how many crazy different kinds of people they have! I mean, what are they thinkin', man? They're never going to get that coalition together."

And I said, "Oh, that's interesting. Um, you know, that was *ironic*. The whole point of it was that it's a nice effort to *try* to get those kinds of people together. It was really kind of a celebration of what they were doing, and the idea that the Republicans are all one voice is a criticism of what is essentially the patriarchal power structure still propped up by the white, Christian male leadership of the Republican Party."

That was generally the idea of what I said to him, and he looks at me and goes, "Huh. Well . . . I'll take your word for it, but it was funny as hell, man. We play it all the time."

Then he just walked away, and I went, "Oh . . . Okaaaay."

PAUL PROVENZA: I can't help wondering if that may happen more often than you're aware.

STEPHEN COLBERT: I think maybe you're right, too. I don't put much stock in things like the Pew Research Center study that says young people get more of their news from me and Jon Stewart than any other place. *However* . . . Harvard did a study at the Kennedy School about Jon Stewart's and my demographics. Basically, it said that traditional Democrats watch his show 46 percent to my 29 percent, something like that, and traditional Republicans watch me 49 percent to his 25 percent. So there might actually *be* some "I identify with what that guy's saying." There *might* be a little bit of that in there.

PAUL PROVENZA: And does it matter?

STEPHEN COLBERT: Oh, it absolutely doesn't matter to me. I'm not crafting my work for a demographic. I'm just glad people watch, and I don't suppose they'd watch other than to laugh. So if they're laughing, then that's fine with me.

PAUL PROVENZA: Given that "willful ignorance" is bipartisan, do you consider yourself Left-wing or Right-wing?

STEPHEN COLBERT: There are times that my character's ignorance of himself allows him to say liberal things or even hold liberal ideas without any knowledge of it. In reference to my character, he's generally conservative.

I myself sometimes agree with him. It doesn't matter to me if my audience knows when that is, but I *do* sometimes agree with my character. But generally speaking, if you slap me across the face at three A.M. and say, "What are you?" I'd say I'm a liberal.

PAUL PROVENZA: If your audience doesn't know whether you're making fun of a Left- or Right-wing position at any given moment, does that not get in the way of the point?

STEPHEN COLBERT: I think sometimes it could muddy the sharpness of the satire, but I'm also creating a character, and I enjoy that occasionally the audience gets a whiff of my *personal* honesty out of the character's mouth, and they may not even be aware of it.

PAUL PROVENZA: So you let your own views slip through—

STEPHEN COLBERT: They don't slip through; they're purposeful. I like jumping over the line between who I am and who the character is, to confuse the audience. If my game is continuous, if I'm continually merely saying the opposite of what I mean, that becomes a well-worn rut. From the beginning I've wanted to do things that are (a) self-critical, and (b) also reflecting my honest beliefs at times. It's not all that often, but *occasionally,* because I think then the audience will listen a little bit closer.

PAUL PROVENZA: Does that soften the character?

STEPHEN COLBERT: It adds a layer of reality to it.

PAUL PROVENZA: Doesn't playing a character create distance? Can people not take the point seriously since it's just from a quasi-fictional character? And if they hold views you mock, can't they just say to themselves, "Oh, that guy's just a joke?"

STEPHEN COLBERT: I try to wear his mask *lightly,* but never really take it off *fully,* because it allows me to say things that you would not forgive *me* for saying. For instance: "That Rosa Parks is overrated. Let's not forget she got famous for breaking the law, okay? Last time I checked, we don't honor lawbreakers. I think that gets lost in this whole back-of-the-bus thing. Don't get me wrong, it took a lot of courage, but I think we're burying the lead, here. She's a *criminal.*" I can get away with that through the mask of my character.

I suppose many comedians keep some level of mask between themselves and the audience, and the audience agrees to let them get away with it, but I wear it all the time on my show, to various thicknesses. That's how the character helps me. I can get away with shit. Most of the time.

PENN JILLETTE

AS THE BIGGER, louder half of the Las Vegas magic duo Penn and Teller, Penn Jillette not only performs magic, he often deconstructs it for the audience. As co-producer and co-creator of the comedy/documentary *The Aristocrats,* he deconstructed not just a joke but the art of creating comedy and of being funny. On his Showtime series *Penn & Teller's* *Bullshit!,* he and Teller put the lie to all manner of urban myths, old wives' tales, and other commonly held truisms. In this interview, he calls "bullshit" on icons of satire itself. From Jonathan Swift to Lenny Bruce to Borat and Stephen Colbert, Jillette opines on why irony, sarcasm, and ironic detachment will never be a substitute for speaking from the heart.

PENN JILLETTE: The fact that Colbert can pass off anything he does as "satire" just seems very, very *safe* to me. There's a kind of protection in satire—in that you get to do your emotional acting as someone else, and if you are *wrong,* it's very hard to tell exactly *how* you're wrong.

If *I* say, as myself, "There's been too much collateral damage in Iraq; too many innocent people have died," then you can come back and say, "But it's during a war and we're trying to protect American soldiers. Can you go into a war and worry about the other side's collateral damage more than your own soldiers?" And then we'd get a real discussion going about that. But as soon as I go into a character, like . . . say I'm playing the part of "The Guy Running the Acme Chemical Company, Who Has All the Money in the World And His Hand Up the President's Ass Because the President Is His Puppet," okay? If I'm *wrong* as that guy, well, we can be in an area where I was using hyperbole, or where I was using a certain kind of shading . . . all kinds of stuff like that. As that Acme presidential puppeteer guy, I can go, "Well, the job *is* collateral damage! The more women and children we kill the quicker they'll be broken down," and you can't come back and say, "Wait a minute, you can't make that argument."

Intellectually, it's just all sorts of shading and *sloppiness.* It all ends up being such broad strokes that the interesting stuff gets lost for me.

When I'm watching Jon Stewart, there's a sense that he's speaking from his heart—that's not always true, of course, it's show business—but that's the sense of it: he's being him, it's *his* point of view; it's him and *his* thoughts and feelings. But when you go to Stephen Colbert, that ancient Greek question of "Who am I?" of every poem gets rammed down my throat too much. It seems more of an intellectual puzzle and less of pure balls to me.

Stephen Colbert is *so* smart and *so* talented and *so* cool, but I was so much more interested in talking to him backstage, out of character, than I ever am in watching his show.

I think I don't much like satire. There's a lack of nakedness in it that I often find much less interesting. It seems like in satire, almost by definition, you have to bump up the character enough to say, "This *isn't* me, this *isn't* me, this *isn't* me."

It grabs me when someone is really talking to me; the lack of archness and the lack of artifice just grabs my heart. In Lenny Bruce's classic bit about "Would you rather fuck a black woman or a white woman? How about if the black woman was Lena Horne and the white woman was Kate Smith?" he talks about who *he'd* rather fuck. To me that's so much more profound and there's so much more to think about because it's in Lenny's *own* voice; it's Lenny talking *personally.*

When he did "How to Relax Your Colored Friends at Parties," which is satire, and was a really important bit about civil rights and prejudice and tokenism, if you just read the script, all it says is, "Racism is stupid," and that liberals avoid it sloppily. But to me, the intense part of that bit was that he had one of the African-American jazz musicians in the band come out and play the part of the black man the character talks to at the white liberal's cocktail party. To me, that makes the whole tension, and it humanizes it, you know?

I'm *always* less interested in anyone who is doing a character. The exceptions to that, and I don't know why it is, are in music—like when Randy Newman or David Bowie or Lou Reed and even Tom Waits have done whole songs as characters. They really interest me, and I think that's because of the form itself—when you bring music into it, it's so much more confessional.

PAUL PROVENZA: Is it that the music itself evokes feelings and makes a connection?

PENN JILLETTE: The clearest examples of Randy Newman doing this are songs that I love: "Sail Away" and "God's Song." And, as satire, "Sail Away" is the hardest example to make any sense out of for me, because I kinda think the parts of that song that kill me dead are actually the parts that are *not* satire.

The slave trader sings, "Don't have to run through the jungle, scuff up your feet." That part fries me, because at the time he wrote that song in the early seventies, it probably *was* better to be an African-American in the U.S. than to be an African in wherever it was they took him from. And Randy Newman is *so* into the character there that it almost makes it seem like there really *is* a justification, and he's actually *making* it! Those are the parts that are really, really scary.

When satire crosses over into seeing the

point of view of the enemy, it becomes really fascinating. Is it even still satire?

PAUL PROVENZA: I think that makes it really *good* satire, and why so much of it is misunderstood and upsets people. Abbie Hoffman comes up for me along those same lines of "Is it even satire?" Even as a kid watching things he was doing on the news at the time, as my very conservative, hawkish dad railed against nutty things Abbie Hoffman was in the middle of—people holding hands surrounding the Pentagon trying to levitate it, throwing dollar bills down onto the floor of the stock exchange and creating havoc—even then I had a sense that this was some kind of comedy going on. But it was on the *news*! He was very funny on talk shows while he made serious points, but he was arrested, charged with conspiracy to incite riots, was even mentioned by Nixon himself on the infamous White House tapes as someone they needed to go after and get out of the way. What he was doing was not *about* silliness, but it was clearly *very* silly. And being silly got him in trouble and made him a real threat.

PENN JILLETTE: Abbie Hoffman, because of my age, was very important to me. I read *Steal This Book* . . . He meant everything to me.

In the late sixties, when all that stuff was happening, I thought that what I loved about Abbie Hoffman and what he was doing was the politics. I loved that it was real; I loved that he really believed in things. But Abbie was really interested in not getting too close to the other hippies and Yippies! He'd take a cab away from the scenes of the things, throw his hair under a hat, and get out of there, because he wanted to go back to someplace and laugh about it. *That* was really important to him. So I now realize—and it's, like, the hardest thing to admit—that Abbie Hoffman probably now comes under my category of artist/comedian, and the political stuff is actually pretty insignificant.

I remember when I was in high school having a huge screaming argument over an article in *National Lampoon*, where I believed that all that mattered in it was the political content, and the person arguing against me had the foolish point of view that maybe some of it was in there to be *funny*. That was the most *appalling* point of view that I could imagine! And when I saw the movie *Lenny,* with Dustin Hoffman playing Lenny Bruce, at the end of the movie—I believe the last line of it—they say "He was a very funny guy." I was appalled by *that,* too. Lenny Bruce being funny was *totally* unimportant to me. Abbie Hoffman being funny? *Totally* unimportant. There was a much higher calling than that.

But you know, my wife occasionally has to tell people, "I don't mean this as an insult—it's one of the reasons I love my husband—but you've gotta understand he takes *everything* seriously."

I was complaining that my three-year-old daughter was being thrown into this whole "princess" culture. I watched a little bit of *Aladdin* with her and there's all this stuff about being a princess, all her friends have these "princess days," she has this Disney princess game where she moves these little

princess puppets around the board . . . And I said to her, "You're not my little *princess*—you're Daddy's little *freedom fighter.* You're not Daddy's royally born, with no egalitarian spirit and able to keep down other people because of your ancestry and birth. You're an individual, and you will accomplish in life what you *want* to accomplish. Your friends, *they* are their daddies' little princesses—*you* are Daddy's little freedom fighter. If you want to dress up, dress up like Betsy Ross! Dress up like Susan B. Anthony!"

And I was saying things like, "Lady Di was an evil whore! Why did anybody in America like her? She's a symbol of everything bad! Susan B. Anthony—women's rights, atheist, abolitionist . . . Everything Susan B. Anthony did was right! Dress up like her! Dress up like Madame Curie! There are female *heroes* that you can dress up as. Don't do the *princess* thing."

And my sister-in-law looked at me and said, "You know, Penn, I don't think it's meant that seriously. I think it has more to do with playing dress-up and the nice pretty gowns. I don't think she's thinking all that much about keeping down the proletariat."

But I feel a horrible guilt come over me when she pulls out the princess book for me to read and look at the gowns. I just feel, "This is so *wrong*."

PAUL PROVENZA: If satire or character stuff seems detached or impersonal, has anything that's clearly satire ever been able to make the leap across that distance to affect you in a visceral, emotional way?

PENN JILLETTE: Randy Newman's "Rednecks" is the easiest example of that for me.

When I heard it, I was living in Massachusetts, and I'd been brought up to believe there were no civil rights problems in New England, and that Northerners understood that blacks were okay, and Southerners were poorly educated, bigoted, bad people, and they had all the problems with race. I was brought up to hate Southerners the way Southerners were brought up to hate blacks. So the song "Rednecks" was a baseball bat to my chest.

These aren't the actual lyrics—which are beautifully written—but it starts out with the redneck character singing about how Lester Maddox was on TV "with a smart-ass New York Jew," and how the Jew and the audience all laughed at Maddox. And he goes into how they all think they're better than Lester Maddox but, he says, they're wrong.

And he proceeded to sing *exactly*, precisely about *my* point of view—as a *satire* of it. He was satirizing the way *I* saw rednecks!

It turns at the end—so much so that it was banned from radio play in Massachusetts, because the character says that down South they're just too ignorant to realize that "niggers" up North have been set free. And basically he says, yeah, sure black people are free up North—free to be put in a cage. He says they're free to be put in cages in all these black ghettoes he names in all these different cities—including "in Roxbury in Boston."

I'd been to Boston only three times, to see concerts—one of them Randy Newman—and I'd never even been to Roxbury, but hearing that . . . my world collapsed. Randy Newman made a point in "Rednecks" that sticks with me to this very day and informs my very shallow, uninformed thinking about racial relations in America.

It changed my thinking from "I know everything I need to. I'm from Massachusetts; we didn't have cotton plantations, we were on the correct side of the Civil War, I'm totally okay on the racism thing all the way back" to "Wow, I really don't know *jack shit* about this."

PAUL PROVENZA: And, by extension, "I might be part of the problem?"

PENN JILLETTE: Yeah, exactly. Sure. And what's interesting is that at first blush you could say it's an example of satire making a huge political and emotional difference in someone's life, but if you graph it out, it wasn't the *satire* that blew my mind. What blew my mind and made me think differently was the point of view that was *being* satirized. It was my own!

RANDY NEWMAN

RANDY NEWMAN HAS long worn two hats, one as a venerated, Oscar-winning film composer, the other as a sardonic singer/songwriter whose incisive, disturbing lyrics lay bare many of our nation's assumptions and great hypocrisies. With melodic, seductive tunes like "Sail Away," "Rednecks," and "Short People," Newman affected a generation of future satirists. Sometimes misunderstood, he courted controversy by often assuming the first-person voice of the undesirables he portrays. But in this thoughtful discussion he explains why, like a broken heart, racism is easier to understand if you put it in a song.

RANDY NEWMAN: The point the guy in "Rednecks" is ultimately making is that he's offended by the way Dick Cavett and his audience treated Lester Maddox on his show—being morally superior to Maddox and people of the South—because there's racism *everywhere*. There is *no* basis for anyone anywhere in America assuming moral superiority over citizens of Georgia.

Lester Maddox was awful, no doubt about it. It's public record; you *could* hate him, and if they had let him talk he would've indicted *himself*. But they didn't let him speak—as if they all had black friends at home. Bullshit, y'know? An audience of New Yorkers has no right to scream and not let him speak as if they were on some moral high ground. I set up a character that used *that* word for black people, and uses it on purpose, but the point he makes? He's right. That character's vile, but his point of view is *not*.

The only "cheat" in that song is that the guy knows the names of all those ghettoes and he *wouldn't*, okay, but he's an American, and he's *not* Lester Maddox, and he's right that there *isn't any* moral high ground in this country where racism's concerned. It's been our great sin. And despite all the songs I've written about it, it's not cured.

PAUL PROVENZA: You *have* dealt with that issue quite a bit.

RANDY NEWMAN: I really have. I wonder when I'm gonna stop. Apparently, it bothers me a great deal that this kind of thing exists.

It's *always* bothered me. My father was a rough feller who hated a lot of people and a lot of things, but he didn't have an *ounce* of that kind of bigotry in him. A black woman from Texas brought up my brother and me, to a large extent, and my mother was from the South, so as a kid I'd see the COLORED ONLY and WHITE ONLY signs—and I'm not saying I was oh so sensitive and ran home crying and ate a madeleine, but I *noticed*.

It's astonishing, the disparity. You just can't put it in words. It comes from something so *clearly* unfair. It's complicated, but it's simple in that affirmative action *is* required. When an African-American is born, he's born behind, because he's going to encounter that kind of fear, no matter what. Unless he's wearing a sign saying I'M A MILLIONAIRE, he goes into a market and women grab on to their purses.

PAUL PROVENZA: Has hip-hop and rap altered the way the white middle-class relates to the African-American experience in any way?

RANDY NEWMAN: If it has, it's just been the kids, but I don't think so. I think people still get scared when black kids come into their shop; they're not any more comfortable just because they like Jay-Z.

But people don't get along in Switzerland, or in Belgium either, you know?

PAUL PROVENZA: That's an important point: in no way have we solved or addressed every aspect of race in America; we certainly have far to go and much injustice that desperately needs correcting, but I've traveled the world and worked with comics of every race in many different cultures, and it's shocking how much deep-seated racism exists in every other country I've ever been to. Endemic racism is accepted; even worse, *unacknowledged*. The tragic truth is that even with how far we have to go, no country on earth has made such strides, such effort, and has such awareness of racial issues as America.

RANDY NEWMAN: You're right. When it comes to race, no one can throw stones at us. We *agonize* about it. And America's doing absolutely, unequivocally the best when it comes to immigration, too.

In Europe you don't even have to be a different *color*. I don't think people can get along if people are just *different*. I don't know what the hell it is.

PAUL PROVENZA: Do you find people who may sing along a little *too* enthusiastically with something like "Rednecks"?

RANDY NEWMAN: Yeah, I do, actually, but there's nothing I can do about that. It comes with the territory; what can you do? There's something about the beat that makes you sing along. It's a powerful thing.

In any number of ways it's a very strange medium to do what I do—to write first-person songs and comedic songs; songs that aren't love songs, like, "I fell in love with a woman, but she wasn't my type"—so if you make someone *laugh*, you kind of know you're all right; you don't have to wait for applause or anything. A laugh is, like, "They like me!"

But I figure if you're up there and you have a lyric, you should *say* something. Most of the repertory of song-writing is love songs; that's what people like, they always have and always

will, so it's the wrong medium for what I do.

And people don't really listen to music like we used to in the sixties and seventies. It's now background while doing something else, and my stuff doesn't work too well if you're doing something else. If you're hearing it at a party or while driving at seventy mph, you're not going to go, "Oh, that guy's being ironic." You're either not following the story or the jokes, and will lose a little bit. So it's a strange choice I made, and I'm very lucky to have done as well as I have.

PAUL PROVENZA: Do you set out to make points that are important to you, or does your sense of humor just seem to take you to those places?

RANDY NEWMAN: I'm out to make people laugh. I like comedy; it's my favorite form of entertainment, along with classical music. I'm trying to make people laugh, almost first and foremost. Naturally I want minds to be changed about certain things I write about, but I never believed that music could change the world.

Maybe I'm *wrong*. Maybe it did help the whole movement to get us out of Vietnam faster; maybe it did do some good things. But it's had more effect on fashion than anything else.

PAUL PROVENZA: Can music or comedy or anything artists do change any *minds* about anything?

RANDY NEWMAN: No. In your life, how many arguments have you won? I can't think of three.

PAUL PROVENZA: Well, there's another one I

just lost. So do you think of yourself more as a comedian or as a songwriter?

RANDY NEWMAN: Songwriter. Comedy's a really important *part* of my songwriting. I like to make people laugh, maybe inordinately, which is why I write songs the way I do even though that may not be what people like about them.

PAUL PROVENZA: With the risks you've taken and challenging subjects you've tackled, did you expect that "Short People" would be responsible for the only serious flak you've ever gotten? That looked to me like a classic example of missing the point. What was your intent and how was it misconstrued?

RANDY NEWMAN: What I intended was an "up" song for the album. I needed something that moved. I had that rhythm going, and I just thought of this idea about a crazy guy with a psychosis about short people. It *wasn't* about prejudice; it wasn't about anything bigger than just somebody who was loony. As a matter of fact, I think I *was* a little insensitive to people about their height. I just didn't think it was a big deal. But it made a lot of people very angry.

I had to *say* it was about prejudice and racism, because it reached people that I've never reached before or since, but it really *wasn't*. There isn't some cabal against short people—the guy was just crazy!

PAUL PROVENZA: Have I ascribed aspects of the rest of your work to this particular song and given it more credence than it deserves? A guy who singles out and hates short people wasn't meant to be an absurd analogy for an irrational hatred toward *any* group of people?

RANDY NEWMAN: There wasn't any hatred to that group of people, and they weren't meant to *represent* anything. If I wanted to write a song about prejudice, I did it about seven, eight times about black people, or people that are different. "Davy the Fat Boy" was about that kind of thing.

It's often *individuals* that interest me. It interested me that *this* guy was so nutty about *this* one subject, that's all. It *is* giving too much credit to that song to extend it to being about prejudice.

PAUL PROVENZA: You've just pulled the rug out from underneath everything I believed from the moment I heard it. But that brings up an interesting point about how what we do simply because it's funny to us ends up meaning other things as people interpret it.

RANDY NEWMAN: And sometimes things take you places you didn't even know you were going. I've got a song about America, "A Few Words in Defense of Our Country," and the last verse is *sad*. The end of any empire is particularly sad to me, but I didn't know it would go there until I arranged it and realized, "Hmmm . . . This is kind of a sad picture here."

I do feel somewhat sorry for Americans. We're brought up to think America's the best place on earth, but you don't measure a nation's greatness by how many guns they have, you measure it with boring things like infant mortality, standard of living, health, and how they care for their poor or aged—of which I am one. I'm sad that people's idea of this country has been disabused by what's happened recently.

PAUL PROVENZA: Since I was so wrong about "Short People," I'd better ask about "I Love L.A." Is *that* ironic, or do I have to rethink that one too?

RANDY NEWMAN: Ha! Well, it's true that the weather's great and it *is* great to drive in an open car with a redhead listening to the Beach Boys, but it's *also* true that there are bums on their knees, and I purposely named streets in it that aren't exactly the Champs-Elysees.

It's not a straight-out "New York Is My Kind of Town" song. And when people chant "We love it!" at Lakers games, they *know* it's funny; they know a *real* "chamber of commerce" song about a big American city shouldn't mention a bum and all that in it.

PAUL PROVENZA: That's such beautiful satire, *because* of its ambivalence. Two people can hear it, one can take it literally, the other ironically, and *both* are kinda right. It's on that razor's edge of irony/not irony.

RANDY NEWMAN: You're right. But whom would *you* rather have in the audience? I can't decide which one I'd rather have in the audience myself.

It's a "toe-tapper." That the song is played at Lakers and Dodgers games, that it's got "the bum on his knees" and the raggedy streets, none of that diminishes its appeal—but it's got some things in it. If it didn't have that stuff in there, I wouldn't have written it.

PAUL PROVENZA: *Do* you love L.A.?

RANDY NEWMAN: I don't know anymore! I like the weather, but I've never been through a real winter, so I don't know. *I don't know!*

PAUL PROVENZA: Then I'm okay on that one. That's what makes your work so compelling to me—it's often in a shade of gray; the ideas, the understanding you give to your characters even when they have really ugly points of view create tough, conflicting emotions. "Sail Away" is a perfect example. While not a laugh riot, it's funny as well as moving and disturbing.

RANDY NEWMAN: If I don't announce that it's about a recruiter for the slave trade, I'm not sure most people would get it. Since the guy's trying to recruit people into slavery, he's making it as attractive as possible, like someone recruiting a high school ball player.

People don't expect something like that to come in that kind of a package, in a song. It sounds pretty and you wanna sing along, and then you realize what you're singing along with, and . . . It's an *odd* song. I'm glad I wrote it.

PAUL PROVENZA: It feels like there's a "meta-joke" in the fact that people get lulled into this *horrible* character's third-person point of view.

RANDY NEWMAN: You're right. It *does* lull you, and you don't want people laughing out of the side of their nose, saying, "Oh, we can't enjoy this music because of what it's about." But if you really think about it, it *is* a jarring contrast.

PAUL PROVENZA: I wish that *all* of us in comedy had more license to play with all those other emotions. I feel like comedy's the only art form where the emotional range is limited by the audience: emotions A through M are acceptable for comedy; emotions N through Z don't belong in comedy. Like any other art form, comedy should be able to evoke a lot of different emotions along *with* laughter, as your work does so richly.

RANDY NEWMAN: It's hard to do. I have music going for me, so I can get through it. It'd require quite an acting job to bring off something like that. Writers that are good enough—Harry Shearer, Albert Brooks— could bring off something like that. Lenny Bruce did things like that and brought it off. I couldn't.

Take the lyric in "Sail Away": "Won't have to run through the jungle and scuff up your feet." If that were prose, you'd have to get a laugh pretty quick just to continue. You'd have to be a great actor to make comedy out of that character, but in a song I can just go on singing.

PAUL PROVENZA: Which brings us back to "Rednecks." You use "nigger" in "Rednecks," said by the *character* you portray in the song, not by you. Do people get past that explosive word to understand the point and reason you're using it?

RANDY NEWMAN: Not everybody, I don't think. There are places I don't play it. Sometimes I'll intro it by telling the story of how I happened to write it. It's a close call, that word, whether to use it or not. If there's just been some kind of incident it may be even worse, but the word's *always* been ugly.

It's always been the worst thing a white person can say—but I didn't think twice about using it. I always knew the character was going to use that word. I felt he *had* to; there was no way I could write that song without it.

Even so, it's not something I'm completely comfortable with.

PAUL MOONEY

IT WOULD BE far too reductive to label Paul Mooney as simply a "black comedian," as his range and audiences are much broader than the term suggests, though it would be perfectly apt to do so. He has been and remains a leading African-American satirical voice, and his career follows somewhat the evolution of modern black comedy itself. In the 1970s he wrote for Richard Pryor, helping to craft some of his best-known and most incendiary material and the use of a certain word that we all know and shouldn't say. In the wake of Michael Richards's racially charged, epithet-laden meltdown at L.A.'s Laugh Factory, Mooney's got a lot more to say on the subject. But even as his language has changed, his antiauthoritarian opinions and his refusal to care what anyone may think of them have not.

PAUL MOONEY: Michael Richards was a godsend. He was. He put the N-word on the table, that's what he did. It stopped the world. Everybody wants to say that it's just one person, it's just Michael Richards, but it's not. It's everyone. America is responsible for him; America has to take the responsibility. Everyone in this room has to take responsibility.

I took it, and that's why I stopped saying it.

PAUL PROVENZA: *Paul Mooney* stopped saying the N-word??

PAUL MOONEY: Of course I did. Because of that incident.

PAUL PROVENZA: You've used it more than every gangsta rapper *combined*.

PAUL MOONEY: Oh, I was an *ambassador* for that word. I was a lover to that word—and like a lover, I stayed right with it. Richard Pryor and I made a lot of money saying that word. Then Richard went to Africa and came back saying that it wasn't in any African language, and he wasn't going to say it. But I couldn't see the N-word for the trees. Richard Pryor couldn't stop me from saying it, but Michael Richards did.

I've known Michael for over twenty years, and what's funny is that everybody came at me saying he's not funny. Well he started out in stand-up, and he was *very* funny, but he got caught up in that Hollywood bullshit. He was the "darling of the discotheque." They sucked out of his ass on that hit show of his, okay? When that show went off the air, he was looking for that same thing he always wanted: that *attention*. So he came back to this arena, but,

like Jesse James, if you hang those guns up you're gonna get shot in the back.

He had hung those guns up. And it also wasn't the same arena, it wasn't the same audience, and he fell. Comedians, we don't like to fail up there. If you listen to the tapes of the audience, the Mexican gentlemen and the black gentlemen who were heckling were more vicious to him than he could ever hope to be, saying, "You ain't funny, you ain't never *been* funny." They talked shit to him, so he reached into hell to pull out all that shit he was talking.

When it went down, Reverend Jesse Jackson and everybody else called me. They brought me over to the Hilton to a room with Michael. That boy grabbed on to me—I told you how long I've known him—he clutched on to me, didn't know if I was gonna hit him or curse him out or whatever. He just hid. He was scared to death. He told me he didn't even know he had that in him; that it wasn't a performance, it was a meltdown.

He freaked out from what was going on, and he was real sorry. He said white people were calling saying he should be the leader of the Klan, that they agreed with him, all this other bullshit. It fucked with him and scared him, and he was *really* sorry.

I couldn't believe that all the Christians in America didn't have the forgiveness for him. We're all human beings; we can all screw up. My kids, everybody, came to me, "How can you go near that asshole?"

People are vicious, okay? I think everyone saw a lot of themselves in Michael Richards, and that's why they all freaked. And *every-body*'s responsible for it and has to *take* responsibility for it before we can change any of this, so I stopped using that word. I knew I was a *part* of it.

We're *all* part of it. These fucking pedophiles in America, where are they coming from? Mars? They're coming from our society. The wife beaters, the assholes that get up on buildings and shoot people—we're responsible for all of it. It's *us*. We're *creating* it.

PAUL PROVENZA: If you feel you have great responsibility for what you say, do you feel that you also have some obligation?

PAUL MOONEY: Yes, I do. And for us as comedians, as truth-sayers, as satirists—political, social, and otherwise—we have a very hard job with this new environment we're in now.

What the whole Bush administration did, it's very scary. They tried to make America not America, you know? It's like with that "Are you now or have you ever been a Communist?" crap. Who would think that could happen in this country called America? If you wrote that in a script, people would walk out of the theater and call it unbelievable.

I got fired from a TV show at The Apollo for talking about Bush. Whoopi Goldberg was hosting the series, and she couldn't host all of them so they had me host some. I talked about Bush and his girlfriend, Condoleezza. I said the question of the evening was, "Does Bush eat Rice?"

It brought the house down, brother. But they *freaked*. You'd have thought that it was 9/11 again. They shut the show down for an hour and a half because Time Warner saw the taping here in Hollywood by satellite, and put a stop to it. The woman producing the show told them she could change it, and they told her, "No, he's a Bush-basher. We want him out of here."

I had two witnesses in my dressing room, thank God. After that I went to the press and got on their case. I told Howard Stern. I brought the witnesses. Time Warner denied it. Said, "That's ridiculous. We'd never fire him for that."

We actually owe President Nixon—remember him?—an apology. Nixon eavesdropped and we crucified him, and Bush did it every five minutes and they loved him for it. It's disgusting. It really is. We have to stick to our guns, we really do.

But it's the Jim Jones syndrome. People drink the Kool-Aid simply because it's there to drink. There's no thought process.

And I resent the idea that we don't help our own, that we run to help everybody else spread democracy. We want to free people? Our *own* people aren't free. I don't know where Americans get their balls from. Somewhere out of a book? I don't know where they get their nerve. That's very nervy to tell somebody, "I don't like the way you're living. Live like me, in a democracy." It's crap.

PAUL PROVENZA: You thrive on confrontation with audiences, don't you? Confrontation is as much a part—or more—of what you do as the laughs are.

PAUL MOONEY: Well, that's who I am, I had nothing to do with it; I don't have any choice.

When I get onstage, I can only in my heart be earnest about what I feel. I'm as American as apple pie; I didn't drop here from Mars. This shit was here when I got here; if I drop dead right now it'll be here when I leave. People need something to blame: "It's him. He's the troublemaker," but I had nothing to do with none of this. I had to learn to *survive* in this bullshit. Every trick in the book. And I've turned a few.

People say to me they're shocked by some of the things that come out of my mouth, but *I'm* shocked by some of the things coming out of me. I don't know where it comes from. It's innate; it comes from some sort of process I'm unaware of. Maybe I'm an alien, I don't know. I'm shocked by things I say, and I'm also amused by them.

It's great to shock people. A lot of times people walk out on me, they'll pick up and leave while I'm performing. Lately that hasn't been happening, though, and I thought I was losing my touch. I think it's the best that people get so emotionally involved with me I can make them get up and walk out of a club. It's the best. What *power*.

People have been programmed that if you get out of line, you're the enemy. See, us comedians, we cross the line, which is good. We open people's eyes. Also, comedy is a time bomb. We give them time bombs. They might not get it that night; it could hit them six, seven weeks later.

I love my audience. Without them, I'm nothing. I want them to learn and I try to give them knowledge.

Black and white, I try to make people feel good about themselves, to feel that *one* person makes the difference. A majority doesn't rule; a lynch mob is a majority. Harriet Tubman made a difference, not Harriet Tubman and her little sister, not Harriet Tubman and her next-door neighbor. Harriet Tubman.

PAUL PROVENZA: So if you're trying to make the audience feel good about themselves, what do you think is really going on with people who are so taken aback by things you say?

PAUL MOONEY: It's almost like church. Some people don't get it, and that's not my problem; some people do get it, and it's great and it's wonderful.

In America, I can sit here and talk about religion, about sex, and people will sit on their ass here all night. I talk about race, give it fifteen minutes and they'll run out that fucking door.

Because they're caught up in this thing in their heads. They're brainwashed about it. Certain subtleties are put out there, and they believe it all.

Women do the same thing. Women are a minority, and like you say "Uncle Tom," there are "Uncle Women" who go along with it not to have trouble. They burned women; they said they were witches. They fucking *burned* them, okay? They didn't burn men for being witches, but burned women for it. It's like this fucking insanity and hating their mothers and beating women and all this crazy shit that goes on.

While I'm talking right now, there's some woman in a river just because she's a woman.

And what we do to our kids, besides the molesting and the brutality? It's *insane*. A fucking baboon has more sense.

They taught a monkey sign language, you know about that? And it gave them the finger! Now they're trying to figure if it was just imitating us or whether it *meant* it. That's the best. There's nothing funnier.

PAUL PROVENZA: What's been your biggest frustration doing what you do?

PAUL MOONEY: *White* Hollywood.

Hollywood's been like a woman wrestling with me. California? The phoniest state on the planet. Los Angeles has burned three times, and it's all been racial. It's a scary place, but they play this wholesome Gidget/Beach Boy attitude. It's not the City of Angels, don't let that fool you. It's the city of demons. This place here bears watching.

I'm from the South; from Louisiana. When I see Malibu burning down like it does, I just think, "You want some water for that? You don't have enough water in Malibu? No water out there in the woods? Come to Louisiana. We got *plenty* of it."

PAUL PROVENZA: Do you think audiences are more or less receptive nowadays to the kinds of things you challenge them with?

PAUL MOONEY: People are listening now, because they want to hear the truth. Especially the youth. The youth wants to hear the truth; they *want* to hear it, because they've been lied to.

And timing is everything. You could say something at the wrong time, and it's nothing. Say it at the right time, it means everything. Let me give you an example: I was in a class in high school, talking about something other than the class, and the teacher said, "This is science class. We don't discuss that here, so be quiet."

And I waited. If I had told him, "Screw you," or gone after him then, I would've been sent down to the office, maybe even gotten expelled. Instead, I waited. I waited *three months*. Then one day in class, he told me to shut the back door. I told him to shut his own back door. He said, "What did you say to me?"

I said, "Are you deaf? I said for you to shut your own door."

He said, "Why are you talking to me like that?"

I said, "Because this is a science class, not a domestics class, and you can shut your own door."

The kids in the classroom screamed with laughter. But they weren't laughing at what I said, they were laughing that I waited so long to talk back to him—and that I used the same weapon on him that he had used on me.

And you know what that teacher said to me? "Touché."

Timing is *everything*. Timing is powerful.

THE SMOTHERS BROTHERS

IN THE LATE 1960s, the Smothers Brothers turned what should have been a conventional, bland variety show into an outspoken vehicle of protest against the Vietnam War and the Johnson administration. Outwardly squeaky-clean, nonthreatening, and perfect for a prime-time Sunday night show on middle-of-the-road, conservative CBS, their image proved a Trojan horse from which burst forth a torrent of anti-authoritarian, counter-cultural comedy that shocked their gatekeepers and polarized America. Successful in spite of their own network's wishes, the Smothers Brothers wielded their popularity uncompromisingly and with great comic inventiveness, and gave a platform to countless others of their subversive ilk. They became the frequent subject of personal calls from a nervous President Johnson to the president of CBS, imploring they be reigned in as a threat to America's security. Censored repeatedly and ulitimately canceled under false pretenses, the silencing of *The Smothers Brothers Comedy Hour* stands as a chilling reminder of the dangers of speaking truth to power, and of the power of comedy to rile even the most daunting of powers that be. Tommy and Dickie reflect on the spirit of protest of the sixties, and where it's gone today—for themselves as well as others.

TOMMY SMOTHERS: This friend of mine is a mechanic, he fixes some things for me now and then, and I saw this little magnet on the refrigerator in his garage, and it says:

"When your timing is off, nothing else matters."

—TOMMY SMOTHERS

He's a mechanic!

But it not only works with comedy and engines, it works with *everything*. The decisions you make about your life, everything you do. It's very obvious with comedy, but I didn't think about its application to so many other things in life.

Someone is putting out four of our sixties shows, and so I looked back at them. And I just thought, "Jesus Christ." So I made Dickie watch them—'cause like most straight men, he's just going out racing cars, playing golf, having a good time—but I made him watch them, and he comes back and says, "How the *hell* did we become stars?"

And part of that was the *timing* of it. Because of the timeframe, the environment. People watched our show 'cause so much was happening, but nothing was being said on TV in the sixties. But when our show was on, there was always that danger that "They're gonna say something." So people watching it would see the dancers, the songs . . . then all of a sudden . . . *boom!* "Jeez, did you hear what he said?!" People would say, "God how did you get away with that? How'd you do that?" There was always that tension that something was gonna be said in the course of that hour.

But here we are, thirty-five, forty years later, and you take it out of that context and you're looking back, going, "What the hell was that about? What was the big deal?" I thought, "God, it was filled with observations and political pithy and fuck-you's, wasn't it?" And it wasn't. It just had that brinksmanship. And only a *little* bit, not as much as I remembered.

I look at the old Carol Burnett shows, and *The Honeymooners,* I look at some of the historical shows and, God, they hold up. You'll see a Flip Wilson show, and Jesus Christ they were funny shows. And I look at ours, and even though ours had a bigger impact politically and artistically and comedically, they weren't *near* as good as those other contemporaries. But there was this magical thing of "truth" in there that we had that they didn't have. But it doesn't hold up in hindsight or in retrospect. I'm seeing it now and it's just. . .

PAUL PROVENZA: Don't you think a lot of that has to do with the feat of doing an hour every week? The concepts and ideas in the show are so strong that while perhaps the craftsmanship isn't as fine as you may like it, if you look at a sketch like God talking to guys in the foxhole and all the other classic moments from it, together those are bigger than any individual moment or scene. That is where craftsmanship also lies; in the show and series and entity as a whole, not just in individual moments.

DICKIE SMOTHERS: Tommy has this microview of everything we do where he gets into the pores and every frigging flaw. It's like, if Clint Eastwood really looked at his hairline he'd never make another movie, you know? Every single step you could cut it apart and say, "This is flawed, this isn't as good as it could have been."

TOMMY SMOTHERS: Our first albums before we got in television were really pretty creative. I mean, it's improvisational all the time, eleven albums. And then we got the *Comedy Hour* show in the late sixties and it was just, "Whaaa . . ." It was *my* fault. I was a head; I smoked, I was a weed dude. I'd come on and try to be so cool. And I was so involved in the production.

We had done a sitcom first and it was just vacuous, silly shit. It went thirty-two shows and won all its time slots and whatever, but it put us off. I said, "Man, if I ever have another show, I'm gonna have creative control. There's gotta be some substance in just about everything." So we get the *Smothers Brothers Comedy Hour,* and I say, "I don't wanna do it unless I have creative control."

"You got it."

Little did they know that during the course of the show I would experience an evolution of consciousness as the war ramped up, and people were protesting and everything.

Just about everybody on the show was under thirty. I said, "I didn't like that director," and fired him. Brought in new, young writers.

"But they've never written."

"I don't care," I said, "who did that bit on that local radio show? Who the fuck was that? It was brilliant." Bob Einstein. Steve Martin was twenty-one, Rob Reiner was twenty-two.

Lorenzo Music was a banjo player, and I got him writing on the show. It was great; I loved the power of it.

I had no vision, I was just doing what I liked. I liked Pat Paulsen, I wanted him on the show. Pretty soon he was in every sketch; if we had a problem, "Put Pat in it."

Mason Williams, who was like my moral guide before I got politicized, would read the scripts over and say, "Bullshit, bullshit, bullshit," and I'd go to the meetings and I'd say, "Well that's bullshit; it's not written very well." I was very young too, and I wasn't very crafted—but I knew what bullshit was.

But when we were doing it, we were exactly *right.* I wasn't trying to save the world, but all of a sudden, when you start saying things, by accident you become like a poster child for the First Amendment and free speech. That comes to you without asking. When you feel passion about something you just always try and put it in your show; it's always just a personal thing.

Now I look back and see the old shows and say, "God, the whole show was bullshit," you know, but that was the fun of it. That was the *joy* of having a television show.

But then there was a time, about two years after we were fired from CBS, where I only heard the dark side of everything. I took the serious side.

DICKIE SMOTHERS: He's not *funny* when that happens.

TOMMY SMOTHERS: I saw Jane Fonda on *The Tonight Show* around that time, and she was talking about burning babies in Vietnam, and workers' rights . . . and all the things I *agree* with. And I'm going, "What's wrong with this?" Epiphany: no *joy*.

There was no joy, she had no sense of humor! And I realized I'd been doing that for two years at that point. And I just realized: to have a message, you can't be deadly serious or they're not gonna hear you; you're just an advocate of a point of view.

DICKIE SMOTHERS: You gotta be funny first. The art's got to be there. If you can't do that, you're just doing nothing.

TOMMY SMOTHERS: And a friend sent me something that Alistair Cook wrote: "Any generation takes the problems of the world so seriously that they forget why they were put on earth in the first place: to enjoy your friends, hug a baby and bounce a ball." If it's gonna be done, you *have* to do your art first, really *good*.

So by then we couldn't get any jobs, and we started from the bottom again opening for everybody else, working *discos* . . . Then we did Broadway shows, we did a lot of dinner theater . . . And after I got my sense of humor back in the theater and stuff, we just worked our way slowly back. A couple of national commercials, a television special. . .

And I look at the live work we did in 'eighty-eight, 'eighty-nine, 'ninety . . . God it was *good!* Took all the "Tom and Dick" spots from the TV show and put them together—that's *ours,* that's *our* statement. It wasn't filled with politics or any of that. Just really good art, good comedy, great timing, eye contact . . . Just fucking *great*.

PAUL PROVENZA: Even with your criticisms of the craft and the flaws you see in your CBS show, that show did have real impact. Yes, it was a particular era and maybe that's *why* you stood out so, but you made waves. Prime time on the most conservative network, in the typically sterile variety-show format, and reaching middle America with subversive and controversial views—*successfully*.

DICKIE SMOTHERS: Well, satire's *always* been a very powerful force. And you don't go unpunished.

PAUL PROVENZA: But you had *serious* impact. Lyndon Johnson himself was asking the network to drop you guys because he believed you were having a major effect on turning the public's view on the Vietnam War. I don't see impact like that from anyone anywhere now. Do you think it's even *possible* for anyone in comedy now to have the kind of impact that you guys had then?

TOMMY SMOTHERS: Absolutely, but there's something else too, you know? Look, Tom Brokaw was doing a "greatest generation" thing, and I flew out to New York to do an interview with Brokaw and Jon Stewart. Jon wasn't there yet, so Brokaw and I were talking, and I said, "I notice *The Daily Show* is getting a little bit softer."

And Brokaw said, "Yeah, I notice that too. I wonder what that is about."

So Jon arrives and the taping starts, and Brokaw says, "You know when the Smothers Brothers were on, they were thrown off the air. They lost their job. It was a lot more oppressive in the sixties than it is now."

And Jon Stewart says, "Yeah, we've got such *freedom* now; we've got cable, we can do what we want, we have the freedom to say anything . . . But back *then,* boy that was *tough* back then. Jeez."

And Brokaw says, "What do you think about Fox News?" and Stewart says, "Well it's not really news, it's opinion . . . There are different sides, liberals and conservatives, those are kinda just labels, there's room for both . . ."

And my head's spinning! I'm going, "Jesus Christ! We were on for *three years* before they threw us off. The Dixie Chicks say one line and no one plays their albums on the radio for two years! There's *wiretapping*!" I mean you look ten years ahead, and it's a *fascist* country.

It's already done. The coup took place, and he *sees* it.

I said, "Are they holding one of your kids hostage at the White House or something? What the hell *happened* to you?"

And he says, "Nothing, there is room for different points of view . . . I don't think everyone should be so adamant, God Almighty!"

In terms of the bigger picture, his work is just softening down. Just like most of the Baby Boomers, going, "Don't say anything and get fired from your good job by expressing yourself."

Where are the fucking Baby Boomers who were out there with signs in the sixties? Fuck, we stopped the *war,* basically. They're all in their forties, fifties, early sixties—where are *their* voices when they see the same things happening again? Well, they've now got jobs, they got kids in school or going to college . . . And the money thing, the *greed*. You did anything just for money in the sixties you were a piece of shit. What *happened* to the Baby Boomers?

DICKIE SMOTHERS: Garrison Keillor said that, at a particular fork in the road of his life, "I thought about telling the truth and being a prophet, but they come to very bad ends. Flayed, hung, beheaded. And people don't like them very much. Or I could become a liar, and be highly paid and revered, and successful. So I weighed the options and thought I'd become a liar. Because we love liars and they get lots of money."

PAUL PROVENZA: Sounds to me like even though you went through a phase of feeling like your politics had gotten in the way of the funny, you're feeling more fired up politically again.

TOMMY SMOTHERS: I've been feeling it for a long time, but this is so . . . Orwellian, what's been going on. It's so fucking obvious.

If I had the intellect, the intelligence to write and create a more powerful scream against the darkness, I'd do it, I'd take it as far as I can—*without* becoming a preacher, 'cause I've been *there* before, and it's not funny and it's not rewarding.

I just think it's so important that all artists reflect something more than their art. There's gotta be some substance beyond it.

I think Bill Maher's probably the finest political satirist we've ever had; Bill Maher doesn't pull a punch at all. If I could do a Bill Maher I'd be doing that in a minute. If I was smart enough. But I've always been slow-witted, kinda inarticulate, and it's hard to get clever.

PAUL PROVENZA: Are you both feeling like you might want to be more politicized onstage again now, or is it mostly just you, Tommy?

TOMMY SMOTHERS: No, my brother is by nature a would-be conservative. I think it's in the DNA; you run into people who are basically conservative by nature. But he's always, always appreciated *my* passion. He's always allowed me to do it. He just said, "Don't fuck up the show, though, okay? Don't get us fired."

I said, "Don't worry."

And *boom,* we're fired.

CONAN O'BRIEN

FROM HIS EARLY days writing *Saturday Night Live* and *The Simpsons* through his *Late Show* years and controversially short reign on the *Tonight Show* throne, Conan O'Brien found a rabid following for his edgy, inspired lunacy. Abruptly thrust into the center of a highly public exhibition of network television's cruel, hard vagaries, Conan discovered emotional depth in his relationship with his audience that enabled him to eschew cynicism, and may even have strengthened his commitment to, and love of, pure, childlike silliness. Though his post–*Tonight Show* future remains unclear (yet undoubtedly assured) at the time of this writing, he was still on air when we discussed not the ugly business of late-night TV, but his particular take on comedy: what fuels it, why a joke can be just a joke and a laugh just a laugh, and how we'll never really know why one produces the other.

CONAN O'BRIEN: The censorship *The Smothers Brothers* were up against in the late sixties is almost inconceivable today. There are, like, 900,000 shows on TV now. The bottom is out of the bathtub; it takes so much content to keep it filled, so there's less reason to be afraid of censorship. If you have a funny and interesting idea, yeah, you may get some letters, but there's so much to choose from, people will just watch something else.

PAUL PROVENZA: Except that it's driven by advertisers who regulate content based on what they think appropriate for shows they advertise on, and they draw the lines in very close. Like what happened with Bill Maher: a small group of people brought just enough pressure to bear on his advertisers.

CONAN O'BRIEN: Right. And thirty years ago he'd be *gone*. It would be, "Whatever happened to Bill Maher?" He'd be doing his act somewhere in the Catskills. But in the current climate, he can just slide over to cable, where there *are* no advertisers.

PAUL PROVENZA: We have all these new outlets now, but the flip side is that there's that much less impact one can make, and less attention given any of it.

CONAN O'BRIEN: That gets trickier and trickier. When *Saturday Night Live* started in October 1975, it was the *only* show with a subversive and satirical point of view. Today, when every show is trying to be the bad boy, the show that takes on the system, sometimes you think there's almost no system for us to work against. At some point, 25 percent of our economy is going to be satirical TV shows making fun of the country. It's much more difficult now, which might actually be *good*. It's probably forcing us to think a little more and try even harder. You're *constantly* trying to figure out what's going to break through the television set and cause a ripple of some kind. It's not as easy as it used to be, so, like evolution, you have to get better or you're gonna just go away.

PAUL PROVENZA: You cut your teeth at the *Harvard Lampoon,* which has a decidedly satirical bent. Did you want to say something or make any satirical point in those early days?

CONAN O'BRIEN: I felt very strongly that I *didn't* want to make a point. My comedy heroes were people I felt weren't trying to make a point at all, like the Marx Brothers or W. C. Fields. I have a lot of admiration for talented comedians that have a social cause or try to say something about society, but that's never how it worked for me. The instincts that I'm working off of in comedy now at the age of forty-six are *exactly* the same instincts I believe brought us all to comedy when we were seven years old, making people laugh on the playground—just that pure desire to make people laugh.

PAUL PROVENZA: You actually do some pointed political satire on your show, so it seems surprising that you claim to not care about it much.

CONAN O'BRIEN: A lot of comedy has an edge to it and *has* to be pointed, but I remember someone from Fox News was on my shows a few years ago, maybe Bill O'Reilly, and he said, "You really go after President Bush. You're such a Left-wing show."

I said, "We did a show for eight years while Clinton was president, and we went after *him* then."

Comedians bounce off the structure that exists in their lives, and that includes things like who is the president? Who is doing what within the structure we live in?

I remember reading an interview with Groucho Marx, and the interviewer said, "I love *Duck Soup* because you attack fascism and show how totalitarian societies are misguided and insane and that the democratic process is the way to go."

Groucho said, "What are you talking about? We were five Jews trying to get a laugh."

That resonates with me. Of course *Duck Soup* was inspired by what was going on then in Europe, but that's just what they were working off of. I always felt Charlie Chaplin was really making an overtly political point with *The Great Dictator*, whereas the Marx Brothers were using what happened to exist in their world just to be *funny*. And I gravitate toward the Marx Brothers.

Do you remember the original *Batman* series from the 1960s with Adam West? That was actually very influential to me. As a kid, I watched it on one level, which was that it's just plain fun—it's Batman and Robin fighting The Joker, it's all colorful, there's "ZAP! POW! BANG!" and all that fun stuff. But suddenly you're fifteen, sixteen, seventeen,

watching reruns and there's this whole *other* level, which is the *absurdity* of it. And there are jokes in there about the Vietnam War, and about things like unions and class struggle. All that stuff is in there, but it all goes down easier because of the silliness of it. Throughout my life, on any of the shows I've worked on, whether *Saturday Night Live* or especially *The Simpsons,* I always wrote things with a silliness and almost childlike appeal to them.

I know these are serious and scary times we're living in, and I'll hear people say comedy needs to be more relevant or tackle issues, but it's *always* been rough times, it's *always* been scary, and I think comedy needs to be *natural.* It needs to come from the desire to just make people laugh. The biggest danger in comedy is trying to inflate it or give it an importance of any kind.

I'm very wary of the analysis of comedy. Doing comedy is like being a chef who sprinkles a pinch of salt, sprinkles some oregano, throws in a dash of this and a bit of that. He doesn't measure everything or think about it and work out the chemical formula. For all of us it's ultimately just what makes you laugh. At rehearsal, that's still what I go off of. "Gee, this doesn't feel very funny to me." Or, "Wow, this really makes me laugh." If the interns on the sidelines are giggling about it, then we've probably got *something*. I never stop and think, "What was the relevance or satirical impact of it?" I just think, "Good. I see some people laughing. It feels funny to me, let's go."

PAUL PROVENZA: Your show is one of the

most permissive in terms of material that comedians can do; I did a piece on your show that no other talk show would let me do. It's not just because you're on at a late hour, there's a *feeling* of more freedom than on other talk shows.

CONAN O'BRIEN: That's 'cause at one point in the early days of *Late Night* I realized that nobody was really in charge. We were being watched by eighteen-, nineteen-, twenty-year-olds, but executives weren't really minding the store. So we started pushing it and doing weirder and weirder and stranger things almost from the beginning. Then another dynamic kicked in, which is that when a show becomes profitable and the network is making lots of money off it, they just figure, "These guys seem to know what they're doing, so let's just not rock the boat."

PAUL PROVENZA: Is wanting to affect change or add to the discourse through comedy just wasting time? Is it ultimately pointless?

CONAN O'BRIEN: No, it's not pointless. I read a lot of American history, and I'm always coming away with, "This person was great and did a lot, but how did this person move things forward? How did they really *change* things?" Even when I look at people who had a huge impact on and in their time, like Napoleon, for example, I always come away thinking, "All these battles, what did that really mean? Did any of it move the chess piece of humanity forward? Did it really accomplish anything? Did it change anything?"

I can get very cynical about things like that, but in the most abstract sense, people using

their talent is never wasted. People using their talent in good faith will always be good for mankind in *some* way. I just can't tell you how.

Here's the thing, really: whatever fuels someone's need to be funny, their need to express themselves, they need to follow that direction. It pleased Richard Pryor and George Carlin to be funny the way they were funny; that was *their* fuel. Whether that fuel is something you read in the *New York Times,* what you saw in the street, what you saw when you were walking through Afghanistan, or what happened to you in the third grade—it's all valid; it's all good. We're all just looking for *our* fuel.

I don't know what the Marx Brothers' fuel was; maybe it was growing up in New York at the turn of the century, being Jewish immigrants and being stereotyped. When you think about it, who are the funny people? The Jews are funny, the Irish are funny, black people are funny—if you're making huge blanket statements, you'd say those are groups that historically have been thought of as very funny. Well, you're looking at three groups with *huge* amounts of fuel, like repression and cultural insecurity and all of that. I'm certainly mining my experience growing up Irish Catholic just outside Boston.

All of us are grabbing on to our insecurities, whatever they are. In *my* life, I'm the middle of six kids in my family, and it was always, "What's my place here? How do I fit into this pecking order?" It's the most primal thing, you know? "Do I belong with all these smart people at this school? Am I the mistake?" It goes all the way through to "Do I *belong* here on television?" That's the constant. That's the stuff I mine a lot and get a lot of my humor from. That's some of *my* fuel.

I always tell the young people who come to work for our show, "If you learn one thing here, learn that we don't really know what we're doing." And I don't mean it as a joke. I've spent tens, hundreds, thousands of hours thinking about what's funny, trying to *be* funny, and it's still a struggle. It's *always* a struggle.

PAUL PROVENZA: Does that sort of become insurance that you don't fall into pomposity or self-importance?

CONAN O'BRIEN: That's almost a religious belief for me. I really don't think I'm better than other people, and my comedy should reflect that. One of the beauties of doing shows like ours is that you can never get too pompous, because of the sheer volume of comedy you have to do. You do five hours a week in front of an audience, you're simply going to fail a certain percentage of the time. If it's going really well, you're going to fail, say, 20 percent of the time—and that's if it's going *really* well. There is no 100 percent. It just can't happen at that volume.

Comedians are constantly reminded that they're mortal in ways like that. I always envy musicians, because I think they're judged differently. Once a musician has his thirty songs everyone loves to hear, they come out, play their songs, and everyone applauds. It always looks to me like it's very nonjudgmental. Whereas for a comedian, the crowd will tell you from joke to joke exactly how you're doing and what they think about it.

PAUL PROVENZA: Comedy is the only performing-art form where the crowd gets to determine its *existence*. People can sit back and go, "That didn't make me laugh, it's not comedy." With the cheesiest music, stupidest book, or crappiest painting, nobody argues that it's not music or a novel or a painting. Comedy is the only art form where the recipient of it gets to decide if it even exists. If it doesn't make them laugh, they don't think "It's not *good* comedy," they think it's not even comedy at all.

CONAN O'BRIEN: I've always thought of laughter as coming from our reptile brains somewhere, because it's actually some weird bodily process. It's an art form where we're dealing with ideas and language but the response you're looking to create is like trying to get people to sneeze or hiccup. You're looking for them to react by an involuntary physical process. And if they're not sneezing and hiccupping, it means you've *failed*. It's not enough that they're happy or entertained or amused or thinking about something, it *has* to achieve that weird, involuntary, physical response. I always find that very strange.

A sense of humor is very democratic, really. With many kinds of art, people can feel, "I'm not qualified to tell you if that Jackson Pollock painting is good or not." Or, "I don't really know if this wine is good or not, because I don't have the training." But *nobody* says that about comedy. Nobody thinks they might not know enough about what's funny. It's an absolute—they laughed or they didn't.

If someone doesn't think something is funny, no one can ever really say, "Well actually it's *very* funny, you just don't have the refined palate for it. You don't know enough about it." There's no such thing. They'll punch you in the throat if you say that.

Early on, when I thought something was really funny but the audience just stared at it—which still happens, too—your first inner reaction is anger: "How dare you people not laugh at that?" But you've got to let that go. You just have to get to that place where there's no right or wrong to it. I thought it was funny, but I can't be mad at them because they didn't think it was funny.

And if you *are* mad about it, then just go home and bitch to your wife about it, but never let *them* know you're angry.

DAVE ATTELL

ON COMEDY CENTRAL'S *Insomniac,* Dave Attell traveled from state to state, lingering in bars and all-night diners, poking at the pale, fetid, after-hours underbelly of America. Those travels only seemed to reinforce the perverse and often disturbing sense of humor on display in his shockingly funny stand-up. Attell talks about the importance of saying things that shouldn't be said as he finds an ever-increasing audience rabid to hear a voice that doesn't care what anyone thinks—he's saying it anyway, 'cause it's *funny.*

DAVE ATTELL: If the crowd doesn't get a joke, I *will* attack them.

I'm coming up there with jokes I worked on or things I'm thinking about, and if they don't get it, then I just start attacking. I have a "three strikes" rule with audiences. I've never really told anyone this until now, so this is a big scoop from me here, Jimmy Olsen: I always go up there with new stuff and try it. The audience doesn't get it, I'll try the next audience. That audience doesn't get it, I'll try the next one. After that one I'll just get *angry*. And that's usually when the funny stuff comes out. I guess that's not very professional, but you just gotta keep working it until you find the funny angle on it. Some people just aren't *going* to get it.

PAUL PROVENZA: Do you think what you do is satire?

DAVE ATTELL: That's a little Marcel Marceau of you to put me in a box like that.

I don't know. Satire doesn't exactly fill up seats. No one's, like, "Let's go down there and hear that great satarian." Is that even a word? Fuck it, let me try that again: no one's going, "Hey, there's some great satire going on down there! Let's go!" It sounds a little fruity.

It sounds like some chick on Flava Flav's show. If I was a stripper, that's what I'd call myself. I'd dance around the pole and the announcer would go, "Give it up for . . . *Satire!*"

As I've just illustrated, I'm more sarcastic then I am a satirist. I like to think of myself as "the thinking man's hack." I like to do the dick joke and pussy joke and all that, you know? I

don't like middle-of-the-road stuff. I'm not a fan of jokes about going to the Walmart and having problems with the wife. I think you have to pick a side, and I pick the side that's more shocking.

PAUL PROVENZA: I'd say your material is satirical, because everything you do is subversive of the accepted way of looking at things. The point of view in all your jokes is from a perspective that, by any decent standard, is just plain *wrong*.

DAVE ATTELL: I always thought of satire as having more of a political element to it, and I do *some* of that, because I have to; no one has that exciting a life that they can just talk about themselves over and over. But I'm not really a "change the world" kind of guy. A lot of people try to be political, because with *The Daily Show* and Colbert it's a trendy thing now. As long as it's funny you can say anything you want, but if you're just up there preaching your agenda, then I turn tail. I'm sick of all that.

PAUL PROVENZA: Well, colloquially, we put political commentary in the realm of satire, but you're actually satirizing social conventions and norms in a dictionary definition of what satire is.

DAVE ATTELL: Hello! Someone reads over here.

PAUL PROVENZA: Your onstage character has a perspective that we laugh *at*, not *with*. Which is why some people get you, and others don't. And some people not only don't get you, they have to leave the room.

DAVE ATTELL: Well, we live in a very conservative country with heavy religious overtones to it. What used to be considered just funny—like Sam Kinison, balls-to-the-wall, crazy stuff—is now seen as, "Whoa!"

America's different now. It's taken a step *back* from how cool things were in the eighties and nineties. It seems now if you talk about drinking and smoking and sex and drugs or that kind of stuff, sometimes the crowd gets uncomfortable. For a lot of the younger comics, clubs want them to work clean and mainstream all the way now.

A friend told me he did a joke about abortion, and some people in the crowd were of course offended, but the club owner took the side of the crowd instead of the comic. I think that's wrong, you know? Manny, who used to run the Comedy Cellar and passed away not long ago, *always* took the side of the comics. You come to the show, you're going to hear the word "cunt." You're going to hear all these things. It's a comic show. Let it go! It's nothing. It's not real. This is not like at your job; it's not office-speak here, you know?

PAUL PROVENZA: Would Manny have taken Michael Richards's side?

DAVE ATTELL: Yeah, he definitely would have—even though what Michael Richards did was wrong and incredibly unfunny. *That* was the problem: he didn't make it *funny*. If you say those kinds of things, you'd *better* back it up with the funny. And that was a crowd-work situation, so he should've been able to handle crowd work if he's gonna do crowd work. You're supposed to size up the scene, see what's going on. There's craft and skill involved.

It's a great YouTube moment, but I think it was blown *way* out of proportion. The fact that the guy was banned over it is ridiculous. This isn't *Survivor*, where you get kicked off the island.

Since then I've been saying: "I remember when saying the N-word would *help* your job. When it meant a raise or a week off." And that's the point, really.

PAUL PROVENZA: Satire again, by the way.

DAVE ATTELL: You don't let up, do you?

But yeah . . . There's Michael Richards, and then there's *real* racism. People get upset over the words instead of the deeds. The Jena Six, that is *real*. Real, serious, old-fashioned, cracker, "You ain't from 'round here, boy" racism, and that's what people really should be getting upset about. That shit happens for *real*. But everyone focused on Michael Richards—because he's a celebrity.

That whole thing really showed once again how audiences only lock onto people they've seen on TV. People who know me from TV will come to see me and I'll do an hour of new, original material and they'll go, "The TV show this, the TV show that . . ." I just did an hour of original material, but it's still all about the TV thing. That bothers me.

PAUL PROVENZA: Quit whining. At least people are coming to see you. You're way ahead of Michael Richards there.

DAVE ATTELL: Well, I've been taught to keep my racial opinions to the confines of my trailer park.

PAUL PROVENZA: Do you find that people often turn off to just a single word before they even hear what the rest of a bit is about? That they can't hear any irony whatsoever once you've pushed their hot button?

DAVE ATTELL: Oh, yeah. I was doing a joke about the tsunami—as it was happening, that's how cool *I* am—and it took people a long time to get that I was just using it as a reference. I wasn't even talking about the tsunami itself, but just the word got them all, "Whoa, ease up."

The word is just a word. It means "an overwhelming thing." What if it was a "tsunami of blow jobs"? They ruined it for themselves.

PAUL PROVENZA: Do you find when that happens you amp it up and push them even further?

DAVE ATTELL: Yeah, you always attack it more. Because you're really fighting for the most precious thing in your life: your *ego*.

Here's another one that people hate, although it worked here at the Comedy Cellar *one* time. See, that's the problem, it's worked one time, but no one else *ever* gets it: "I live in a high-rise building, and I realized that I'm closer to God than I am to the ground. So here I am, high in the air making a sandwich and masturbating—much like an angel would . . ."

And the audience kind of titters a little, "We get it, you live up high. Angels masturbating. That's cute."

And then, this is the point where they hate me when I say, "You probably think it's easy sleeping in a high-rise apartment, but it's not, because the prayers of homeless children keep coming up through the windows. I have

to shout out the window, 'Could you keep it down down there? *Some* people have a mortgage! Stop grumbling for food and methadone so I can get some sleep here!' "

People don't like that part at *all*. I guess people take it as I'm anti-homeless people.

PAUL PROVENZA: I don't get excited much by comedy that *doesn't* fuck with my head a little. I think that comes from the notion that as comedians, we have a license to do things that can't be done in any other form, so if you don't take the opportunity to say something ballsy or challenge something, you've just squandered an amazing opportunity.

DAVE ATTELL: I agree with you about that; those are always the most fun comics to watch. But they're not for everybody. I think I'm setting myself up as an asshole to begin with, so I'm kind of baiting them to hate me. I actually like that part of it. I kind of like the negativity sometimes more than them going "Whoo!"— you know? Sometimes that's just way better, because I hate myself.

I come at my comedy with my very-low-self-esteem, verbal-abuse family background. That's helped me in comedy more than anything else. Any negativity I get from a crowd almost, like, *warms* me. It's like going home.

Truth is, the best comedy comes from the *losses,* not the wins, in your life. "I just banged five strippers, and they're all hot!" Where's the comedy *there*? See, *I'm* the loser; the guy who went home alone and masturbated while the other guy was banging the hot strippers. I *like* that guy. Everything is about winning in our society, and it's fucking boring. *Dancing* with the *Stars*. You want to win that? Really? "I'm a better dancer than Heather Mills, a one-legged whore!" Does that make you feel better at the end of the day?

But America sure loves that shit, so it's really hard to come at them from a different angle. People are so complacent with just buying what they're sold, and it's really hard to break that. I guess if I'm making any points with what I'm doing, it's breaking up that whole through line of "I've been told this is what's good; I'll buy anything they tell me I should."

I always feel bad when I do a college. They're at that age where anything goes, right? You'd figure these kids are like you were at that age, you know? But all they really have is this shopping-mall, consumer mentality. That really bothers me. Very conservative. Spoon-fed. And *sneaky*. There's like a sneakiness. Now I sound like the old guy who lives down the block, "You're sneaky! You kids are *sneaky*!" But they're sneaky. You know they're doing all the stuff that we all did at that age, but they're pretending they're not. Like they've learned how to gloss it over or hide it from their parents or something like that.

And they seem very happy with their lives in the world. They've been taught that they're all special. They've been taught through You-Tube, *Dancing with the Whatevers*, and all that crap that *they* should be famous. So it's very hard for them to give you a moment and listen to what you or anyone else but them has to say. They suck! That's what I'm saying. The kids are asses, goddammit. *Sneaky asses*.

PAUL PROVENZA: Audiences in general seem to have that sense of entitlement. Rather than see what a performer has to offer, it's more, like, "We want the show we want, and if you don't give it to us we're going to walk out or be pissed off and complain."

DAVE ATTELL: If everybody acted as prim and proper in their real lives as they do when they come see me then we'd live in this fucking fantasy world of just do-goodism. Everything would be just great and Jesus-on-Earth perfect. But they've been *taught* not to laugh at certain things.

I have this joke about abortion—which I think is a different take from anyone else's abortion joke, by the way: "Ladies, they could take away from you your right to have a safe, legal abortion at any moment. But they can never take away your right to get drunk and throw yourself down a flight of stairs. No one can arrest gravity, ladies." And of course, that gets *big* groans.

But you look out in the crowd, and it's, like, girls in their twenties. If this was 1974, they would be picketing Washington singing the theme from *Maude* to keep their right to an abortion. And it's not that they're really religious, any of them, it's that they've just been taught that abortion is something they shouldn't laugh about no matter what.

But if you say it through a hilarious puppet, people might get it, because ventriloquism is the best way to get bad news.

PAUL PROVENZA: I wish you worked on *Sesame Street*.

DAVE ATTELL: People think comedy's not that

important, but let me tell you something: if you go see a comedy show, and at some point after that show you're molested by a priest, well, then you just weren't listening. 'Cause priests are boy fuckers; every comic has a joke about it, so you can't go, "How could this happen?? Oh, right, I remember. The comics were saying how the priests fucked a bunch of kids. Right."

I mean, come on! Does it have to be a ringtone before anybody takes it seriously?

PAUL PROVENZA: Well, since you're loath to call what you do satire, what are some things you like that *are* satire?

DAVE ATTELL: I think of something like *Blazing Saddles*. If you really look at *Blazing Saddles*—a great movie, and *still* funny—Mel Brooks really did something very cool there. He confronted racism in that movie in a really funny, over-the-top way. *Blazing Saddles* is what I think of if you're talking about satire.

Spaceballs, not so much.

South Park is another great example of really well-done satire. I don't know how they turn it around so quickly, but whether it's a celebrity issue or something political, what they do with it is just great. It's *super*-funny—but what they do and how they do it is also *important*. It's, like, *meaningful*.

But for the rest of us who aren't animated, we need things like *food*, you know? So sometimes we just gotta whore it out.

DOUG STANHOPE

MANY ARE FAMILIAR with Doug Stanhope from his brief tenure on Comedy Central's *The Man Show*, but watching Stanhope on basic cable is like watching a snuff film edited to run as an in-flight movie— you're just not getting the full effect. His fearlessly challenging Showtime special is a better example of just what it is he does, but the live stand-up arena is where Stanhope has few if any artistic peers. He offers up the boozy detritus of his own life, seeking out truth in the most depraved, shocking corners of human behavior and exposing numbness in the comfortable and cozy ones, all with dark, hilarious intensity. From his ultimate outsider vantage point, we see the forest, and the questions about where we stand among the trees can often be unsettling. Here, he sums up his worldview—or is it a nihilistic lack thereof? Ah, who gives a shit.

DOUG STANHOPE: When you're onstage, you're just a fucking whore. No one ever complains about the blow job you get from a girl that sucks your dick because she *wants* to, but if you *pay* for a blow job, you'll critique it, bitch about how it wasn't worth the money, it wasn't the way you like to get blown, and all of a sudden you're some reviewer.

I get onstage, and it just all seems like a fucking scam. What "funny" *really* is to me is hanging out with other comics around a table. Real, genuine "comedy" is making the guy stocking shelves at Walmart laugh when he's having a shitty day. You just say shit no one else ever says and you break the social mold and make someone laugh or guffaw or gasp on the job when they don't expect it. Then it *means* something, you know?

The only time it's *truly* rewarding is when you make someone laugh just 'cause you *wanted* to, then you leave. You don't ask them to buy a CD in return, you know? That's how it is when comedians are just hangin' out: no commerce, no "job to do," just some funny shit we're giving away free to each other and laughing our asses off.

PAUL PROVENZA: I know you spend time over in the U.K. where there's a really cool comedy scene; nutty stuff can happen anywhere. Comedy seems more alive and vibrant there, and there's more of an enthusiastic audience that supports and encourages that. There's an audience there that comes out for comedy *now* the way it used to be in the early days of the comedy boom here when people came out spe-

cifically looking for something *different*. Now they mostly want the same sanitized, boring stuff they're already familiar with.

DOUG STANHOPE: Yeah, I remember when I started in 'ninety or 'ninety-one, you'd be in some fucking Red Lion Hotel lounge on a Tuesday, and the emcee would go, "Is everyone ready for comedy?"

They'd all go, "Yeahhhhh!" And they would *mean* it. They were *alive*. They were excited to be there. Now they just come in, sit, and cross their arms.

PAUL PROVENZA: The comedy club scene's gotten so institutionalized and programmed to where everything's so predictable. I think that happens to everything in this culture at some point. What are people excited by in the general culture, *American Idol*? Can they genuinely be passionate about that stuff?

DOUG STANHOPE: I don't know. *American Idol*—Jesus, do they hand out these fuckin' I LOVE CLAY AIKEN signs? Are they making the studio audience do that shit so the public just assumes, "Everyone seems to love it, I must love it too?" I don't know, man. Television is such bullshit.

You know when you do stand-up for TV, they have "fluffers" doing fucking warm-up, making the crowd practice screaming like idiots, pretending to be excited about something? For the taping of my half-hour special, they rounded up fifteen hundred people for the audience and went through the paces with them to the point where when I was introduced, they fucking went ape shit, like I'm

The Beatles or something. I thought, "You people don't even know who I fucking *am*!"

So I opened up with that. I walked out, "It sounds like all my fans are here!"

They all screamed, "YEEEAHH!!!"

I went, "Then what's my name?"

Fucking *dead silence*.

Of course they cut that out of the show, because they don't want any truth or reality to anything. When it aired, it went, "It sounds like all my fans are here"—*CUT*—"Wow old people complain a lot . . ." Some dumb, obvious edit; the fucking frauds.

I don't know. I don't sit around analyzing this shit. I'm a drunk; I'm not one of those guys, "I see comedy as the satirical voice of blah, blah, blah . . ." Shit *sucks*, that's all I know. I'm not the scientist of why everything melts into some bland flavor. I just usually go, "This sucks," then head to the bar and bitch about it all.

But America dulls down *everything*. Maybe everywhere does, but I live in America, and everything always seems to be dulled down. Music, cars, movies—everything. I guess it gets dull for a while until people get sick of it, go, "Fuck this," then everything's different and crazy with Mohawks and slam-dancing. It's probably cyclical, I just don't know if I'm gonna live through the cycle.

PAUL PROVENZA: I always say that in live comedy, where we can say anything we want and there's no FCC or advertisers to answer to, the only real censoring comes from the audience.

DOUG STANHOPE: I've heard you say that, and you're right. It's like the populace has gotten in lockstep with the media or something and just recite, "Ooh, that's bad." Come *on*. And it's like people have some sense of entitlement: "My dad died of cancer, so for you to say anything about cancer . . ." *What??*

I had a whole fucking problem a few nights ago over mentioning Ecstasy in a positive light. That's like the *tamest* thing you could pick out of my set, but that's the thing some girl went into histrionics over, because, "My sister died from one hit and anyone can, blah blah blah . . ." You can get flak over everything. If I just did dick jokes, they'd get mad 'cause I said "titty fuck" or whatever.

Everyone will find a reason to get mad at anything if they want to, and it's all the same. At one gig recently, this Christian group sat through all the "kick-fucking a girl with cerebral palsy" jokes and every other horrible thing in my act, but then I got to some Jesus stuff, and as a group they all marched out, making a big show of getting upset. It said right on the fucking bill: "Triple-X Rated"—which I didn't put there, but it's the only buzz word they could think of to keep the weak out—so it was like, "Oh, I see; *this* isn't the triple-X rated stuff your Christian group was *looking* for."

You can't talk logic with those people. They *need* their Jesus. If your life was working in a chain factory outside Carbondale, Illinois, with bleak fucking winters, and you've married that girl you got pregnant when she was sixteen because that's what you were told you're supposed to do, and now you're thirty-five—you're not gonna start second-guessing those beliefs. It would fucking destroy everything your whole life's been about. You need that Jesus and structure and those "family values" just to get you through the fucking day. You're not gonna go, "I've lived my whole life wrong. Fuck my wife and kids, I'm gonna learn ballet like I always wanted."

I assume most of that comes from fear. And belonging. People join churches the same way some people join gangs, just to *belong* to something. Things like religion work because people are hopeless and want to believe in *something*. They don't wanna end up like me, fuckin' sitting in a basement all day with *you*.

PAUL PROVENZA: I consider this a good day for me. Anyway, the flip side of all the people who walk out is all the people who are *thrilled* to hear that same stuff, and to find out *they* belong to something, too, even if it's just you and them.

DOUG STANHOPE: That's the only good thing, and why it's nice to play all the shitty towns I play instead of David Cross–ing it up and just playing among your own element, never taking gigs you just know are gonna be miserable. Occasionally that one kid comes up to you; a fat, loser Goth kid, alone, no one will fuck him, so he has no chicks or drugs, but he'll come up and go, "I've always thought that, but no one's ever *said* it."

PAUL PROVENZA: A couple of years ago, Steve Hughes was accused of anti-Semitism in the Edinburgh Fringe press over a joke he did, and then they came after you and a few others with similar accusations. What do you think that was really all about?

DOUG STANHOPE: I don't think those stories come from any real place. Writers are looking for an angle; I don't think he really saw racism there but he saw an *angle* where he could *push* racism. He could push a fear button and justify it somehow to get attention for himself and his paper. On any genuine intellectual level, if you're sitting with him drinking a beer, would that writer go, "Yeah, I believe Steve Hughes is a racist"? No, you saw an *angle,* you fucking scumbag.

PAUL PROVENZA: But audience members do the same thing, twisting something someone's crafted usually to make entirely the opposite point.

DOUG STANHOPE: But they follow the lead of the guy that's looking for an angle. Very few people in this world are actually conveying their own opinions. People parrot ideas from some media garbage they heard, or *half*-heard, or their friends heard somewhere. It's all so media-driven, you wonder, "If there were no media, what *would* I worry about?" It sure as fuck wouldn't be terrorism, you know?

Really, when you think about it that way, all the comics doing Jerry Seinfeld kind of observational stuff are the *real* social commentators, because all that little stuff they talk about actually is the stuff that bothers you in your life: things like traffic and assholes on line at the overpriced coffee place. You don't *really* worry about terrorism or wars for oil or pedophilia in the Church; they're not *real* in most peoples' lives. Most people are not in the military and don't have kids that are being fingered by priests. What *actually* matters to all of us on any average day is the fast-food guy that forgot your fries and the fees they charge at the ATM, *not* immigration or gays getting married or any of that shit everyone's always jackin' off about all the time. So really, in those realistic terms, I'm *bullshit,* and Jay Leno's the real deal. Jerry Seinfeld is the meaningful social commentator; he's talking about things that really *do* matter to us.

PAUL PROVENZA: To be honest, that's a perspective I never considered, and frankly, it scares me.

DOUG STANHOPE: That's why I try not to fucking think so much. I'm kind of a reluctant nihilist. I *want* to believe in something, it's just that as much as I search the gray matter, I can't find hope. So I just try to be the happiest miserable guy I can be; I'll *enjoy* my misery. I keep rooting for the home team and hope for a small victory here and there, but there's no fucking utopia in the mix that I can find. I keep stacking that puzzle and it keeps falling down.

PAUL PROVENZA: And yet, you actually considered running for president. *What?*

DOUG STANHOPE: Yeah, I figured I'd take a stab at that before I quit. Might as well take a shot at being the leader of the free world before I drop out of society and take a beachfront in Costa Rica, right?

PAUL PROVENZA: But this wasn't some joke, right? You were seriously going to run as a legitimate candidate.

DOUG STANHOPE: Oh, it wasn't a joke, I was going to run as the Libertarian Party presidential candidate. The party leaders were committed to me running as their guy in the 2008 election. I went through all the paperwork and legal crap you have to do just to be president of this fuckin' country, but I would've had to stop making a living in order to do it. It turns out that doing my stand-up constitutes "campaigning," so if I got paid for it, I'd be in breach of campaign finance laws, so I had to drop out of the race. Probably better for everybody.

PAUL PROVENZA: What was your platform?

DOUG STANHOPE: Individual freedom, and limiting government to a government so limited even *I* could run it.

PAUL PROVENZA: Oh, you mean like what it was meant to be?

DOUG STANHOPE: Exactly.

I think it's time for entertainment to take over politics. They've used entertainment for so long to divert and distract people from what's going on politically, it's just ripe to backfire on them.

But I really think there's no political structure that can work. There's always gonna be assholes to fuck it up. That's why I love "last guy on Earth" movies, where a guy wakes up after an apocalypse and he's the only guy left on the whole planet. It's hard to fuck that movie up for me, 'cause I daydream about it so much.

I don't know, Provenz . . . You always seem to be in a good mood. What makes *you* happy?

PAUL PROVENZA: Are you kidding? I'm *constantly* fighting my demons. I just try and live the way I want it to be, and just keep hoping it'll become that. It's a constant state of *trying* to be happy.

DOUG STANHOPE: Well . . . You're not buying it off a guy, like some of us do.

ROSEANNE BARR

WITH HER GROUNDBREAKING eponymous television series, Roseanne brought the voice of America's working class to prime time, joining Ralph Kramden and Archie Bunker among television's great blue-collar heroes. With the Connors and a rocky relationship with fame and fortune behind her, her stand-up has become even more outspoken, while a questionable-award-winning blog and a new series on FreeSpeech.org provide more outlets for her rage against the machine. She discusses her success, and how average working moms just might be the real instruments of radical change.

ROSEANNE BARR: I hate the word "happy." It's such horseshit. I'm fifty-six, and until I was about forty-eight I went through a period of all heavy-duty mental illness.

PAUL PROVENZA: Did you feel like you didn't know who you were then?

ROSEANNE BARR: I knew exactly who I was— all twenty of me. Every one of *them* knew who *they* were, they just didn't know each other. But they're all on the same team now.

PAUL PROVENZA: Are you as political in your live shows now as you are on your blog?

ROSEANNE BARR: I put the literate stuff where you can read it in my blog and do the jokes on stage, but I do *my* point of view always. My whole life is a statement about the way I see things. I don't know why, but I'll get this piercing ache in my head, going, "I must say this."

When I said Oprah was a fucking closet Republican, which she is, it was all over the fucking news. Whenever that happens, I think, "Hmm . . . Musta hit a nerve *there*."

I always say the stuff that isn't being said. It's like a door that hasn't been opened yet, and somebody has to open it before anybody else will talk about it. I'll try to kick that door down for as long as I'm on the planet, because I can't help it. To me, I was chosen for it. I heard it in my head when I was three. It said, "This is what you're gonna do," and I've done it ever since.

PAUL PROVENZA: So as a kid you were already preparing for stand-up?

ROSEANNE BARR: I was onstage long before I did stand-up. I was a preacher in the Mormon Church when I was six years old. I know, nobody knows about that; it's in my books that nobody reads. At twelve years old, I was talking to groups of Mormon bishops about the Old Testament. It's crazy, right? I can't believe it myself.

PAUL PROVENZA: Where do you stand on religion now?

ROSEANNE BARR: I think religion is the enemy and soon as it's gone, things will be better. My conclusion came after suffering the type of terrorism they shove down your throat from the time you're born. I've suffered from it my whole life.

I never said, "I don't believe in anything," I just redefined it for myself. Underneath every religion's big ol' books—the ones they use as an excuse to bomb each other—it just says to be nice to people. I like *that;* that's a good message, but I'm passionate about religion's brainwashing.

I was raised in an apartment house with all these Holocaust survivors; Jews with tattoos. It was in Salt Lake City, but it was like being in Poland or something. We got all the real *scary* Jewish stuff. Just horrifying. They'd point to me when they talked about horrific things you don't want nobody who's three years old to hear. It was mental terrorism. I believe it takes a lot of abuse and terrorism to make a believer, and that's what they do to kids. They do it so a kid'll keep quiet when the priest molests him or something.

But if you read my books that nobody reads, I'm totally into Jesus. I love the whole myth of it. It really is the greatest story ever told. I think we're wired to believe *something;* some story, myth, whatever.

And that's what being a stand-up comic is to me: a whole mission from God. I know a lot of comics don't feel that way, but a lot do and we wonder, "What is this thing that drives us to correct everything?" So I follow Jesus.

Jesus would be a stand-up comic today, for *sure.* He probably wouldn't go to comedy clubs, because he wouldn't want to be around that filth and sin, but he'd probably do it in a park under a tree, for free. He might be homeless, too.

And I say he's a girl this time.

PAUL PROVENZA: You say you do it for Jesus, but people who claim to devote their lives to Jesus take offense at you.

ROSEANNE BARR: Because they have that other Jesus, not the one *I* got. They want to force theirs on me, but I won't force mine on them.

Comedy is a spiritual act, really. You give the audience something, they take it, and they leave something behind for you. It's a perfect exchange.

And here's another thing I love about comedy: as a woman, I don't have any place to force my will on people, so I do it onstage. I've had from nine to fifteen thousand people or more, and to be one lone being controlling that room with nothing but your own body, mind, and a mic is high, spiritual shit. It feels *so* good!

I talked for a while in my show about how Bush tried to make the world safe for democracy so other countries can have Walmarts and sell Chinese goods for discount prices, because that's what freedom is all about. That, and shooting abortion doctors. When young people at colleges heard it, it was like being a rock star. They just loved it. They'd say, "*This* is what you're saying? You're our TV *mom!* We grew up with you! You raised us!" I'd say, "That's why you are how you are. You were my TV children, and I raised you to be citizens of an enlightened future." And that's what I meant to do: teach them something.

PAUL PROVENZA: You've gotten a lot of flak for your views on Zionism and Israel's treatment of Palestinians, and you're still putting it out there on your blog. So many people try to tackle those questions but can't get a word out without being labeled anti-Semitic.

ROSEANNE BARR: *My* ancestors go *way* back before the Jews to something that crawled out of the ocean.

Some people believe "Zionism" stands for "justice and peace," as opposed to "apartheid and war," but every piece of earth on this planet is holy, not just one. I believe in *no* separatism, *no* mental terrorism against children, and a lot of Jewish people think like that, too. It's up to Jewish people who think that way to challenge the Jewish people who don't.

My father always said, "I am a Jew, I am not a Zionist." And I, Roseanne Barr, am a Jew and not a Zionist. Most Jewish Americans are like me. In fact, most Jews in Israel think exactly like me, but the top tier—the first and second estates, politicians—all block that message, because they're making too much money off things as they are.

My father also said, "Israel's just another walled ghetto." I don't support walled-in ghettos where Jews live, I don't care *who* builds the wall. It ain't right and I don't like it.

This is a big example of knowing I have to say things no one else is saying. They've got all the Jews scared shitless. All the famous Jews are right on board; none of them are going to say *anything.* I thought, "This *has* to be said by a Jew." It can't just be said by Arabs anymore.

I'm well aware of the risks I take, too, but what the fuck? I'm living my beliefs. If I don't say it, if I live only for myself, as it says in our Talmud, then what am I?

PAUL PROVENZA: I'm guessing Lenny Bruce influenced you a lot as a comedian.

ROSEANNE BARR: I have the world's second largest collection of Lenny Bruce; everything he ever recorded. My dad bought all his records, and we'd listen to them together. It was the *only* thing we had together. He'd say, "This guy is a *prophet.*" I liked a lot of comics, but the ones I kept listening to were Lenny Bruce and Johnny Carson.

Me and Bill Maher are, like, the only ones that think this way, but I always say if Johnny Carson was still on the air, we never would've gone to Iraq. He was the conscience of the whole TV community.

PAUL PROVENZA: You think Johnny would've taken a political stance?

ROSEANNE BARR: I thought he was extremely political.

PAUL PROVENZA: But he always made sure he was balanced, never really stating any position.

ROSEANNE BARR: That's what was so great! He was down the middle. The middle is the biggest, most powerful way to go. You gotta bring things to the middle to manifest. My stand-up was bringing the Left to middle. That's what *Roseanne* was always about. It's what my position on Zionism is: it is the middle, it needs to *go* middle and I'm *bringing* it middle.

To get into the middle is *extremely* powerful. It's "the path of the mother." The middle is the filament for the negative and positive to come together. To take what someone else might make look radical and make it middle takes a *lot* of thought.

PAUL PROVENZA: Do you get credit for being as fearless as you are? Do you feel respected for that?

ROSEANNE BARR: No, I get nothing at all except my points in heaven. I don't give a shit if anybody likes it or not, I gotta live for myself and that's that. And that is being *a comic.*

At the Comedy Store, we'd say, "Where's the most important place on the planet Earth? It's the Comedy Store. Because that's where the comics are, and comics tell the *truth.*"

As you and many other comics know, it's a lonely road to take to voice the outsider opinion. Or else you're a phony fucking asshole. I want to *be* who I *say* I am. I want to do the right thing with my beliefs. I want to encourage the youth to be fighters—and that's pretty cool, because old people don't usually do that, they tell 'em to shut up. But I'm gonna be that other type of grandma, going, "Let's tear this thing down!"

I haven't been *excited* since I did that whole *Roseanne* show/class thing, but I'm excited now. Talking to kids who are cheering like sons of bitches. I'm, like, "Jesus! *This* is what my fame can do? Encourage warriors and thinkers?" What a great reward to encourage people who think and want the world to be better. It's freaking awesome.

PAUL PROVENZA: I want to mention the dubious distinction your blog has gotten: voted Worst Blog Ever.

ROSEANNE BARR: AOL voted it the "worst, most incoherent thing on the Internet," ever! I love my blog so much 'cause I don't have any ads on it so I can say whatever I want. I pay for it out of my own pocket—because money can buy freedom—so I'm ad-free, and fuck 'em all.

And I just *know* it was some gay guy or fat woman working at AOL saying, "I'm gonna do Roseanne a back-handed favor here because I read it, and she *is* fucking crazy but it deserves attention."

It *was* a favor! I had millions of hits from it. It crashed my site. And a lot of *extremely* coherent people found it, and now they're writing on it, too.

PAUL PROVENZA: Did you consider *Roseanne* political?

ROSEANNE BARR: Of course. I wanted to show blue-collar people as intelligent and hardworking, because they always have been. That I even mentioned the word "class" in America is a political triumph. Stanley Kubrick even gave me props for that!

I always thought *The Honeymooners* was ex-

tremely political; it was one of my favorites. Back then everyone watched one of only three channels, so Gleason's populist, middle-of-the-road message wasn't that foreign, but by the time I got on TV, things were different. And I had the great reference of *All in the Family*, another groundbreaking show about class, but my show was as groundbreaking for its time as those were for theirs.

Cab drivers would ask me, "How did you get away with doing that show?" And I'd go, "Well, you got two years before they figure out what you're doing, and I managed to stay two years ahead for a decade."

PAUL PROVENZA: You came from the working class, but now you're *very* wealthy. How has that affected your perception of or relationship to class?

ROSEANNE BARR: I went through this phase of, "I'm one of *them* now. What does that mean that I'm one of them?" So I went out and got face-lifts by the fucking fistful and bought two of everything. There was about ten or twenty years of that, and then I had a moment of reckoning, and it all crashed down. It has to.

It went full circle. I was, like, "Now I got this fame, which to me is on the negative end, I have no enmity, which is really freaky for someone like me, and I have lots of money. What the hell does that make me, and what am I gonna do with it?" So I gave a lot of my money away. It was fucking *awesome*. I gave millions of dollars away in the street. Anybody that asked me for it, I gave them money. I gave millions and millions of dollars away, just to give it away. And it really was a great, great thing.

I wanted to see what it felt like if I actually practiced what I preached. I started thinking, "How cool would it feel to be that fucking honest, to actually live your beliefs?" And it was *really* fucking cool. To let go of money was *cool*. So awesome. More rich people ought to do it.

PAUL PROVENZA: Is this a well-known thing about you? You didn't take a camera crew to Africa and do a prime-time special I missed, did you?

ROSEANNE BARR: Nah, I just did it when I felt like doing it and I'd go, "Don't make a big fucking deal out of it, okay? Don't let me read it anywhere, ever."

After that, I was, like, "Man, I gotta make it my dream now to only make fifteen dollars a night." I mean, that's been my goal for a long time. I want to work someplace where you get paid, like, fifteen dollars. Or even doing it for *free*. Because that's when you're back on track.

UPRIGHT CITIZENS BRIGADE

FROM THE EARLY tutelage of Chicago improv legend Del Close, Upright Citizens Brigade has become a significant force in alternative comedy. Their cultish, innovative Comedy Central series may have been short-lived, but they've had immeasurable impact through Upright Citizens Brigade Theaters in New York and Los Angeles—performance spaces where comedy talent can gestate and find creative voice, unfettered by the usual commercial restraints and supported by a nurturing, collective-

like atmosphere disdainful of the predictable and encouraging the new and adventurous. Like Second City and ImprovOlympic before it, the UCB Theater has become a launching pad for a career in artful comedy and an incubator for ambitious new forms. The founders of the UCB Theater and actual Upright Citizens Brigade themselves—Matt Besser, Amy Poehler, Ian Roberts, and Matt Walsh—sound off on the need for confrontational comedy that challenges the way people think.

IAN ROBERTS: The way we run the UCB Theater business is that nobody gets paid for performing there, and conversely no one is charged for using our space. So you're not gonna make any money or spend any money, and I think that has an effect on things artistically. People can give something a shot that they might be nervous about giving a shot somewhere else if they have to pay to rent a space or answer to a venue owner or booker who's paying them.

Some shows start slow, but if they're really good, word of mouth builds them up. We can afford to let that happen here. We've never looked at the theater as a place to make money. It just about breaks even and pays the rent, and then on classes we make a little money.

PAUL PROVENZA: I was particularly impressed with the *God Sux* shows you do every now and then. You dedicate whole shows to atheist comedy and antireligious material and provide a platform for some smart, provocative performers and material that comedy clubs aren't generally enthusiastic about.

MATT BESSER: Most stand-up clubs are really conservative. They figure, why take that risk? They're in the business of selling drinks. We *can* do it.

PAUL PROVENZA: What you guys have is really like an incubator, with an audience that feels the same way you do about supporting and encouraging artists and different kinds of work.

MATT WALSH: Truthfully, it's like a clubhouse. Say Matt has an idea for a show, some musical where it gets all bloody or whatever he wants to do, he can just do the show. He can treat it like his clubhouse, and that's a benefit for us on a real simple level.

AMY POEHLER: It's also nice because we all have to keep one foot in commercial stuff, but we've made a place where we can have those kind of shows, too. During the writers' strike, we performed *Saturday Night Live* live onstage at the New York UCB Theater. Then *30 Rock* and *The Colbert Report* did episodes of their shows live, too. It was super-inspiring to see all these performers doing live in the theater what they do on television, because, at the end of the day, it's encouraging to know you can always get up onstage if it all goes to shit, you know?

IAN ROBERTS: I keep both my arms and both my feet in commercial stuff. Then I try to dip my hips in, like I'm having sex with commercial stuff.

AMY POEHLER: You love to fuck commercial stuff. As you can see, it's a nice way for us to extend our adolescence well into our forties.

PAUL PROVENZA: When the Upright Citizens Brigade themselves do shows, it's almost always pretty dark and edgy stuff. Even in your improv, it's consistently crossing lines. Is that conscious, or just who you guys are?

MATT BESSER: When we started out onstage in Chicago, we enjoyed making a certain percentage of the audience angry. As much as we enjoyed people getting what we were doing, it was just as funny to us when people didn't get it. So our shows were always very agro and confrontational with the audience.

IAN ROBERTS: And uncomfortable, too. We

liked people not knowing whether something was real or fake.

MATT BESSER: In retrospect, we sometimes did stupid stuff, but it was fun. We did a fake "interrogation" once, where we just grabbed an audience member—who didn't volunteer—and stuck a hood over their head and blew cigarette smoke into their face pretending it was weed smoke, but, even worse, it was cigarette smoke. And it was supposed to be making fun of interrogations and CIA stuff or whatever, but in truth we were really just grabbing someone and blowing smoke into their face.

MATT WALSH: We told someone their car was blocking the entrance and an ambulance couldn't get to the place so somebody just died as a result of them not moving their car. We just, like, bummed the audience out.

AMY POEHLER: I'm totally the least brave of the group, I have to say. I'm probably the one that feels the most nervous about doing that kind of stuff.

IAN ROBERTS: You know, Amy, I'd have a hard time explaining what you just said without using the word "pussy."

PAUL PROVENZA: What *is* it about provoking audiences that is as appealing as getting laughs?

IAN ROBERTS: It gets you excited. It's that same kind of fun you had making prank calls and throwing eggs at houses.

PAUL PROVENZA: I think a lot of what we do is really just a fundamental life-long commitment to being bad boys and girls, doing and saying stuff we're not supposed to.

MATT WALSH: Or *not being afraid* to say the wrong thing.

MATT BESSER: Or actually even being effective, too, by pissing off the people who are in the way. The enemy, you know? That's how our pranks were. We would always take them out into the street so we could really pull off a prank, because in a theater you always know something's fake, but once it's taken out into the street, who knows *what's* happening. That became the prank element of our Comedy Central show. We just talked our premises to people and had them react to them, and sometimes they were really uptight people, and that's *always* funny.

But even beyond the pranks, even just doing the "ASSSSCAT" show really is outrageous to some people. Unless you're a comedian and you're used to that freedom of language or the kinds of topics we get into, it's really outrageous to some people. It's surprising.

MATT WALSH: Often in "ASSSSCAT" we'll take on the opinion of an ignorant, terrible human being and play that to the nth degree. Sometimes people don't think it's funny, because we're assuming they understand that we're not *endorsing* what any character might be saying.

MATT BESSER: People don't always get that level, but the people who don't get that level, I don't think we really care about. We kind of laugh at the fact that they don't get it.

MATT WALSH: Unless they're the majority.

PAUL PROVENZA: To me that's sort of the whole point of subversion in this context. I believe complacency and conformity are really the biggest parts of the world's problems. Politicians and governments get away with war crimes because we the people have become complacent. Anything that challenges complacency I think has tremendous value. Saying and doing the "wrong" thing may be exactly what's needed.

MATT BESSER: Have you read *The End of Faith,* by Sam Harris? His whole thing is that sometimes, like in response to 9/11, the people who are moderate are more to blame than the fundamentalists, because they don't allow there to be any discussion about religion. It's not PC; it's considered intolerant to question religion, so people don't feel comfortable talking about the Koran and Islam or the Bible and what's fucked up about any of it and no one talks about it.

MATT WALSH: Just lay off the Catholics, that's all I say.

MATT BESSER: I'll shut up then.

MATT WALSH: I'm kidding. I was just being satirical.

MATT BESSER: Oh. I didn't recognize it. Sorry.

IAN ROBERTS: Surprisingly, though, I *do* have a cutoff point for some stuff. I remember a guy at our theater who did jokes about fucking babies and killing women, and I just didn't like it. I thought, "This guy shouldn't be performing at our place."

MATT BESSER: That guy was just being shocking; there was no comedy to it. There *can* be, but there wasn't.

IAN ROBERTS: That's the thing, you can do

any *topic,* but you gotta be on the right side and you gotta have something to say.

MATT BESSER: We've been asked by people in the audience to ban concepts. Like, "Don't do anything about the Holocaust," or whatever. We wouldn't make fun of the Holocaust but we might make fun of someone's *perception* of the Holocaust, and some people just don't get that level. We'll apologize, like, "Well, I'm sorry that offended you but it wasn't offensive and we're not gonna stop." We are *not* gonna ban all references to the Holocaust or 9/11 or the N-word.

IAN ROBERTS: We might be making fun of idiots that are really out there who say that word. How else are we supposed to do that without *being* that kind of person and using the word to show them to be the idiots they are?

MATT BESSER: We would never ban a word from UCB. It's not any *word,* it's the *hate* behind the word. Lenny Bruce had a famous bit about exactly that. I could be really hateful against black people without ever saying the N-word, so does that make it okay as long as I don't use that word? Of course not.

And look at how gays are treated in comedy. I hope people will someday look back on this era the way we look back on humor against black people in the past. I hope someday it'll be, "I can't believe people openly ridiculed gays so much." Just saying the word "gay" or "homo" is a punch line for so many jokes and no one blinks an eye at that. "Faggot" is said freely; no one gives a shit about that. So, how can you ban *one* word? You gotta start banning words all across the spectrum.

AMY POEHLER: I would like to ban the word "panties." I really don't like that word. It makes me feel weird.

PAUL PROVENZA: I'd like to ban the word "butthead," because it's the lamest replacement in sitcoms for "dickhead." I cringe when they use that.

AMY POEHLER: I'd also like to ban "bumfuck."

PAUL PROVENZA: The word or the action?

AMY POEHLER: Just the word. Like when people say, "I was out in Bumfuck, New Jersey." It's just . . . *arrrrgh.*

PAUL PROVENZA: Back in the day, when I was doing *Comics Only* on Comedy Central, standards and practices went through all the stuff we submitted and sent a formal letter with specific guidelines for what we could and couldn't say. It was hilarious to read a formal document clarifying things like, "The phrase 'ball sack' is acceptable; however, it is *not* acceptable if preceded by the modifier 'sweaty.'"

So we could talk about a ball sack, but it had to be a clean, dry ball sack.

MATT BESSER: On our TV show, I was smoking pot in one scene, and they specified the number of bong hits we could take. It wasn't that I couldn't take *any*, but I couldn't take too many. They said, "You can take up to three," or something like that. I guess, you know, "We don't want you to be enjoying pot *too* much."

MATT WALSH: Anyway, here's my thing about what people say and what they do: nobody thinks they're a bad person or thinks they're making terrible choices. No one wakes up and says, "I'm gonna figure out how to go to hell today. I'm gonna be an awful person and say and do horrible things." What people do is try to accomplish what they *believe* are good things: "I'm going to improve the economy and make the country safe. To do that, I'll get rid of all the Jews."

That's how people think. They do what's *right* to them. So if you wanna make fun of it, you've gotta *support* their point of view. You have to commit to it in order to see how all this horrible stuff follows from their simple intent to do the right thing. That's how you show how fucked up and idiotic the logic is. You can't just say, "These people are wrong!" That's just polemic. That's for politicians.

IAN ROBERTS: I always ask my students to accept the principle that all people pursue pleasure and avoid pain. People have car accidents, get in fights and get their ass kicked, break up with the girl they should have married—and at each of those moments, nobody was thinking, "Let me wreck my life right now. Let me become paralyzed." They were thinking, "Let me get there quickly," or, "Let me get with that other girl, I don't know about this one."

You've got to play it like the person really believes what they're doing makes *sense* and is a *good* choice. That's what's really hysterical: people, all of us, we're *idiots.* That's what's funny.

I think that's something in the way we perform that maybe adds to it having a feeling of satire. We try to play things completely straight and *real* in our sketches. We've talked among ourselves about how some of the sketch now for younger kids is real goofy; talking in a voice you'd never use, playing it really broad. That just makes it less real. Instead, we play it like it *matters*. We make the guy in the scene who's getting fucked with *really* be affected. We try to really feel what *he* would feel—right or wrong, good or bad.

FROM *LAUGH-IN* TO *Saturday Night Live,* and from feature films to her own award-winning one-woman Broadway shows, Lily Tomlin has created an unforgettable array of characters that capture all elements of the human condition. In her performance, she threw pointed barbs at the establishment. In her uncompromising personal life, she thumbed her nose quietly at convention as well. Tomlin reflects on the origins of her characters, what we might learn from them, and how similar even the most disparate of them—and us—truly are.

LILY TOMLIN: I guess I was really trying to depict another human or culture type that I was either just enamored of—or, in some cases, appalled by.

Growing up in an old apartment house in Detroit in a black neighborhood, with so many different kinds of people, with parents who were Southern and had come north to work in the factories, every apartment was like a microcosm of life. Their foods, their furnishing, the way they spoke, their prejudices, their advances, their failures—they were all so different, yet so similar, and I was just mad for all of them. In some ways, I wanted to just communicate something about humans in general. Perhaps I wanted people to see them as affectionately and as sympathetically as I did.

By the way, I think I'm actually articulating all of this to you right now perhaps for the first time ever.

PAUL PROVENZA: I'm honored, thank you. What you do is very much about looking at those ordinary lives that are overlooked or unrecognized. They're human beings, not clichés or archetypes, and you give voice to their unique perspectives. To me, giving voice to those otherwise invisible individuals and ideas is really a political act.

LILY TOMLIN: Well, I like that you say that. I couldn't say it myself, but I like to think that's absolutely so. If that's what you get from it—it sounds like a much better thing than just wanting to get famous and get laughs.

PAUL PROVENZA: *Was* your motivation just

to get famous and get laughs?

LILY TOMLIN: I used to put shows on all the time when I was a kid, but to me that was all "play"; I didn't know people made a *living* doing it.

I was pre-med in college—believe me, it was a pretense of the highest order—but thank God I got into a college show. It was *The Madwoman of Chaillot,* and I was one of the "capitalist women," who was banned to the cellar. I had to improvise my entrance, and I was just a big hit. I felt totally comfortable on the stage. I thought, "I wish I could make a living doing this."

Then I got into another college show, this time a sketch show—very collegiate kind of stuff. A takeoff on *Gunsmoke,* a takeoff on the Academy Awards . . . And I thought, "Gee, this material is void of any content. It's sort of cute, but that's about it." Before the first performance, the kid who was the producer was pacing up and down going, "Man, if I just had *one* more sketch or monologue . . ."

Now, we had "society pages" in the paper back then, and Charlotte *Ford* was making her "debut" that year; it was a $250,000 event—a *huge* amount back then. The lid has just been blown off the fact that Grosse Pointe, the rich suburb, was a covertly segregated community; if you were anything other than white, if you were even *swarthy,* you would get demerits and couldn't buy property there. They did their best to keep anybody ethnic, anybody the wrong race out of Grosse Pointe.

So I improvised a woman being interviewed

on a show called *Distinguished Guest,* and ad-libbed all this stuff about my daughter's debut party, and all that topical stuff. And at the end, after the character was so elegant, so careful in her language and so proper, as she gets up out of her chair, she puts a hand on each knee and spreads her legs. I was just a sensation doing that monologue because it was *so* topical and *so* relevant—

PAUL PROVENZA: Was *that* the genesis of your "Tasteful Lady" character??

LILY TOMLIN: Yes! It was! I did it on *Laugh-In* because I'd shown her to George Schlatter, the producer. Everything she did was "tasteful"; she'd say things like, "I'm appealing now to the *tasteful* people in the audience . . ." Of course, we all know what "tasteful" requires or implies, so it was about breaking all that pretension with her crude kind of rise out of the chair.

Then after doing that sketch show, I started working in the coffee houses in Detroit, where I started consciously developing monologues.

PAUL PROVENZA: It's interesting that you first found yourself being funny improvising in *The Madwoman of Chaillot,* a play that focuses so much on class struggle.

LILY TOMLIN: Yeah, that *is* interesting . . . Because I *was* class-conscious. I lived in what might be thought of as a "ghetto," and in concentric circles spreading out from my neighborhood—which was my whole world—with each block the houses got progressively bigger. I went to school with kids who lived in some of the big houses. And in Detroit in those days,

rich gentiles moved out to Palmer Park and rich Jews moved to Sherwood Forest, leaving the rest of us behind with a diminishing tax base, and I knew people in both of those communities too, because I was always hyper-mobile, socially.

All through my life, I was eager to somehow be with all these different kinds of people—but I knew the difference; I knew what it meant to people. My mother was a nurse's aide and my father was a factory worker—and a big gambler, too, and I probably shouldn't have, but I used to go to the track with him so I was hip to all that, too. I knew what money was and what it meant. And I knew what sex was, too—when you live in a tiny apartment, you just know *everything* that goes on with people.

All of that creates a compassion for, and understanding of, people. You see them at their highest and lowest; you know that for people who put up a good front or are high and mighty all the time, they're *not.* They're *all* pretty fragile. I got very early that everybody had been a baby once, you know? It's a leveling realization; suddenly *nobody* had any authority. I got that my mother had been a baby, my teachers had all been babies; they all had been a kid like I was, and I knew they didn't really know a whole lot either.

It may be a cliché, but it's true that *all* people can do the most noble, elevated things when you least expect it, and they can all also do the most base things.

PAUL PROVENZA: Having been raised Southern Baptist, how did you process that very particular experience and how do you think it manifests itself in what you do?

LILY TOMLIN: I so often meet "born again" people who think God singled them out. Like if they survived an accident, God *particularly* saved them—because they were Christians or whatever. That God has something in mind for them to do; "Their work here is not finished," in the parlance of that subculture—which is really a *major* culture. There seems to be an arrogance in all of that.

Until I was about ten years old and had any consciousness about it at all, I lived in *terror* that I would not be "saved" before I died. The preacher would call for people to "come forward," you'd go to the front of the church where there were people for you to confess your sins to and to accept Christ as your savior to get "saved." The adults all just acted so out of control, weeping and wailing, beating their breasts and carrying on . . . and I just thought, "Oh, this is *so* absolutely embarrassing."

I said, "I'll *never* be able to do that." It didn't feel genuine; I couldn't transcend that. I knew if I did it, I'd be playing a part. But it puts a lot of terror in a kid's heart. Every time you'd step out of the church after services, somebody'd say something like, "Oh, the sky looks funny. The end of the world could be coming."

And you'd think, "Holy mackerel! I don't get another chance to go forward till next Sunday and what if the end of the world comes before then??" For a seven- or eight-year-old to be thinking this all the time is a bit . . . oppressive.

What opened my eyes was Faye Mathis, a girl I knew in grade school. Her parents were a bit intellectual, and Jewish as well, so they had a whole 'nother perspective. One day Fay said to me, "Do you think God made man, or did man make God?"

That had never occurred to me. It was so revelatory, I never worried too much again.

PAUL PROVENZA: Well, you went on to lead a life that is completely antithetical, by fundamentalist standards.

LILY TOMLIN: You mean because I'm gay?

PAUL PROVENZA: No, because you're in show business. And *also* gay.

LILY TOMLIN: Yeah, well, that's true. But that doesn't seem to be too much of a factor. Maybe the older relatives would have been more shocked or dismayed about my being gay, but you know what? Fame supersedes everything. They probably excused me because I was famous and I could get them tickets to Jay Leno.

PAUL PROVENZA: When you became a star in the seventies, it was pretty risky to be "out," and you handled it in such a way that was pretty fearless and really honest. I particularly remember a moment on *The Tonight Show* with Johnny Carson that to me was so bold and disarmingly honest.

LILY TOMLIN: You mean when he asked me about not having children? Well, that was very much *of* that time. "You don't want to have children?" was something they could broach in public rather than whether or not you were gay. So I remember Johnny asking, "You're not married, are you?"

I said, "No, I'm not."

Then he said, "Don't you ever want to have children?"

And I said, "You mean biologically bear children? No, I don't have any desire to do that." Remember, this was 1973—and the audience just stopped *dead*. They went totally silent. Even just that short time ago, for a female to say in public that she didn't want to be a mother was really *divisive*. It's hard to believe, but it was a very strong thing to say publicly. It was, "Well, what's *wrong* with you that you don't want to be a mother?" It was un-American, you know?

And I could feel a *huge* amount of tension, so just as a joke, to break the tension, I said to Johnny, "Well, who has custody of yours?"

PAUL PROVENZA: That was a pretty ballsy line, since Johnny was notoriously touchy about anything to do with his personal life.

LILY TOMLIN: It didn't *seem* ballsy to me, it was just kinda the truth. I mean, who *did* have custody of his kids? I'm sure he didn't have to expend too much effort raising them. That's often how it is.

I'm sure I wasn't aware or intending to make any kind of powerful statement . . . it was just the truth. And it was a way to make him laugh.

PAUL PROVENZA: Do you care to, or think that you make any kind of difference?

LILY TOMLIN: Especially when you're young, you want to believe you're the one who is doing something that is going to make people believe things or affect their lives, or that you're going to bring people together, but, you know, we're like little drops in the bucket. I think it's all

good, because a lot of drops fill up the bucket, I guess. But I certainly don't overthink or overstate whatever I put out into the world. I'm glad I didn't put out anything that I'm ashamed of or feel that I cheapened myself or other humans. That's about the most you can hope for, really. You can maybe minimize the downside, but I don't know if you can maximize the upside.

PAUL PROVENZA: As you've said, "I always want my comedy to be embracing of our species rather than debasing of it."

LILY TOMLIN: I definitely do. That's why I think so many men don't think women are funny. They have a different sensibility, basically.

Or really, I should say that very *often* that's the case, but not *entirely*. I've noticed that in movies like *Juno,* or in *Superbad,* the Judd Apatow movie, that they've introduced a certain kind of tenderness into movies that they never would've taken a chance like that with before.

They're funny and ribald and all that kind of stuff is going on, but then a kind of tenderness shows, a shade of it that I think is kind of lovely. It's not heavy-handed or anything, it just kind of gets a little tender—which you don't expect in that kind of a movie.

Of course the tenderness is very often between the guys, and that's okay. In *Superbad,* when they're going off with girls, it's a point of passage, but they look kind of longingly at each other, in that kind of "buddy" way. They tell each other they love each other, you know?

With movies like that, on the surface you think, "This is going to be a *boys'* movie," but they actually seem more thoughtful, more textured than you'd expect. They're not just showing all the obvious fronts or posturing. They're finding some kind of loving impulse. They're finding the *humanity*.

THOUGH HE FELT unable to find his own unique voice and persona as a stand-up, Judd Apatow's outsized comic gifts and originality were immediately apparent, and earned him the respect of some of comedy's biggest names. A gifted writer, he moved easily into writing and producing television, yielding cult hits *The Ben Stiller Show*, *The Larry Sanders Show*, *The Critic*, *Freaks and Geeks*, and *Undeclared*. He transitioned deftly into features, producing *The Cable Guy* and *Anchorman* before breaking out as a writer/director with the sleeper hit *The 40 Year Old Virgin* and becoming the most in-demand—and profitable—comedy guru in Hollywood. Subsequent producing and/or directing efforts *Superbad*, *Pineapple Express*, *Forgetting Sarah Marshall*, and *Knocked Up* cemented that position, and Apatow has raised the bar for exploring heartfelt, touching human experience through sometimes profane, always smart comedy.

JUDD APATOW: Even my wife says, "What's with you and the bro-mances? What's the deal on all the man-love?"

I'd never really looked at it that way, but something affects what you respond to, I suppose. Steve Carell said, "I want to make a movie about a forty-year-old man who's a virgin," and instantly I think, "It's the greatest idea ever!" Maybe it's because of who I am and what I've been through in relationships that I connect to that loneliness or need or terror that makes that a funny idea to me.

For me, the emotion is the *reason* to do the comedy, it's not tacked on to make the jokes hold together. It's the part I'm most interested in. If you care about something, if what you're saying is genuine to you, it's much easier to be funny with it.

When I wrote for *Larry Sanders,* Garry Shandling always talked about "writing from your core." Whenever we got stuck, before we'd work on any jokes, he'd say, "What would *really* happen? What would the *truth* in this moment be?" He said, "*The Larry Sanders Show* is about people who love each other, but show business gets in the way. *All* stories are about people who love each other but something's getting in the way. It's *always* about something blocking love." It never would've occurred to me that *that*'s what *Larry Sanders* was about, but it made perfect sense. I realized, "Yeah, Larry loves Hank, but Hank really wants to host the show himself. Larry's ego needs him to be number one, but Hank's getting in the way so Larry's afraid of him . . ." It's all those permutations.

That idea changed the way I looked at *all* stories.

PAUL PROVENZA: All your movies are very much "guy" stories, but they're not afraid to wear their hearts on their sleeves.

JUDD APATOW: I think it's fun when men open up. That's why in *Knocked Up,* they take mushrooms so they can say what they're really thinking—which *I* did once; I was on mushrooms on a first date with this woman and after she rejected me, for three straight hours I just asked her why.

PAUL PROVENZA: Two women opening up to each other isn't as comedically interesting to me, because women tend to do that naturally. But guys trying to be open and vulnerable while trying to be macho and strong at the same time is pure comic fodder.

JUDD APATOW: I think a lot of that's just being uncomfortable being a man and the struggle to "own" your masculinity and cockiness as part of all that. I've always found that funny. The goofy guy *trying* to figure out how to be confident is one of the funniest things of all to me.

I also think there's an interesting dynamic of women "straightening out" men or trying to manipulate them into being something different. *That* struggle is always human, and *really* good for comedy.

PAUL PROVENZA: And they're usually both right and both wrong—that's what's really funny.

JUDD APATOW: I learned slowly over the years that I'm wrong about most everything. In every fight, there's that struggle to accept the fact that you're wrong about something and how hard you'll hold on to being right.

PAUL PROVENZA: Your movies all say a lot about the male-female dynamic, evolution into manhood, and our assumptions about *all* that sort of stuff, I think. But they're not always appreciated for that, are they?

JUDD APATOW: People see the movies through their subjective eyes. Some critics said they're sexist, but to me the whole point is that there's no way the guys could be worse with their behavior; it's about their *struggle* to grow up, to be *able* to handle a family and kids and whatever. With something like Seth saving his bong during an earthquake before thinking about his pregnant girlfriend, I'm *trying* to show the worst side of a man.

And I should also be able to show the worst side of a woman, which sometimes is being pregnant and hormonal and kicking your boyfriend out of the car in the middle of a major intersection. You go into nesting mode, your hormones are kicking in, you're in a panic trying to hold it all together, and once in a while it just blows—at the man you're with, or at someone you bump into walking down the street. That is *very* real, *very* human, and also very *funny*.

In *Knocked Up,* I tried to show a really unpleasant relationship; two people that don't really work well together. I always thought, "These two might not last three weeks after this movie ends." It doesn't even *imply* they'll be together forever, but I like that they're saying, "We screwed up and got pregnant, but we owe it to the baby to at least find out if

we could like each other. It'd be wrong to *not* find out." That's the point of the movie: they don't just blow each other off. It's an original premise, because people don't *do* that. People usually just head out of town.

And some people say, "Oh come on, a woman like that would *never* go for *him*."

Well, a goofy Jewish guy being with a gorgeous woman is not all that crazy. If you need proof, Google Image me and my wife. Look at my wife, then look at me.

PAUL PROVENZA: I love that *Knocked Up* ends bittersweet. It evokes *The Graduate* with that looming sense of, "Now what?" at the end.

JUDD APATOW: I *hope* people think it's open-ended. It's not exactly *The Graduate* with them staring at each other on the bus, but it would be illogical to think it's not going to be a very problematic relationship. In fact, an inspiration for *Knocked Up* was David Denby's review of *40 Year Old Virgin*. He wrote that Steve Carell's relationship with Catherine Keener would be very difficult, but that it would clearly be worth it. I thought, "That's what I want to write more about, people working hard to make their relationships work."

Because no two people get along perfectly.

PAUL PROVENZA: So it's the journey that's more interesting than the actual outcome of whether they're together or not together. These kinds of subtexts and underlying themes aren't usual fare in younger-skewing, box-office-hit comedies.

JUDD APATOW: What I've done is brought a little bit of a television comedy aesthetic to it. I often see a movie and think, "I liked it, but really . . . That *could* have been a *lot* funnier."

I always ask myself, "How can I make it as real as possible and be about all these bigger things and also be *super*-funny?"

PAUL PROVENZA: I walked out of *Pineapple Express*—a *very* funny movie—thinking, "I don't know whether this is a pro-pot or anti-pot movie."

JUDD APATOW: That movie started because I watched *True Romance,* and Brad Pitt played this guy who was high in *one* scene, but he was so funny I wished they were chasing his character instead of Christian Slater, because it must be really hard to run away when you're *that* high. And I thought, "How great would it be to do a Cheech & Chong movie but with Jerry Bruckheimer–level action?" A big action movie, but they are just high out of their minds.

I had read *Superbad,* but couldn't get anybody to make it, so I thought, "If Seth Rogen and Evan Goldberg wrote this stoner/action-movie idea, maybe that's more commercial." I don't know why we thought the *pot* movie could be more commercial than the *liquor* movie, but *Superbad* ended up happening, and in the middle of shooting that, the studio said, "Since the alcohol movie seems to be going well, maybe we should make that pot movie too."

Now, Seth and Evan always said, "*Superbad* is the kind of movie we *wish* someone would make. It's the way we talk, the kind of comedy we like, the kind of action we like," so it's been like hooking into two people with this unique perspective as young guys; how they look at the world and what they want to see. I can talk to them, like, "You have these friends in *Superbad,* but other than trying to get liquor, what's the movie *about*?"

I said to them, "It's *really* about two guys that love each other and are about to separate probably for the rest of their lives, and they're heartbroken and mad that they can't stay together." That's the *engine* of *Superbad.*

With *Pineapple Express,* we kept saying, "What is this *about* underneath all this action and comedy and this tone?"

PAUL PROVENZA: Is it about class division? Self-delusion? Alternative realities?

JUDD APATOW: Our friend Ian Roberts from Upright Citizens Brigade did the table reading and said, "My favorite thing is that it's a story about a guy trying to figure out if he's really friends with his drug dealer or if he's just his drug dealer."

And that was *kind of* in there, but suddenly that became the story that motored the whole movie: "Am I really *friends* with this guy?"

But it's about Seth's character, who smokes pot, thinks it's okay to smoke pot, doesn't think it's dangerous, doesn't think there's any collateral damage, but he looks down on the guy who *sells* it to him. He slowly realizes smoking pot causes so much damage to him—and to other people by supporting, like, a whole *crime industry.*

I kinda wanted to say there are probably as many people getting killed from pot dealers as from coke dealers. Seth and I had an ongoing debate while making the movie; Seth always said it was *not* an anti-pot movie; I always said it *was*: "He smokes pot, has a terrible job, dates a high school girl, for the whole movie the dealer's trying to kill him, then at the end he realizes, 'Maybe I shouldn't live this way.'"

Seth said, "Nah, he'll probably just keep smoking pot."

So you *can* see it and think it shows the joys of smoking pot, but . . . all *I* know is he gets his ear blown off, almost dies, and basically gets about twenty other people killed—so you'd kinda hope that the next day he wouldn't run straight to the pot dealer.

But that's for people to debate.

PAUL PROVENZA: For me, it's easy to sidestep all of that and turn it into an anti-War-on-Drugs movie either way, since if it was legal, none of that would've happened. But that's the way I see things *a lot*. But again, rarely do you get a movie with such over-the-top action and huge comedy set pieces but you can actually debate the ending or what it all means.

JUDD APATOW: My daughters are twelve and seven, and I think a lot about what they're going to make of my movies. Will they think they're unethical? That I'm promoting pot use? What I tell my twelve-year-old is that I find idiots to be really funny. *That's* why they curse in my movies or smoke pot all the time: because they're a mess, and it's funny to watch people who are a mess try to get it together.

What's funny is some conservative Web site had *Knocked Up* and *Superbad* on their list of top ten movies. They said, one says, "Don't have an abortion," and the other says, "Don't have sex before marriage." Neither is specifically what we intended to say, but . . . Beneath

it all, hopefully, is something positive to think about.

At the end of the day, I want to get my thoughts across *and* give the crowd a great time. Those things *can* work together.

PAUL PROVENZA: *The Graduate* and *Groundhog Day* are two films that really clarified for me that balance between broad comedy and genuine introspection in comedy.

JUDD APATOW: *Tootsie* is a big one for me. Couldn't be more enjoyable. Then there are movies that are meant to make you uncomfortable or leave you unsettled—like Cassavetes movies. I'm always trying to think how I can slip a little of that kind of thing into my movies.

I love *Borat* and movies that are deeply uncomfortable—which is ironic, because when I was a kid, *The Honeymooners* made me so uncomfortable I'd shut it off when things started going badly for Ralph. I've only seen the first twelve minutes of every episode.

PAUL PROVENZA: My parents couldn't stand *The Honeymooners*. They said, "There's enough screaming and yelling in this house, we don't need to watch it on TV, too."

JUDD APATOW: When we were making *Freaks and Geeks*, NBC said, "Why can't they ever win?" They tried to turn it into a wish-fulfillment show like they were used to making.

We said, "The whole point is they *don't* ever win—but they have each other. They *may* win in the end, but not right now."

I had a sense of that myself as this funny kid, bad at sports, reading comic books and writing reports on the Marx Brothers—not for school, just for myself. I used to think, "One day, these things will be *cool*."

When I moved to L.A. at seventeen, I started hanging out at the comedy clubs. I felt like that "bee girl" in Blind Melon's "No Rain" video, walking through the field and finding all these other people dressed like bees. I couldn't believe there were that many people with the same interests as me. I felt alone in high school; nobody else cared about comedy or was obsessed with Bill Murray or Monty Python or any of that. It was a great feeling to be in the comedy world, where suddenly, "Oh, I'm *not* that weird? People *value* that I know minutia about John Candy?"

PAUL PROVENZA: What other film comedies influenced what you do now?

JUDD APATOW: Hal Ashby's a filmmaker I often look toward. In a short span of time he made *Shampoo, Coming Home, Being There, Harold and Maude*—it's pretty remarkable. *The Last Detail* is one of my favorites. Very little happens, but it's so dense and rich. It's very powerful *and* funny.

Being There is the bar. That's the kind of movie you look at and think, "I'll never get *there*. I'll spend my whole life trying, but I don't think I'm going to get there in terms of originality, meaning, comedy, performance . . . It's just unique, and one of the most hilarious movies ever made.

And, obviously, *The Graduate* was a gigantic influence. On *all* of us.

MIKE NICHOLS

AFTER A FORTY-YEAR Oscar- and Tony Award–winning career directing movies like *The Graduate* and musical extravaganzas like *Monty Python's Spamalot,* it's easy to forget that Mike Nichols was a groundbreaking comedy performer, too. In partnership with Elaine May, he helped propel the Chicago improv movement, created best-selling comedy albums, and took their act to Broadway. Here, the "veteran" multi-hyphenate holds forth on the thing that inspires you to start doing comedy, and the only other thing that can sustain you if you want to survive.

MIKE NICHOLS: *The Graduate* was really about a very specific thing: it was about what happens to your life. It was about drowning in objects, becoming an object—and saving yourself through passion. Madness and passion. That's why the sense of Ben and Elaine's liberation at the end, fighting to be free, brought such joy.

And I *meant* it. Buck Henry and I bullshitted about it for a year, and meant it *all*.

PAUL PROVENZA: Do you feel you've lived that way over the course of your own career?

MIKE NICHOLS: It's very hard to be proud of yourself for anything, but I'm "not displeased" with myself for having tried to do a lot of different stuff. I don't want to be the master of everything. Once you are, then you're sort of an eminence instead of what I get, which is "veteran." And that's fine—but what I don't believe in is "icon." Nobody becomes an icon without working on it, and it's not worth it.

You do, in fact, have to take *chances*. But only *you* know what they are.

PAUL PROVENZA: In terms of what each of our own challenges may be?

MIKE NICHOLS: Nobody else can tell. First of all, we're very lucky in a way, because "selling out" is an idea of the past; there's no such thing. If you're lucky enough to get two million bucks for a commercial in Japan, more power to you, man; wish I could. There's no selling *out*, there's only selling. But I've always thought about disassembling the whole thing, and have enormously enjoyed putting that into effect.

I always suspected that moving toward in-

visible would be good. Because you then get to have what happens to you every day, and it's yours, and it's *life*. And I'm loving it more and more. You have nothing left to prove to yourself; you're the only one you ever pay any attention to. And you can look and listen and love and have your actual life.

So much of our work—a comic's work, writer's work, actor's work—is *instead* of life. It's great, it's like a constant orgasm, it has great joys and depression in it—it's *living*—but it's not exactly *life*.

PAUL PROVENZA: Some people do comedy—specifically stand-up—that's aggressive and confrontational and harsh. But I really feel the root of any anger they demonstrate comes from a place of beauty. Theirs is anger at a *lack* of kindness, at a *lack* of compassion, at injustice and pain people suffer or perpetuate upon one another. That's all really life-affirming, I think, despite any harshness in their approach.

MIKE NICHOLS: That's a tough, complicated one, because kindness is one of the *last* things you'd look for in stand-up, capital-letter "COMEDY." Because comedy's sort of the opposite. It's a place to vent our *rage* by making as much fun as possible of those who've made us mad.

If you go all the way back to Aristotle, comedy is like tragedy in its concern with the fall of someone in a higher station than us. In comedy, though, nobody gets hurt.

PAUL PROVENZA: It goes through some sort of alchemy, where rage somehow becomes joyful.

MIKE NICHOLS: How smart you are. It turns a corner—and it happens to be my favorite corner—from rage to kindness. And that connection is right before our eyes, which is the hardest thing in the world to do with farce. We tried to do it with *The Birdcage;* you try to do it here and there. It is a beautiful thing.

There's something about revenge, too. Revenge drives most of the plots we love. *Cinderella* is the ur-plot, made over and over in a thousand different ways, whether it's a maid at the Plaza, a working girl, you name it— it's *Cinderella,* and what drives it is revenge. I think that's what drives comedy, and a lot of theater and movies too. And that revenge is sweet, because it's laughing at that prick that beat you up in school.

You find that more in America than other places, for obvious reasons: high school is the central American experience. And *popularity* is the central aspect of high school. In fact, a friend of mine has a kid who, when asked, "How are you doing in high school?" said, "I'm the most popular of the unpopular kids."

What we do in life is always, I think, based on revenge for humiliations suffered in high school. Even if it was mild, or invisible to others, there are humiliations. And I think the joy of comedy for comedians—and laughers; we're all both—is revenge. Talk to anybody smart, anyone beautiful, anybody who manages well and succeeds, and invariably they were miserable in high school; they were outcasts.

When Elaine May and I were on Broadway,

this guy came up to me afterward and started, "You don't remember me, but—"

And I said, "I remember you very well. You're Eddie Pompadour. You're a *prick*." When I was ten years old, he had pushed me under water in the lake and stood on my head and kept me under. He looked dumbfounded. I said, "So, what are you doing now?"

"I'm selling used cars."

"I'm *so* glad."

And that was it! It wasn't like I've dwelled on this person since the age of ten, but it felt as if I'd lived all those years just for *that* moment, and now I *had* it.

PAUL PROVENZA: It is, ultimately, revenge, but unlike most of our tormentors, we don't need to make them smaller to feel bigger ourselves. We're really just trying to even the playing field.

MIKE NICHOLS: And if the revenge shows, it's not funny. The minute you *see* a flash of revenge, it's out of the question; it doesn't work. You've revealed that you're really just still that high school kid going after whoever made you miserable.

PAUL PROVENZA: How does that relate to satire or social commentary, where it's not revenge against an individual or a specific incident, but against a mindset or culture or some injustice?

MIKE NICHOLS: In order to stay funny when going after people in politics, one has to remember to some extent the idea of democracy and justice for all. You can't be all the way to the Left or the Right. You can't be Ann Coulter and be funny. It's *pseudo*-funny because it's very shocking; it's almost like a parody of an actual position. But it's not *funny*. It has nothing to do with comedy. Comedy is vastly more diplomatic.

Now, when you take it to its outermost edges, you have Lenny Bruce—or, more recently, Sarah Silverman, who clearly in some way is going for the Lenny bar; it's one of the reasons she's so interesting. And all those clichés about funny girls aren't there—she's *very* hot; *very* pretty. She's hot and pretty *and* she's going for the Lenny Bruce bar? I'm interested.

But in order to do that, you have to live with going too far all the time, because that's what you've set before yourself. And everybody has a different temperature of "Well, now you've gone too far."

PAUL PROVENZA: I find Sarah one of the most interesting comedians working today. In many ways, there's no difference between what she's doing and what Stephen Colbert's doing. She's embracing an absurd point of view. And when she makes fun of somebody or something that might be in bad taste to make fun of, she's really commenting on our *relationship* to that.

MIKE NICHOLS: That's a brilliant description, and it's accurate. It takes both intelligence and a certain amount of training to understand that she's *representing* a viewpoint and that she's not the person *espousing* it. That's already pretty sophisticated. She does it pretty clearly and well.

Stephen Colbert is somewhat to the right of that, because he's on night after night, and

each night has an advantage and a disadvantage. The advantage is that you can educate people as to your tone and where you stand over time. The disadvantage is that you can't *appall* them night after night; you can only delight them. And in order to delight them, you have to move back a little. You can't go to the extremes every night.

PAUL PROVENZA: Right, whereas Sarah's stand-up is more of a concentrated nugget that we consume once in a while. And I believe that she does it in a way that's not always immediately apparent. It sneaks up on you.

MIKE NICHOLS: Exactly. Whoopi Goldberg ran into that trouble now and then. The problem with what you could call "intellectual comedy" is that you are either talking to the anointed few, or you're confusing people.

PAUL PROVENZA: My instinct would be that you're *confronting* people, but *confusing* them is a much more subtle and interesting thing to do.

MIKE NICHOLS: I say "confusing" because, in general, we're no longer accustomed to somebody who goes too far. We don't see a lot of that.

Contrast that with Jon Stewart and Stephen Colbert. I watch them a lot, and it seems to me that they're possessed by a kind of joy of *getting it right*. "Making a difference" is such a hideous, used-up idea, but they have a *joy* in making the difference of saying something so clearly that everybody can hear it and see it.

Watching Jon Stewart is how I know I'm living in a free country. If you take him and Colbert away, I worry a lot more about things like Guantanamo—coming, as I did, from Nazi Germany, that subject really pushes a button for me.

And like every good satirist, I think they're beyond not only politics, but also beyond revenge. I think Jon Stewart and Stephen Colbert have gotten to a point where they really make everyone *happy*. Which changes your life.

It's funny . . . I've thought a lot about comics like Jack Benny and Steve Martin, for example, who are, or who seem to be, immune to "the comic's disease" the way some people are immune to certain viruses.

PAUL PROVENZA: The comic's disease?

MIKE NICHOLS: It's an absolutely consuming self-obsession: the inability to consider anything but whether they got the laugh. And it's the corruption of spirit that comes from the reward—the work and the reward being at the same moment.

PAUL PROVENZA: Is that where people begin to compromise their integrity?

MIKE NICHOLS: Well, they begin to *not develop* their integrity. Or, if they had integrity, they begin to dismantle it. Because for them there's only that one God: the laugh. And there's no arguing with the laugh.

To live that way for any length of time, to have only the work and the instantaneous reward, to have the laugh and only the laugh as a God, is to *not* do good things to the spirit. If not to the spirit, then to the personality. You have to spend that six months or a year just being with your *love*. Just being with your kids, just *living*—or else what is it for? The work just becomes a recording.

Without even thinking for a minute, we could both name a dozen people who are unbearable everywhere else except onstage, where they're hilarious or lovable or whatever is useful to get the laugh. But imagine you're stuck with this person for any length of time at all. That is a hell that makes the old-fashioned, narcissistic movie star look like Mother Theresa. Those comedians are incapable of considering anything but themselves, after a certain point.

PAUL PROVENZA: And Jack Benny and Steve Martin are examples of comedians who are somehow immune to that?

MIKE NICHOLS: I believe so. Both technically *and* emotionally, Jack Benny, as I'm sure you know, didn't care who had the laugh line. He would find another one *after* the laugh. He wanted to time the laugh. He didn't care who got it.

PAUL PROVENZA: People these days think of Jack Benny as old-school or sort of retro; he was actually postmodern. His comedy was about the space between the lines. It was all about when he *wasn't* speaking; that's where he found comedy that only *he* could've found.

MIKE NICHOLS: Precisely! The biggest laugh anybody ever got on radio, one he built toward for twenty years of defining his character as a miser, was where a guy held him up and said, "Your money or your life." It's the most famous pause in comedy history, and the biggest laugh ever on radio. From not a line, but a *pause*.

Then, of course, the most brilliant line *after*

the pause: "I'm thinking it over!"

He was also the *exemplar* of comedy that is sweetness. If there was a joke on somebody, it was always on himself. Never in his working life did he go after anybody else. That's not so easy to do. I knew him a bit and he was, in fact, a saintly man. He and George Burns are my memories of a kind of happiness that can only be achieved through *love*. Love of their wives, love of each other, love of their work, their world, their golf club, lunches together. . .

It was real. And nobody paid for their laughs. Ever.

Steve Martin is certainly like that. Steve's figuring something out. He's trying something; building something; making something. He's much more like a mathematician.

PAUL PROVENZA: There's something very intellectual about his approach, yet as a stand-up he was completely childlike. Silly, goofy—all those things that belied the intelligence behind it.

MIKE NICHOLS: I once sat at a table of Nobel Prize–winning scientists—it doesn't matter how I got there—and the thing that struck me, forcefully and constantly, was that they were like little kids. They were extremely innocent. They were *geniuses*.

They didn't develop all these defenses and vices, because numbers were what concerned them and fascinated them. And they couldn't develop numbers to do *for people*. Steve has a touch of that, as if he's moving forward with the sense that he's from another planet and has just learned our ways perfectly. I think it has to do with something not unlike those mathematicians. He's someplace in his head that's not exactly earth, but he's adapted beautifully. And never, in almost a lifetime of knowing him, a moment of unkindness.

CRAIG FERGUSON

FIRST DRUMMING FOR Scottish punk band The Bastards from Hell, and later performing monologues as the provocatively named Bing Hitler, Craig Ferguson is a performer not afraid to zig when others are zagging. Out of the crucible of the Edinburgh Fringe Festival, Ferguson emerged white-hot in the vanguard of "alternative" comedy in the U.K. He survived his decade-long bad-boy bacchanalia to emerge sober but still sharp as Mr. Wick on *The Drew Carey Show*, and now, as a global comic conscience, is able to simultaneously embrace and embarrass America five nights a week as the host of the *Late Late Show*.

CRAIG FERGUSON: That weekend when Britney Spears shaved her head and got a tattoo? I've *had* weekends like that. I *know* that thing. I know how it feels—and it don't fucking feel good. And when *I* went through my own shit like that, *I* didn't have all those fucking cameras around me everywhere all the time. Well, I *thought* I did but it turned out I was just hallucinating.

I did that monologue about how I was not going to do any more Britney Spears jokes, because she was having one of her meltdowns at the time, and I just felt so strongly that this poor, very young girl is clearly a fucking mental patient, and you just don't *laugh* at mental patients. You try to *help* them. You laugh at fucking Donald Trump and all that kind of shit. So I just didn't wanna join in with the gang on that one.

What got my goat that day was the glee with which everybody expected me to slice and dice the poor woman. I got to work that day, and everybody was all geared up to do it. And I just felt, "Fuck you. Watch *this*." Because the minute you expect me to do something and I do it for you, I'm your fucking puppy. I'm your hooker. So whenever you expect me to do that, I'm not gonna do it; I'm gonna do something else. *That's* born from punk rock. That's born from "No, fuck *you!*"

PAUL PROVENZA: That decision and your openness about it on the show demonstrated a certain humanity, which in the arena of late-night television talk shows is perhaps professionally . . . questionable?

CRAIG FERGUSON: I don't care! I'm not a late-night talk show host, I'm a guy who's hosting a late-night talk show. That's what I do, not who I *am*. Not for a fucking second. There are guys who do this and it's what they've always wanted to do, but *I* don't care. I do this 'cause I have fun doing it, and when I'm done I'll do something else. I don't do this because it was my life's goal.

And I was very careful that night when I said all that to make sure I wasn't projecting a manifesto for comedians. I'm not at all. This is for me, not for anybody else.

Jay Leno, Conan, David Letterman . . . I admire their work, and they do it their way, but that's not how *I* do it. And I don't fucking *have* to do it that way.

You have to attack *something*, I know, but my feeling is you have to attack *power*. Power is what I attack. I don't attack weakness, because it doesn't feel satisfying to me.

It's always an ongoing process for me; I don't even have a manifesto for myself about all that. I just know that *iconoclasm* is what this thing—comedy—is meant to be. For me, at least. That's why I chose to become an American citizen, for Christ's sake! The whole idea of this country is that those in power must be told the fucking truth. They *must* be. And that's a really good idea for a country.

PAUL PROVENZA: It's counterintuitive, but at that point it was more iconoclastic for you *not* to go down that path, because going after Britney Spears had already become not only easy as comedy, but institutionalized and mainstream.

Having said that, your motivation came

from a very personal place. It was quite the opposite of satire; it was sincerity.

CRAIG FERGUSON: It came from my own personal experiences with alcoholism, which is not her issue, but I certainly had gotten to a similar point in my own life to where she was at.

I would go after Mel Gibson for his drunken, anti-Semitic rant, but then at a certain point, I'd think, "Oh God . . . Can I? Really? The guy is alcoholic and troubled . . . Can I feel okay about going after him like that?" But then I'd think, "Yeah, of course you can," because the things he said were *so* horrible! Case-by-case, you know? Now, you might ask yourself about some joke: "Is this against my own personal philosophy? Is this violating my own principles?" But then you may end up thinking, "Yeah . . . But it's so funny, I'm gonna fucking do it anyway." That happens every now and again: "This is against what I stand for, but it's so funny that I'm just gonna have to let the audience know that I know it's wrong, and I'm going to say it anyway. Just because it's too funny *not* to do."

Sometimes I listen to guys like Dave Attell, who just pushes the edges so far, and I'm like, "Dave! Too much, Dave!" Then I think, "No, no. It's too funny to *not* do. You're right, Dave. You *have* to do it."

PAUL PROVENZA: The Ferguson stories over in the U.K. comedy scene are the stuff of legend.

CRAIG FERGUSON: Well, I was drinking then.

PAUL PROVENZA: And you were hard-core punk—very different from who you seem to be now. Your early comedy was very in-your-face, very . . . Glaswegian. I mean, you went by the name "Bing Hitler," and you'd say things that would get somebody glassed real quick.

CRAIG FERGUSON: Yeah, but to be fair, there were plenty of things you could say that would get you glassed in Glasgow in the 1970s. But yeah, if you start doing comedy in Glaswegian punk rock bars, you develop a certain aggressive style. I've been introduced with: "Here's a cunt that thinks he's funny." *Not* a great way to start. You have to be fairly tough just to stay alive.

But just naturally, over the years, as my balls get lower, I've become gentler in my approach. I still have a wee bit of fire left in me, but not much.

PAUL PROVENZA: That punk mentality was behind those first flashes of alternative comedy over there. Was that all just about "Fuck the power, fuck authority, fuck all rules," or was there a real social consciousness to it as well?

CRAIG FERGUSON: There were some who were very politically motivated at the time. I wasn't, myself. I think I was more about this terrible rage that I believe all comedians have. I was a drinking alcoholic, so that fueled it in many ways, but all the comedians I know have a bitterness, a fucking anger, a malcontent and madness about them. Which, you know . . . they use for cash.

PAUL PROVENZA: The alternative comedy scene in the U.K. didn't really "evolve," did it? It actually happened suddenly, almost as if someone flipped a switch in 1980.

CRAIG FERGUSON: I think what happened is

that in the sixties and seventies, it became a little better. There was a pop combo around at the time called The Beatles—I don't know if you've heard of them—and everybody got into music for a while. Then comedy became "cool" in Britain around 1980.

PAUL PROVENZA: So you're not only an American TV personality now, you're also an *American* now, and I wonder if you feel like you're in a bit of an uncomfortable situation at all. You have a forum to talk about politics on your show, but you're newly a citizen.

CRAIG FERGUSON: Yeah, it's difficult, because you can't choose to become an American and then within the first six months start telling people, "No, here's where you're going wrong." 'Cause then it's, "What the fuck are *you* doing here anyway?"

But what it does allow me to do is to truly say I am a voter who is uncommitted right up until I hear what you have to fucking say about this or that. I don't get to say, "I'm a Republican, so that's the way I think!" or, "I'm a Democrat, so that's the way I think!" As a new American, I'm new to all those kinds of affiliations, so I can admire the policies of the Democratic Party and *despise* the Democratic Party for their arrogant infighting. I can despise the policies of the Republicans and admire the fact that they know how to get elected and how to reach Americans who live outside of just New York and Los Angeles— all those good people who give a fuck about things, you know? It allows me a certain freedom in the way I see the politics here.

But the reverse side of it is the restriction of

being an immigrant, and always being aware that I'm a new immigrant. I don't feel like I can say, "Hey, everybody . . . Know that I'm here now, and that there's a few things I'd like to get sorted out." I think that's a terrible arrogance. So I watch my mouth a little bit.

I mean I kind of speak out in certain ways, you know, because everybody that runs for power is always questionable. Anybody. Obama is questionable. I know everybody around me thinks he's fucking great, but he's questionable, because he wanted to be president in the first place. And anybody who wants to be president, well . . . you've gotta question that. What is that? And you've gotta fucking needle away at that.

Power should be made fun of. *Anyone* who seeks power should be got at. They have to be fucked with in a big way. Even if they're vetted and they pass, they're gonna change, because they're going to get the power anyway. So let's fuck with them. The guys who started this whole deal, the Founding Fathers of this country, knew that. They got that whenever anyone got into power, they'd turn into fucking jackasses so we need to limit the amount of time they're there. They understood that, and that was a huge fucking leap forward in human thinking, I think.

PAUL PROVENZA: Was your choice to become an American citizen based on economic opportunities for you or was something else going on?

CRAIG FERGUSON: Nah! I mean, I had been paying taxes in America for ten, twelve years before I became an American. There's no tax break if you become an American. You pay what you pay. Would it make me more successful? I don't think I was worried about that.

My son is one of the reasons. My son was born here and he's an American, and I wanted to be like him. He's also Jewish, but there's no way I'm getting fucking circumcised; never mind, it's too fucking late. I'll deal with my maker when the time comes: "I missed it. Sorry. There was a window of opportunity and it didn't happen, so . . . Sorry, God, but you gotta overlook this one."

But, I think, emotionally I'm an American. I've always felt more comfortable here than anywhere else. It's where I belong; certainly more than England and a lot of the time more than Scotland. I think it's because I became myself, I turned into who I am here. It seems kind of weird saying that; it seems hippie-dippie, but I ended up here because it just *felt* right. It just felt *inevitable*.

It's a hell of a thing to change your own nationality, but I didn't change my ethnicity—and that's one of those things about being an American. You can be an American and still be Scottish. You can be an American and be Jewish. You can be both an American and whatever your ethnicity is as well. That's *specifically* America.

I think America is more than a country: it's an idea and a dream. It's a dream that's become nightmarish at times, I don't think anyone could deny that, and I'm not blind to the problems and the horrible issues that we have, will have, and have had in this country. But it's the best idea for a country anybody's

fucking had, *ever*.

PAUL PROVENZA: That's the other thing that's interesting to me. Because one of the responsibilities we have as Americans is to criticize what's wrong.

CRAIG FERGUSON: It's your job.

PAUL PROVENZA: And yet, that's been portrayed as being unpatriotic.

CRAIG FERGUSON: Oh, that's just lies per our own corporate culture. And I'm saying that from my own comfortable office at the CBS Corporation, but corporate culture has sold itself as two things: one, corporate culture has said, "*This* is truly American," which is fucking bullshit, and two, corporate culture has said that capitalism and corporate culture are the same thing. That's fucking rubbish as well.

You know what I believe? I believe that's fucking lawyers and middle management. That's the fucking problem. You think that the Indians, the Russians, the Chinese, and, to a lesser extent, the Europeans—all of the economic competitors to the U.S.—do you think they're having middle-management seminars on how their workers and people are fucking feeling today? Don't be fucking ridiculous. There's this strange kind of "Everybody gets a trophy; everybody gets a prize" thing that corporate culture's become. It's fucking nonsense.

I think it'll come, and it'll go. It's a new economic model that doesn't work. It has nothing to do with patriotism. You get patriotic fucking bums, you can get patriotic punk rockers, patriotic comedians. In fact, one of the best patriotic speeches I've ever heard was in *Team America*, at the end, where it's, like,

"You need dicks, pussies, and assholes." That was a wonderful speech about how America works. I liked it.

My personal belief is that the political process has been hijacked by corporate culture and I don't know if there's a way up that very steep, slippery slope. What will happen is that it will become economically nonviable, that's all. When it becomes economically nonviable, it falls apart. When the dollar fucking collapses against every other major currency in the world—what's happening right now—and it becomes economically nonviable, it will no longer exist.

I think what will happen is that as people get more disadvantaged they personally get more political. What we'll see is a rise in political interest, which will eventually disseminate corporate control. Because corporate control is about minority interests and issues that *should* be *majority* interests.

Not enough Americans are political in their own mindsets. That's all.

PAUL PROVENZA: Do you think through comedy, or whatever, someone like yourself, on TV every night reaching millions, can change anybody's minds about anything?

CRAIG FERGUSON: You know, I think you *do* change minds sometimes. I suppose in order to maintain any form of mental comfort I have to believe there is value in what I do on a daily basis, but personally, I feel it's necessary to realize that you *may* change someone's mind—and that you may also change it in a direction you were not intending them to go, too.

That's why I truly believe that if you want people to vote Republican, then you want to have Hollywood endorse the Democratic candidate. Because if Gwyneth Paltrow is telling me how to vote, I'm going the other fucking way, Buster; that's the way it's gonna fucking be. You want somebody to vote Democrat? Give them an hour and a half of Fox News, and a lot of them will end up going, "Oh fuck you, you overbearing, lying, fucking windbags." That happens—and it probably happens a *lot,* too.

What I think we're guilty of in the media is that we don't attempt—or even want, really—to change anyone's minds. What we want is people in the same business as us to like us and give us awards; that's all we *really* want.

We don't even want numbers; we don't even want ratings! You know what was the best fucking rated show ever on late-night TV? Well, I know *you* already know who it was: It's Jay Leno—by a *million* fucking miles. You know why? Because he doesn't fucking talk down to his audience, that's why. To assume an intellectual superiority over your audience is a terrible arrogance. I think I am guilty of that occasionally in my weaker moments, and others are, too.

That's the *only* fucking reason Leno stayed ahead in the ratings, and why he was always so *far* ahead. Leno's not a better comic than Dave; his show wasn't a better show than Dave's. But that's got nothing to do with it, because that's not the point.

The point is that *Jay Leno does not talk down to his audience.* Period.

STEVE MARTIN

JOHN CLEESE

ERIC IDLE

EUGENE LEVY & CATHERINE O'HARA

FRED WILLARD

DAN AYKROYD

LARAINE NEWMAN

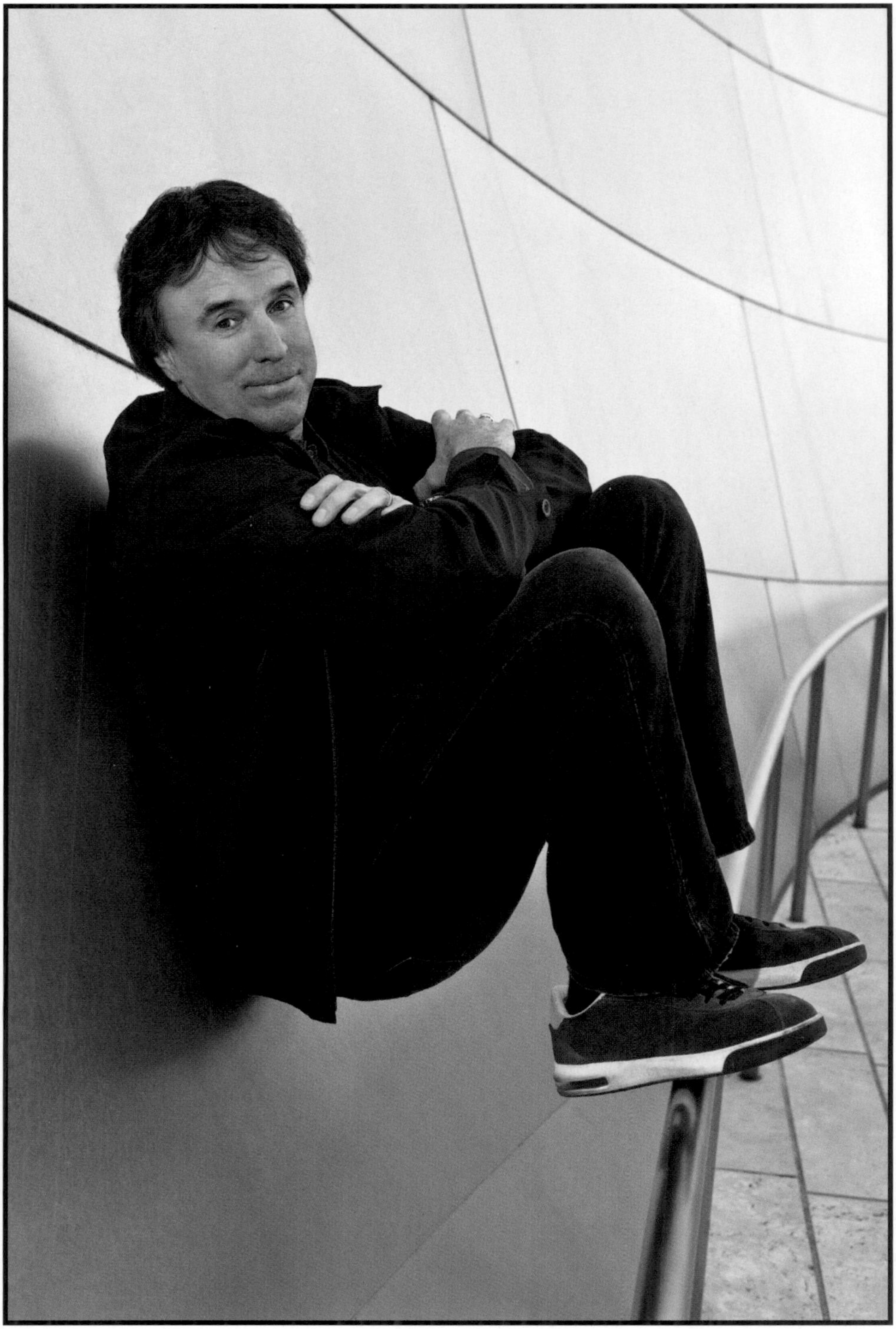

KEVIN NEALON

DANA CARVEY

CHRIS ROCK

DAVID SPADE

HORATIO SANZ

NORM MACDONALD

ROBERT SMIGEL

SPINAL TAP

JAY
LENO

WHETHER AS TWO-TIME host of *The Tonight Show* or on his TV-history-making NBC prime-time debacle, Jay Leno has always made it standard policy to gently knock both sides of the aisle in his nightly monologues while remaining seemingly neutral himself. Even in times of dire political polarization, Leno keeps to the center—despite ongoing criticism from many comedy peers and some of the public. America's un-deposed late-night king explains why that's ultimately a more difficult and admirable thing to do.

JAY LENO: The trick is not to know more than everybody else knows, it's to know *exactly* what everybody else knows. If a story's on the cover of the *New York Times, USA Today,* the *L.A. Times,* the *Boston Globe,* if they all have the same story, *that's* what you write jokes about.

My job is not to give the audience new information—sometimes you *can,* but the trick is to take the information they already have, then turn it on its head a little, or exaggerate or blow it out of proportion to make it funnier than it is in real life.

A classic example is a joke I did in front of the Reagans at the White House Press Correspondents' Dinner when he was president. I said, "I want to congratulate Nancy on winning the Humanitarian of the Year Award . . ." There was big applause for her, of course, and then I said, "I'm glad she beat out that conniving little bitch, Mother Theresa."

It got a big laugh, and I was able to say, "Okay, we know you got that award; congratulations," but then: "How ridiculous that you're 'humanitarian of the year' over someone like Mother Theresa," at the same time.

PAUL PROVENZA: Actually, I happen to think Mother Theresa *was* a conniving little bitch.

JAY LENO: That's *your* opinion, but not the one the audience has. A joke that's contrary to what most of the audience believes won't be a joke to them; they don't buy the premise. Another joke—I don't know why I'm going back to the Reagan era again, but this comes to mind as another good example of what

we're talking about—was, "President Reagan has come out against the electric chair . . ." In fact, he was *not* against the electric chair at all, but establishing that as a premise got their attention; it surprised them, they *thought* this was new information, but I said, "Since there are so many people on death row, he'd like to have electric *bleachers*."

So we're back to his true position on the death penalty, but exaggerated for comic effect. It worked because it took them one way, then brought them back to what they sort of already knew or believed. I'm going far back with these examples, but that's still sort of the basis for all the jokes I do.

Did you *ever* see any comedian doing material about what a great tactician President Bush was, or how fifty years from now his Iraq policy will be seen as genius? No, because most people don't believe that premise. *Some* people may believe that, but it doesn't work onstage because most people don't. So you'd see a million comics doing jokes about what an idiot he was, because most people saw him that way. Most people go to see performers who believe as they do, who think like they do. Rarely do they go to see people who think differently.

Comedy is basically a cowardly act. It never changes anybody's mind. It only reinforces what they already believe.

PAUL PROVENZA: When Stephen Colbert did the White House Press Correspondents' Dinner, he didn't seem to be reinforcing what that crowd believed, he seemed to go right up against it and contradict it. Was he not doing the job of a comedian?

JAY LENO: I'm a *huge* fan of Stephen Colbert, but Colbert is, I think, a classic satirist—a *great* satirist—but he's not a stand-up. He's playing a character, so it's very different from what I do. I couldn't get away with what he does, and as far as I know, he doesn't go to Vegas and do personal appearances. It's a very different thing; not better, not worse, just different.

If you want opinion and satire, go to Bill Maher or one of those guys; they do that *really* well. That's not what I do. *My* terms are very clear: if you want jokes, I'll come in and do the job. I will not give you a lecture; I will not try to change your opinions or criticize you for having them.

And I've never had any problems playing for all different kinds of audiences. I've noticed a lot of comics, particularly younger ones, only want to play to audiences they think they'll do well in front of. I meet young comics who go, "I just want to do colleges." Or, "I want to be like Chris Rock and just play those kinds of gigs." You'll hear a lot of new comics make fun of the Bob Hopes and those kinds of old-school comics, but those guys played to *every conceivable* kind of crowd. I've always tried to challenge myself to be able to work in front of anybody, any audience. I've done the White House Press Corps Dinner with Reagan, Bush Sr., Clinton, George W. . . . just to see if I could do something that would make both Democrats and Republicans laugh equally.

Not long ago, I deliberately booked myself at Oral Roberts University just to see if I could play a white, Christian, straight-arrow, Republican audience—to see if it would work. In my mind, I said, "Okay, they probably don't like sex jokes. I'll take any of those out and do all the other stuff I have and work around it." And, in fact, it *killed*.

When I was starting out, I used to play a primarily black club in Boston, called The Sugar Shack, just to see if I could work in front of *that* crowd. I toured in front of predominantly black audiences opening for a brilliant black jazz artist named Rahsaan Roland Kirk. He was really outspoken and radical, and also happened to be blind. He'd go onstage in a dashiki before I went up, and say, "I want to introduce a young brother who knows the black experience and knows all about the white devils . . ." He'd do that whole radical Black Panther, "white devil" thing, and then: "Please welcome Jay Leno!"

I'd walk on and whisper, "*Shhhh* . . . Don't tell him I'm *white*."

Of course there'd be a huge laugh, because all you have to do is *be funny*.

To me, the real test of a comic is when you can play any audience—all black, all white, all female—whatever it might be.

PAUL PROVENZA: What's your response to criticism that your monologue jokes on *The Tonight Show* never really took any stand on any issues?

JAY LENO: My response is that *The Tonight Show* was not a bully pulpit. You try to give equal voice to all sides. For example, when Bill Maher made that comment after 9/11 about the terrorists not being cowards, he got a *lot* of shit for that. I called him a week later and said, "Bill, why don't you come on my show and explain yourself?"

We got lots of grief for it, a lot of angry letters, but I thought he had an unpopular opinion that was misinterpreted; I don't believe Bill's a "traitor" or anything like that said about him, so I said, "Come on our show," because that's what we *do*. I've had everybody from wacky Ann Coulter to so many others who had strong points of view; we didn't say, "Oh, no, *you* can't come on *my* show." Unless it's a viewpoint so abhorrent, like a David Duke or someone of that nature, you try and give equal voice and let the audience decide who or what they want to believe.

I always remember a comic, who will remain nameless, coming on *The Tonight Show* once and opening with, "I'm a Democrat, so blah blah blah . . ." He proceeded to do his jokes, but he only had *half* the audience; he'd already alienated the half that wasn't Democrat. I said, "Why don't you just do your material? People will figure out that you're a Democrat; or maybe they'll think you're some outraged Republican that's pissed off—whatever. What difference does it make what party you belong to? Do your *jokes*."

I think what some comedians call "satire" is often just opinions mixed up with some comedy.

PAUL PROVENZA: Did you not care at all about any point that you were making in *The Tonight Show* monologue? Was it always just about getting the laugh regardless of what you personally agreed or disagreed with?

JAY LENO: Obviously you care about the point made, but my main responsibility is as a *comedian* and trying to get the *laugh*. If an audience gets something out of it afterward, fine, but I just write jokes and try not to hurt anybody. It's like the Hippocratic oath to me: "Do no harm." Other people have different agendas.

The Michael Vick story is an example of *perfect* monologue fodder, because no one can defend abusing and killing puppies no matter what the details are, so you can do all these Michael Vick jokes and everybody's always on the same side, *all* appreciating the jokes the same way.

PAUL PROVENZA: What about those who call themselves comedians, as you do, but who feel the political point of view or what they're committed to saying is more or equally as important as the laugh? Are they being less professional, somehow not doing the comedian's "job" because it may not appeal to everyone?

JAY LENO: You can do whatever you want, but don't blame me if it's not working.

Here's *my* thing: if you're a police officer, an emergency room doctor, a nurse, whatever, you work your ass off all day long and see the worst side of life every day and you want to come home, turn on the TV, and just see somebody that makes you laugh. If your life is one of reflection—maybe you're pretty well off or have enough money not to worry about it and can do whatever you want—maybe you prefer a little more introspection or stimulus, so *you* go there instead.

PAUL PROVENZA: If, as you said, comedy doesn't change people's minds about anything, do you think comedy that challenges people's opinions or beliefs is a worthwhile endeavor at all?

JAY LENO: Yes, of course it is; it's brilliant. But the tricky part to me is that you're always preaching to the converted.

I always liked Lenny Bruce, always thought he was a great, funny comedian, but when he was in jazz clubs doing material about sex and drugs or whatever, he was preaching to the converted.

Whereas when Mort Sahl went on *Ed Sullivan,* the "Eisenhower jacket" was a popular trend at the time, and Sahl comes out and says, "They just came out with a *Joseph McCarthy* jacket: it's got an extra flap that goes over your mouth."

That was, like, "Whoooa!" He *really* took a chance. He wasn't saying stuff like that in some jazz club, it was on *The Ed Sullivan Show.* Prime-time on Sunday night, when *all* of America was watching, this Jewish, smart-alecky comic goes out and does sharp, pointed jokes against America's biggest Commie hunter at the height of Commie-hunting paranoia. To me, that took a *lot* more guts.

I don't think Sahl quite got the credit he deserved. He was much more of a trailblazer, really. He reached people who didn't want to hear that material, people who were completely unaware that this kind of comedy even *existed*.

PAUL PROVENZA: So much has changed since Sahl was blazing a trail, and Lenny was thrown in jail for things you hear every night on HBO now. Is it even possible for comedy to cross lines anymore? Can anybody really *challenge* in comedy anymore?

JAY LENO: Yes. I think Colbert does it on a nightly basis. Jon Stewart does it, too. People challenge all the time. It's just how you go about it.

I remember Mort Sahl came to Boston when I was a kid, and I always thought he was a *terrific* comic, a *great* humorist, so I went to see him. But at that point he was so immersed in the Kennedy assassination and the Warren Commission and all that, to the point of *obsession*. He came onstage with graphs and charts, he showed the trajectory of the bullet, and on and on and on. About five hundred people were in the club when he started, and by the time he finished there was maybe me and another guy.

You *gotta* be funny first. *Then* slip in your opinion.

PAUL PROVENZA: Did you ever consider *The Tonight Show* an opportunity to speak your mind and consciously hold back?

JAY LENO: Personally, I do not care what *anybody* in show business has to say about *anything,* and I assume most people feel that way about me. My job is to go out and make people laugh; that's what I do.

We're in a *business,* you know? What happens to a lot of comedians is that they start out as comedians, then become humorists, then become satirists, and then they're out of the business. Just go out there and tell jokes— that's my job; I don't read into it any more than that. And sometimes I get picked on for that.

MOST SATIRISTS WILL tell you that the audience's laugh always, always comes before one's own political agenda. Ever the contrarian, Janeane Garofalo will tell you the exact opposite. A strident critic of Right-wing policy and ideology, she believes that a comic's voice is an instrument to be wielded for a cause, and that to believe otherwise is simple cowardice. It's a position that's made her—both as a stand-up and as a radio and television pundit—the object of boycotts, partisan vitriol, parody at the hands of *Team America: World Police,* and even death threats. In this interview, Garofalo stands her ground and takes them all head-on.

JANEANE GAROFALO: Leno choosing not to take any position is just fear of not being well-liked. It's just fear, straight up, I don't care how anyone wants to parse that.

He's a nice guy, Jay. He is really, *genuinely,* very, very *nice.* And he likes *being* nice, and he wants everybody to like him. But to say "I'm not taking a position" on anything is *irresponsible.*

That's why I don't understand when people say, "I don't want to talk about religion or politics." Why? Like, what could be more important? What *do* you want to talk about then? *American Idol*? You don't want to talk about politics, religion, or what-have-you? Then you're a coward. If you don't want to rock the boat, then you're just as guilty as the person that rocks the boat in a negative way. You don't get a free pass just because you don't talk about it.

PAUL PROVENZA: Your activism is, I think, to a certain degree, separate from your comedy. They're obviously woven from the same cloth, but it seems to me that you have a place as an activist and a pundit that is different from your place as a stand-up. I think there is a disconnect between them.

JANEANE GAROFALO: I never got into punditry because I thought I was any good at it or articulate or anything. The problem at that time was CNN, ABC, NBC, FOX, all these alleged news outlets would only book people in entertainment for the antiwar side, for some reason.

PAUL PROVENZA: Setting them up as straw men?

JANEANE GAROFALO: Yeah, so they could mock and marginalize the antiwar position. I was asked to do it by MoveOn.org and a group called Win Without War. They said, "We're so sorry, but they'll only book people in entertainment, and we're having a hard time finding people willing to go out there and do it, will *you* do this?"

And I felt like, "Well . . . I can sit here and yell at my TV on my couch, or I can try to get involved and say something of value, if I possibly can." And I *knew* I would be mocked for it.

PAUL PROVENZA: So you believe they had you on precisely because you lacked real credibility?

JANEANE GAROFALO: Yes. The networks knew the average American believes I lack credibility. That's why I was on. I understood that. And that's why I had explosive diarrhea 99 percent of the time I was doing it.

PAUL PROVENZA: Did you ever feel like you were playing into their hands?

JANEANE GAROFALO: Yeah, but I didn't know what else to do. I could see this freight train headed toward a wall. And I don't say that from a position of arrogance. Any thoughtful idiot could see the war was a bad idea, right?

But again, I would stress that I didn't do it because I thought I was *good* at it. And it doesn't enhance your career, believe me. What does anybody gain from being the Right-wing's punching bag du jour? I got so much hate mail; death threats that came right to my apartment. I had to hire a security person to go through all the mail, because some of these people had criminal records and histories of mental problems and stuff. But, you know, what are you gonna do?

PAUL PROVENZA: Do you believe that it cost you? That it hurt your career, for you to be so politically active?

JANEANE GAROFALO: It didn't cost me for stand-up. It may have cost me television-wise. As soon as one of those letter-writing campaigns started, my pilot died at ABC. But who gives a shit? It's not like I was ever Drew Barrymore. I didn't have very far to fall. When the *South Park* guys mocked me in *Team America*, they gave me far more status than I've ever had in real life. My puppet actually had a scene with George Clooney's puppet, which is, like, the highest I've ever been in show business.

PAUL PROVENZA: Do you say you co-starred with George Clooney?

JANEANE GAROFALO: Well, technically, as a puppet, before I got my puppet head blown off.

PAUL PROVENZA: How did you feel about that?

JANEANE GAROFALO: I was angry. I was *really* angry. They had my character say things like, "I just repeat what I read in the newspaper as my own opinion."

First of all, that's not at all what I did, and it infuriated me that that's how Matt and Trey wanted to portray it. I was mocked for saying "I don't believe there are weapons of mass destruction. We're being lied to." And then I had my head blown off to cheers in the audience.

PAUL PROVENZA: Well, Matt and Trey suggest it's not that you were mocked for that, but you were mocked for a certain stridency, a certain absolutism in the way you said things.

JANEANE GAROFALO: Well, how *else* would I say it? Everything I said turned out to be exactly correct. Their point of origin was that we're all dicks, you know? We're just dicks, and because we are in the entertainment industry, we have no right to speak. Even though they are doing the exact same thing. They are in the entertainment industry positing their thoughts. There were tons of people—who were not women in the entertainment industry—saying the exact same thing I was saying. It's just easy to marshal cultural hostility toward women and women who are in entertainment, whether it's Natalie Maines, Susan Sarandon, or me, or whoever. I've run into Matt and Trey a couple of times since then. I told them the least they can do is send me a puppet, and they've declined to do so.

PAUL PROVENZA: But in being satirized in *Team America*, you are in the same place as the victims of *your* satire, of your own comedy. How does that sit with you?

JANEANE GAROFALO: If I was being satirized for something I thought was worthy of satire, that's fine. Being mocked for that particular thing made me angry. When I'm mocked for other things about my personality, I think it's funny.

PAUL PROVENZA: Matt and Trey's attitude is that they want to make fun of the stuff that they believe in, too, because it's right to do that. If you're going to call people on their bullshit, sometimes we have to call ourselves on our own bullshit.

JANEANE GAROFALO: Yeah, that's their interpretation of it. I'm going to have to disagree wholeheartedly. I love *South Park;* that's not my problem. But what they are doing is not taking *any* position. In a way, they're taking the coward's way out: "We're too cool for school." In fact, the conservatives have taken *South Park* under their own wing. There is a book called *South Park Conservatives* where young campus conservatives have decided that Matt and Trey speak for them. That's what bothers me.

That's what pisses me off about these alleged news shows. "We want to have somebody who opposes the war, and somebody who thinks it's okay to destroy these videos of interrogation because we're torturing people. Let's get an opinion from both sides." Torture is wrong, and it's illegal. I don't need another person to sit on the side of the pro-torture contingent.

If a comedian is going to be fearful about stepping on any toes, or if they don't want to piss anybody off, what's the point? You can get that from any schmuck on TV. A person goes, buys a ticket, goes to a venue to see a comic, hopefully, to hear somebody with a distinct point of view. What is the point of going to see a comic that doesn't believe in what they are saying or is just trying to please everybody or not to offend anyone?

PAUL PROVENZA: That's why guys like Jim Norton actually are interesting to me, because Jim Norton says the unthinkable. He's rude, and he's vile, and he's like the turd in the punch bowl, and I think that's really important. There needs to be a place for that.

JANEANE GAROFALO: I would like to make a distinction about different types of turds in the punch bowl. Again, I don't think it's wrong for society to try and extend the courtesy of dignity to people of color, to women. There's a difference between defending First Amendment rights to speak against the military-industrial complex and defending Don Imus's "nappy-headed ho" comments. They're not the same thing. So the turd-in-the–punch-bowl thing, if you're talking about Bill Hicks as the turd in the punch bowl, amen. If you're talking about Jim Norton as the turd in the punch bowl, no thank you. I want a new punch bowl.

PAUL PROVENZA: How did being seen as an activist affect your stand-up shows?

JANEANE GAROFALO: At the height of the pro-war fever, there would be people who deliberately came to the shows to heckle. They were even in cahoots with different morning-drive deejays in different towns to do it. It became like a fad, you know what I mean? It was like, "Burn the witch." It was shocking to me.

After September 11, certain people built their identity around hate. September 11 gave a lot of people *someone to be.* Dennis Miller is a great example of it. Dennis Miller is just an asshole. He's a straight-up asshole, but what he gets to do is pretend to be a Republican. You can be an asshole but pretend it's politics. I mean, there's a reason why a lot of Right-wingers are assholes. You couldn't be on the Right without being an asshole.

PAUL PROVENZA: But the whole Right/Left, liberal/conservative thing is a bit misleading. I think it traps people like you in a lot of ways. The truth is that most people are in the middle and would like a reasonable combination. At the top of the bell curve, I think most people don't really care about gays getting married, but at the same time they might want smaller government, certain conservative economic principles.

JANEANE GAROFALO: No, when I say Left and liberal, I stick by that. Without liberals, we got nothing. Without liberals and liberal thinking, we would still own slaves and women wouldn't vote. There's a wonderful tradition in this country of liberals making great strides to bring society forward. Conservatives like the hierarchy the way it is, and they don't want to change it. And when I say Right-wing, as it pertains to Ann Coulter and Rush Limbaugh, I mean exactly that. They are Right-wing and their loyalists are extremists. They're radicals. That word fits there. The GOP is a big-tent party: all manner of assholes are welcome in the tent.

PAUL PROVENZA: Your dad is a Republican. Is your dad an asshole?

JANEANE GAROFALO: Politically, yes. As a grandpa, not really. But he believes in a mythical guy in the sky, yet he doesn't truly care about people suffering on Earth. He doesn't want to pay taxes for social programs, like midnight basketball. A lot of Republicans, they get to be the good cop, but the way they vote outs them as the bad cop. You get to pretend to be a nice patriot, but you vote for these assholes. They do your dirty work for you, but you don't get your hands dirty.

PAUL PROVENZA: It's like subcontracting it out?

JANEANE GAROFALO: Yeah, you contract out your meanness, your morality, or lack thereof.

Look, you can't divorce behavioral psychology from voting patterns and from political affiliation; you can't. If you look up "liberal" in the dictionary, it means tolerant and open and progressive. "Conservative" means an adherence to tradition, and—I would add to that—fear of change. There is a reason that Roy Cohn was Roy Cohn. There is a reason that Dick Cheney is the way he is, that George Bush is the way he is, that Ann Coulter's the way she is. It is not separate from their political affiliations. You have to be a certain type of person to be on the Right. The repression, the fear, the guilt, the shame, sex is bad and wrong, I'm a closet queen—whatever.

So whenever someone on the Right tars me as "anti-American," I know I'm not dealing with a serious person. I'm dealing with an infant.

When somebody brings up the religion thing with me, same thing. This is how I feel about *that:* about a year ago, I went to a play on a quasi-date with this guy. We were sitting there waiting for the play to start, and he goes, "You know, I've seen you on TV, and I have a theory about why the country seems like it's falling apart right now, but I don't think you're gonna like it."

And I go, "Uh-oh. What is it?"

"I think it all started in the fall. The fall from grace in the Garden of Eden."

That's what he said: "Garden of Eden." This is not an exaggeration. This is not a joke.

I literally climbed over the seat to leave. I *climbed over the seat*. I will not go on a date and sit next to a person who is forty years old and is talking about the fall from grace in the Garden with me, because then I have to question his judgment on everything. There are not always two sides to every story. Sometimes there is absolute truth, and if you're a walking, talking adult, and you're going to bring up Adam and Eve, a fictitious story, a fairy tale, to explain to me why 9/11 happened and why there's terrorism, I'm going to have to climb over the seat to leave to get away from you.

TREY PARKER AND MATT STONE

MATT STONE AND Trey Parker like to push limits. From puppet porn in *Team America: World Police,* cartoon bestiality in *South Park: Bigger, Longer and Uncut,* and just about everything else over *South Park*'s thirteen-season run on Comedy Central, they've redefined limits of what can be said on television and in film. But just below that seemingly sophomoric surface lies keen intelligence and social critique more on par with the writings of Jonathan Swift than those of a potty-mouthed eight-year-old, and a richly textured, through-the-looking-glass view of America's values. Deftly multilayered, their work often makes our perception of it an integral part of the joke itself, and its actual, bigger point. Many satirists provoke anger and outrage in their time only to be fully appreciated and embraced later on, and, like them, *South Park* will long be regarded as a masterpiece of modern satire despite any baseness in its approach. In relating their run-ins with America's appointed and self-appointed thought police, Parker and Stone illustrate the hypocrisy and ultimately ineffectiveness of those who would impose conditions on the First Amendment.

MATT STONE: It wasn't intended, but we had kind of a "triple crown" of religious anger all in just one year, from the Catholics, from Scientologists—I don't know if that really counts as a religion—and from Muslims for a "Mohammed" episode we did.

We wanted to do a Scientology episode for years, because it's just so fucking *funny*. It's just this big funny thing that we were ignoring, and we were ignoring it just because Isaac Hayes, who played Chef, was a Scientologist. Finally, we just decided—

TREY PARKER: We decided, fuck *him*.

MATT STONE: We went after everyone else; Scientology was all that was left.

TREY PARKER: So we did the Scientology episode, and Isaac Hayes *and* Tom Cruise got pissed off. They wanted to pick a fight. Tom Cruise decided he would try to get it pulled off the air.

PAUL PROVENZA: Did Isaac Hayes get all "Shaft" on you?

MATT STONE: No, through all of this, Isaac was a *really* nice guy. I think someone put him up to trying to make us pull it. When he asked us, there *was* some creepy, cultish stuff going on in the conversation.

Three months later, when the first rerun of the show was scheduled, we got a call from Comedy Central, saying, "The producers of *Mission: Impossible III* want the show pulled."

We were, like, "Tom Cruise?"

They said, "THE PRODUCERS of *Mission: Impossible III* want the show pulled. We're gonna pull it tonight, and, uh, you guys can't say anything."

We decided, you know what? We don't *have* to say anything. The truth will come out. And it did.

TREY PARKER: In, like, six hours.

MATT STONE: On the Internet. Everybody was calling us—the *New York Times,* CNN, *The O'Reilly Factor* . . . There was a temptation to really go to war. Unfortunately, we have to get a show on the air, so we just issued this brief statement—

TREY PARKER: See, the whole Scientology gig is that you have alien souls attached to your body—

MATT STONE: —And their Satan is named Xenu. We're not making this shit up.

TREY PARKER: So we put out a press release that said, "Ha ha, Scientology! Alien souls will be attached to your bodies forever and you cannot save the human race. Hail Xenu!"

MATT STONE: It turned out to be much more effective than starting a fight, 'cause then you'd get into a pissing war with Tom Cruise.

TREY PARKER: And you don't wanna be covered in Tom Cruise piss.

MATT STONE: Even if you're right, you're on *that* level of bullshit.

And, really—and I don't know why this makes us proud, but—that whole show was basically only *barely* legal. It shouldn't even be legal, but it just *barely* is.

Scientology is known for taking people to court, so we had called Comedy Central's lawyers, who said, "Well, if you follow these guidelines, you can do it." And we did, but the way we do *South Park* is the reason that show got on the air. We do an episode in a week; if that show had sat on a shelf at Comedy Central, it would never have made it to air because they would've gotten cold feet.

TREY PARKER: When we started thinking of that show, I said, "We'll have Tom Cruise on it, all super-flamboyant."

And the lawyers said, "No, you can't do that."

"Well, what if he's really closeted?"

"You can't do that, either."

"Well what if he's *literally* inside a closet?"

"You can do *that*."

It's all nuance. We had Stan saying, "Scientology is just a pyramid scheme."

And they were, like, "You can't say that."

MATT STONE: See, Trey just said that, and now he's gonna get sued.

TREY PARKER: No! I said, "Stan said it." I didn't say *I* said it! There's actual, legal reasons why that's different.

So we said, "What if Stan says, 'It's a global scam.'"

They went, "Okay, that's good."

As long as something's worded just the exact right way, it's okay.

MATT STONE: To give Comedy Central credit, they were *really* cool about it.

PAUL PROVENZA: Aren't you a little upset that nobody burnt shit down over *your* Mohammed cartoon?

TREY PARKER: Funny thing is . . . We had this episode called "The Super Best Friends" with Mohammed on it as a superhero who turns himself into a beaver for some reason. It first aired about seven years ago, but I turned on the TV and saw Muslims rioting, and, "Mus-

lims upset over Mohammed cartoon."

I went, "Oh fuck! They *just* saw it!" Honest to God, I thought, "Oh man, it took *this* long!"

I called Matt, "This is great! We have our next episode for sure! We've already shown Mohammed, so let's do a show about what *qualifies* as showing Mohammed." Like if I draw a little stick figure with a Chinese hat and say, "This is Mohammed," is *that* showing Mohammed?

We eventually decided to do the South Park boys watching *Family Guy,* and Mohammed's on *that* and it causes all this uproar. Of course, the real joke was that we put Mohammed on *Family Guy* so if any stills of it came out, *Family Guy* would get blown up, not us.

MATT STONE: We weren't being brave at *all*, really.

TREY PARKER: We showed Comedy Central a little clip of Mohammed just standing at the door—no bombs in the turban, *nothing* offensive at all—and they were, "No! No Mohammed! NO! You can't do this."

We said, "You *do* realize an episode from seven years ago with Mohammed on it is re-running on your network right now, don't you?"

They went, *"WHAT?!"*

MATT STONE: They didn't want us to do a show *about* showing him, much less show him. But to be fair, *no one* in America would've done that, and still no one has. *No one*'s had the guts to do the simplest thing.

PAUL PROVENZA: What was the Catholic controversy?

TREY PARKER: That was our first episode to ever get pulled: "Bloody Mary." Stan's father thinks he's an alcoholic, and he turns to God since that's what AA tells you—even though they're not supposed to tell you that, that's basically what AA tells you. There's a Virgin Mary statue that's crying blood, and Stan's father thinks it's a miracle and maybe the statue can help him. But it turns out the Virgin Mary is actually crying blood out her ass.

The pope comes to determine if this really is a miracle, and the Virgin shits blood all over his face, and the pope says, "This isn't a miracle, because she's not bleeding out her ass; she's bleeding out of her vagina, and chicks bleed out their vaginas all the time."

PAUL PROVENZA: I just love that the pope calls them "chicks."

TREY PARKER: Some Catholics were upset about it, and for the first time ever we got THE phone call: "We're pulling the episode." In ten years, we'd never had an episode pulled. We told Comedy Central, "You're setting a scary precedent here, because if you pull this for the Catholics, then you'd better pull that for the Jews, this for the Muslims, that for the homosexuals . . ." Where does it end, you know?

MATT STONE: We wouldn't have *any* shows left!

TREY PARKER: So they said, "We'll just pull the repeat scheduled for Christmas Eve."

And we said, "Well, okay . . . that's probably cool."

But for about two days we were thinking, "Here it is; we're being censored! Things are changing; they won't let us do what we wanna do anymore!" But then we thought, "Well, really . . . It *is* Christmas Eve, and to be fair, the Virgin Mary *does* shit blood on the pope . . ."

PAUL PROVENZA: People not all that well-versed in your work tend to assume you're Left-leaning liberals, but then you do *Team America*, blowing the brains out of Michael Moore and Janeane Garofalo, and it fucks with everybody's head. No pun intended.

MATT STONE: We've purposely stayed apolitical, because there's funny shit on *every* side. We've never had any group we've ever made fun of get more mad at us than liberals got over *Team America*. They were humorless about it, like, "Whoa! The joke is *never* on us!" It was a learning experience. We've done plenty of shows totally ripping on Right-wing stuff, and then we'll do a show that rips on Left-wing stuff and people go, "Which side are you *on*? What's *wrong* with you?"

PAUL PROVENZA: I believe, and this is an illustration of it, that most censorship in America now actually comes from the Left.

TREY PARKER: Absolutely! We've seen that personally. Everyone always says, "Wow, you guys really fight the religious Right," but the truth is, we've *never* heard from them.

MATT STONE: The Catholics were the first time in *ten* seasons at that point.

TREY PARKER: But when we ripped on liberals in *Team America*, Sean Penn wrote to us, "Fuck you guys!"

Matt called and said, "Dude, we got an open letter from Sean Penn!"

I was, like, "What??"

And he starts reading it: "'I've been to Iraq, and let me tell you something . . .'"

I said, "You're making this up!" 'Cause it sounded *exactly* like he did in *Team America:* "I've been to Iraq! Fuck you! You don't know anything . . ."

MATT STONE: It was such a trip.

PAUL PROVENZA: Blowing up Michael Moore in *Team America* has a bit of a back story to it, doesn't it?

TREY PARKER: He asked us to do an animated piece for *Bowling for Columbine,* but we said we didn't have enough time to do it or whatever.

MATT STONE: Then he asked me to be in it, because I grew up in Littleton, and I agreed to talk a little about growing up there. He didn't misrepresent me in the interview, but about five or ten minutes after me, he put in this *South Park–looking* animation someone else had done. It looks *just* like *South Park,* and most people who saw it thought *we* did it.

That's what Michael Moore does: the way he cuts things together, he creates meaning where there isn't any—and now we were personal victims of that. He pulled *South Park* into it, which pulled Trey into a movie he didn't want any part of—

TREY PARKER: So I made him into a puppet, filled him full of ham, and blew him up.

PAUL PROVENZA: What were some particular issues the MPAA had with *Team America?*

TREY PARKER: The biggest problem submitting *Team America* to the MPAA was the names Matt Stone and Trey Parker on it. They smelled blood; they were just, "Fuck those guys, we're not even gonna watch it."

For the first cut, they said we could only have three positions for the sex scene, for, like, three seconds each. Matt didn't think they were gonna cut out much, but I was, "Dude, they are so gonna fuck us on the sex scene, I *guarantee* it."

We learned from the *South Park* movie that you gotta give them shit to cut out, so I was, like, "Let's have him piss on her face, and have her shit in his mouth, and they'll cut *that* out and everything'll be fine."

The MPAA got it and said, "You can have them do it missionary, that's it."

There's no genitalia. There's no pubic hair. There's two pieces of plastic rubbing against each other, that's all there is!

MATT STONE: Truth is we *never* wanted any piss or shit in the movie. We really didn't think that was Gary and Lisa's relationship; we had long arguments about it.

PAUL PROVENZA: They're just not those kinds of puppets?

MATT STONE: It breaks the reality, believe it or not. But when we released it on DVD, we could release an unrated version, and of course the unrated version sold about 90 percent of the DVDs sold and the R-rated sold 10, so most people in America have now seen shit-and-piss puppets solely *because of the MPAA.*

TREY PARKER: If it wasn't for them, we would never have shot it.

MATT STONE: The MPAA made the *South Park* movie more anti-American, and dirtier, too. They did it. We didn't want to, they just kind of forced it on us.

TREY PARKER: They make no sense, either. In the *South Park* movie we had a scene where the boys find Cartman's mom blowing a horse on the Internet. The scene is just Kyle going, "Dude, is that a horse?" You didn't see what he was looking at; you didn't *see* anything. Well, the MPAA came back and said, "No bestiality. You can't do that."

They don't realize that with *South Park* we can animate something overnight, so we were, like, "Let's fuck with them. Let's have it be a German shit video with people shitting on her and stuff and send them *that*."

They watched that and said, "Okay, that's better."

MATT STONE: The original title was *South Park: All Hell Breaks Loose*. The MPAA said it couldn't have the word "hell" in the title. We said, "What about *Hellraiser* and *Hell's Angels* and all these other movies?"

They said, "This is animated, so you're under different guidelines."

So we made it *Bigger, Longer and Uncut*, and they went, "Okay."

They had no idea. Three weeks later, they called, "We just got it. You can't do that."

We said, "We've already printed a hundred thousand posters, we can't change it."

So that's the title.

VERNON CHATMAN AND JOHN LEE

VERNON CHATMAN WAS a consultant on *South Park* (and gave voice to the lovable Towelie), won an Emmy for *The Chris Rock Show*, and wrote for *Late Night with Conan O'Brien* before joining creative forces with John Lee to cocreate, write, and produce the now-defunct MTV series *Wonder Showzen*, the brilliantly twisted anti–*Sesame Street* for the nihilist child and bipolar Muppet in all of us. They are the team behind the ethereally funny *Xavier: Renegade Angel*, and the deadpan un-reality show *Delocated*, both for Adult Swim. Along with their partners in PFFR, their production company/band/art collective kinda sorta, they just may be the darkest, most inventive, imaginatively subversive minds working in television comedy today.

VERNON CHATMAN: On *Wonder Showzen,* we put all our darkness and cynicism through the vessel of a child. That's it. That was the entire premise of that show.

JOHN LEE: Because if *we* do it, we're assholes, but if a little kid does it, it's cute and funny.

VERNON CHATMAN: Ironic and deep.

JOHN LEE: It *says* something.

PAUL PROVENZA: Well, you know . . . It *does,* actually.

VERNON CHATMAN: But we weren't, like, "This is an important thing." Mostly, it was, "These are scrappy little shitty, cynical things we want to say and if we get a kid to say it, it's funny."

I don't think we ever think much about a point. We're not that smart. The degree to which we put any statement in is "just enough to keep things interesting."

PAUL PROVENZA: That show grabbed me right away, because I despise prepackaged, one-size-fits-all sentimentality. To be cynical about it in the context of a kid's show I think is substantive.

VERNON CHATMAN: We want to smash those smiles off people's faces.

PAUL PROVENZA: On *Sesame Street,* my favorite things were the fact that one puppet is homeless and lives in a garbage can, and *somehow,* one puppet contracted AIDS. That fucks with your head; whatever you feel *has* to be original and surprising.

JOHN LEE: Early *Sesame Street* was really somber and strange. A lot different than it is now, which is a formula. Early *Sesame Street* was kind of a downer—but in a *good* way. We just think about the puppets now, but it used to have a really weird, political slant to it.

VERNON CHATMAN: They would go to a prison and just talk to inmates.

JOHN LEE: Like a Fred Wiseman documentary.

VERNON CHATMAN: I think Oscar got raped.

PAUL PROVENZA: We're always surrounded by so much artificial sentimentality, which I find vulgar. Whenever I see those sweatshirts with cute little kittens and puppies on them, I always think of the factories where five-year-olds make them for 2 cents a month.

JOHN LEE: This book should come with a sweatshirt with puppies and kittens on it made in a sweatshop. That feels right.

VERNON CHATMAN: All the emotions that go into all that are fuel, sure, but it's also a dark black hole to go down; it's not that creative. It wasn't just cynicism with *Wonder Showzen.* A lot of it was that kids are just funny and fun. They're anarchic and goofy. Their personality and energy bring out the kid in *us.*

PAUL PROVENZA: Was your voice as a stand-up similar to your voice on TV?

VERNON CHATMAN: I definitely indulged in rape and abortion jokes and the darkest, bleakest shit. But there are limits when you have a live audience. When you're on TV, you're not in the room, so they can't punch you.

JOHN LEE: Were you punched onstage?

VERNON CHATMAN: I've been punched as a result of *Wonder Showzen.* Doing the Clarence puppet with strangers in Central Park, we got knives pulled on us; I got punched in the head in a restaurant—

PAUL PROVENZA: It seems endemic for many of us in comedy that, for some twisted reason, it's more compelling when someone gets upset about something *we* think funny than just to see them enjoying themselves.

JOHN LEE: Somehow what you're talking about is kind of sad. Being cruel and pushing somebody is much more somber than someone going, "Hey! Here's ten jokes about rednecks."

PAUL PROVENZA: Are we just hiding cruelty because it's funny enough on the surface?

JOHN LEE: We just can't think about it. People ask us, "Should you really have little kids saying stuff like that?" And we're, like, "Yeah, it's fine; they know about it." But really, ultimately, probably not.

There *is* something cruel to it, but the larger point of it being funny and somewhat interesting makes it okay in *our* world. I feel fine with it because I *do* think it's funny and it *was* interesting to show that contrast.

VERNON CHATMAN: We put our Clarence puppet on the street to provoke people, just to get people mad at a puppet. It *is* a shitty thing to do, that if *they* get angry, *you've* got a good shot. And I see people I fucked with walking down the street, too. I saw this crazy hippie we had harassed, and he recognized me and punched me two years later. He's like a gnome with a blanket and he flipped it on me. I inhaled all of those germs.

JOHN LEE: Ewww, hippie dust.

PAUL PROVENZA: In his defense, when Clarence provoked, it was from a heady place. Harassing joggers in the park with "What are you running from, your fears?" and "You can't run away from the truth." Pretty big ideas for a puppet.

VERNON CHATMAN: That's inevitable with a show that's "cute" on the surface. For the contrast, you go to the darkest place possible and put the brightest colors on it. That's sort of our personality. Thematically, we don't *really* talk about the big things. We just focus on the joke.

People who are thinking about "the grand statement" are probably working at Kinko's right now.

JOHN LEE: How's that going, by the way?

VERNON CHATMAN: Pretty good. $5.75 an hour.

PAUL PROVENZA: Have you had much resistance?

VERNON CHATMAN: Yeah, we got canceled. And it took six years to even get *Wonder Showzen* on the air.

PAUL PROVENZA: On your "Beat Kids" segment, this cute little kid was obviously being fed lines, but the adults he was screwing with never seemed to register that. It's amazing.

VERNON CHATMAN: We'd go right up to him and whisper stuff right in his ear! Everyone *always* saw it.

JOHN LEE: They'd be arguing with the kid, we'd whisper right into the kid's ear, the kid would say it and they'd literally go, "Where'd you *get* this kid? It's incredible what this kid says!"

VERNON CHATMAN: Weird psychological trick. Very strange. We'd have the kid say something offensive and then we'd go, "Trevor! How *could* you?!" clearly acknowledging the obvious charade, but people seemed to still buy it. They don't seem to notice the camera, the whispering, *anything*.

PAUL PROVENZA: Have you had any dealings with—

VERNON CHATMAN: Death threats? Have I had dealings with death threats? I've had a death threat. White supremacists, wasn't it?

JOHN LEE: Yeah. But it seemed like some kind of a prank.

VERNON CHATMAN: I hope it was real. That'd be comedy cred, right?

JOHN LEE: That's cool. Like getting raped in prison.

VERNON CHATMAN: We did this thing celebrating white culture: "This episode of *Wonder Showzen* is brought to you by . . . white people." And we guess someone saw that and said, "You're making fun of white people? That's not right."

JOHN LEE: There were online debates where people liked *certain* points of the racism. "I like *that* racism, but are they making fun of white people in *this* bit?" I guess people like that get easily duped.

VERNON CHATMAN: We'd have a joke that's ironically racist, but then you'd see people who are. . .

JOHN LEE: . . . *really* racist.

VERNON CHATMAN: *Happy* there's racism there. There's a lot of paranoia that we have the wrong people with us sometimes.

JOHN LEE: But you can't let stupid people stop you from doing stuff.

VERNON CHATMAN: People who misinterpret your jokes, that's *their* problem.

PAUL PROVENZA: It's usually all bullshit. Somebody who is part of some organization with some agenda.

JOHN LEE: We *wanted* some kind of controversy.

VERNON CHATMAN: We wanted press. We did a bit at Ground Zero—a little kid asking people, "Is it okay to laugh again at Ground Zero?" The network almost pulled it, but they said, "We'll air it if you write an apology beforehand."

JOHN LEE: A pre-apology!

VERNON CHATMAN: "We pre-gret this."

JOHN LEE: It was great; just pure total nonsense.

VERNON CHATMAN: "We take back what we haven't yet done."

JOHN LEE: "In advance, we're telling you we're sorry." That's a great way to approach any relationship, right? It's like a comedy prenup.

VERNON CHATMAN: We wanted to do something there because of the *comedic challenge*. The show was about doing the darkest stuff, so could we take the *most* horrific thing and somehow be funny with it?

JOHN LEE: We wrestled with it for a long time.

VERNON CHATMAN: The premise was the answer for us: "Can you laugh at this?" We were struggling with it. It was one of the only times that we did a bit about something we ourselves were actually, literally struggling with. We both live really close to there—

JOHN LEE: We experienced the whole thing firsthand.

PAUL PROVENZA: That's not necessarily—

VERNON CHATMAN: Funny? *Exactly.* What happened was something we truly related to and respected. This was not like making fun of cutesy Care Bears cartoons. This was *real* stuff.

JOHN LEE: I think people understood the bit right away, too. They understood the question really was, "Can humor help us deal with this crazy, abstract emotional thing?"

VERNON CHATMAN: If we took it to the point where people described how they felt when they saw the towers fall while wearing Groucho glasses, that might've been a little fucked-up.

JOHN LEE: And put fart noises over them.

PAUL PROVENZA: Sounds like you actually considered that.

VERNON CHATMAN: Just for a second. But we were trying to raise—or lower—the bar, depending on your limbo.

We had a little kid dressed up like Hitler asking people, "What's wrong with the youth of today?" And that only came up because we wrote another bit we thought would never get through, so we thought what's the craziest, stupidest thing we could come up with?

JOHN LEE: We'll put *that* in the script, and they'll say, "You can't do this *and* that," and we'd go, "Okay, we won't do *that*, we'll just do *this*."

VERNON CHATMAN: But they went, "Oh. Okay."

JOHN LEE: "Can't *wait* to see the kid in the Hitler outfit."

VERNON CHATMAN: We were, like, "Holy *shit*." We were legitimately, like, "Is this *right*?"

JOHN LEE: We went back and forth on it

for, like, . . . a minute. Ha! No, overnight.

VERNON CHATMAN: Then it was a matter of convincing a kid's parent to let us do it with him, and can we convince ourselves that there's *any* actual legitimacy to the whole thing?

JOHN LEE: It at least has a legitimate question: What *is* wrong with the youth of today?

VERNON CHATMAN: There's nothing I regret in that bit, but I think some people were hurt or offended.

JOHN LEE: The saddest thing was that some people saw the kid and said, "Is that little kid dressed up as somebody? Who's he supposed to be?" One guy asked, "Is he that Korean guy?"

VERNON CHATMAN: He's got the moustache, the hair, armbands, swastika—everything. Marching around, arm stuck up. . .

JOHN LEE: Some people had *no* idea, that was the most disturbing thing about it.

VERNON CHATMAN: The kid's going, "What's wrong with the youth of today?" and I'm thinking, "What the fuck is wrong with EV-ERYBODY??"

JOHN LEE: We were, like, "He's dressed like *Hitler*! That's, like, THE number one bad guy, isn't it?"

PAUL PROVENZA: I can't help wondering what the network *didn't* let you do.

JOHN LEE: The censors never saw us, never met us, and we did some black satire and they asked us over the phone—

VERNON CHATMAN: "Is one of you black? Maybe if it was a black person . . ." And I'm half-black, so I said, "Yeah." And then they had nothing more to say to us!

JOHN LEE: Crazy, right? That's completely nonsensical.

VERNON CHATMAN: That's the scary thing about network standards people: if somebody's white, they don't feel comfortable judging what's acceptable to blacks, whether it's okay to say "nigger" here or there, so they just don't touch it. So . . . Hey! How about you hire a black person? There's an idea!

PAUL PROVENZA: So you guys get to say a horrible word on TV, and in return a major network finally hires a black executive. That's an interesting conundrum.

VERNON CHATMAN: Right. Of course, throwing it back in their face like that doesn't usually help.

JOHN LEE: I'm a quarter-Asian. That's why we hooked up; we thought we could cover a lot of racial territory.

VERNON CHATMAN: My favorite example of that is in *South Park*. The Mr. Garrison character can say "faggot," because *he's* gay, but another character—with the same guy doing both voices—couldn't.

JOHN LEE: So they really believe the character's a real person and acknowledge him as a citizen.

PAUL PROVENZA: Should everybody have the right to say things or nobody have the right?

JOHN LEE: Are we contributing to the moral demise of the country? Yes.

VERNON CHATMAN: Only nigger faggots should get to do it.

JOHN LEE: They're the only ones who can say "chink."

VERNON CHATMAN: Nigger faggots get to say "chink."

JOHN LEE: Chinky Jews get to say "kike."

VERNON CHATMAN: We're working on a chart for this.

JOHN LEE: They were always sensitive about religious stuff, too. That was kind of the biggest thing. We had a little puppet on the cross, and they said, "You can do God, you just can't do Jesus. God is just an abstract idea, but Jesus? People will get offended."

VERNON CHATMAN: MTV actually told us, "You can make fun of God because he doesn't exist—

JOHN LEE: —But you can't make fun of Jesus, because he's God's son."

VERNON CHATMAN: Someone actually said this to us. Please print that; I want it on the record. I'll say it again so you get it right, and you promise you'll print it. Someone at the network said: "You can make fun of God because he doesn't exist, but you can't make fun of Jesus, because he's God's son."

PAUL PROVENZA: I will print that you told me *both* times that the network said, "You can make fun of God because he doesn't exist, but you can't make fun of Jesus, because he's God's son."

VERNON CHATMAN: Of course, the big thing now is Mohammed. That's the big thing.

JOHN LEE: That's the *crazy* big thing.

VERNON CHATMAN: But the reason that Muslims get upset if you show Mohammed's face is because he's got a cock for a nose.

JOHN LEE: And it's not very big.

DON NOVELLO

WITH BRILLIANTLY CONCEIVED characters like Father Guido Sarducci, Don Novello has satirized, skewered, and stood up to authority for decades. As Lazlo Toth, he authored the infamous *Lazlo Letters*, a seminal piece of what came to be postmodern satire and a direct line to Sacha Baron Cohen. As a performer and writer, Novello has been in the foreground and background of everything satirical, including *The Smothers Brothers*, *SCTV*, and *Saturday Night Live* as well as his own books and published collaborations. Looking back, he offers insight on what he feels comedy can and cannot accomplish, and how, with enough rope, authority will always hang itself.

DON NOVELLO: I first did Father Guido Sarducci in 1972 during Watergate, Nixon, and hippies. I started doing the character because I thought, "I'm this thirty-year-old guy from Ohio. Who am I to talk politics?" I thought doing it as a foreigner would give me a perspective, and to do it as a priest gives you authority, *kinda*.

Funny, first they said, "He can't smoke. Priests don't smoke."

I said, "I'm playing a Jesuit priest, they *all* smoke." It's true. I don't know if it's a Philip Morris sponsorship or what, but they all smoke. Ask anybody.

PAUL PROVENZA: When I look back at some of that Sarducci material, I think it couldn't be more relevant today. What do you think when you see how religion has become such a political force now?

DON NOVELLO: It doesn't have a lot to do with religion at all, really. It doesn't matter what religion you belong to, the Sunnis or Shiites or whatever, it's all the same: "We're right, the rest are wrong." I don't know if anything will ever change that.

PAUL PROVENZA: Do you think comedy can ever change *anything*?

DON NOVELLO: I think the Smothers Brothers helped to end the Vietnam War. They were clean-cut guys, their father was a West Pointer who was a POW and died in the war, so they weren't Mick Jagger and Keith Richards, you know? They could *get* on prime time and have an impact there.

But I don't think comedy changes minds. If it does anything, it makes people less afraid.

I don't know a lot about Judaism, but they believe questioning God brings you closer to God, whereas Catholics think if you question God you'll get hit by lightning. So I think comedy says, "People, don't be afraid!" I'm not *afraid* to question religion in my humor, and I think when you do that it helps people become a little freer, I guess.

PAUL PROVENZA: Because if *you* haven't been struck by lightning. . .

DON NOVELLO: Exactly. I never got called on it, either. When I was doing Father Guido on *Saturday Night Live,* NBC *never* got a mean letter from the Church. Not one. And we were a block away from St. Patrick's Cathedral, where the cardinal lives.

I always thought they kinda liked it. I was criticizing the bullshit of it, not Jesus or anything it's supposed to be about. It's like criticizing the war, but not being anti-American. I wouldn't make fun of Jesus; he's the last person I'd want to make fun of, after Frank Zappa, maybe.

PAUL PROVENZA: Did your early advertising career influence your comedy?

DON NOVELLO: Advertising teaches you to write really tight, because ads are only thirty seconds. I learned that that works for *all* writing. Everything I write is short, because I learned how to edit myself.

At one point, I wrote an ad for Lavoris mouthwash—and, by the way, I wrote it for Cassius Clay, as Muhammad Ali was known then, but they wouldn't put him in a commercial because of his political stance at the time, so we got the football star Bernie Casey to do it. Lavoris got three letters complaining about the spot. They were all from the South and all blatantly racist, but they took the ad off the air because of those three letters! So I saw the influence a letter could have at the time: if a network received ten letters from different parts of the country, then they were right and you were wrong. It's just ridiculous. I mean they're just letters, they're not bullets. But they were *so* afraid, a letter could have that kind of effect.

That experience is what inspired me to do *The Lazlo Letters.*

PAUL PROVENZA: *Lazlo Letters* is a great example of a kind of satire where the target of the joke actually writes the punch line for you. It was an inventive idea, and presages things like *Borat* and *Bruno.* How'd it come about?

DON NOVELLO: Starting out, I thought it'd be a magazine article, and I decided to use the name "Lazlo Toth," the name of the guy who attacked Michelangelo's *Pieta.* He went to mass every day and then to the Vatican library to read the Bible in Hungarian, and one day he just decided to put on a tuxedo and attack the *Pieta* with a hammer and chisel nineteen times. I thought that would be a great name to be receiving all these letters from Spiro Agnew and all these fascists.

What's interesting was that I pretty much just parroted back to all these Right-wingers what they were telling us; all that "stand by our flag," and "stand by our president because he's the only one we got" stuff. I think that's why they wrote back. I wrote to them as someone supporting them or who cared about them.

Like after Nixon resigned, he'd gotten a buzz cut, but then grew his hair out, kinda long for Richard Nixon, so I wrote to him, "You shouldn't let your appearance go just because you lost your job."

He wrote back, "I can assure you my new haircut isn't because I lost my job, and I will continue to stand by my flag as you urge."

Even with corporations, you could write, "I like your soup. I also like Adolf Hitler."

And they'd write back, "Thank you for your kind words about our soup."

PAUL PROVENZA: The early years of *SNL* were really bold. You got away with so much I don't think you'd ever get away with today.

DON NOVELLO: *Saturday Night Live* got away with stuff because it was so hot. I've thought about this and always thought it was weird, but they would bargain, "You can't say this *and* this. Pick one, but not both," so people would put more and more in to see what they could bargain and get away with.

We did a nativity scene with Gilda Radner as the Virgin Mary and Bill Murray gives her noogies. We got a note saying, "You can't give the Virgin Mary noogies." It was always so arbitrary and ridiculous. Like, you could say "penis," but no slang word for a penis. Of course then they'd just overdo it with putting "penis" into everything.

I wrote a bit about getting the bill for the Last Supper. I don't know why, but they said we couldn't say there was a bill for the Last Supper. This guy from standards and practices tells me this, and I say, "How 'bout it's the Last Brunch?" Which is much funnier than the bill for the Last Supper, anyway. They're eating eggs, one guy gets soft-boiled, one guy orders waffles . . . It's much funnier as a brunch than as dinner, really.

And they said, "As long as there's no bill for it."

PAUL PROVENZA: Your work pretty much always avoided taking sides, but in the best of ways. It's apolitically political, like the through line is just "Question authority," no matter who or what it is. Keep asking questions, keep making them squirm, and eventually they'll reveal their own bullshit.

DON NOVELLO: That's right. It's *all* a mind game, and you'll see that both sides are the same. Democrat or Republican, they're all the same with all that money and the PR and the private planes and scandals and deal-making . . . It's just two rocks that look different. Turn 'em over, and they've got the same things underneath 'em, man.

THOUGH BEST KNOWN for his epic role as David St. Hubbins in *This Is Spinal Tap* and as one of the core of improvisational actors in Christopher Guest's mockumentaries, McKean has crafted a richly textured career as both a serious and comedic actor on Broadway, in television, and in film. Less recognized now is the groundbreaking work he did, along with Harry Shearer, among others, long before their *Saturday Night Live* days, as part of *The Credibility Gap,* a now-legendary radio show of the late sixties that spawned albums and countless imitators and shook up comedy and talk radio on the West Coast. McKean explains how satire, commonly seen as a cold and mocking art, can, in fact, come from kindness, thoughtfulness, and even love.

PAUL PROVENZA: My greatest recollection of *The Credibility Gap* was fearlessness. Like *National Lampoon Radio Hour*, it seemed ballsy and often shocking. Correct me if I'm wrong, but it seems like you guys influenced a movement in comedy.

MICHAEL McKEAN: "Movements" become more attractive when one feels they might yield a profit. Nobody was doing political satire for the money. That really didn't happen until *Saturday Night Live* in 1975.

The Credibility Gap really started in the wake of the RFK assassination in 1968. Everybody was pretty on edge in those days. There was the Democratic Convention in Chicago, Woodstock, and by 1970, when I got there, everybody was pretty politicized, and there was *something* every day. We'd wake up one day to find out we'd just invaded Cambodia, so we'd do a sketch about that. We were all pretty political, and we did little stuff *and* big stuff. It was fairly radical for AM radio in the sixties and early seventies. In 1971, we moved to KPPC FM in Pasadena—the *other* English-language station in Pasadena then—and we got a little bolder. I think we broke the word "asshole" on FM radio. That was ours. A true legacy.

PAUL PROVENZA: Did you find an audience that was looking for that, craving that?

MICHAEL McKEAN: Not enough to get upset and write in when we were canned. The famous line we were fired from KRLA with was from the station manager, who told newspapers: "We're letting *The Credibility Gap* go because the times are too serious for humor."

If that was the case then, it's just too *apocalyptic* for humor now, I guess.

PAUL PROVENZA: Just the show's name, *The Credibility Gap*, is a dictionary definition of satire.

MICHAEL McKEAN: That's what satire deals with: that lag between what they're telling you is the truth and what you perceive the truth to be.

PAUL PROVENZA: I'm not so clear on David Lander's later work, but it seems like that sensibility's maintained itself through almost all of your work, and much of Harry Shearer's since then.

MICHAEL McKEAN: I'm fairly active politically, and certainly get the red ass about things happening in the world. My politics haven't changed all that much, but a lot's changed around us. Harry Shearer and I were talking the other day—and by "the other day" I mean five years ago; that's what happens when you get older, every year is a smaller percentage of your life—but anyway, we were talking about how we used to use the N-word all the time in sketches, if we had, say, a Klansman character.

And there was a news story that some trade commission okayed some clothing manufacturer to use the word "Jap" as the name of their clothing line. So, in response, we did a series of extremely racist TV commercials for things like "Jigaboo's Carwash," "Mr. Spic's Taco Tavern," "Dago Men's Wear."

You play that stuff for people now and they're, like, "Where did this *come* from??"

"From FM radio—in 1971." And nobody

shot us! The only time we were really threatened with action of any kind was when we did a parody of Scientology with "Alientology," which was actually invented by a Martian. The very next day, that weird Easter Seals–looking letterhead showed up on our desk and we had to apologize.

PAUL PROVENZA: In the days of *The Credibility Gap,* there was a groundswell of people doing really risky things. Today, so many things get "Dixie Chicked." The Dixie Chicks would've been way too tame to be martyrs for free speech back then. Do you think satire or confrontation like that is more dangerous now?

MICHAEL McKEAN: I think the goal post gets moved. There are certain things you can say now with impunity, but if you wanted to do a sketch, just to grab one out of thin air, about a member of the "Greatest Generation," and wanted to do, say, a World War II scene where GIs committed atrocities, you couldn't do that *anywhere,* not even on Comedy Central. The reason is because we haven't touched that yet.

Of course, there *were* no atrocities committed by U.S. soldiers during World War II. Being bad to the enemy was invented later, by William Calley at My Lai in Vietnam.

PAUL PROVENZA: Which, of course, is a myth.

MICHAEL McKEAN: And a myth we're not ready to blast yet. I can't think of anything terribly funny to say about it, but even if you had a great idea for it, you couldn't do that sketch. So, things do change in that way.

The main thing with satire is you gotta be fucking *fast*. Sixty years ago, you could've done a pretty funny satire about a bad science-fiction writer inventing a religion but instead of being laughed out of the marketplace, becoming a millionaire; a billionaire, probably. You can't do that satire now, because it's been done in *real life*. And don't get me started on a pope who used to be in the Hitler Youth. Terry Southern would've *invented* that, but nope, too late; it's been done. Every day you see something in the paper that could've been pretty funny if only it weren't real.

PAUL PROVENZA: *Spinal Tap* satirizes specific cultural elements, but it seems to resonate in a way that's political to me. It's an indictment of the music industry, of people who make rock and roll their "religion" and put faith in it while it's really just a big charade, which seems metaphoric. Am I just full of shit about that?

MICHAEL McKEAN: It's certainly a parody of the rock documentary form; that handheld, fan-driven mania to capture a band, like Martin Scorsese's following The Band, except Rob Reiner's character got the wrong band, which was the gold. In particular, it's about Marty DiBergi, Rob Reiner's filmmaker character, too; that guy who probably always wanted to be in a band and probably stood in front of his mirror with a tennis racket pretending he was John Lennon. He wishes he was *in* the band, but instead he'll *film* the band. I've always felt that was the hidden lead.

But the other thing it's about, which is also true for Chris Guest's other films, is the bubbles that people live in. It's now a cliché, seeing the lines for a new *Star Wars* movie, but the world of hard-core fandom is an amazing thing. Those people really do live in a bubble. And it's fine; I understand it, because the world outside the bubble is full of police sirens and all kinds of shit. But anyone living within a constant bath of self-assurance like that is very much like a political party. Political parties are groups of people who live inside *political* bubbles. I gravitate toward one more than the other, but you still wouldn't catch me there, because I live in the real world.

In that sense, it's political: it's about choosing a side very early in your life and not budging. That's an invitation to be slapped anyway, because you *gotta* be a little fluid.

PAUL PROVENZA: Doesn't it seem like comedians just have to constantly "poke" at things like that? It seems we're not even happy for people to like us unless they like us *after* we've been annoying.

MICHAEL McKEAN: Like the British expression, "taking the piss." You take the piss out of somebody because they're droning on and on about something and you have to puncture them. I know this woman who's this astrology maven, with her big book of concordance and all that stuff. She'd show me all this, going, "When's your birthday? What time of day were you born?"

I'm sitting there, thinking, "Jesus . . . When can we go home?"

She said, "You look like you don't believe this."

I said, "I believe astrology's nonsense."

She said, "Well, I'm not saying it isn't, but it's a *tool*. For getting to know people."

I said, "Well, it's not the *right* tool. You can wipe your ass with a hammer if you want, too, but it's the wrong tool." There are better tools for getting to know people: talking to them, telling them about yourself, and all that.

I think that's part of what it is for us: the more self-assured people are, the more fun it is to kick the ladder out from under them.

PAUL PROVENZA: Satire usually takes down a target that's an object of scorn, but in movies like *Spinal Tap* and *A Mighty Wind,* you guys deftly satirize things you *love*. Your targets are things you have affection for and embrace rather than scorn. That's a huge, fundamental distinction as satire.

MICHAEL McKEAN: It's because I don't think satire has to be thoughtless. In fact, it works better if it's not. It works better if it's thoughtful and learned on its subject. *Spinal Tap* was obviously created by four rock 'n' roll fans. I don't think anyone comes away from it thinking, "That rock 'n' roll stuff really stinks. I'm gonna stay away. It's opera or nothing from now on!"

Nobody has that reaction, because we have great affection for the subject. The same thing with *A Mighty Wind.* Satire can come from a place of kindness, though I don't think that comes naturally. Satire has a point to it: it's meant to wound or to correct. It's the work of the muckraker, to a certain extent. "Burlesque" is something different, "parody" has some specific set of rules, "pastiche" is a form of parody; there's all this stuff that defines things like that, and I think ridicule to make you feel better than what you're ridiculing is not really satire.

PAUL PROVENZA: Another sorta rule of thumb is, "Are you ridiculing the individual or the point they're making?"

MICHAEL McKEAN: Exactly. There's a Mark Twain quote for everything in life, and there's one to the effect of "laughter is the one thing no idiocy or tyranny can stand up to." Once you've become a laughingstock, you'd best just crawl off and die. How many times did Nixon crawl off and die in his career? If a joke tells the truth and the truth cannot be denied, then that's a powerful joke.

PAUL PROVENZA: There are people who say that Ford's defeat had to do with the fact that Chevy Chase made him a laughingstock.

MICHAEL McKEAN: The only person I ever heard say that publicly was—

PAUL PROVENZA: —Chevy Chase?

MICHAEL McKEAN: No, actually, Gerald Ford's press secretary Ron Nessen wrote an op-ed piece saying, "It's not funny if a decent man doesn't get reelected president because of Chevy Chase."

PAUL PROVENZA: It's an interesting case study, if you will, because a lot of people who do this kind of work doubt that it actually has any impact. They feel it's important to do only because someone's got to keep doing it, and every drop in the ocean adds up.

MICHAEL McKEAN: Yes. But not mimes so much. They can all die.

BILLY THE MIME

SINGLE-HANDEDLY REJUVENATING A justly ridiculed art form, Billy the Mime accomplishes the unthinkable for a mime—*and* for many in the audience. Best known for his scene-stealing turn in *The Aristocrats*, the self-proclaimed "mime for people who hate mimes" studied in master classes with Marcel Marceau and at Ringling Brothers Barnum & Bailey Clown College before turning his skills toward the most difficult, daring subjects any artist could possibly attempt to make funny. As disturbing as they are moving and funny, his routines cover such topics as 9/11, abortion, Christopher Reeve, JFK Jr., Kurt Cobain, AIDS, rape, Karen Carpenter, Terry Schiavo, the Columbine shootings, David Carradine, slavery, and the entire second World War. More than just for shock or mime derring-do, Billy finds deep humanity, sincere emotion, and meaningful comment in his unlikely subjects, revealing mimes' unexpected abilities to amuse, shock, and profoundly move an audience.

PAUL PROVENZA: Which is more meaning-ful for you, the comic moments you physically create in your pieces, or the meta-joke of a mime performing such subject matter?

BILLY THE MIME:

PAUL PROVENZA: Are you accepted by the mime community, or are you regarded as some aberration and treated as an outcast?

BILLY THE MIME:

PAUL PROVENZA: Audiences often don't really know if they should even be laughing at some of your routines. Is that frustrating?

BILLY THE MIME:

PAUL PROVENZA: The sign you hold up an-nouncing your next piece can get a huge laugh, but then as the piece unfolds, it may evoke deep sadness instead. Do you consciously try to keep the audience off balance like that?

BILLY THE MIME:

PAUL PROVENZA: You seem to find sympathy toward, and the humanity behind, even your ugliest of characters. As you explore their truly inhumane behavior by committing to such characters, do you worry that your point of view may be missed because you embrace rather than criticize their evil?

BILLY THE MIME:

PATTON OSWALT

ALONG WITH COUNTLESS roles in film and television and giving voice to the charming rodent of Pixar's *Ratatouille*, Patton Oswalt has also emerged as one of stand-up's funniest, most biting cultural critics. A major force in *The Comedians of Comedy*, Oswalt helped reclaim stand-up from the stifling strip malls to which it's been relegated since the comedy boom of the eighties, bringing it back to its gritty, iconoclastic roots in alternative venues and rock clubs and reinvigorating it for an audience that turned its back on the institutionalized, predictable stand-up that had become all too common. In the process, Oswalt spread his wings more expansively, spoke his hilarious mind more freely, and has come to learn that the proper tone is everything—and that the Left's oft-heard, well-practiced condescension can only get you so far.

PATTON OSWALT: I don't like the kind of satire that points to things and says, "See how stupid this is? See how much smarter *I* am by pointing out how dumb this is?"

I like it better when you embrace what you can't stand to the point where you strangle it: "Let's let this horrible thing flourish. Let's see what would happen if this grew with no boundaries and no restrictions, and see where this takes us." That's what the best satire does.

PAUL PROVENZA: Isn't that *precisely* what Colbert does?

PATTON OSWALT: Exactly. And it's never improved since episode one—because it hatched fully formed from the forehead of Zeus. They were right on the money right out of the gate. And he *knew* it was a perfect thing—particularly how it taps into this thing that was evident but nobody could see because it's too much a part of us: this undercurrent, especially in cable news, of "You're *welcome*. I *know* I'm doing something amazing." It's that tone of the Bill O'Reillys and Sean Hannitys; like that guy who never left his small town but kinda rules the sports bar he hangs out at. He's the loudest, most violent, psychotic one all the time so everyone just goes, "I don't wanna argue," but *he* thinks he's *won* the argument. He doesn't see that people go, "He's just loud and crazy. He's not even worth talking to."

PAUL PROVENZA: More and more people are seeing those pundits as just bullies.

PATTON OSWALT: But it's not your classic bullying, it's more like they're *pitying* you, looking down on you for not being able to grasp the great truth that they understand. Colbert tapped into *that* thing. A lot of those guys have this phony "I'm just a humble journalist, just a truth-teller" attitude, whereas Colbert comes at you, like, "You're *lucky* I'm a pedagogue and that I'm telling you what to think. You can thank me later."

On the Left *and* Right, there's usually the subtext: "The truth just showed up." That's such a poisonous attitude. You're shut off from the danger of actually being wrong. It's how a smug fundamentalist Christian or smug atheist acts if you say, "I have doubts."

They're, "Of course; someone of *your* intellect would. *I* can deal with bigger concepts." They preemptively dismiss any disagreement.

PAUL PROVENZA: So, is it "smug" to hold absolutely, firmly to the belief that an administration is corrupt and dishonest and have manipulated the press and people? To me, there are no shades of gray there.

PATTON OSWALT: Right, except a smug *attitude* stops any forward movement. I think that's one factor that lost Kerry the 2004 election. A lot of people had this smug attitude that said to Republicans, "You fucking idiots who voted for Bush, here's your chance to correct your big mistake, asshole."

So people got defensive and said, "I'll vote for him *again*, goddammit!"

I used to come at comedy from a very smug attitude, because I was so disgusted and disappointed with the government. I'm not the most politically astute person on the planet, so I look at myself as a bellwether: if someone as dumb as me can see how blatantly awful something is, everyone else *must've* seen it before me. But when I'd start talking about it, people would react *so* violently. I was getting booed off stage and confronted after shows.

My attitude now is that I'm trying really, really hard to find out the truth, and say it in a way that will make people laugh. I don't *want* to say, "Hey, stupid fuckers, let *me* tell *you* what the hell's going on." I don't think that gets anything done.

PAUL PROVENZA: I think one of the things Judeo-Christianity has done to us is to demand dualities on everything. We tend to have no place for any middle.

PATTON OSWALT: Unfortunately, there's also no voice for the mass of Christians out there who actually treat Christianity like a spiritual journey rather than, "I just got born again! Now I have superpowers. I'm *right* all the time!" There's nothing scarier.

We had a president that thinks God *chose* him, like in some bad *Highlander* movie. He's James Bond, Superman, all those things— but anyone who's studied religion or knows anything about true faith knows it's that you *search* for God. God never answers you, you never find him, there are no actual *answers,* and it's that *search* that makes you a better person. The truly religious live in nothing *but* the gray area.

The truly faithful embrace the mystery and wonder and have no answers. George Bush is not that. He's dogmatic, but I think he has zero faith. Bush *and* Osama think their gods were searching for *them* and singled them out—that's how sociopaths and serial killers

and dictators and people in mental asylums think. Basically, we watched two very wealthy mental patients fighting over the fate of the world.

PAUL PROVENZA: I've always said the difference between Bush or Osama and Son of Sam is really just one of scale.

PATTON OSWALT: It really *is.* Ask Son of Sam why he did what he did: "This demon searched me out because I'm special. I was sent on this 'holy' mission because I have superhuman powers other people don't have. I hear dogs talking."

He says it was some weird "test of faith." It's a rough draft of Bush's thinking: "I was a wayward drunk, and went through all that because God was testing me. I was Luke Skywalker, this superhero in disguise, and now I shall reveal myself."

That's a dangerous way for the shift manager at Wendy's to think, but for a guy that's basically running the planet? *Bad* times.

PAUL PROVENZA: I loved the bit you did about how it was completely inappropriate to compare Bush to Hitler, because Hitler was democratically elected. It's an important point about how fragile democracy really is.

PATTON OSWALT: And Hitler did it by championing family values and religious purity, too. I actually look back on the days when I'd compare Bush to Hitler as being *more* hopeful, because being in a pre-fascist state would actually be better at this point; I think we've been in a pre-*inferno* state.

Neocons want to see what happens if the world just burns to the ground. They were told that when everything burns to the ground, super-beings will come out of the sky and fix it. It's been this deadly combination of like-minded crazy believers and mediocre opportunists—like Karl Rove, who couldn't give a fuck about religion; *I* think he's a closet atheist. Those people figure, "This sociopath *may* just go all the way. I'll attach myself to him for *my* own agenda."

It's been this perfect storm of all the worst people all coming into power at the same time. And not just here, all over the planet, and on every level—politics, business, entertainment, religion—the worst people won, all got power at the same time, and, in a weird way, all support each *other*.

I don't wanna get too paranoid, but a lot of these awful TV shows like *Keeping Up with the Kardashians,* the Britney Spears stuff, all the stuff that just celebrates dumb consumerism . . . that's just another way of supporting this overall structure. Shows like *Keeping Up with the Kardashians* are victory gardens for neocons: it grows the lettuce and the cabbage that'll keep our nation going the way it is. "Help the neocons—Keep people dumb and buying shit."

One advantage I have over some political comedians is that I'm *way* susceptible to stuff like gossip magazines, TMZ, Paris Hilton—*all* the distractions, all that shit. But instead of saying, "This is bullshit!" and extricating myself from it, I go *deeper* into it and try to show what happens when you indulge it. I'm as damaged by the entertainment system and the TV monster as everyone else—maybe

more so—so a lot of my comedy says, "See what this has done to my thinking?" I *love* big, loud, clangy movies and bright, tasty junk food. Because I love it, I also find out what's wrong with it.

PAUL PROVENZA: "Hey kids, don't do drugs. I do them, and look what happened to me."

PATTON OSWALT: Yeah, "Stop watching everything on VH1. Look what it did to me."

And I wouldn't be outraged if I didn't think this country was awesome. It's an awesome thing in the hands of numb-nuts who are ruining it. It's like seeing P. Diddy take over the Pixies and "take them in a new direction." You'd be, "What the fuck? Goddammit, no!"

When I see those ads for the Arby's sandwich that's a Reuben sandwich in the middle of a burger, and the Pizza Hut pizza that's just two pizzas stacked on top of one another—*I* wanna destroy the country. Maybe we need a zombie attack; then we'd see, can you grow your own food? What can you do without?

It's an easy, knee-jerk thing to say, I know. I'm trying hard not to be smug and dismissive, because that's as worthless as everything I just named. It's just standing around going, "See? I'm right!" while you watch everything burn to the ground. So I change the way I say things; I want to really try and change people's minds, not just show how smart and hip and cool I am. That just gets people angrier and gets you nowhere; you seal yourself in your own little bubble of coolness, and nothing happens.

PAUL PROVENZA: As a comedian, where's your place in that equation?

PATTON OSWALT: As a *comedian*, I have *no*

place in that equation. I can point things out all I want to, change my tone all I want, but it really comes down to things I do privately. I do fund-raisers, I work with a couple of charities—I won't name them, because I'm always suspect when people say, "Here's the amazing charitable work I do"—but I do some things quietly that I hope will show progress down the road.

I'd prefer for people individually to say, "I'm gonna help some independent journalism organization uncover stories," or "I'm gonna help out at a veterans home," rather than everyone getting together in a room going, "Bernie Madoff sucks! Fuck that guy!" and then going home and making fun of Paris Hilton and nothing gets done. We're at the point where we need small, individual actions rather than a big, group hate.

I want people to go, "We can all change this; we can *all* benefit, rather than just keep fighting and nothing happens and we're *all* miserable." That goes back to tone and line of attack. The antiwar effort and the Left wing's lines of attack were archaic. They didn't embrace this media climate and how you get things through—especially satirically. If you're out there wearing body makeup and banging a drum, everyone's going to ignore you. The Bill O'Reillys and Ann Coulters know how to get complete lies through as if they're truth. But then the other side gets angry, starts waving their hands and screaming, and it's, "Ah, those liberal moon bats." We're in a war. Why lose it for yourself by coming to a rally wearing fucking bunting with firecrackers up your ass? All anyone's gonna see is the nuttiness. Just calm the fuck down!

I have no patience for people who are unsavvy about how to comport yourself in the media.

LIZZ WINSTEAD SPENT her youth beating her independent head against the walls of a conservative, Catholic childhood, a trend she's continued as a creator of *The Daily Show* and cofounder and on-air host of the Left-leaning radio network Air America. Particularly intrigued by media and its effect on how we process the world, Lizz, along with an array of other brilliant talents, currently writes and performs a weekly live show in New York, called *Wake Up World*—an ongoing, relentless, subtly audacious skewering of bland, anodyne morning television and how it seeps into our consciousness, trivializing everything that matters. Taking a break from that monumental task, Winstead explains how an inquisitive mind is born and the challenges it must face.

LIZZ WINSTEAD: My goal in creating *The Daily Show* was that it wasn't just about newsmakers; it was about who presents the news and decides what's important. The indignity of what happened to journalism is that people stopped being journalists.

I'd hear friends who worked in mainstream media say, "When I worked at CBS News there were no Native American stories, no stories about the environment . . . It's boring." Journalists would prioritize things that'd keep people tuned in rather than make things that really matter gripping enough to keep us tuned in. During the first Gulf War, when cable news had just sort of started coming into its own, the build-up to the war felt like a mini-series. I felt like I was watching something that was not real. It felt like the graphics department was CNN's highest-funded department, like, "Let's take that research money and put it into graphics and music!" You felt like you were watching some kind of docudrama that wasn't really going on.

PAUL PROVENZA: It seems real confrontational journalism is actually mostly happening through comedy now.

LIZZ WINSTEAD: There's a very valuable place in comedy for people who are flamethrowers. In the world of sound bites and stump-speeching we live in now, none of it is very inspiring, and a satirist's job can be to break through. We have a freedom that politicians and journalists don't have; we have no agenda other than to speak our minds.

It's a fair question whether Al Franken will be able to make as big an impact as a sena-

tor as he has as a satirist. His books and radio show mobilized people in a really powerful way. I've never seen a comic writer with more researchers and fact-checkers; any news network should take a page from Al. I think he was responsible for getting people on board through his work, mobilizing them to join the fight in a way that I don't know a senator can.

I myself try to present my thinking through asking questions, like, "If you're Mitt Romney and want to appeal to mainstream evangelicals, is denying Mormonism and saying your favorite book is written by a Scientologist really the best way to go?" I present facts and ask questions, because I don't have the answers. To write political satire you have to have information, and once you spend your time getting the information, you're left with nothing but questions. That's the whole point of information: so you can ask questions to try to get to the bottom of it, to the truth—to the comedy. Satirists are the ones putting it out there, because they're the ones asking questions.

PAUL PROVENZA: Did you always have an interest in satire?

LIZZ WINSTEAD: I was always interested in why powerful entities did what they did.

I never liked babysitting as a young girl. I loved Barbie, because she didn't have any kids; she had a house and a boyfriend and a car and cool clothes and was fucking *awesome*. It was the opposite of feminist thinking, where they see Barbie as this oppressed woman with a fucked-up body, but . . . whatever. So when it came to making money as a kid around twelve years old, my mom wouldn't let me have a paper route, because it was too dangerous for a little girl to be out in the Minnesota early morning; it's dark there until fucking whenever—and there's *wolves*. So I thought, "Altar boy! That's good; that's easy enough." I thought it was a job where you could make some money, but the priest said, "You can't be an altar boy, you're a girl. It's called altar *boy*."

That sounded easily fixable; just start calling them "altar kids," or whatever. I started a petition, went to the archdiocese . . . and started this whole *thing*. My mother was completely mortified, but I simply didn't understand why the boys who ate their boogers got to stand on the altar.

Then the first time I ever had sex, in high school, I got pregnant. I knew I wasn't having a baby, but the way to get an abortion was so insane. Being brought up Catholic, I didn't know where to go, but one day I saw a sign on the bus for a place that said, "abortion options." I thought, "Oh. There are *many* options."

So I go to this place, and it was run by some group called The Lambs of Christ. This woman comes out wearing a lab coat, so I'm thinking she's some kind of doctor. Then I realized the women at the Clinique and Lancôme counters wear lab coats; she's not really a doctor, lab coats are pretty much available anywhere. She shows me blow-ups of mangled fetuses and a picture of a kid on a bike. I'm, like, "A *bike*?" It was insane. I left completely confused. As I walked out the door, she was yelling after me, "Just remember, the choice you make is *mommy* or *murder*."

I thought, "I'm sixteen and here's an adult, a 'person of God,' impersonating a physician, just scaring the shit out of me." Even as a kid, I was, like, "That's fucking *weird*."

From that point forward, I just thought, "There's something really fucking wrong here." I couldn't wrap my head around it. So my activism really grew out of self-interest more than anything else. Those events propelled me into looking into other stuff.

PAUL PROVENZA: What's your take-away from your experience with Air America?

LIZZ WINSTEAD: The weirdest thing was that since there *was* no progressive radio, you could never satisfy everyone. Ninety percent of talk radio is Right-wing—and not moderate; it's rabid—so people were so starved to finally have any kind of political viewpoint that wasn't from the Right that you couldn't give them enough. So the clean-coal assholes would call and go, "You're not talking enough about clean coal!"

It gets confusing trying to please everybody. People have a tendency—and I used to, too, and try not to—for their thing, their issue, to be the *driving* issue, when, in fact, there are *many* important issues. Like biofuels may be the thing that gets you going about the environment, where my thing might be dependence on foreign oil. There's no number one priority, so you get all this infighting for attention even though we have the same broader goals.

And guess what? Progressives are assholes, too! That was fun; to find out you can work for a progressive organization and have just as much corruption and weirdness and megalomania and assholery as anywhere else. I've always said I'm glad I'm not a lesbian because once you're sleeping with women you can't blame men for being the fucked-up assholes in relationships. It's kinda the same thing.

PAUL PROVENZA: I assume some of it has to do with the fact that progressives have money issues like everyone else.

LIZZ WINSTEAD: Money issues, and power struggles. At Air America, lines were blurred about shareholders who were big Democratic Party donors. There were agendas, like, "Careful what you say about the Clintons, or about this, that, and the other thing."

I was, like, "*Careful* what I say?" I thought we were a media consortium that threw the words "careful what you say" out the window. Instead, people would say to me, "Don't be so hard on John Kerry in the 2004 election, 'cause he's our guy."

I was, like, "I don't *have* any guy. I want to talk about injustice and hypocrisy and whoever walks through my path." If John Kerry's letting himself be Swift-Boated into some abyss, I'm *not* going to say he's the right guy for the job.

PAUL PROVENZA: How much of that was about advertisers' demands?

LIZZ WINSTEAD: There weren't a lot of advertisers we worried about pissing off, because we didn't have a whole lot of advertisers. I felt it was more about which powerful people on the board had connections with Washington politicos.

PAUL PROVENZA: That's exactly what happened to the Smothers Brothers, where the head of CBS happened to be Lyndon Johnson's friend, and Johnson would call and say, "Make them stop." Nothing's changed, on the Left as well as on the Right.

LIZZ WINSTEAD: On the other hand, we *did* get people motivated. People would call and say, "I live in rural Oklahoma, and the only signal I ever got on my radio was Rush Limbaugh, but now that I can listen to you on the Internet and hear your point of view, I've completely changed my mind."

You hear that and you think, "Wow, that's pretty unbelievable."

PAUL PROVENZA: That surprises me, because I always felt that people who listen to Rush Limbaugh already agree with Rush Limbaugh, and those that listen to Air America already agree with Air America, and it's all just cheerleading.

LIZZ WINSTEAD: Sometimes people listen to these giant AM or FM stations because it's the only thing they get or that comes in clearly, so it must be the truth.

That was a whole narrative during Katrina: the veil hiding the poorest of the poor was ripped down. Who knew those people existed? We're shocked that young girls get pregnant because they don't know any better, but it's because we ignore this sub-sect of people who have zero information to work with. They're really out there; a lot of people can't even *get* cable let alone afford it. School systems in oppressed, impoverished areas don't even have buildings that can accommodate wiring computers.

PAUL PROVENZA: Some argue that censorship doesn't really matter, because there are so many outlets, so while you can't say some things on broadcast TV, there's hundreds of cable channels and the Internet where people say whatever they want. Is that argument hollow?

LIZZ WINSTEAD: I think it's completely hollow. People who are trying to survive don't have time to scour the Internet to find the truth every fucking day. If giant broadcasting conglomerates are just allowed to manipulate regions, people trying to raise their kids, pay for healthcare, and work two jobs just to scrape shit together just aren't going to have the time to sit at the computer going, "I wonder if what I'm hearing on the news is the truth."

And why should people have to *dig* for the truth? That's the part I find incredibly upsetting. People say, "With the Internet people can find out whatever they want," but *lots* of people can't afford computers, and, again, that's no reason not to demand truth of the media.

People that need the most representation often don't have a lot of the stuff we assume them to have. "Pull yourself up by your bootstraps?" What about the people who don't have boots? People who have boots are not the bottom; the real starting point, the real bottom, is the people without boots. Until we get them boots, everybody else is fucked.

PAUL PROVENZA: Do you think your work as a satirist makes a difference?

LIZZ WINSTEAD: I think it does. If you can unsettle someone who may think they're gonna disagree with you, if all of a sudden they're laughing at something you say, you find a common ground in a weird way. It's a great way to say, "Look, we're laughing at something *together,* maybe there's something here we can talk about in a real way, too."

It's pretty hard to change dogmatic ideologues. I'm not necessarily ever gonna agree with people who are anti-choice or who believe this war is right. That's also why I like telling personal stories. I'm not afraid to tell my abortion story, because people can't argue with my experience; no one can say, "You didn't have that experience."

RICK SHAPIRO

WITH A TROUBLED (to say the least) past fueling improvisational, highly personal comedy, Rick Shapiro was a legend in the underground comedy scene. Louis CK introduced him to wider audiences on his HBO sitcom, *Lucky Louie,* and stand-out appearances on *Tough Crowd with Colin Quinn* gave a platform for his uniquely enigmatic worldview, but live stand-up is where Rick's work truly shines. He is perhaps the most jazz-like comedian working today. Rick's art is best appreciated over time and successive performances rather than any one show or individual jokes. His wildly caroming comedy takes you on unpredictable, hilarious journeys into his personal hell and back again to ours, with surprising poetic sensitivity and appreciable prosaic anger.

RICK SHAPIRO: Something happened when I was a hustler: this big, rich, powerful guy would put on straight porno to get me hard and then he'd blow me. One time he dropped to his knees, and behind where he'd been standing I saw a picture of his son in military school, and one of his wife posing with a nun.

PAUL PROVENZA: That moment's got pretty much *everything* represented in it.

RICK SHAPIRO: Exactly. I saw what, to me, was all just "The Big Lie." The guy'd say things like, "You're such an energetic kid, you gotta get your life together."

I'd say, "Yeah, *you're* the guy I should listen to about straightening out my life."

I started doing stuff that was more "political" when I watched the presidential primary debates and it all looked like satire to me. They didn't look like leaders at all; they don't even look human. John Edwards blinked impulsively all the time; Martin Luther King, with a *real* fight and *real* truth on his side didn't fucking blink. To me, those people are all completely satirical. Somebody made them up to mock the citizens, but the citizens don't fucking know it.

At some gig a few years ago, Ralph Nader was on the green-room TV and some girl goes, "*Ewww!* Change the channel!" Because Nader looks like a real human being looks: cheap suit, wrinkled sleeves, he sweats, doesn't fix his hair or fake smile, and tries to say important details no one else does. She goes, "Put on *Six Feet Under*."

I said, "Ah, that show sucks."

She goes, "Don't insult my friends!"

She's an actress, so she might know actors on the show, so I said, "I'm sorry. I said the *show* sucks, not the actors."

And she goes, "No, the actors aren't my friends, the *characters* are." So she's a total satire now; a completely satirical being. Somebody drew her and put her in a cartoon.

Man! The only time I feel really alive is when I'm saying things like this. That, and when I'm with my girl and she's hard for it until I put on my motorcycle pajamas and become the satire that *I* am: a guy who wants a motorcycle more than anything but spends too much money, so I have to settle for motorcycle pajamas. With little Harleys on 'em. Double nickels. Put those flannel babies on, it's like you're torqued up to 350, man.

Anyway, I didn't even know I was doing satire when I started. I'd just got off drugs and I'd go to these AA meetings and my sponsor would tap about fifty people on the shoulder and say, "Hey everybody, watch Rick do comedy. Rick, imitate their shares."

I'd imitate everybody's "share" and characters—real inside, really personal shit—and they'd be *cracking* up: "My name's Ray and I'm an alcoholic . . . *and* a closet homosexual." Or, "My name's Ellen. I'm really more of a spritzer-holic."

I think I was getting at some truth, even though to me it was just funny. The whole fuckin' *world* is already satire to me, I'm just pointing it out most of the time.

PAUL PROVENZA: Whenever I read the papers, watch financial news, or just walk through a mall, to me everything seems like self-parody.

RICK SHAPIRO: I have to say, though, I love malls, because I grew up in New Jersey. My mom's a mall.

I think you can have more fun when you're on the outside knowing that we're all self-parodies; knowing that basically we all live in *I, Robot*.

Here's a point about comedy being real: a comic I know who always does generic shit like, "Hey, I'm a Jew, so cliché, cliché, cliché . . ." was fucking with me at a gig, denigrating me in that harmless fun, comic's way. So I stood near the stage as he went on and said, "At least *my* brother ain't dead." He was completely thrown.

PAUL PROVENZA: His brother *was* dead? And you pushed that button just as he went on?

RICK SHAPIRO: Yeah, I know, I know . . . I'm an asshole.

He looked at me in shock, like a scared little kid—but turns to the audience and goes, "Christmases are weird . . ." Then this long pause . . . "Because my brother's dead."

It was *hilarious*. The crowd never expected that fuckin' opening line. And that was the first time he ever took any *risk* on stage. Fresh off his head, 'cause he *had* to deal with it just to be able to do his set. If you're gonna be a *real* comic, you *gotta* go for it, and he had no choice then.

He sent me a long e-mail, and I realized he really loved and missed his brother and it was so painful for him. I've never been close with any of my family, so it took a while for me to get it was *really* cruel of me. But he also said he started coming up with a whole show

about his brother's death because I forced him to finally confront it all on stage. He *had* to be authentic up there. Comedy's absurd, man, isn't it?

People in crowds will break through their own shit when they get raw honesty from you, too. People in the business always used to say, "Get them to like you first," but I never did that. I'd yell, lash out about things, or just blurt shit out without thinking. When I quit drugs I'd sleep all day, so I'd say things like, "I sleep all day . . . because I really *hate* brushing my teeth."

Cute, silly joke, right? But then I'd blurt out, "Because every time you brush your teeth, you get that thought everybody gets, 'Oh, *I'm* the one who's supposed to kill the president!' And then your mirror winks at you, your toothbrush starts to dance, and a cockroach on the wall's whackin' off going, 'Do what *you* want buddy! *You're* in charge!'"

People figured out quick that I'm not your typical middle-aged white guy.

I don't know if I'm making much sense at all . . . because it's kind of a wide tarmac to throw over the *Grapes of Wrath* truck.

PAUL PROVENZA: I think you mean "tarpaulin." "Tarmac" would be throwing an airport runway over it.

RICK SHAPIRO: See? I just talk, I don't really know what I'm saying most of the time. I have trouble putting my thoughts together. But why do they have to be put together so concisely all the time? Who made that rule?

PAUL PROVENZA: And so you play with form as well as content: you say what you want however it happens to come out—regardless of rules of grammar. We have to get inside *your* head to figure out what you're trying to say.

RICK SHAPIRO: I guess so . . . I never really went to college; I tried three of 'em, then just fucked up. But the first thing anyone should learn about any writing class is that your professor's wrong and every thought is yours to write. They'll say you can't go against what the "authority" says. Who *is* the goddamn authority? That's the real question: who the fuck *is* "the authority"?

PAUL PROVENZA: Isn't railing against authority and convention the substance of all your comedy?

RICK SHAPIRO: When Louis CK wrote on *Conan O'Brien*, he got me a gig there playing an "Angry Poet." That's when I first saw what fuckheads TV executives are: "We'd like you to hold up a Barney doll for the next poem."

I was right off drugs then and had nothing left to lose at that point, so I was, "Fuck you; I'm not holding up any Barney doll. My shit stands on its own, period."

And they'd go, "You're right. Sorry we mentioned it."

So Tweedle Dee and Tweedle Douchebag admitted they don't know any more than anyone else. The only thing that makes them more successful is that they can carry more fucking Gap bags over their shoulders.

PAUL PROVENZA: I know you seek more than laughs onstage. Your performance almost feels like a *yearning*.

RICK SHAPIRO: It's weird, because on one hand I'm just doing jokes, but I really think

people could be . . . freer. I see struggle in their eyes. Why should they only hear jokes that don't rattle them? Why shouldn't they laugh *hard* at stuff they've been told is wrong? They get it, they laugh, they forget after a while that it's "wrong" to laugh at. I feel they get me in spite of it all.

I didn't plan any of this, I just wanted to do comedy and make somebody laugh. Sometimes it's just that: "Don't worry, another guy will be on after me who'll make you feel comfortable, but *I* want to take you on a rollercoaster ride. That's fun, too."

I feel like we just have to work to keep our brains *alive*. That's all we have in the long run. It's *not* an easy thing to do, but at the same time it's a *really* easy thing to do: know what gets you mad. People will talk you out of it, or go, "I just don't want to think about it anymore."

Well . . . I *do*.

PAUL PROVENZA: Is stand-up therapeutic for you to help manage anger and handle your "outsider-ness"?

RICK SHAPIRO: I never felt like it was therapy. People go, "Acting class is therapy; comedy's therapy." I'd think, "If it was therapy, then why ain't I happy?"

PAUL PROVENZA: Well, it feels like if you *don't* do stand-up, you could go on a shooting spree instead.

RICK SHAPIRO: Yeah, there was a time that coulda happened. Or I'd be in the corner of a room trying to die with heroin.

PAUL PROVENZA: It feels like you confront a lot of your own demons when you perform, but they're just *barely* under control, like Sigfried and Roy's tigers.

RICK SHAPIRO: But I also do simple, silly things everyone can relate to easily, too. Like I do that guy who gets all crazy asking for his pen back: "Can I have my pen back? Gimme my pen back . . ."

"Shut up about the fuckin' pen! Your pen needs to live without you. It needs to live somewhere else now, with *real* men. Have you heard about Darfur? Who gives a fuck about your fifty-cent pen? Why are you wasting energy chasing me down three flights of stairs? Adopt a dog, throw him a ball. Feed that baby you saw on TV in some desert somewhere. Stop with the fucking *pen*."

Maybe that guy drives me nuts because I was never taught to respect anything I've ever owned. Maybe they're into *self-care,* and I just can't relate.

Is that confrontational? I don't think so. Is it? I guess it is. Is it?

PAUL PROVENZA: I see *all* your comedy essentially as: "I've figured out the hard way what's important in life, and you want me to care about *stupid* shit? Why am *I* the bad guy for not caring about *stupid* shit?"

RICK SHAPIRO: That's kinda it, isn't it? I even used to yell that on stage: "I'm the bad guy! I'm the nut! I'm the pile of shit!" I guess I spent so much time on the other side just watching.

I used to go to an acting class when I was drinking. I was really shy; I acted with my back to the class and never turned around. One guy from class would hang out and listen to me tell my crazy stories till three in the morning. He called once and said, "I really liked hanging out with you tonight."

I hung up on him. I was really fucked up. If you're gonna hustle, you're pretty much fucked up, right? But I called him back and said, "Thanks, but . . . What does that *mean*?"

He said, "It means I want to be your friend."

I didn't know how to *have* a friend. I'd never really talked to anyone before, but we had *great* talks, became good friends—and he went to AA and helped me with that. He also said, "I think you're a comedian and *you don't even know it.*"

In AA, they say, "Go where it's warm."

I'm such a moron I took it literally: "It's warm inside this comedy club; I'll go in." *That's* how I stumbled into comedy!

I'd get embarrassed because my stuff was so different and weird compared to everyone else, and I'd just run. One night this girl calls me, "I'm a comedian, too. You were like a breath of fresh air."

The next night, I'm screwing her from behind thinking, "*This* is where I want to be: telling jokes and screwing around. I could do *this*."

But I'm such a child; nobody taught me how to not be afraid or how to deal with fear. I still get scared walking into a club sometimes. But I just gotta go up with what I know, right?

PAUL PROVENZA: Where did your particular fear come from?

RICK SHAPIRO: My father was really broke and ashamed of his background, so I guess he felt powerless, and we were his toy soldiers. You couldn't have any independence; he'd freak out when I had any idea of my own.

I used to write poems and stick them under everybody's door. He'd rip them up, shake me and yell, "What's wrong with you?" in my face.

"WHAT'S WRONG WITH YOU??"

And he had this thing of never apologizing. My mother would say, "Your father's sorry for smacking you."

He'd give me a look during dinner that meant he would hit me, and I'd jump up on my desk, open my window, and run away. He'd line us up Sunday nights and hit us over the nose with a rolled-up newspaper, like a dog. He did weird shit to my brother with enemas and . . . whatever.

We didn't know we were allowed to, if we ever needed to go to the bathroom. I'd be so scared all the time, I was afraid to raise my hand in school, so I'd piss my pants. I'd have a puddle under my desk every day. That was normal for me.

I think this year, at *forty-something,* I finally learned instead of waiting until after being onstage, you can go right fucking *now.* Because I'm up for the new *Desperate Housewives* or whatever, I feel like I can finally just take a piss when I need to.

SANDRA BERNHARD

IN THE 1980s, Sandra Bernhard slipped the comedy world a roofie and had her way with it. As her stand-up took unique and innovative form, she took on a persona as daringly outrageous as it is vulnerably intimate. Amid the traditionally desexualized world of stand-up, Sandra joyously celebrated her sexuality and challenged our assumptions about our own. After three decades of torching formerly unexamined identities of gender, sexuality, and even race, Bernhard explains how she did what she did, why she did it, and how through comedy she became who she dreamed she could be.

SANDRA BERNHARD: The most interesting comics have been born with this weird way of looking at the world and have been victims of estrangement and alienation from things we *should* look up to.

When I was ten, my family moved to Arizona, and it wasn't a very comfortable place for me, so it forced me to really look inward to find a world I escaped into. I had to rely on my imagination and projections of my future. A lot of the stuff I address comes from that.

My whole high school experience was just waiting to get out of high school. With my few friends, we'd talk about how we were going to travel to Europe and be these interesting, creative people. In reality, I was skinny and awkward, but I already had a certain kind of self-confidence that came out of all that uncertainty about myself. I knew exactly what I wanted to accomplish: to break out and be the sophisticated, sexy, exciting person I *wanted* to be.

When I started performing at eighteen, *that* was where I was coming from.

PAUL PROVENZA: So when you went onstage, you went on as the person you *wanted* to be, and then actually *became* that person?

SANDRA BERNHARD: Precisely. I created my own world, my own reality, and my own happiness for myself. I didn't look for someone else to go, "You're beautiful! You're fabulous! We accept you!" I was always on the outside, so I took that and turned it around and found some sort of happiness and understanding of myself, and with others who have a similar way of being in the world.

When I'm onstage, I become the persona of the all-knowing, sophisticated, totally-comfortable-in-her-own-skin, I'll-handle-every-situation woman I always wanted to be. Once I walk offstage, I'm back to who I am right now talking with you, but I'd never walk onstage and do what I'm doing now. When I walk onstage, I take on the "Sandra Bernhard" persona.

PAUL PROVENZA: It's an interesting paradox: you've created a character that you're able to hide behind, but the character you hide behind is one who's open and vulnerable.

SANDRA BERNHARD: Exactly. I've *got* to step into that character. You've got to be in that hyper-state or you can't *do* what you're doing onstage. It's too much; you'll implode and fall apart at the seams.

PAUL PROVENZA: You've always had a very different approach to stand-up. How much of that was just who you are, and how much was a conscious effort to do something different with the form?

SANDRA BERNHARD: When I started, we had Phyllis Diller, Joan Rivers, and all these women doing self-deprecating things: husband jokes, kid jokes, ugly jokes. I was just, "This is a bummer. This has got to change." I was postfeminist; I had a strong, natural belief that a woman can be and do whatever she wanted to no matter what she looked like or where she came from. I said, "I'm not going to put myself down."

It was a battle between how *I* looked at it and what the audience was *used to* seeing: women who act like men, or like a man's idea of women. It seemed like women took on all the trappings of what male comics were doing, so I was going to come in *being* a woman, doing what I wanted to do *as* a woman.

PAUL PROVENZA: What kind of obstacles did you run into?

SANDRA BERNHARD: In L.A., I was dealing with the sexism of a woman who owned The Comedy Store and the sexism of a man who owned The Improv. They both looked at me, like, "What the hell's she doing? Singing, talking about these things, being confident? This isn't what we're used to." Of course, they'd seen all that from male comics for ages, they just weren't used to it from a *female*. I had to break through all that just to get stage time.

And then there was the content of what I was doing. Every night was one comic after another, mostly all white males doing their thing, with the occasional female doing something pretty familiar. I was getting onstage after all that every night, and I wasn't in that rhythm. It was hard for people to make the adjustment.

If you can make it through the comedy circuit and still be committed to your point of view, it must be a really *strong* point of view, because at any moment you just want to run home and write fifteen minutes of easy jokes and scatological stuff just to get through the night. At the end of the night you're, like, "I can't believe I put myself through that *again*."

At The Improv one night, Paul Mooney walked in and sat next to me and I started crying. He said, "*Never* let them see you cry, Bernhard. They want to destroy you."

There is that schadenfreude of that scene. They want to crush your spirit. Ten years later, that trial by fire makes you the kind of great performer you could never be if you hadn't gone through it, but it's brutal.

PAUL PROVENZA: In the notoriously desexualized arena of stand-up, you're one of the few who are sexualized onstage. Lots of comics talk *about* sex, but you were *being* sexual as an organic element of your character. And your sexuality has always been proudly mysterious and ambiguous.

SANDRA BERNHARD: I was revealing the fluidity of sexuality. The idea that nobody has to commit to anything in that "gay/straight/what-am-I?" way people grasp onto an identity and hold on for dear life. You might be somewhere today, you could be somewhere else tomorrow, you know?

It's about the interaction of people, what turns you on from unexpected places, about the *adventure* of sexuality. The excitement, the fun, the sophistication of sexuality. It's not about what gets done in dark rooms, or guilt and shame and remorse. If you're connected with and turned on by somebody, that's a groovy thing.

I always brought that to my performances, because I was just barreling through it all myself. I don't know that I was savvy or sophisticated enough to really understand and disseminate all these things I was thinking about, but I knew instinctively that there are roadblocks for all of us sexually, so I just barreled through them and came through the other side. Now, all these things I talked about are part of the lexicon.

PAUL PROVENZA: If you believe, as I do, that the personal *is* political, all those very personal things you dealt with make yours a very political act.

SANDRA BERNHARD: Fashion, beauty, and *concepts* of beauty had always informed my life, and all of that is inherently political, too. I'm from that postfeminist era where we were trying to question or break down what was perceived as beauty, and I was expressing all of that, too. I wasn't explicitly saying it, I was *doing* it. That's what I've always tried to do: *be* it, not just *talk* about it. I *am* the result of that era and those influences.

PAUL PROVENZA: You create the same kind of fluidity with race as you do with sexuality. You deal with the black/white divide as if it doesn't even exist, and challenge assumptions about how we perceive it all. It's pretty risky.

SANDRA BERNHARD: One of my biggest core audiences is the black audience. They know me from television; they *love* me. Wherever I go—in airports, on the street—they hug me and give it up to me.

PAUL PROVENZA: That doesn't surprise me. You're a white "sassy black woman."

SANDRA BERNHARD: Exactly! I think I also have a certain leverage from being a white, Jewish woman who hangs out with Paul Mooney. I already have that stamp of approval, so to speak. I can say the N-word onstage if I want to. If I say, "Nigger, please!," they know I'm coming from a place of having been prac-

tically anointed as a black artist myself.

Any time you put yourself on the periphery and stand on your own saying what you believe, you automatically become part of the "other." Nobody's *ever* questioned my feelings about race or sexuality or feminism. If you're coming from the right place in your heart and have that connection to your soul, nobody's ever going to take you down for it. With me, black people are never offended. They love my ass. My black, Jewish, white, mixed-up, crazy fuckin' ass. Whatever I am.

PAUL PROVENZA: Comedians and musicians are probably two of the least racist subgroups on Earth. I've never met a racist musician in my entire life, and I can't think of any comedians I've met who are racist. That comedians are taken to task so heavily for ideas that are seen as racist is truly ironic.

SANDRA BERNHARD: Well, we're being watched by people who are racist. Studios and networks are racist institutions comprised of many racist and afraid people who project their own limitations onto artists who say things. They don't have the ability to be ironic or get underneath something or understand any *art* of it.

They don't want it to get out that that's actually how *they* feel. People like Richard Pryor, Dave Chappelle, Paul Mooney, and a few others have broken through, been honest and challenging, and that *terrifies* them. Believe me, I've seen it firsthand, and I know it still exists. I was approached by a high-profile management company, and one of them said to me, "You've got to stop hanging out with

Paul Mooney. He's no good for you."

I was, like, "Excuse me? I'm *never* going to stop hanging out with Paul Mooney." He was influencing my take on the world of comedy, and it freaked them out. They thought "guilt by association," and that he would rub off on me. Or, worse yet, maybe they thought I was having an affair with a black man, and *that* was a problem for them.

PAUL PROVENZA: It seems like any comedians wanting to deal with issues of race in any intelligent, positive ways are hamstrung, because we're afraid of a knee-jerk response, or we're not sure irony will be appreciated, so it's just too risky to even "go there." And audiences are on eggshells; they get uncomfortable if they think something could be *seen* as offensive, justified or not. In truth, we could learn a lot from comedy that goes out on that limb. There are white comedians who have things as interesting and thoughtful to say about black/white relations as Dave Chappelle does, but they're certainly not going to get on TV doing it.

SANDRA BERNHARD: That is another problem. But if you don't have layers and layers of understanding about the issues between the races historically, you're just jumping on some bandwagon—and that happens a lot. If you haven't done your homework, haven't really dug down deep to reveal something new or important to bring to that very complex situation, then you have no business talking about it.

CULTURE CLASH

SINCE THE LATE eighties, Culture Clash has been widely regarded as America's preeminent Latino performance troupe and a major comedic voice of the Latino experience. Through sketches, plays, screenplays, and a short-lived Fox TV series, their unique blend of satire, vaudeville, spoken-word, and performance art digs deep into America's racial consciousness, challenging assumptions and bringing fresh perspective to all-too-often cliché-ridden Latino comedy. Earning innumerable awards, commissions, and grants as well as an ever-widening theater audience, Culture Clash continues challenging themselves and audiences with bravery and fearlessness, finding unique insight and outrageous comedy in territory where few dare to tread—and fewer survive.

RICK SALINAS: More and more, we're exploring the multi- and intercultural stuff going on in America now. Dealing with just some of that could be a lifetime's work, so we've moved away from only focusing on the Latino and Chicano experience. That's in our DNA, so it influences all our work, but looking into what's happening *between* different people now really justifies our name, "Culture Clash." We're doing things now about Latino racism against blacks, Asian kids assimilating black culture, white people confused by different cultures rubbing up against one another . . . And being three brown guys portraying different races and ethnicities, it's yet another variation of that theme.

RICHARD MONTOYA: Our new work's about cultures *merging* now, in surprising ways. Like about how Sephardics fled the Inquisition and settled in Texas and that whole area, so there's, like, sixty thousand kids there who've been Latino or Caucasian their whole lives and are now finding out they may actually be Jewish: "Umm . . . Why is there a menorah in our New Mexico farm shack?"

How delicious would it be to mix the movie *Crash* up with *Jackass,* you know? To take the lid off *Crash* and find more truthful, *fun* moments when races, classes, and cultures clash in these unexpected ways?

Like, you know these "car gangs," with their party crews and all that? They're on a cutting edge in a way, merging so many different cultures together. It's part hip-hop, part techno, car culture, gangsta . . . all at once. It's still mostly unknown, but we do this "Asian Car Gang guy" character.

We think of the Asian kid in the research library or doing extra-credit reading on Saturday nights. He's not; he's skateboarding on a wall somewhere, or out in parks trying to be dangerous, like other kids do. That's a new idea to most people in the audience, because of the preconceived notion that Asian kids are all working on computers and advancing when our own kids aren't. No, actually, lots of them are outside behaving very badly or just being typical American kids. In Orange County, a "hate crime" is just as likely to be a Latino student sending hate e-mails to an Asian student, and that's news to many people.

All kids co-opt lots of different cultures at once, so I play the Asian Car Gang guy just like the rest of them: "Wassup my nigga? Where yo' other nigga at?" It's *so* wrong and they *so* shouldn't be doing that shit, but to observe it without a filter is quite something, and to report it back to our audience is great fun—and we feel to do that is a kind of responsibility we have. We don't understand exactly why, but "Asian Car Gang guy" is not just comedy, it's "information sharing."

And we really owe a lot to Mel Brooks, by the way. With things like *Blazing Saddles,* he didn't just pave the way for stuff about ethnicity and mixing cultures, he went, "Fuck it; this shit is *on*."

PAUL PROVENZA: How'd you end up playing arts centers and having places like The

Mark Taper Forum commission you to *create* comedy/theater for them? I'm guessing not through comedy clubs.

HERBERT SIGUENZA: We intended to *not* be theater; we *wanted* to hit in comedy clubs.

RICHARD MONTOYA: Before Culture Clash, we'd each done eight to ten years of hard-core political theater in the San Francisco area, and that had gotten kind of stagnant. By eighty-four, comedy clubs proliferated all over the Bay Area and we felt maybe we could blaze some kind of trail there.

HERBERT SIGUENZA: We did *Comedy Tonight with Alex Bennett,* a local San Francisco TV stand-up show, and thought, "Great! This *is* our road. We're on our way." But we quickly discovered it was hard, being a group doing sketches in comedy clubs.

RICHARD MONTOYA: We realized that stand-ups have very specific points of view and personae and whole worldviews right from the start. Playwrights *develop* all of that, in a roundabout way, so it never quite worked for us. It was a weird, odd fit.

Performance art was also becoming big around then, so a lot of weirdo, artsy-fartsy things were going on around us too, and there was this uneasy tension for us between comedy clubs and all these other possible kinds of performance. Not wanting to go back to that old, stale political theater of El Teatro Campesino or the San Francisco Mime Troupe, we took the best of what we learned in the stand-up world into theater, and kinda made a new kind of theater for ourselves.

RICK SALINAS: Herbert did impersonations, I was rapping in Spanish and English, Richard's comedy had a more "suburban" identity . . . so we began connecting all these different performance elements and sketches with through-lines of our politics and ideas into a three-act form, kind of like a play. We just pieced it all together, and ended up with something different from what others were doing.

RICHARD MONTOYA: It was more a combination of characters, stand-up, and performance art than it was either political theater *or* stand-up, and satire and social comment fit *perfectly* into it.

HERBERT SIGUENZA: We're a product of the politics you get from just being in San Francisco, so our material had that point of view and sensibility, but we were more irreverent than the didactic kind of theater people had seen before. And we weren't talking about the plight of farm workers or Latino immigration, we talked about being bilingual, bicultural, urban Latinos; about *personal* neuroses being Latinos in the United States.

We found a huge audience, because *no* one was doing that. Paul Rodriguez was already a star, but he just played into the stereotypical way mainstream America saw Latinos, with all those jokes like, "Why do I wear pointy shoes? To crush *cucarachas* in corners."

PAUL PROVENZA: I remember him in his early days, flinging tortillas to the audience like Frisbees.

RICK SALINAS: And he'd pull out a knife, "This is my Mexican Express card."

HERBERT SIGUENZA: But we were just being *true;* being totally honest about girlfriends, about going to college, about just *being.* It wasn't any stereotype; it was our real experiences.

RICK SALINAS: We made fun of ourselves and Latinos, too, but in a very different way. Before us, everyone treated Latino icons reverentially, but along with white icons we'd slam sacred Latino images too, from Che Guevara to Frida Kahlo.

RICHARD MONTOYA: We got flak from conservative Hispanics who felt we should be constantly projecting a positive image, but we're not going to. We'll portray a Latino cop going down the wrong way, we'll do corrupt Latino politicians. We're not gonna say Latinos are all criminals or drug traffickers, but we want to do stuff about *that,* too. That's part of what makes it more universal. That's how we play a 99 percent Anglo theater audience and an all-Chicano university crowd and get the same laugh. We balance it.

We're not gonna change who we are, we're not gonna sugarcoat anything, and we're gonna *have* to talk about how there are just too, too many Mexicans hanging around the Home Depot in Orange County, 'cause that's *hilarious* to us.

Our humor is what makes *us* laugh. Like during some primary debate, CNN interviewed locals at some "Carlos and Charlies"–type bar nearby, but it just so happened it was "Wetback Wednesday! Dollar Coronas

and dollar tacos!" For *real,* man! Big banners everywhere, on live TV! The reporter even confronted the guy running the place, and he was, just, "What's the problem? I gotta move some Coronas."

That was *so* funny to me. "'What's the *problem*?' Dude . . . Seriously? You think it's okay to have 'Mick Mondays! Half-price Guinness and potato skins?' Like Italian-Americans wouldn't have any problem with 'Wop Wednesdays'? Hey, wanna move some chicken wings? Any day of the week could be 'Nigger Night.' Try *that* one."

RICK SALINAS: We did a show in Berkeley with some "politically incorrect" jokes like that, and they fucking freaked out. They were so condescending; the kind of crowd where you can't make any joke involving someone disabled without, "You can't say that about the disabled!"

You want to go, "Are *you* disabled? No? But you know what disabled people *feel,* is that right? If you *were* disabled, would you like being singled out even more than you are already in life by now being the *one* person in the entire theater who can never have any joke made about you?"

PAUL PROVENZA: People rarely get that about disabled people—or is it "differently abled" now? I'm never sure. Is there some crippled Al Sharpton I can get a ruling from?

Comedians know from *lots* of experience that unless you're actually a cruel scumbag or such a shitty comic that no one knows it's all in good fun, dis-differently-abled people are almost always *thrilled* by jokes about themselves. Most are so sick of condescension, of being treated like babies, that treating them no differently from anyone else and making fun of them, too, makes them want to get out of the wheelchair to hug you for *including* them in something for a change.

A friend of mine had some dis-differently-abled guys in a crowd and did some joke about them being vegetables or something. *They* laughed their wobbly heads off, but some people in the audience were outraged. They don't know that the next night, those guys came back with about a dozen friends in wheelchairs wearing T-shirts with pictures of different vegetables. They had a blast and told their friends, and they couldn't wait for him to see them wearing those T-shirts, hoping *they* could get made fun of, too.

Most people can't get their heads around that, but comics *know* it.

RICHARD MONTOYA: That's why Asian kids love "Asian Car Gang guy." They're, "Thanks for *including* us."

We once worked with an out gay director, and were tiptoeing around doing any gay jokes. We went after everybody else, as usual, but respectfully felt self-conscious about any gay jokes we had, even though they're not malicious; we don't do *anything* malicious. One night he said, "You're being very condescending not including gay people in the fun. Let us play, too. Do a fag joke. Just make it a good one."

That was a good lesson. We left out a whole group that should be *included* in good-spirited, equal-opportunity offense.

PAUL PROVENZA: As soon as some people *sense* "un-PC," they'll shut down before even hearing it.

HERBERT SIGUENZA: Certain *words* shock that way.

RICHARD MONTOYA: There's a lot to be said for that shock, though. In our Home Depot sketch, this guy says to an undocumented worker, "Are you an illegal alien?"

Someone says, "How *dare* you call him an illegal alien?"

And the guy goes, "Oh. Excuse me. Are you a wetback?"

We *want* that to be shocking—both to the ear *and* that the guy thinks that's *better*.

PAUL PROVENZA: I can't think of any high-profile Latino stand-up who's not reinforcing stereotypes rather than subverting them. They claim to, but if you deconstruct it, the jokes ultimately rest on accepting clichés, not challenging them.

RICK SALINAS: That easy stuff is what audiences want, in a sense. At more "bonehead" comedy clubs, Latinos will play into what they think the audience wants to hear. It's what gets the quickest, easiest laughs, and what crowds are used to.

RICHARD MONTOYA: I myself tried getting laughs off a fucking switchblade, and we had our lowrider sketches and all that shit in the beginning, too, but somewhere along the line you realize if you take that road, before you know it you're Marlon Brando in the backseat in *On the Waterfront*. We decided that since stereotypes and archetypes exist, we'll use the fuck out of them, but try to flip them over somehow.

Our *cholo* gangbanger character ends up doing a Shakespeare sonnet; something else is going on, he's different from what you'd assume. That's how we turn *using* stereotypes into *satirizing* them. Our farm worker would end up on top in some way, with some dignity, some respectability. Most other Latino comedians end up the butt of their own joke; the stereotypes remain true for them.

There's this really great collective on the Internet called the Latino Comedy Project. They do really great edgy stuff; *so* smart and *so* knowing. They did a parody of the movie trailer for *300*—

PAUL PROVENZA: It's fucking *brilliant*! I'm glad you mentioned that piece; it's a perfect example of subverting stereotypes or contextualizing them to make bigger, important points. And an excellent illustration of elevating parody to satire, nailing the look and feel, and using actual lines from the original trailer about Spartans, but about Mexican immigrants: "The mightiest army couldn't defeat them. An entire nation couldn't stop them . . ." Instead of spears and swords and maces, they're wielding brooms and rakes, swinging bags of oranges—

RICHARD MONTOYA: And the *300* becomes 300 million as it counts them coming across the border—

PAUL PROVENZA: —"Coming soon . . . and bringing cousins."

They used all those clichés, but for a reason. By showing stereotypes they're basically saying, "Whatever you believe about them, they *will* come over the border, you *can't*

stop it, you will *not* win that battle, period." It's a powerful joke, and a powerful statement: Mexicans will come here no matter what, accept it and deal *realistically* with it.

Modern immigrants juxtaposed with ancient Spartans also, to me, evokes a comment on the idea of putting up a stupid fucking wall: China did that in 200 BC! Are we seriously doing that *now*? It subtly drives that home, too.

RICHARD MONTOYA: It's all of that. Such a wise, knowing bit of comedy. That's what we try to do in *our* work. It's not the kind of thing someone like Carlos Mencia does. It just isn't.

I'm very proud of this group and how we've always been handling dynamite with some of our stuff, generally with great care and much thought. I watch Mencia and feel like there's dynamite there that's not being handled very well at all. And sure, his show's hugely successful, but . . . Come on. That kind of stuff just adds to the clamor and noise; we all know that Lou Dobbs take already.

It's hilarious that we're the second most vilified group in America now, right below Al Qaeda. They're not even *looking* for bin Laden but they'll do anything to find five Mexicans hiding in a trunk trying to support their families. And no one cared much about all those "jobs those foreigners took from Americans" when janitors and maintenance people died in the World Trade Center. They only seemed to care about middle class, white businessmen and -women who died there.

That's the kind of dynamite *we're* talking

about, so we have to inspect and handle it carefully.

RICK SALINAS: And gleefully. Political theater groups were always so *heavy*. With comedy, we talk about racism, homophobia, classism, sexism, all these really heavy subjects, and they're *digging* it.

We did "American Border Gladiators," a takeoff on the gladiator/sports thing, but also a serious comment on what happened recently in Riverside County where sheriffs beat up all these immigrants. The prize is a green card to live and work in America if you can survive that, which is "The American Border Gladiator Challenge."

People laugh and high-five through the whole piece, but later on, it's, "Whoa . . ." And the real meaning behind the comedy hits them: what price does one actually have to pay to become an American citizen?

DAVID FELDMAN

AS AN EMMY-WINNING writer behind the scenes at *The Daily Show, Real Time with Bill Maher, Dennis Miller Live* and *Roseanne,* David Feldman is responsible for some of America's most biting satire and comedic commentary of the past decade. You've just never heard of him. Perhaps because in his own stand-up career, Feldman's taken the ultimate contrarian track, making sure at every turn that the audience hates him. He explains why an audience's visceral reaction is more important than any joke itself, and why "cunt," "nigger," and "kike" are so bad they're good.

DAVID FELDMAN: My next project is a documentary called *I Hate My Cleaning Lady*. I interview white people who complain about their cleaning ladies. It's like the ultimate pornography: white people complaining about someone who crawled through a sewer and ran hundreds of miles through a desert, dreaming and hoping to make their life better by cleaning people's toilets. It'll just be all these white people bitching and whining.

I think that'd make a great documentary. I'm just afraid that half the people who see it will walk out, going, "Wow. It really *is* tough to get good help."

PAUL PROVENZA: I will *never* understand why you're not bigger in this business, Feldo.

DAVID FELDMAN: I *know* why I never made it big in stand-up: I make people feel dirty for laughing.

It's been an interesting spiral downward. When I started, the audience *hated* me before I even said a word. I think it's because I look like the guy who fired them or gave them an F. I tried to get onstage and just be silly fun, you know: "I was going to get a new car today, but they were all locked."

But people were, "Ah, fuck you. We hate you; we don't need that shit from you."

So I put on a clown suit. Actually wore a clown suit onstage and did political humor. I discovered hiding behind a character gives you all kinds of freedom. Eventually I took off the clown suit and began doing this faux Right-wing character, kind of my version of what Stephen Colbert's doing now with far greater success and way bigger paychecks.

Then I heard Dana Carvey say in an interview, "You need to 'slide into the skid.' Find what people hate about you the most and pursue that." To find your biggest fear on stage, dive right into it, and poke around there.

I thought, "The audience absolutely *hates* me, so maybe if I make myself *so* despicable, *so* hateful, they'll tolerate laughing *at* me."

I asked, "What do I find most despicable about a human being?" Self-righteousness, immorality, lying, hypocrisy . . . and I decided all my jokes would reflect all that and reveal a horrible human being.

It doesn't matter if I mean any of it or not, it's how does it affect you when I say it? If you think something's offensive, I'll play with that—and with the fact that I *know* it's offensive; I *know* I'm being an awful person.

I want to provoke; I want you to go, "Ooh," and then antagonize you with it. You know when you play with a cat he'll swipe or bite you a little, but it feels kinda good 'cause you've made a connection and he's just playing and it's fun to get him excited? But *you* know that *he* knows if he cuts too deep it hurts, and neither of you wants that, 'cause then everybody's fun is over? It's *that* very thin line I like being on with a crowd.

PAUL PROVENZA: That biting and scratching is "affectionate."

DAVID FELDMAN: Yeah. So's the way his tongue feels on my balls, but audiences *really* couldn't handle when I did that.

I get off on pushing the crowd away and luring them back in. And when they get close again, pushing them away again. Oh, wait—that's my parenting skills.

It's just fun to make people think differently from what they assume. I look like your next-door neighbor or the guy in the next cubicle at work, so as this average-looking family guy, where can I take you? Maybe I'm an average-looking family guy with a Vietnamese kid tied up under the floorboards.

Really, I would *like* people to like me—

PAUL PROVENZA: That ain't gonna happen.

DAVID FELDMAN: I know! So if I just get them laughing I feel it's a successful evening.

PAUL PROVENZA: Do you care about changing people's minds?

DAVID FELDMAN: I think you can change people's behavior, but can't really change minds. Supreme Court rulings force racists to serve black people at lunch counters, but they still hate them as they serve them. It's like when I courted my wife: I *acted* as if I were a normal, decent human being; acted and changed my behavior till eventually I kind of outwardly resemble enough of a human being that she doesn't leave me.

But you can't change anyone's mind, certainly not with political humor. I think all you can do is provoke them.

PAUL PROVENZA: Then why even bother with political or social commentary?

DAVID FELDMAN: To encourage seeing things differently.

Example: during the primaries, I did something about Rush Limbaugh hating John McCain. What was *that* about? It didn't add up to me. So I started with the presumption

that Limbaugh was, as always, just working for his corporate paymasters. All those pundits are just businesses, making money off the Republican Party and corporations. So . . . *Why* would Limbaugh's "patrons" want McCain portrayed as moderate? To lure unsuspecting Democrats over *to* McCain! They know everyone *hates* Rush Limbaugh—and his brother Ann Coulter, who's hung like, unbelievable, by the way; I saw him in the shower once. They knew undecided Democrats would think, "If Coulter and Limbaugh hate McCain, how bad can he be?"

I honestly believe that's the true angle on that story, too.

PAUL PROVENZA: I want to deconstruct that little bit of comedy. You're making a big satirical point in that bit, but along the way mention Ann Coulter's dick.

DAVID FELDMAN: I was very complimentary about her penis.

PAUL PROVENZA: I'd be thrilled if you talked about mine as generously, but mentioning Ann Coulter's dick (a) plays into the status quo idea that strong women playing hardball with big boys are not real women, and (b) feels a lot like making fun of Ronald Reagan's haircut or neck flaps. It's not political commentary, and deflects discussion from a substantive challenge to her, which is what really matters.

Nick Doody, a terrific U.K. comedian, did a great bit about this, regarding Bush: "To criticize Bush for being dumb is to ignore a whole *tsunami* of wrong."

Easy jokes get in the way of important things. Summing it up, he says, "It's a good thing Hitler didn't have a lisp." Granted, Ann Coulter's dick was just a grace note to a substantive point, so you deftly get the best of both worlds, but you see my point?

DAVID FELDMAN: Yes, and I *used* to agree, but the older I get, the more Freud is dismissed, the less we delve into anybody's past and really look at who they are personally, the more I believe attacking them personally is the right way to go.

I've dealt with Republicans; I know their game. They'll argue politics until it gets too rational, then they'll attack you personally, knowing that because you're enlightened and liberal you won't stoop to that level, but it all boils down to: "Look at YOUR life."

You want to talk family values? Then let's look at *your* family; at *your* values. Every Republican I know who's for the war either has an incredibly small penis or is impotent, racist, hateful, in a horrible marriage, or is just some money-hungry pig. So *where* is the discussion? You still think the war in Iraq is right? Let's talk about your penis then, because that's part of the problem. Because Freud is no longer so highly regarded, nobody is discussing your penis. I need to discuss your penis.

PAUL PROVENZA: It's so hard to tell when you're being serious and when you're not.

DAVID FELDMAN: I know. The Vietnamese kid says the same thing.

And I *am* being serious. When discussing politics with Republicans, I believe it's necessary and right to attack them personally. Rush Limbaugh's a thrice-divorced drug addict talking about family values; how can you *not*

attack him personally? That's all that *matters*!

Attacking people in the audience personally is right, too. Going after what they claim to believe or are lying to themselves about is *important*.

PAUL PROVENZA: It's substantive to talk about Larry Craig looking for a blow job in a men's room, because since he is an anti–gay rights guy, the hypocrisy is meaningful. But the same jokes wouldn't have the same meaning if it was Barney Frank.

DAVID FELDMAN: Barney Frank should be arrested for *not* getting a blow job in a men's room. He's letting down his core voters.

PAUL PROVENZA: We'll get back to that later in private, but by your logic, jokes about Bush as "stupid" qualifies as actual political commentary, not just easy jokes. What about Clinton blow job jokes? Was *any* of that substantive political commentary?

DAVID FELDMAN: Going after him for lying about a blow job sidetracked us. We took our eye off the ball because of it. We weren't joking about Osama bin Laden or foreign policy or anything else substantive. We focused on the obvious, which was ultimately just blow job jokes, since it was pretty much covered long before it ended. But I see your point. Maybe it's just . . . moral relativism?

PAUL PROVENZA: Like the infamous Supreme Court definition of pornography: "I can't define it, but I know it when I see it?"

DAVID FELDMAN: Yeah. And by the way, I've still never seen any pornography yet, because everything *I've* ever seen was just beautiful.

The thing about that Clinton episode is that

Newt Gingrich was getting hummers from a mistress the whole time; Livingston, who replaced him, was having an affair; Henry Hyde was, too. There was substantive material to be had there about hypocrisy, political opportunism, lots of things. But we were too busy doing blow job jokes handed to us on a platter.

I've got other bones to pick with comedians, too. Like the word "fuck." It's destroying stand-up comedy. I have one simple rule for any comic opening for me: "Don't say 'fuck.'"

They go, "What about freedom of speech?"

I say, "Say 'cunt.' Say 'nigger.' Say 'kike.' I beg you to say 'kike' or 'cunt.' Just don't say 'fuck.'"

They'll say, "Those words are worse than 'fuck.'"

And I say, "Exactly. There's no challenge in using 'fuck.' You're not being edgy, not saying anything new, not challenging any conventions or offering anything about society or the human condition. 'Fuck' is easy, so you're just using it to punch up weak material. I've done this awhile; I know the only reason you say 'fuck' is because this joke is so weak it can't get a laugh without it, this joke needs attitude because there's nothing else there, that one needs it for rhythm. You want to be edgy and confrontational? Say 'cunt' or 'kike' or 'nigger,' because if you say *those* words, you're in very dangerous territory and will have to have a damn good reason for having said them, and that's a challenge. If you're getting away with using those words then you've somehow

elevated them, and most likely it's because you're doing compelling, well-thought-out comedy with them, and *that* would be truly edgy. 'Fuck' brings nothing of value, and it's harder to do things that aren't coarse or lowbrow after you've been saying it all night."

I really believe if you rid stand-up of the word "fuck," we'd all be able to talk about more important things on stage more often.

PAUL PROVENZA: So "nigger," "kike," and "cunt," create a degree of difficulty that *raises* the comedy bar?

DAVID FELDMAN: They're *far* from easy to use in comedy, so if you're getting away with them after the first time you did and got the shit beat out of you, you'd *have* to be playing with truly substantive, meaningful material or you wouldn't be able to use them a second time. But there's *nothing* challenging about saying "fuck" in a nightclub, and it won't make any material anything more than it is without it.

I don't like comics talking about their own religion or race much, either. I think it's un-American, a distraction from the real issues in this country. Like the vast economic divide and the control that corporations have. That's all that matters to me. The only candidate worth voting for is one who says, "You're not black, not Jewish, not Hispanic, not gay, not whatever interest group. What you *are* is not rich, and one paycheck away from losing your house and health insurance, *that's* what you are." Forget this identity politics we've fallen prey to, it's just haves and have nots, that's it. When you talk about being black or being Jewish or anything else, you bore me.

I'm sure it's a profound, complicated experience being a lesbian in this country, it's just irrelevant to what's *really* wrong with America, and you'll continue to have all those same issues unless we all get together and deal with the people who control the money.

PAUL PROVENZA: But there's no significant presence of non-white power and wealth. Don't race issues matter when addressing class divisions?

DAVID FELDMAN: Here's how I judge it: is your material or the idea *easy*? If you're talking about race and it's hard to accomplish, then you've probably done something worthwhile that I'd enjoy. If it's easy comedy to do, it's not going to be anything we don't already know and I don't enjoy it. If it's difficult, takes me out of my comfort zone, challenges what I think about it, then I feel you've given me something of value. But 99 percent of it is overbearing Jewish mothers, Mexicans riding in one car, Asians can't drive, and, yes, I know, "Jewish women don't give blow jobs."

PAUL PROVENZA: But you *do* provoke people when you say that, so at least there's that.

DAVID FELDMAN: That must be why I said it even though I'm completely against saying it.

It's instinctive. I can't help being hateful. Growing up, I took perverse joy in trying to prove there was no Holocaust to my Jewish parents over dinner. I'd convince kids at Hebrew school that Israel is actually just a real estate concern and we invented this Judaism "myth" to justify it, but it's really just a big gated community, and we invented this fake spiritual path to convince people we're "entitled" to the property so we could get it at a deep discount.

It even pissed *me* off as I was saying it.

TOM RHODES

TOM RHODES WAS meant to be Comedy Central's answer to Pauly Shore—complete with long hair, a love for weed and a smart-ass grin—and his ascent was swift. But even if the spots he did for the network in the nineties relied too heavily on his rockstar good looks and bad-boy image, his comedy never suffered for it. As the decade closed and NBC cancelled his sitcom *Mr. Rhodes* after one season, Rhodes absconded to the Netherlands to find a second life successfully hosting his own comedy talk show, *The Kevin Masters Show starring Tom Rhodes*. Having matured into a new sense of artistry and international vantage points, Rhodes holds forth on his experiences as a subversive American comic performing all over the world.

TOM RHODES: It's a real talent to find something that'll rub someone the wrong way. God, what a *gift*.

I used to say I was a communist just because it upset my family. Not that I even knew what communism was, I just knew it upset them. I didn't have the courage to say I was a homosexual, and communist was next on the list.

I was a smartass my whole life. My uncle once told me, "You always choose the most unpopular angle on anything, the one that's going to cause you the most grief," but it's really *fun* to upset people. I had two older brothers that bullied me, and I could always push their buttons with just my tongue. It's better than kung fu or muscles. It happens in bars, where there'll be some guy my animal instinct tells me is a bully, and I can find the two or three words that'll make him lose his fucking mind. It's a gift. I'm grateful for it.

PAUL PROVENZA: So being a confrontational comedian is not even a choice?

TOM RHODES: I always thought I was moody and arrogant and bitchy and argumentative, but my mother's from Argentina, so I went there for the first time last year, and it turns out I'm just Argentinian. There's nothing wrong with me at all; it's just the way of my people.

PAUL PROVENZA: You didn't start doing comedy in Argentina, so did you have a tough time with crowds, starting out?

TOM RHODES: I think taking the Lenny Bruce route is just difficult in general for anybody. You're just going to get your knees skinned up. I remember opening for Bill Maher years ago in Atlanta, and it was packed with his fans. He did things that were so confrontational even some of his own crowd's feathers got ruffled.

But who knows if anything we say really affects anyone? In Bakersfield, I did a bit about this antigay protest in Texas, and I said they were yelling things like "Gay is not okay!" and "God condemns homosexual acts!" And some hillbilly in the audience yelled, "You're damn right!" The bit I was doing was actually a "love everybody" kind of message, ironically, so I just kept going and finished the bit. And I don't know . . . Maybe it got through his little pinhead. Just maybe it penetrated his concrete skull and made some tiny little difference. Maybe not. Who knows? Maybe he's choking some gay guy in an alley right now in Bakersfield.

PAUL PROVENZA: Or getting sucked off in a men's room.

TOM RHODES: That's equally likely too.

PAUL PROVENZA: Have you paid a price for doing the kind of stuff you do?

TOM RHODES: Some woman wrote a letter to the club I played in Indianapolis, saying I had completely ruined her mother's sixtieth birthday party. I save all those kinds of letters, by the way. Anyway, the club wrote her back saying they've used me in the past, but I've adopted this new, "rebel" approach, and they wished me well on my "new endeavor" but wouldn't be having me back.

Rebel? I just wasn't the boring, conservative puppet act they were looking for, that's all. That kind of thing didn't help on the Southern circuit, that's for sure.

PAUL PROVENZA: That's ironic, given their refusal to stop flying the rebel flag.

TOM RHODES: I know. And they're just stupid *jokes*. With all the violence and pornography available at the push of a button, who can possibly be offended by just words in this day and age?

I've actually been back to Indianapolis, because there's new owners now, and some soldier who had just come back from Iraq got really upset about jokes I did about the war. But the guy was cool; he actually started crying . . . It got pretty heavy.

It turned out he was conflicted about whether or not we were doing the right thing in Iraq, and wanted to know my opinion further. I was, like, "Dude, I'm from an Army family myself. No matter what, nobody has anything against the soldiers."

That's why people should be pissed off anyway—that our lovable soldiers are being sent to fight for bullshit. Maybe the guy just had some epiphany, but who knows what he went through over there.

I did shows for the Marines in Okinawa and met a lot of guys returning from Iraq. Some guys were really tightly wound; their buddies would say things like, "He's a little fucked up over it." That's another thing: remember how for about twenty years after Vietnam it was like at any moment a vet might just lose it and flip the fuck out and grab hostages on a bus or something? That's what we'll have on our hands for the next twenty years after Iraq, too. These powder kegs that are gonna be going off from being in another unpopular war that

it's hard for them to be all that sure about.

I was living in Amsterdam when this war started, and on TV there I had CNN International, BBC World, and EuroNews—and it was like three different wars happening. And the common perception of a lot of Europeans was that Americans were easily brainwashed. Easily deceived and naive.

Because everyone else in the world *knew* that there were no weapons of mass destruction. The UN was on Saddam's ass for years and he complied with nuclear checks. We destroyed it all during the first Gulf War, and Iraq's biggest weapons supplier just so happens to be America. And with our technology, intelligence keeps close tabs on every country in the world. *Everyone* knew Iraq didn't have anything.

PAUL PROVENZA: Do you think it's true that Americans are easily brainwashed or manipulated?

TOM RHODES: I don't think so. I know I have a *lot* of intelligent friends. But a few years ago my brother's nineteen- or twenty-year-old stepson was saying how we *had* to go to war there because Iraq blew up the World Trade Center. I was politely telling him that he was an idiot and explained how we should be having a war with Saudi Arabia, not Iraq, since sixteen of the nineteen hijackers, Osama bin Laden himself, and most of the funding came from Saudi Arabia, and that, in fact, Saddam Hussein *hated* bin Laden and wanted nothing to do with any of it, while the Saudi royal family, however, has been saying America is the great evil for about seventy-five years. So this kid's mother heatedly goes, "What is it that you *hate* so much about America?"

The fucking *twat*. I love America more than anybody, and I'm standing up to lies, trying to tell the truth *because* I love my country. In my opinion, it's the people who *don't* love America who, right or wrong, just put on a uniform and march. The people who just go along with whatever the government says, never questioning any of it.

We're talkin' *America*! Where you *can* rage about your feelings and ask questions; most other countries will drag you through the streets for having any subversive opinion. My mother's cousin in Argentina was one of *Los Desaparecidos*, "The Disappeared." He was a professor and said some things against the government in class and nobody knows what ever happened to him.

There was a Spanish comedian in the fifties, whom Franco dragged through the streets because he made jokes about him.

PAUL PROVENZA: The Moustache Brothers in Burma got five years and seven years hard labor for one joke about the leader of the country. That's something that makes comedians here actually have some kind of *responsibility* to speak out. Because we *can* here, and elsewhere they *die* trying to.

TOM RHODES: I agree. And *all* Americans have a responsibility to live up to the hype America's created about itself. You've traveled loads, so you know how Americans are held to a higher standard around the world. We have got to be *dazzling*. We've got to live up to the high expectations we set for ourselves when we created this fucking dream to begin with.

America has done and will continue to do more for the rest of the world than the rest of the world could ever do for us, yet the rest of the fuckin' world hates us. Maybe the next time some little punk-ass country has some big disaster, America should go, "We're just gonna sit this one out," just to remind them what impact we really have.

But Americans also need to wake up and see the global vision. To understand the perspectives of everyone else in the world, not just our own. Comedy and humor making a political statement is part of that.

I saw a *brilliant* photo exhibit in Amsterdam by a French photographer who did this covert project with Palestinians and Israelis. He took close-up portraits of both Jews and Palestinians—old men, children, women—all making their silliest, goofiest faces. Beautiful portraits of all these people, mortal enemies, happily making themselves look ridiculous and silly. And he posted them on the barrier between Israel and the Gaza Strip. It was *beautiful*.

That's how people should be, you know? When you're angry at someone, think of their silliest moments. Everything changes when you can all laugh together.

PAUL PROVENZA: I think a lot of comedy is filled with ideas that maybe really should be taken more seriously than just as a joke.

TOM RHODES: I have a plan for our country. You know, Fidel Castro's dream was to play Major League Baseball. He had a tryout with the Washington Senators and didn't make it, right? Well, Hugo Chavez, big enemy of this country, tried to play Major League Baseball, also. He had a tryout with the Houston Astros as a shortstop, didn't make it either.

So, for our country's future, I think Major League Baseball needs to let more scrub Latin players into the league, just so we don't have to deal with these pesky dictators years down the road. I mean, if the guy is batting .185 . . . For America's security, "Come on in!"

PAUL PROVENZA: Well, the world would be different if Hitler had gotten into art school.

TOM RHODES: Right. That's just a joke I thought of, but you know . . . it's not completely crazy.

I think it was in *Thank You, Masked Man* where Lenny Bruce said that if the world wasn't filled with so much hate and evil and corruption, we'd have no need for people like the Lone Ranger. And we'd have no need for people like Lenny Bruce, either. If it was sunny every day and everybody was running to the park with balloons and happy all the time, we wouldn't need stand-up comedy at all.

I did an interview on some TV show in Australia, and since I perform all over the world, they asked me if some comedy themes were universal. I said, "Yeah. Pain, suffering, heartbreak, misery . . ."

EDDIE IFFT

THOUGH JUST NOW gaining prominence here in America, Eddie Ifft has long been a favorite among English-speaking expatriate audiences all around the world. In his work and travels, he's developed a unique perspective on how America is perceived, and made fun of, abroad. While compiling those thoughts, jokes, and observations into a documentary called *America the Punchline*, Eddie found himself both more proud and more questioning of his country than ever before.

EDDIE IFFT: I do a joke where I say that America should not have sent more troops to Afghanistan, because you can't rebuild a country with military force. The only way you can really rebuild a country is with the Olympics, because they bring in parades, Ferris wheels, pizza shops, bottled water, toilets . . . It's a boon to any economy, and all kinds of stuff gets built quick whenever the Olympics are involved.

I also say that another way to rebuild is with a good gay population, because any time a gay population moves into any neighborhood, they *Queer Eye for the Straight Guy* everything in sight and send real estate values through the roof.

So what's the solution to the whole Afghanistan situation? The Gay Olympics.

PAUL PROVENZA: I genuinely believe the State Department should consider that as a legitimate strategy.

EDDIE IFFT: Right? It's true that the greatest victory you can ever have is to infiltrate with culture, not weapons.

PAUL PROVENZA: You perform throughout the Middle East, but to civilian English-speaking crowds, not on military bases. What's that experience like for you?

EDDIE IFFT: Amazing. Middle Eastern people are *exactly* the same as us. Just like we have Christians that will walk out and be offended by what you say, they have really strict Islamic people that walk out.

PAUL PROVENZA: Well . . . Fundamentalism is fundamentalism.

EDDIE IFFT: But there's also people that are,

like, "Fuck yeah!" there, too. Just as many people feel one way as feel the other, just like here. People aren't really all that different. It's everywhere.

It's more nerve-wracking performing over there, though, because you're in this culture that's not really free. You can't just say anything you want to, like we're used to. You're always reminding yourself, "Jokes here could actually get me *beheaded*." Or at least get your tongue cut out. For real. So you're riding the edge, teetering on lines you're not supposed to cross. But that's really exciting as a comic. It's why people do drugs; it's why people do anything they're not "supposed" to. It's the same buzz you get as a comic playing there. And you *do* get a buzz doing it, because it's ultimately about changing their minds or addressing their fears or giving them a different perspective that's really a big deal over there. You're taking this risk and saying, "Look, *I* did it. You can, too. It's ridiculous that you have these beliefs, that you're this restrictive. That you're this *archaic*."

That's what Lenny Bruce did in our own culture here back in his day. He went, "Fuck you, fuck your dumb fucking words. How dare you keep me from speaking?" But you know, I don't *really* want to be Lenny Bruce. I don't ever want to go to jail. I love my anus, I really do.

PAUL PROVENZA: Do you find foreign audiences to be any different anyplace?

EDDIE IFFT: Audiences are all very similar. A lot of people say they're different, but wherever you go, it's pretty much always that

"80/20 rule." In any crowd, 20 percent are hip and cool and smart and 80 percent are dull and boring or idiots. That's the "80/20 rule," or, as the 80 percent call it, the "20/90 rule."

So you just find your 20 percent in any audience, and go for that. I used to go for the big laughs and try to get that 80 percent, but then I realized I don't even like those 80 percent. Those aren't the people I would ever hang out with. So now I just go for the 20 percent that I want to be friends with, whatever country I'm in.

Before I got into comedy, I was the funny guy among my friends and the joke was always on everyone else. We were always playing jokes on people; we were the outsiders, and the other people weren't in on our joke. When I got into comedy, I had to let everybody in on the joke. I was pandering. Club owners wanted you to do that because that's the masses; that's the people drinking the most and buying the most quesadillas. I *had* to make them laugh; I never *wanted* them to laugh, or cared if they did. Eventually, I came around to wanting the joke to be on them again.

That's probably why I'm not making any fucking money.

PAUL PROVENZA: What constitutes "pandering"?

EDDIE IFFT: The answer is a question: do *you* go to the audience, or do you have *them* come to you? You can go to them and kill and destroy and get laughs and high-fives and blow jobs after the show, or you can try to retain your integrity and do what *you* think is funny and original and different and honest and walk out having a lot of explaining to do. That's taking a risk.

And it doesn't matter where your audience is. I've performed for tough urban audiences, where you think, "Oh, this audience gets nothing but dick jokes and they want me to fuck a stool." Then I'll perform at some country club full of corporate CEOs, where you'd think, "These are the most intelligent men in the world," but they *still* want me to fuck a stool, only they want to pretend that the stool is "urban" people. They're just as dumb in their own way as uneducated people. It has nothing to do with socioeconomic status.

Most of us all think the same things, eat the same things, drink the same things. The number one restaurant in America is TGI Friday's, and we all know that's not the best cuisine in the world. No food critic's going, "Those sizzling fajitas were *to die for!*" Or, "Put Applebee's on your *must do* list when you're in Quad Cities, Illinois!" But that's what America loves, because it's all just pandering to the majority. You get the big portions, and you always know what you're gonna get and it's always gonna taste exactly the same. That's TGI Friday's. That's Applebee's.

That's Dane Cook. That's evangelical mega-churches. We're all chanting the same thing, all drinking the Kool-Aid. It's groupthink: when you see everybody else do it, you think, "This must be the thing to do."

PAUL PROVENZA: Maybe what comedians do in general is try to illustrate the groupthink that goes on around us.

EDDIE IFFT: Absolutely. Politicians are always

trying to rally people *for* themselves or their ideologies, right? Well, with comedy you can rally people *against* them. Humor really is the only weapon some people have. I would never pick up a gun, I would never hit a person. Using any intelligence I have—which is not a lot—is the only weapon I have. With a sense of humor, you can rally people.

I think a satirist is a cynic to begin with. I once read that the role of ancient Greek satirists was to embarrass politicians to the point where the politicians would sometimes even kill themselves just to save face. And I was, like, "How amazing is this power you can have that you can embarrass somebody to death? That I could have that power; that I could be so funny that George Bush would have gone, 'I can't believe I went into Iraq!'" *BANG!*

And jokes grow, too; they travel through lives. You're performing to people who hear those thoughts, and because they laughed at them and maybe felt the truth of them, they'll relate those thoughts to other people. So you're perpetuating thoughts, and in some way actually have a little power against the powers that be.

It's amazing how many times I hear Chris Rock quoted, and not as a *comedian,* not, like, "Chris Rock said the funniest thing . . ." It's more that he said something *insightful.* He's quoted like a president or a scholar. Ultimately, even though he's trying to make people laugh, people use those jokes as a guide to their thoughts. If you say something so profound that it actually causes the laugh, then it can actually change the way people think.

If you go back in history, the court jester was the only one allowed to make fun of the king. And he was allowed to make fun of him as long as it was funny. The second it crossed the line and it wasn't funny, that's when he got his head cut off.

PAUL PROVENZA: A lot like a suburban New Jersey gig.

EDDIE IFFT: A *lot.* But it's any gig, really: you can get away with murder up there, say anything you want, be as offensive as you want, cross all kinds of lines—as long as you're making them laugh, you'll get away with it. It's when you cross some line where for some reason it's not funny that you can't get away with it anymore. "Not funny" is the really offensive thing.

PAUL PROVENZA: You're producing a documentary called *America the Punchline,* where you're compiling comedy by non-American comedians *about* America. From my own experiences performing around the world, it's pretty disturbing to hear America as the brunt of all the jokes.

EDDIE IFFT: Here, everyone makes fun of Puerto Ricans, Mexicans, Italians . . . whatever. In the U.K., it's the Scots, the Australians, and so on—every country has their favorites to pick on. But no matter who else foreign comedians make fun of, they *all* make fun of America and Americans. America's never felt that. There've always been American satirists criticizing America, but from *within.* When you hear it from so many different voices all on the outside, it's actually *shocking.* It's a rude awakening.

And too many Americans believe this country is, or *should be*, immune from criticism. I always hear people defending America against criticism by listing all the good we do in the world: "We're the most charitable country in the world!" As if that gives us a pass for all the stuff we're also responsible for that's not exactly *charitable*. That's like beating your wife then giving her flowers afterward, going, "Come on, it's okay to beat the shit out of you, because I also buy you roses and take you out for a steak dinner."

And there's that whole chip-on-the-shoulder thing they're pissed off about, too. They think of America as this big, dumb football player. You're having a high-school party, and you let them in—not because you want them there, you're just afraid of getting beat up. So you let them in and they start drinking your beer and getting loud and picking fights, going, "I'm the fucking *best*! *Yeah!*" and trying to fuck your girlfriend while you're in the corner, going, "What assholes."

So of course they're going to make fun of America. But as an American, even if you agree with them about a lot of what they're upset about—and a lot of it *is* justified, in my opinion—it still hurts to hear it, and to hear it so *incessantly*.

I was getting booed before I'd even said a word overseas. They'd say, "The next comedian is American . . ."

And right away, *"BOOOOO!"*

I was, like, "Hold on, hold on! I want to earn my 'boo.' I don't represent a whole country here; I represent a lot of bad jokes. Hold on

at least until you hear them, *then* boo me." I wanted to be treated just like anyone does, like an individual. The fact that they were stereotyping and generalizing was just racism. So I started going up on stage, like, "Fuck you, you fucking racists! How fucking dare you?! You know, you're criticizing America for being a racist country when you're being the same fucking way, so fuck you!"

PAUL PROVENZA: Is it counterproductive to lash out at them? Does it just reinforce their negative image?

EDDIE IFFT: You know, you gotta fight fire with fire. I love America, but I know it's certainly not immune to criticism—and the greatest part of being American is that you *get* to criticize it, and I do it all the time, myself. But if you kick a dog long enough, it's going to bite you, and that's what happened to me. So I would refer to Britain's own history, and I'd point out, like, "Your country's right beside us, you dumb fucks. Your hands are just as bloody as mine are." I like to turn it all around and play on their own ignorance—'cause they're really just as ignorant as they believe Americans are about everything that's going on.

I don't know who it was—Nietzsche? Whoever the fuck, one of those guys said, "You can't fight an extreme attitude with a moderate attitude. It's got to be another extreme."

When I first started doing comedy, someone said something really interesting to me: "You want to be edgy? Edgy is not being dirty. Edgy is saying things people *don't want to hear*."

Like right now, the edgiest thing you could do is to do a joke about how you don't support the troops. You can show *2 Girls, 1 Cup* over and over onstage and people will be, like, "Oh, I've seen girls shit in their own mouths before," but if you say anything that even suggests you don't support the troops, you're saying the most anti-American thing possible—and you'd better be able to prove *why* you don't support the troops, and it'd better be *real* fucking funny. 'Cause if it's not the funniest thing they've ever heard, you're a *dead* man.

ROBERT KLEIN

A TRUE STAND-UP icon, Robert Klein emerged in the mid-1970s with a fresh style and intelligent approach that immediately and profoundly influenced the college-educated generation of stand-up that followed in the 1980s comedy boom. From Yale Drama School, Klein went to work with Second City before merging his considerable acting and performance skills with his smart, collegiate sensibility to forge a new kind of stand-up that altered the conventional form from deep within it. Proudly embracing his educated perspective and laced with savvy social and political commentary, Klein's comedy spoke to a post-sixties generation ready for stand-up with modern values, new observations, and performance flair. Through HBO specials, comedy albums, books, songwriting, and acting roles, he continues "bringing intelligence to bear," and challenging even himself.

ROBERT KLEIN: People ask, "Is any subject off-limits?"

Well, no . . . But if you want to joke about nuclear war, cancer, the Nazi Holocaust or anything at that level, you'd better be at least *twice* as funny as talking about anything else.

There *is* humor in those kinds of things, for sure—people in concentration camps, America's slaves . . . they had their own humor in the midst of all they suffered; the destitute or terminally ill have their own humor—but you'd just better be *real* good at it.

PAUL PROVENZA: Did you consider yourself subversive when you started out?

ROBERT KLEIN: Some would've said I was. I was certainly introducing something kinda new. So much so that on my first *Tonight Show*, January 19, 1968—I'll always know the date—they had me sit down and talk with Johnny for two minutes first, *before* my stand-up. They thought it would help if people got to know me a little first, because what I was going to lay down was so different from what they were used to. It wasn't so much the material, it was the style. I *wanted* to be different, and I was.

I wanted to bring intelligence to bear. I *loved* the Borscht Belt comics I saw as a kid working as a lifeguard in the Catskills, and all the comedians I saw on television were truly great—I just knew I wanted to be *smarter*. I felt that stand-up in one—one person standing there making people laugh—had so much farther to go than had been explored.

Lenny Bruce was a great inspiration. Jonathan Winters was absolutely *brilliant*—he made stand-up a theatrical event, not just sitting on a stool talking. He was an improviser of the first order and I was a Second City guy, so he meant a *lot* to me. Some other people were making a mark doing interesting things at the time: Bob Newhart, Bill Cosby were different; they were changing the form. Shelley Berman was doing these long, one-sided telephone conversations—and killed with them on *The Ed Sullivan Show*, the toughest show in the world, so I just knew stand up *could* expand beyond "Ladies and gentlemen . . ."

I still consider stand-up at its best a theatrical experience. Richard Pryor personifies it—he'd do accents, characters, he moved funny . . . and was incredibly, painfully honest. I'm honest too, but I won't *reveal* nearly as much as he did. He's the *best* I ever saw in person, no question.

I would say Lenny, Jonathan Winters, and Pryor are the best comedians of all time. Lenny gets extra points for having no champions.

PAUL PROVENZA: And for working at a higher degree of difficulty, given what he did and when.

ROBERT KLEIN: *Well* put. When I revisit it, some of his stuff isn't as funny as I first thought, but the stuff that is, is *hilarious*—and socially important. It's groundbreaking. His stuff—including his profanity—seems ethereal. And quite harmless by today's standards.

PAUL PROVENZA: Did you ever run into issues with your material?

ROBERT KLEIN: I had this bit about being a kid and carrying the flag for school assembly. You had to be so careful not to drop it, because letting the flag touch the ground was like one of the worst things anyone could *ever* do. They made it so frightening; like if it happened, the specter of George Washington would appear like a genie: "You dropped *me*? After all I suffered at Valley Forge?? You little *Jewboy*!"

They wouldn't let me say "Jewboy" on *The Tonight Show*. They were afraid they'd get letters of complaint. I actually turned *that* into a joke; I'd mention this incident and say, "They were afraid they'd get angry letters from Alabama saying, 'Why didn't he say "Jew *Bastard*?"'"

I had a similar problem with a bit about doing *Merchant of Venice* in college at Alfred University. I've pointed to that performance as the confluence of two elements of my career coming together at that point: theater and anti-Semitism. I played Shylock before an *entirely* anti-Semitic audience.

That experience became a bit where I'd do this elaborate performance of Shylock's third act speech—the most eloquent dissertation against prejudice of all time, no matter *what,* if anything, Shakespeare actually knew of Jews.

I'd act Shylock *to the hilt* in the bit: "Hath not a Jew *eyes*? Hath not a Jew *organs*? If you cut us, do we not bleed?"—really doing it up big. Then, "And the audience went, 'Hell *NO!! Jew-boy! Jew-boy!*' . . ." And everyone's chanting "*Jew-boy!*" and chasing me with German shepherds.

I wanted to do it when I hosted *SNL,* and Lorne Michaels was very against it.

PAUL PROVENZA: You were censored for bits *decrying* anti-Semitism?

ROBERT KLEIN: Absolutely. I persuaded Lorne eventually, but . . . times were different.

PAUL PROVENZA: I think there's actually *less* of a chance to get that on network television today. A while ago, I wanted to do a bit on *The Tonight Show* about how we'd never take anyone seriously if they said, "Have you heard the word of Thor?" And how everyone agrees that Zeus hurling lightning from mountaintops is laughable but gets upset if you make fun of a god who walks on water and speaks through a burning bush.

They said, "Absolutely *no* religion material. Period."

ROBERT KLEIN: Without hearing the whole bit, maybe you pushed it too far?

I remember when Sam Kinison— who was insane, but *very* funny—did the most brilliant bit about televangelists. I thought I was the only one talking at the time about those crooks I couldn't stand to see raking in all that money, but Kinison had a great bit that nailed it. I understand he was one of those preachers himself in his youth and really knew what he was talking about.

But at the end of this brilliant piece, he did this bit which wasn't particularly funny, where he mimes nailing Jesus to the cross. *SNL* cut that part from the West Coast feed; there was a big controversy over it.

He had just pulled off this brilliant, edgy bit that spoke the truth without being offensive, but then does this harsh, cringe-worthy bit that I imagine *is* offensive to a lot of people, and screwed the whole thing up.

PAUL PROVENZA: Actually, I think that part *made* the whole piece. I'm *not* making a joke now, though it could be one, but—why is Jesus sacrosanct? That's a real question he addresses.

Those guys get away with taking people's money claiming to speak for this character in stories *they* claim are "holy truth." Kinison's bit was not just for shock; there's a serious, subversive—albeit aggressive—purpose in stripping away *reverence* for this supposed higher authority, trivializing what so many just accept unquestioningly.

It was iconoclasm in the truest sense of the word: reverence for the icon is what enables those greedy posers to get away with it, so . . . Destroy the swamp, and no one buys swampland.

Why *should* a religious icon be any different from government, politicians, or anything with power over us? Comedy and satire always take those to task, so why is a religious belief—one with tangible political sway, in this case—off limits? Because it offends someone's *sensibility*? A lot of Republicans are offended by jokes about their icon Ronald Reagan, too.

That line we're not supposed to cross with people's religious faith is arbitrary. And it's the refuge for those scoundrels you're revolted by, so Kinison addresses *that* in the bit, too.

ROBERT KLEIN: What you say has a lot of truth to it, for sure. When to be subversive, when to be irreverent . . . It's a difficult question.

I loved his getting at the hypocrisy of these evangelists, but there are ways of making your

point and being hard-hitting, and I recall that part as being superfluous and easily offensive to people who could hate those evangelists, too, but also love Jesus and their faith. So why go that way? It's not necessary.

PAUL PROVENZA: He asks the question you ask: "How do they get away with it?"

But his answer is, "Because we don't question the 'truth' of what they manipulate us with in the first place."

Kinison went after the *root* of that same cancer you recognize, after the "boss" whose orders *they* say we're supposed to follow. They tell us they're *authorized* as "official" go-betweens. And these flawed, often evil human beings decree that to question what *they* tell us is to question the boss in whose name they *claim* to act.

Kinison took down the core premise *along with* those who use it to their cynical advantage.

ROBERT KLEIN: You're right on a lot of this. I agree with much of what you say about these ideas, and I'm really arguing just for show, mostly.

But you talked about "subversion" with Kinison's bit, and I'm talking about "cruelty." Here's *my* point: of course there's no law against saying something like, "That's like Christopher Reeve judging a dance contest," but why is it *okay*? Isn't there some *better* standard of grace or elegance? Isn't there a more thoughtful way to express things?

Filth or raunch aren't any real problem to me; the problem is *cruelty*. Even in some early *SNL* stuff, there was a lot that was simply gratuitous and unnecessary. Chevy Chase had that hilarious bit making faces behind the news anchor's back—that funny, juvenile thing we all did in third grade. The news story the guy's doing isn't important, it's just chatter; you're not listening to it, you're watching Chevy, right? Well, one week there'd been an earthquake in Sicily, ten thousand people killed, and *that* was the story Chevy acted like a third-grader behind. Now that may be subtle, but to me that was gratuitous, thoughtless cruelty. A lot of cruelty goes down like that today.

And a lot of the recent backlash against political correctness is troubling to me, too. First of all, "political correctness" is a terrible misnomer; inappropriate at the very least. "Political correctness" makes it sound like North Korean ideology; like the Communists said you've thought "incorrectly"; your thoughts must be "corrected."

PAUL PROVENZA: It sounds Orwellian?

ROBERT KLEIN: Very Orwellian, exactly. Totalitarian-like. It's a turnoff when you label it "political correctness." When people make fun of it, they already have a leg up because of that stupid label, but people forget that what it's really about is just *common decency*.

PAUL PROVENZA: But regarding art, people all too often use the worthy ideals of it in ways that *feel* Orwellian; actually *feel* totalitarian-like.

Doctrinairism keeps people from considering context or irony; it can obfuscate ideas *behind* words. It's often debased and bastardized from its extremely worthy intent, used instead to suppress uncomfortable, challenging ideas in art.

ROBERT KLEIN: You know, we're not really quite all that hip yet in terms of "bigotry control."

I'm waiting for my luggage at Kennedy Airport, and some guy comes up to me and whispers in my ear, "Didja hear about the Jew who gave to charity?"

Instinctively, I guess, I said, "No."

He says, "Neither did I," and walks away.

It really fucking *stung* me. It was *highly* offensive to me—especially 'cause it's some fucking stranger and it's just some stupid joke, and what am I supposed to do, debate the guy? "The Tisch Pavilion! Jews gave *millions*! Every lung hospital in America—*millions* from Jews! You wouldn't even *have* lungs if it weren't for Jews, you stupid fuck!"

I was born in *1942*, was brought up on stories of anti-Semitism, then at Alfred University I had all these personal experiences with it . . . So when I hear shit like that, my hackles come up.

And I'm not completely sure all the time about these lines myself. I know I have to be fair, and I question myself: "What, so *no one* can make fun of Jews?"

I think about this stuff a lot, but *some* things, you know . . . Like Native Americans protesting the name of the Washington Redskins because the pedigree of the term "redskins" is far from pretty? There were *bounties* on the scalps of Native Americans—that's what that means and where it came from. Good money was paid for actual scalps—the red *skins*— of Native American human beings! It's so shameful that St. John's University changed the name of *their* team, the Red Men—which actually referred to the red robes of Catholic clergy or something like that, but most people didn't know that and assumed it had something to do with Native Americans, so they changed it to the Red Storm so as not to be even *mistakenly* thought of as participating in that kind of insensitivity.

That kind of political correctness to me is decent. It's about caring about other people's feelings, about respect for other human beings.

The use of the word "nigger" is just *disgraceful*. I was of college age seeing Martin Luther King march in 'sixty-three and everyone getting hosed and beaten. After those *horrible* struggles guys now make *millions* saying "nigger"?

And "bitch"? After all women have gone through, we get this *slut fest*?

We're finding out now that people *are* born with different sexual orientations, finally throwing out that "It's your *choice* to be gay" garbage and it hurts people's feelings now more than ever to be called "faggot," but I hear it *all* the time.

I don't see political correctness as a problem. To say "chairperson" because we live in a society where women still have to fight for equality is *not a problem*.

Believe me, I'm not looking for everything to be tepid. I *like* stuff with real bite in it. I've always been self-righteously indignant about things in my life, in my work—in fact, it was something that held me back. I look at myself on old tapes . . . A lot of *scowling*. I was having such fun, but I seem to usually have had a kind of scowl on my face.

PAUL PROVENZA: Was your style perceived as aggressive?

ROBERT KLEIN: A little aggressive, that's true. Intelligent, but aggressively so.

I suffered from "too smart for the room" at first. When I started doing TV, Rodney Dangerfield told me, "None of the intellectual stuff, okay? You're not playing Greenwich Village. This is *all* of America."

But I was determined to push that envelope. For some people, I was a little *too* pushy when I was young. I was a cocky, arrogant kid.

TERRY JONES

TERRY JONES CEMENTED his place in the comedy firmament as one-sixth of Britain's legendary Monty Python troupe, writing some of its most memorable sketches and playing some of its most outrageous characters. When Python made the jump to film, he stepped behind the camera to codirect *Monty Python and the Holy Grail* with Terry Gilliam and then went on to solo-direct the group's other iconic films, *Life of Brian* and *The Meaning of Life*. With an eclectic, post-Python career writing and directing movies, television documentaries, and children's stories, Jones most recently turned his satiric eye on the Iraq War, penning a series of lacerating editorials for London newspapers and later collecting them in a volume titled Terry Jones's *War on the War on Terror*.

TERRY JONES: We had an arrogance. I thought John Cleese and Graham Chapman were writing the funniest stuff on television at the time, and I guess they thought the same about me and Mike Palin, and we all had the arrogance that we'd just do what made *us* laugh.

We didn't want to do satire at all. That's what *The Frost Report* and *That Was the Week That Was* had done, and we came at the *end* of that satire boom, really. Lampooning and specific satire about politics didn't interest me particularly.

PAUL PROVENZA: The way the shows were structured and directed, shot on locations, Terry Gilliam's animation . . . were all innovative and, ultimately, groundbreaking. Did you consciously set out to reinvent the TV sketch-comedy form?

TERRY JONES: I was very concerned about the *shape* of the show. The others weren't much interested, they were just concerned with doing funny sketches, but I thought the show should have some kind of distinct format.

We'd all been writing sketches of three minutes to four minutes with beginnings, middles, and ends, and then a thirty-second "quickie." But I saw the first episode of Spike Milligan's *Q5* and realized he'd just torn up the rule book. He'd start a sketch, then suddenly a marching band would come on and you'd just go off into something else. He just kind of . . . wandered around!

Now Terry Gilliam had done this animation for a kids' show that Michael and Eric and I did, and was a bit worried about it, because it was kind of stream of consciousness; it went from one thing to another, ending up back at the beginning. After seeing the Milligan thing, it suddenly clicked. I thought you could do the whole Python show as stream of consciousness, and Terry's odd little animations could link it all and get you from one thing to another, and you wouldn't even need to *finish* sketches—which was just *great!*

PAUL PROVENZA: That surreality was subversive in itself, but then all your figures of authority—MPs, policemen, archbishops, headmasters, newsreaders—devolve into total silliness every time. Did that mindset seem to have any impact at the time?

TERRY JONES: A teacher at a very tough school in the inner city said she'd noticed a real change in a lot of the teenage boys. There had been quite a lot of bullying going on at the school, but since Python had come on telly, the boys had started doing *really silly things*—I suppose to get attention through laughs rather than through bullying. I thought, "Well . . . That's *quite* something."

PAUL PROVENZA: Even though you say you intended to be not at all political, didn't Python films end up being banned in some places? Did you expect controversy?

TERRY JONES: The bans were religious rather than political, but then again, the more I look at history, the more I realize that religion *is* politics, basically. Ireland banned *Life of Brian, Meaning of Life,* and another film I had made, about a prostitute, called *Personal Services.* They had only ever banned four films in Ireland—and I'd made three of them. I was rather proud of that. I thought, "Well . . . You can't do much better than *that*."

Certainly when we made *Life of Brian,* it was with a definite *intent* to be controversial. That came about when I was editing something else and the others were off doing a publicity jaunt for *Holy Grail.* They were discussing doing another movie, and Eric said, "Why don't we do something about Jesus Christ?" Someone came up with the title, *Jesus Christ: Lust for Glory.* And we all said, "Ooh, that's *very* naughty!"

We thought we were going to do just a funny version of the life of Christ, but then we all read the Gospels again, which we hadn't done, I suppose, since we were tiny, and we all realized that what Christ says in the Gospels were actually great things. The humor wasn't *there;* it wasn't in any of that. The humor is more in how people interpret it: Christ talks about peace and love, and two thousand years later people torture and kill each other because they can't quite agree on *how* he said it—what hats you should wear, how you should dress, or what services you should have in church.

Reading about medieval history and history of the Church, I realize that religion is power. Religion *gives* people power. All the quarrels in the Church were all about political power; the squabbles over the Eucharist were purely about who was going to run what bit of the Church.

A king in Romania worked very closely with a prophet called Zalmoxis, and a Greek historian records that when the king used Zalmoxis's name in pronouncements, people obeyed

more. That was around 500 BC, and people used religion to gain control even then!

PAUL PROVENZA: For what it's worth, I'd like to take the opportunity to say that *Life of Brian* is, to me, one of the three greatest film satires of all time—along with *South Park: Bigger, Longer, Uncut* and *Dr. Strangelove.*

TERRY JONES: Actually, I haven't seen *Dr. Strangelove,* but *South Park,* absolutely, I agree. *Fantastic.*

PAUL PROVENZA: Ten years later, it still seems completely current, as does *Life of Brian.* It's a timeless piece of satire, and will be for as long as religion is abused and used to control people. I'm particularly interested in that film because so much of current life in America is pervaded by religion. I know the U.K. is essentially a secular country—

TERRY JONES: Well, America is *meant* to be a secular country. It was *set up* as a secular country. By your Founding Fathers!

PAUL PROVENZA: Then you know how infuriating it is that people argue it was established as a Christian nation, and that religion's become such a political force. As such, *Life of Brian* is a more meaningful statement now by far than when it was released. Religion was a well you drew from again and again. Was an atheist statement your intent?

TERRY JONES: I don't think any of us were particularly interested in making an atheist statement or saying, "This is all nonsense." It's like exposing the nonsense in any sort of authority.

At the time we made it in 1978, religion was on its uppers in England anyway; nobody was going to church. I actually thought it was a bit unfair on religion. It felt unfair to kick it when it was down. It was really about abuse of power more than about people's believing nonsense.

PAUL PROVENZA: Speaking of abuse of power, your more recent writings during the Bush/Blair era for the *Guardian* were tremendously biting, viciously smart, funny critiques of the abuses of power and lies and came at a time when few mainstream journalists here were speaking out. Why the more satirical approach then, after consciously avoiding it earlier?

TERRY JONES: I was simply so *outraged,* I couldn't *not* do it anymore. It was one of the few times in my life that I've been motivated by anger, but I just *had* to do it; I was just *so* angry. I was so angry about the supine Tony Blair following the Bush/Cheney agenda.

That agenda was all right there, laid out in 1997, before Bush got in, by the Project for the New American Century, this sort of Right-wing think tank. In it, they say we must invade Iraq; Saddam Hussein gives us a good excuse for that, but he's not the real reason we're going to invade Iraq, we're just lucky that he's a nasty character. And they also said, it'd be hard to persuade the American public to buy this, because what we'd need, really, is a catastrophic event, *"like a new Pearl Harbor."* And they got it on 9/11. Fantastic! It's all right there, signed by Paul Wolfowitz, Richard Perle . . .

PAUL PROVENZA: Dick Cheney, Donald Rumsfeld, Jeb Bush, Scooter Libby . . . were *all* founding members of the PNAC.

TERRY JONES: When you're dealing with an agenda like that, actually I find it quite hard to be funny. I didn't write more of those columns because I got bored with my voice, really, since it was always the same sort of character writing.

I went through school being nonpolitical, or with a "plague on both your houses" attitude, and it was actually doing history research on Chaucer and the Middle Ages that made me realize how you could see the same people seeking power then, using the same methods to gain power and the same methods to keep power, as now. That opened my eyes more to what was going on nowadays.

I don't really think we change as animals, as human beings. If you read what Aristotle wrote in 600 B.C., he talks about the same things we talk about now, identifying the same problems.

PAUL PROVENZA: The Native American Hopis had their *heyoka,* or "sacred clowns," whose function was to mock tribal elders and discords in ritualized ceremonies and were regarded as powerful spiritual entities because of the effect their mockery had on the dynamics of the tribe and what they revealed of human nature. In ancient Greece, the Group of Sixty met in the Temple of Heracles for the express purpose of satirizing politicians and influential citizens. I think we need some official government agency like that now with the sole responsibility of making fun of everybody running the show. That could be a much funnier and probably more effective way to check and balance things, don't you think?

TERRY JONES: Yes! "The Department of Mockery." I like that idea.

PAUL PROVENZA: It already sounds like a Python sketch. Is Cleese available?

For people of my generation drawn to comedy, Monty Python is like the comedy soundtrack of our youth. Did you have any idea it would sustain as it has?

TERRY JONES: Python *looks* dated now, but it seems to still work for people. It *is* surprising. While we were doing it for the BBC, I was thinking, "It's a pity we're not doing something that's going to last."

TOM LEHRER

WHEN HENRY KISSINGER was awarded the Nobel Peace Prize in 1973, Tom Lehrer declared that it had rendered political satire obsolete. But Lehrer himself had already quit performing by that point after producing several albums' worth of bitingly funny satirical songs that influenced a great deal of sixties liberal protesters and many comic minds that followed him. In a rare interview as concise and succinct as his career, Lehrer explains why comedy can only do so much, and why he left it behind so many years ago.

PAUL PROVENZA: You performed for a few short years and then just stopped completely. Did you have any idea that you would have such a big impact on so many people so long after such a self-imposed short career?

TOM LEHRER: Didn't hurt anybody, anyway . . . as far as I know. That's the important thing.

Actually, it never dawned on me that, forty or fifty years later, people would still be listening to my songs. Most of them were written for their time. The fact that they're still around is an unexpected bonus, and I'm quite surprised. I think many more people alive today have listened to and enjoyed my song about Werner von Braun than have probably even heard of Werner von Braun, outside of the song.

So I'm really amazed that those records are still selling after all these years. As I've said, though, it has spread not like Ebola but like herpes. So slowly.

PAUL PROVENZA: Do you think that the musical aspect of your satire makes it easier for people to hear the ideas and the content of it in some way?

TOM LEHRER: I think that's one of the reasons that my records have lasted, if I may pat myself on the back. One of the reasons that songs last is because they're songs. I can think of hardly anybody at the moment that does that kind of stuff in songs. There are plenty of comedians and plenty of satirists and stand-up comedians, but there are very few who do satirical songs. Of course, I love Randy Newman, although now he's mostly writing songs for cartoons, which he can do with one hand. He's writing real songs with his other hand, I hope. He's terrific. Stephen Lynch, he has a few. Mostly he's about sex, I think, but still he's pretty funny.

PAUL PROVENZA: You've been known to decry a lack of civility in satire these days, and by extension, culture in general. To what do you attribute that?

TOM LEHRER: The dumbing down of the American populace, I suppose. I always prided myself on at least trying to be literate and use the right words, and if the audience didn't get it then they could go home and look it up. But now I don't think that's true anymore. That is, judging by the little comedy I've seen on television, lately. Irreverence has been subsumed by mere grossness. What we have now, to quote myself at my most pretentious, is "a nimiety of scurrility with a concomitant exiguity of taste." For example, the freedom to say almost anything you want on television about society's problems has been co-opted by the freedom to talk instead about flatulence, orgasms, genitalia, masturbation, et cetera, et cetera, and to replace real comment with pop-culture references and so-called "adult" language. Irreverence is easy. What's hard is wit.

A lot of comedians seem to think that if you say the word "fuck" in a sentence, then that's what makes it funnier. I mean, it's one thing to be able to say that, to be *free* to say that, but that doesn't mean you *ought* to.

I've no objection to the word itself. It's just the fact that I see these Comedy Central things, and even Jon Stewart—whenever they say a naughty word on that show, the audience laughs *harder*. I tried not to do that. I think I say "hell" twice on my records.

And it's not just the words, but the topics. I mean, genitalia and flatulence and just all those things that will automatically get a laugh. It's just too easy.

PAUL PROVENZA: When you were writing and performing, there was a very different politics, a very different populace, and a very different government relationship to it, don't you think?

TOM LEHRER: There was, as I call it, a "liberal consensus" back then among everybody I knew and everybody in my audience. On the Left, there was a general agreement about what was good and what was bad. Adlai Stevenson would make a better president than Eisenhower; most everyone agreed on that. One got the impression, as I certainly did, that anybody who would come to my performances would already be on my side.

But then it began to split up. If you make a joke about Israel and Palestine now, you will alienate half of the audience. The same with feminism and all these other complicated things. The liberal consensus is now split. I've felt it where I've been living, in Cambridge, Massachusetts, and Santa Cruz, California. They are two hotbeds of, well, you're not even supposed to say "liberal" anymore, you're supposed to say "progressive." I live in two of the most liberal/progressive hotbeds in the country, and they are also two of the most *intolerant* communities in the United States. I'm sure you're familiar with that phenomenon

of, "Oh, he said that? Oh, he's a sexist, forget about him. She said that? Oh, she's a racist, forget about her."

And I'm also amused at these politically correct people who will tell a racist joke, but preface it by saying, "Here's a terrible, awful, racist joke . . ." and then they'll say it with great glee, and everybody will laugh, but with the protection that it's not really racism because they've acknowledged it as racist; it's just a good joke.

PAUL PROVENZA: If you were performing and writing now, what are the kinds of things you would tackle?

TOM LEHRER: I don't answer subjunctive questions. If we had some ham, we could have ham and eggs if we had some eggs.

There's plenty of material to make fun of in the papers, the poor things. There are plenty of things that are good for one-liners, as Jay Leno and David Letterman and all those other people do, but to come up with a whole song, that's a little more difficult. How would you write a song about the Middle East? How would you write a song about Pakistan? I don't know. I wouldn't know how to do it. It's too serious. The issues are *really* serious. And I'm a little more angry than I used to be. I'm more angry, I would say, than amused. I don't even know where I stand, sometimes. I'm against everybody. Like Groucho Marx's song: "Whatever It Is, I'm Against It." So that's always a problem. Write a bitter song? Angry songs, as Phil Ochs used to do? It roused the rabble, and that was fine, but I couldn't do that.

PAUL PROVENZA: Do you think there is any value in "rousing the rabble"? Preaching to the converted?

TOM LEHRER: I wasn't *preaching* to the converted, I was *titillating* the converted, because they were often responding with a "Right on!" kind of thing. I think it does make people feel good to be able to say, "Oh, well, that guy really *nailed* it!" I think it does do some good, but mainly it does good to ourselves and to our own egos. The people who think, "Oh, no, we can't say *that*!" are emboldened when they hear someone whom they respect saying it. But I always have to qualify that with ". . . to some slight extent." They're not going to go out to suddenly picket or demonstrate just because of that. Because the people who demonstrate usually don't have much of a sense of humor anyway. I never understood "All you need is love," and all that kind of stuff. That's the biggest lie ever told in a popular song, next to "The best things in life are free." I mean, "Give peace a chance?" That's nice, but, really. . .

PAUL PROVENZA: As a matter of fact, at the time he did that song, lying in a bed with Yoko Ono on international television, John Lennon was confronted by a journalist who said to him pretty much what you're saying. She asked him, "Don't you think you're being silly? Do you really believe singing 'Give Peace a Chance' is really going to make a difference?"

And he said, "Well, a million people just marched on the White House, and they were all singing that song."

TOM LEHRER: Well, yes, I do agree with that. Singing brings people together; it creates a feeling of solidarity. If we're all singing, never mind the content, never mind the actual grammatical errors. We shall overcome using a transitive verb without an object. But I associate that also with the German youth singing in the beer gardens; the same kind of thing. They put their arms around each other and sing. It makes you feel that you're a part of something, which may or may not be good, depending on what you're a part of.

But I was never convinced that anything I did would convince other people of anything. I think one of the only ways it can make a difference is if someone who wasn't already on my side listens to it and hears so many other people laughing that they have to think, "Well, maybe that is an idea worth at least reconsidering." So it *may* have some tangential value, but nobody's going to say, "Gee, I always thought war was good, but now . . . now I'm convinced that it's bad."

PAUL PROVENZA: So why is it that we continue doing it?

TOM LEHRER: Well, *I* don't.

JAMIE KILSTEIN

AT TWENTY-SIX, JAMIE Kilstein approaches comedy with the crusading optimism of youth. Every joke in his stand-up and every rant in his writings for Left-leaning comedy blogs is a sharp rock hurled at the powers that be. For him, comedy is a cause, not a career—though with his breakout success at the Edinburgh Fringe Festival and on the comedy circuit worldwide, it's shaping up to be a very bright career indeed. Here, Jamie describes how comedy radicalized him, and how he hopes to radicalize comedy.

JAMIE KILSTEIN: I became political in my late teens because of comedians. I was the most apathetic fucking person in the world until I met people like you and Doug Stanhope and a bunch of other people—through comedy. I didn't really give a shit about politics, but all these really cool comics I looked up to were really into politics and cared about things so much. I wanted to be like them comedically, and they talked about politics and issues, so I was, like, "Aw fuck, I guess now I have to learn about politics." And now I think I care about that more than comedy.

Any time comics who don't think they changed anything get an e-mail from another comic who's, like, "You inspired me to do such and such," that shows they *did* change something. They passed it on to someone younger.

I almost gave up on this whole social-political thing at one point, but my girlfriend's a writer and she writes about the same kind of things I talk about, and recently we started getting these e-mails from kids who just dug our comedy and were, like, "What can *we* do politically?" They're asking us what Web sites can they go to, so we tell them about Democracy Now and things like that—and that's *huge*. It's really cool when you can get an artist-to-fan kind of dialogue going. They get inspired by it, and I think that's the fucking greatest thing ever.

PAUL PROVENZA: So you got two hundred people in the audience, and one person comes up to you and is inspired in some way. I guess 0.5 percent is not a bad impact for one guy.

JAMIE KILSTEIN: Seriously! If I can tell them

one thing, like, "Go listen to any independent media," and they start watching that instead of CNN, then that is a huge fucking difference. They're going to learn from that, and they're going to pass it on to their friends, and it all keeps spreading.

PAUL PROVENZA: Now, even though you look like you're about twelve, you're actually twenty-six years old, which is still pretty young.

JAMIE KILSTEIN: Yeah, that's why I'm naive. That's why I'm, like, "Yeah, I can change the world." I haven't found out yet that I can't.

PAUL PROVENZA: Do you find that people are less responsive to your ideas or don't take your politics seriously because you're "just some kid"?

JAMIE KILSTEIN: What's weird is I've been doing okay in front of older audiences. I know that if anyone wanted to dismiss anything I say, "Oh, he's just a kid" would be a really easy go-to, so I like to think I'm well-read enough on the things I talk about that it's hard for them to do that.

When I first started comedy, I was talking about politics and this awful, hack club owner gave me all this advice: "You should open up with, 'Hey, I probably look familiar. Sorry your newspaper was late this morning.'" I don't do anything like that. I don't even acknowledge it; I just start talking.

I just talk to people like we're all adults—because adults talk down to adults every day. If you go into any typical office building . . . Casual Fridays? Really? That's what they're excited about? That's the big day of the week?

People are treated like they're in fucking kindergarten. Grown men and women are talked to like they're fucking children. I have more adult conversations with them than their boss does, or than some of their husbands or wives even do. I think that's why I do well in front of audiences who even disagree with me politically—because they're just excited to have a real, adult conversation. They forget you're even *allowed* to talk about this stuff. Even if I'm just a kid to them, I think they're just so excited to not have someone talk down to them that they don't even care.

People want to talk to me after my shows. They'll talk to me about stuff I disagree with. I'll get people who are, like, "I agree with this and this, but why do you say this about religion?" And then I tell them why, and then we'll talk about it. It's awesome. You have to feel really fucking comfortable to go up to a performer you just watched for an hour and dissect their political beliefs, you know? I've sat at the bar after shows for hours and talked personally about religion or my lack thereof, and people listen and talk back. I always talk to them, and we'll usually agree on certain things and disagree on others.

But even if I change their minds in the slightest little way, or have them question something they wouldn't have before, that's good enough. Maybe I've just changed someone's image of a liberal a little bit—like if their idea of a liberal is some elitist poet from the "Left Coast," but now they've connected with one, weren't talked down to, weren't preached at, and instead it was just the sharing of ideas—

that's changing their mind about something right there. About liberals, at least.

PAUL PROVENZA: So just having some kind of dialogue is enough of an accomplishment for you?

JAMIE KILSTEIN: Absolutely. You know that saying, "Don't talk about religion or politics at the dinner table"? Fucking most detrimental phrase to our society. That's all we *should* be talking about until we fix some of the stuff that's been going on.

But we're so red state/blue state, atheist/Christian, CNN/FOX . . . It's all these fucking labels, and no one wants to talk to each other. I've had some of my best conversations with Right-wing Christians, because we're both so shocked that we agree on stuff. We both want to help the poor. *I* want to do it because I think the class divide is too big in this country, and *they* want to do it for Jesus, but we both want to fucking do it, and that should be what matters. A lot of us are working for the same goals, but no one wants to have that dialogue, because we're all subdivided into all these interest groups.

I think humor is the one thing that kind of unites people. I'm a liberal, but I laugh the hardest at Jon Stewart when he makes fun of liberals, because I recognize it and because it's just a good joke. That's where I do care more about the comedy than the social aspects, I guess; you have to make the joke so good that people who do disagree with you will still laugh. Some of mine are there, and some of them certainly aren't yet, but how awesome is that? You can make a joke that's so strong it can break down the barriers. That's fucking *insane,* and you're doing it with just words. It's like a fucking magic trick.

PAUL PROVENZA: Elaborate on that analogy a little for me.

JAMIE KILSTEIN: Well, you have your Republican guy in your average strip-mall comedy club, right? I'll start talking about gay marriage. Now this guy has his stereotype of gays and he's told his share of fag jokes, and a comedian goes and defends gay marriage, and the guy sits there, nudges his wife, and goes, "No fucking *way.*" That's what people do at a magic show: some guy pulls out a blade and a box and a dove or something, and you go, "There's no fucking *way.*"

And the laugh you get is that same kind of gut-punch reaction that you get when you see a good magic trick. You see the guy pull it off, and you just gasp.

PAUL PROVENZA: And like the magician, you've fucked with the guy's reality?

JAMIE KILSTEIN: You've completely fucked with his reality, or his version of reality as he knows it, anyway. And maybe it won't get across right then and there, but subconsciously, maybe a month later, he's watching a piece on the news or reading some article about it and just maybe he doesn't go into it with the same harsh bias as before, because he's taken in some different idea about it, or seen some different perspective on it, or connected with something in a way he hadn't before—because he's laughed about it with you, and he's heard an idea about it that normally he might never have even listened to before.

PAUL PROVENZA: I love the analogy of a magic trick; that's really lovely. People watch a magic trick thinking, "I can't believe that's possible!" For comedy, it might be, "I never thought I could ever even listen to this idea!" But in both cases, they've been forced for just a moment to question something they *thought* they knew for *sure.*

JAMIE KILSTEIN: Totally. You know how when you're onstage, you see people in the crowd hit the person they're with when they recognize something they completely relate to in a bit you just did? It's like they're going, "Wow! Can you *believe* that? How'd he *do* that?"

PAUL PROVENZA: Do you care much if people end up not liking you or what you have to say?

JAMIE KILSTEIN: I was sixteen when I started doing stand-up, and I would be very aggressive, very arrogant. I used to talk down to the audience a lot. I was, like, "I'm gonna be Bill Hicks! And if they don't get it, *fuck* them!" You'd hear stories about guys like Hicks walking people, but the difference was he didn't go into it *trying* to walk people.

So, in the beginning, every time I'd bomb I'd think, "I'm like Bill Hicks! I'm too good for them." But really, it was, "I just ate my balls onstage."

I don't go up with that kind of fuck-you, beer-in-hand, arrogant kind of attitude anymore. I want them to like me—not because of any need on my part to be liked, but because I want them to *listen.* I feel if they listen, they'll get it, you know? And I want them to get it because I care about the message so much. If I'm a dick to them, it just gives them an easy out to disregard everything I say. It's just, "Fuck that guy." Done. And I've lost an opportunity to make a difference.

My favorite compliment is when someone will come up to me after a show and be, like, "I didn't fucking agree with a word you said, but you're funny as shit."

PAUL PROVENZA: Have you had anyone get truly upset by anything you've said?

JAMIE KILSTEIN: I do this new joke about race, and it's all irony—and sometimes people don't see the irony right away, and they'll have that knee-jerk, politically correct reaction to it. It's about how I heard some guy say, "If it wasn't for the blacks, there wouldn't be any crime." And I explained to the guy that crime doesn't happen because of race, it happens because of class. That it's not black people who commit crime, it's *poor* people. And I say, "I've never been accosted by a group of wealthy black stockbrokers on Wall Street. I've never locked my car doors because a bunch of Harvard-bound Negroes were headed my way in their pink, collared shirts with that gang symbol of the little polo horse. 'It's the trust-fund Crips!'" And some people just hear the word "Negro" and immediately snap to, "What the fuck did that white kid just say??" It's frustrating, because if you listen to the context it's completely *anti*-racist.

With black crowds, that joke usually kills, but once I had a black guy come up to me, "Did you just say the word *'Negro??'*" And I was, like, "Did you *hear* the joke?" So I repeated the joke for him, and he paused a minute and then just said, "Oh. That's pretty funny," and walked away.

But if it's an all white crowd, when you say the word "Negro," they all start looking around, you know?

DANA GOULD AND MARC MARON

DANA GOULD HAS been a bright light in comedy since the comedy boom of the eighties. Swinging wildly between hard, recognizable reality and sur-real invention, his comic expansiveness led to a stint as writer/producer for *The Simpsons*, but he's since recommitted to his unique, highly imaginative stand-up. Marc Maron remained a stand-up as he hosted progressive, morning-drive-time radio shows, gar-nering a loyal following on Air America. His com-edy is politicized *and* intimately personal, usually confrontational, and always hilarious.

MARC MARON: To really have any conversation about race, you have to be pretty fucking righteous about it. You've got to make sure your math is *really* good.

I did this comedy "debate" show with a black comedian named Darryl Lenox. The topic was "technology," and my position was that technology's bad because we surrender too much memory to it, what's designed to make life convenient paralyzes us in other ways . . . fairly broad stuff. His argument was that technology's good; it gave us medicine, all *that* broad stuff. At one point he said, "If my ancestors had a Ford Mustang, they could've driven right off the plantation. Technology would've helped my ancestors when they were enslaved."

And my rebuttal was: "Darryl . . . your ancestors *were* technology."

It was completely appropriate, really, but he looked like Sonny Liston taking a punch he never expected. He didn't know what to say, the audience didn't know *what* to do with it . . .

Afterward, though, he goes, "Are you going to use that premise?"

I said, "Run with it, man. It's yours."

'Cause I don't think it's something I could ever do outside of that very particular context. But it was an interesting moment about this stuff we're talking about and what's controversial or not. People still don't know what to do with this stuff.

DANA GOULD: There's a great story in some Lenny Bruce documentary: Lenny's onstage and asks a black guy in the audience for a cigarette. Lenny takes it from him and goes, "He nigger lipped it!," and the crowd *explodes* with this huge laugh. And there was some comic there—I can't remember who it was—who was also working in town and had dropped in to watch Lenny. He says, "I couldn't believe it!," and blatantly admits to stealing the bit: "So I go back for *my* second show, and *I* ask a black guy for a cigarette. *I* say, 'He nigger lipped it,' and they almost *killed* me!"

So there's this weird, ephemeral line, some esoteric divider that you have to nail *just right*.

MARC MARON: We live in a racist culture, no fucking way around that. There are definitely color lines. They're very separate worlds, and they're kept that way—*intentionally*.

If activist gays didn't march through the streets with nipple clamps and assless chaps, how else would they have demonstrated their identity? Their sexuality defined them as a community, so it had to be as out front as possible to make a reactive, revolutionary statement. In the same way, culturally, the black community *wants* to remain different and *needs* a separate identity.

That's where the whole "political correctness" idea was a bust—not in terms of changes in the workplace and treatment of women and race—but culturally, who the hell wants to be on the same playing field? You have a national identity and an ethnic identity you should be proud of. It should be accepted, not ignored or blandified.

PAUL PROVENZA: When the gay community began fighting for rights, it was more of a pansexual thing, about freedom not just to be gay but to be a freak and different and whatever you are or want to be, period. Like your point, Marc, elements in the gay community decry compromising all that in the fight for gay rights, and that gays had to "earn" acceptance by going mainstream, embracing the status quo of conventionality rather than being accepted with a more expansive, outsider identity. Like, "What have we gained if we're only accepted because we've become just like them?"

MARC MARON: And they're *barely* accepting that.

DANA GOULD: I'd just like to point out that all chaps are assless. The *essence* of "chaps" is "asslessness."

Anyway . . . I lived in San Francisco, and when you see a guy screaming for acceptance while Rollerblading down Market Street in a feather boa and spangled jockstrap, it sends a mixed message.

MARC MARON: "Fuck you! Accept me!"

DANA GOULD: "Suck my dick! Let me in the library!" That's kinda like a Stepin Fetchit for gay people. "Stepin Suckit."

And I know this is pointless to mention 'cause all three of us can shoot this fish in its barrel, but the whole controversy over gay marriage is insane. Jesus had no comment whatsoever on gay marriage, but specifically singled out divorce as a sin—and you won't find anything about that in *any* Defense of Marriage Act.

It's not *about* defending marriage. It's the defense of straight people's privileges.

MARC MARON: I think in a lot of straight people's minds, *they're* shouldering tremendous responsibility, but gay people can have the good part of marriage without being saddled with biological kids and all that. So, "Why should *they* get the privileges that come with marriage? What risk do they take? What do they have to put on the line?"

DANA GOULD: But the other side of that, and this comes from a homo friend of mine who said, "Jerry and I live together, have been partnered and built a life together for eleven years. Britney Spears goes to Vegas, gets drunk, and marries a guy she met *that day*, and they instantly have more rights than we do. Does that sound fair to you?"

No, it doesn't. And if what you want is a Defense of Marriage Act, *make* it a Defense of Marriage Act, not just a "Gay People Shouldn't Get What We Have" Act.

PAUL PROVENZA: But of course, the debate is all couched in that religious nonsense that pushes that reality right out of the picture. Which brings me to that phenomenal line of yours, Marc, about religion.

MARC MARON: You mean when I do a Jesus joke that's not as bad as the ones I'm *about* to do?: "Oh, I'm sorry. I'm not here to mock the myths that define any of you."

I do that to get that weird, ironic laughter from the people who understand me.

PAUL PROVENZA: What a nugget of gold that line is.

MARC MARON: I sit there sometimes and just plead with them, "You know it's just a story, right? You're believing in a story. I know you *really* believe it, but there are *lots* of stories."

I have no patience for Christians who do that "If you believe in Jesus, that's it, there are no conditions and there's just our one God" thing. And then there's the "tolerant" ones, "I'm just happy you have a faith," and try to reach out across cultures to other religions, but because of their devotion to Jesus, underneath it all it's really, "But you know you're going to hell, right? There's no way you're not going to hell."

DANA GOULD: I know enough to know that whatever there is, I don't know it. To me being a devout atheist is almost as silly as being a devout Christian. "You know exactly what it is, because you can't rationalize how it could be true?" Because there's no way my dog can comprehend my computer, my computer doesn't exist for my dog?

MARC MARON: Atheists are control freaks.

PAUL PROVENZA: Quite the opposite. *God* is the attempt at control; it's an explanation created to somehow define and structure the mystery and chaos of a world we can't make sense of. Atheism accepts the mysteries of life rather than just making up or accepting explanations that defy reason. I think the idea of a god, frankly, cheapens the wonders of life.

Atheism—"a-" meaning without, "-theism" meaning belief in the existence of a god or gods—is simply a state of not *believing* there's a god. It's not about "knowing" anything at all, it's just *not* believing something. It's not a belief itself, and if there's any "doctrine" it's reason, which leads *not* to the conclusion *there definitely* is no god, just to the conclusion that *believ-*

ing there is is irrational. Atheists don't claim to *know* anything more than anyone else knows, just to *believe* less than some others believe.

Neither of you believe in Zeus or Thor or Xenu or Quetzalcoatl or hundreds of other gods by *precisely* the same reasoning that I've chosen to reject only one more than you've both rejected.

It's like UFOs: I don't believe aliens are visiting us, all the sightings are explainable, it's irrational for me to believe they exist here on Earth. But that does *not* mean that if there *were* some rational indication that aliens have come I wouldn't be the first one to go see 'em, because how fucking cool *would* that be? There just isn't any reason I know of for me to believe it yet.

Likewise, there's no *reasoning* that makes it irrational for me to believe that somewhere in this vast universe, the edges of which we cannot even comprehend, there *aren't* aliens who *could* come visit Earth some day.

But we may never know, 'cause they probably have way better vacation destination alternatives than *this* place.

DANA GOULD: My attitude toward UFOs is the same as my attitude toward a woman's orgasm: I'll believe it when I see it.

PAUL PROVENZA: And by the way, I can prove to your dog that your computer exists. Can you do the same with me for your god?

DANA GOULD: All I know is, I don't know.

PAUL PROVENZA: Neither do I. But I won't accept some mythology in place of knowing.

DANA GOULD: In terms of God or Jesus, that's what I was raised with, so I'm comfortable envisioning the god of my parents' choice, knowing it's just an icon. Like a shortcut on my computer's desktop.

Like when we had our daughters baptized. My parents were upset, my wife's parents were upset, and I just didn't want to deal with it. I was like, "Fine! We'll have a pedophile dunk my kid's head in a bucket so when she dies she can live in an invisible castle in the sky. Let's go! What time do I get up? I read the Bible, I know how much Jesus hates kids with dry heads."

PAUL PROVENZA: Isn't that an atheist statement?

DANA GOULD: No, I think it's an anti-Catholic statement.

PAUL PROVENZA: *An invisible castle in the sky??*

DANA GOULD: An atheist would say, and correct me if I'm wrong, "You die, that's it." But I say, "Maybe I die and evolve into a higher form of energy or a being that no three-dimensional-plane organism can comprehend."

PAUL PROVENZA: That's more reasonable to me that an invisible castle in the sky.

DANA GOULD: I think it's silly, but I will accept that it's *possibly* true.

PAUL PROVENZA: Reason doesn't make *me* reject that as a possibility, either. It's theoretical. I won't accept that it's true just because it *might* be. Do you believe everything that you can't *dis*prove?

MARC MARON: I'm willing to keep the jury out on all this. If you want to build your life on being the guy doing the big work, taking the pictures, discerning the texts, great. Send me a memo when you have something conclusive; I'll be more than happy to look at it.

Faith without works is dead, right? That's a fucking Jesus thing. But faith without God is possible, and I don't think there's anything wrong with that. And if you find yourself struggling with existential fear, the only thing God's supposed to do when you're in your darkest moments, basically, is be a big voice that goes, "Watsa matter, li'l guy? Everything'll be okay."

DANA GOULD: "You'll find your flip-flops."

That's what 90 percent of prayer is: "Where are my flip-flops?" There's the fear that the universe is indifferent, which is terrifying to people, and the inability to accept the fact that decency is its own reward.

See, *I* have no fear in my life. That's why I get on planes and travel thousands of miles to get on stage and beg strangers to love me.

MARC MARON: And then not even believe them: "They don't *really* like me."

PAUL PROVENZA: That need for love can really get in the way of speaking hard truths when you're doing political and social commentary in stand-up—

DANA GOULD: This show I'm doing at the HBO Comedy Festival is a political stand-up show, but the only reason I think I'm on it is, "He's smart, put him on the political show." I'm not a "political" comic.

Most "political" comics are encapsulated one-liner comics that talk about things that are esoteric to most people in a tone that implies all knowingness. Who really wants to be that guy?

MARC MARON: "Two presidents walk into a bar . . ."

PAUL PROVENZA: I was about to say that both of you *also* get really personal and intimate in your work, too.

MARC MARON: They categorize me as a "political" comic, but only by virtue of the fact that I hosted a show on Air America. I had to learn about all that. Before that, it was a very broad range.

DANA GOULD: Bob Goldthwait once introduced me with, "Please welcome the *creepily personal* Dana Gould."

PAUL PROVENZA: And you also go from substantive ideas with real points of view and smart, funny insights and commentary about big, heavy things like abortion, religion—but then you'll just *whiplash* into surreal, absurdist things like John Lennon waking up with a giant cicada one morning because he's run out of women on Earth to fuck.

DANA GOULD: George Carlin is the best example of that. He'd do this amazing bit about God: "Religion has you believing there's an invisible man in the sky who knows everything you've ever done and going to do, and he's created a place of fire and agony where you'll suffer forever if you break any of the things on his Top Ten list of Things You Can't Do—but he *loves* you, and he *needs money!*"

And then he'd just go, "Have you ever farted at a party and had to walk a football pattern?" It's so great.

MARC MARON: You *gotta* lighten it up, let them off the hook a little.

PAUL PROVENZA: For Carlin it wasn't just about letting them off the hook. I asked him about that and he said, "You know what? I think the joke about the fart is *just as funny* as the joke about God. To me, there's *no* difference at all—and that's what makes a well-rounded person. Not *everything* is thoughtful or meaningful; sometimes we're just silly and goofy, and that's the child in us we all embrace and put forth longer than probably is healthy for anyone else."

Especially with a real *thinker* like Carlin, without that streak of playful silliness eventually it can just turn into some free-floating rage at the injustice of mortality. Because lots of the time, we're really ultimately just up there going, "I'm ALIVE! I'm STILL *ALIVE!*"

Someone like Michael Richards may not have what it takes to do it well, but he's still just *gotta* say, "I'm alive. I'm still *here*," you know?

MARC MARON: Well, I've never even acknowledged Michael Richards as somebody in the spectrum of stand-up comedy.

DANA GOULD: That was the whole thing there: that's what happens when you let people who aren't really comedians perform at a comedy club. That's what happens when being a *celebrity* becomes equivalent to being a real *comedian*.

PAUL PROVENZA: George Wallace and I were talking one night . . . And Wallace is just an amazing performer—I've learned so much watching him over the years. He has amazing charisma and presence, such power over an audience, and at a George Wallace show, you just feel huge, expansive *joy* from him, you know? And I envy it. It's really *beautiful*. But I don't think that kind of thing's even *possible* for me. So I asked him what his whole philosophy of comedy is, and he said, "People have hard lives, they come to a show to relax, spend hard-earned money to be here, look forward to it all week. And those people will never all be together in the same room again so it's a once in a lifetime experience, and I want them all to enjoy themselves, enjoy being with each other, forget all their problems, and not think about any of that while they're here with me."

And it made me realize that what really makes *me* happiest is the thought that people leaving *my* show are having an argument on the car ride home.

DANA GOULD: I can't relate to what George Wallace said either. At *all*.

MARC MARON: I heard Dane Cook say that, too, in some interview: "I just want to take them away from . . ." From *what??* In the culture we live in now, all you're taking them away from is some other entertainment option!

This idea that everybody is so weighted down by the world is such bullshit. Most people are just completely consumed with self and the tasks of living their lives. All you're distracting them from is *other* distractions.

DANA GOULD: I want them to look at me and listen to me and hear what I have to say and not interrupt. That's why *I* do it. And if something's not funny, I won't do it.

MARC MARON: Have you ever cried onstage? Seriously.

DANA GOULD: I had a one-man show. I had to cry every fucking night. But my one-man show wasn't just my act with some furniture.

MARC MARON: But I mean a *surprise* cry. Like when you're in the middle of something, and you just break down and cry.

DANA GOULD: During the period I worked on that one-man show, I had a couple of those.

MARC MARON: I hate that. But I constantly struggle, and I bring that struggle onstage.

The only way I know I have any effect whatsoever from all the radio and stand-up work I've done, is that I'll occasionally get really weird, heartfelt letters from people who've seen me saying they identify with my stuff about depression and that it helped them get out of a really dark place of their own. So, I changed their way of thinking about a certain thing, and for that they're grateful.

DANA GOULD: Our biggest fans tend to leave our shows staring at the floor and shuffling. I just came from Minneapolis, "Land of the Sad-Eyed, Shuffling Dana Gould Fans."

MARC MARON: At this point in my career people leave my show saying either, "He's hilarious!" or, "Ooh, I hope he's okay."

DANA GOULD: A lot of Marc's crowd is people from the night before bringing him food: "I made you a little something . . . "

MARC MARON: "I made you some banana bread. It's my mother's recipe . . ."

I'm *fine* with that.

COLIN QUINN

WHETHER AT THE Weekend Update desk on *Saturday Night Live,* as host of his own topical television roundtable, *Tough Crowd,* or in his gravel-voiced, unpredictable stand-up, Colin Quinn brings an everyman's blunt honesty to the sometimes overly arch world of satire. His writing and stand-up have long been regarded by comedy insiders as possessing a highly original, often misunderstood, far too underappreciated brilliance. Here, he discusses how a real-world perspective and genuine honesty are the key to comedy. With them, you can cross any line you want; without them, you'll go down in flames.

COLIN QUINN: I don't consider myself ironically distant; that's not my style. And to me, "satire" implies ironic distance. It's great when it's done correctly, like Jonathan Swift or Mark Twain, but to me, it always seems like, "I'm not emotionally invested in this, so I'll just mock it instead." It implies a lack of emotion. It may have a passion, but it has an attitude like, "I'm not really part of this."

I just said Jonathan Swift 'cause everyone will think it's smart, but—Mark Twain, who, once again everyone thinks is smart, I've never read.

PAUL PROVENZA: Ironically, I sense ironic distance in this conversation.

COLIN QUINN: See why I don't care for it?

I also don't care for comedy that deconstructs comedy. It's too presumptuous for my taste. Reading to an audience and boring them just to see their reaction ain't comedy in my opinion. I'm not saying you gotta do, "Hey, how ya' doin', lady?" But, come on. Where's your bigger point?

A lot of people masquerade having a fucking point as if they're Eugene Ionesco, but they're not. His plays have an overriding point; these guys just wanna watch people's reactions.

I guess somebody can get up there and just jerk off, too.

PAUL PROVENZA: Who books that gig?

COLIN QUINN: I think the guy who used to book "Last Comic Standing."

PAUL PROVENZA: Well, what would you say is *your* overall point?

COLIN QUINN: I don't have an overall point. But I don't presume to.

My opinions on politics are different from most people's in show business in that I'm not a conservative, but I'm certainly not a liberal; I'm not a believer in the idea that the evils of the world can be solved by some sort of "healing dialogue."

But I always believed being a comic means you point out the bullshit on both sides of everything—*and* in yourself, too. If you're talking about politics, you have to see that Republicans and Democrats are *both* lying and hypocritical, and you need to point out how in your own personal life *you* are, too. And you have to at least *try* to get laughs with it.

Some comics are one-sided, and it's just divisive. It's didactic. And really, the fact that hypocrisy is part of our common humanity is what's *really* funniest.

I always ask them, "Is it actually good versus evil in your world? Is it really black and white? Because it must be fascinating to live in such a simple world."

People think too much of their own minor perceptions. I hear people say things like, "The world was better when people respected each other, like back in the 1930s and '40s, when you could leave your door open." Yeah, except if you were a Jew in fucking Europe, when it might not have been that pleasant a time. Have you heard? There was evil back then, too.

"The nineties were *great*! The economy was booming." Except if you lived in fucking Bosnia or Rwanda it wasn't exactly "great." And I don't mean to dismiss any of what's going on now, I just get very cautious when people act like there's some kind of definitive good and evil.

PAUL PROVENZA: So what do you want an audience to take away from your show?

COLIN QUINN: I want an audience to take away the feeling of having had two overpriced drinks each, and then I watch them go, "Did we just spend $104 for three people??"

If my audience isn't laughing, I'm just not doing my job. I don't care if I provoked thought—unless I happen to accidentally provoke a thought that helped somebody cure cancer; *that* I could care about. But you hear some comedians go, "Hey, I don't always have to make people laugh every night."

Well, if you take *money* you do. Unless you're working a thought club instead of a comedy club.

Of course, the ultimate challenge is to have both.

PAUL PROVENZA: As much as we want to make people laugh, shouldn't it be on our own terms? Some people seem to feel like they have some right to "censor" a comedian if they don't like what he or she chooses to do. If you see a movie you hate, you don't demand it be edited to suit you, or that a play be recast to your liking. It's always fascinated me that people sometimes feel entitled to not just *judge* a comic but to demand that a comic actually *change* what they do.

COLIN QUINN: Well . . . Sometimes the audience is right to kinda censor a comic. Like after 9/11, a lot of comics were like, "People are freaking out when we talk about this . . ." And I was like, "Yeah, but they're not freak-ing out because they're trying to be fascist, they're freaking out 'cause it still *hurts*." I mean, I had relatives and friends who died in 9/11, too; I understand it. You can't yell at people for going, *"Uhhh,"* if that's what they feel in their gut.

That's the hardest thing about comedy. We all wanna say, "You have to laugh at this and you can't tell me I can't say it." You can't force people to laugh, even though we'd all love to.

PAUL PROVENZA: But people are sometimes "offended" not from any gut emotion the way you're describing, but from some self-righteous "hall monitor" thing. Or some lock-step mind-set they're in.

COLIN QUINN: You're right, sometimes it's political correctness or a kind of mob mentality, but sometimes it's just a human response. Everyone has their own pain.

There is a question of humanity and complicity in jokes. It's not just, "Who's the victim?" That's just part of it. If you make a joke about some idiot who blew himself up 'cause he lit a cigarette filling up at a gas station, the audience will laugh. But if people know his family's there, they won't laugh. That's humanity; you can't expect them to laugh. They're going to say, "In the name of decency, don't *do* that."

PAUL PROVENZA: I want to talk about the PC thing for a moment. I know it's well-intended, with meaningful goals, and I appreciate *any* effort to promote decency and respect between people. But like so many good ideas it's been co-opted. It's become a tool for some people to arrogantly parade a holier-than-thou attitude, someone's refusal to deal with their own fears can be disguised as socially acceptable righteous indignation, and some people avoid addressing any *real* racism or injustice but still believe they *have* because they once stormed out of a Friday late show at the Chuckle Hut.

COLIN QUINN: I agree one hundred percent. And a lot of times it's people speaking *for* other people. I'll say something about black people and the black people are laughing but some white people are offended *for* them. And sometimes they'll even give you that condescending, "Hey, *I* get the irony or whatever, but *other* people don't, and it's a slippery slope with that language and behavior."

"Really? Other people don't, but you do? Well thank God you're here. They have to live their lives, so it's good that they have you to watch out for them."

I grew up with black people, everybody goofed on everybody. If it's funny you get away with it, that's the way it is, and nobody saw any flak. So I take that license.

I grew up in a mixed neighborhood with a lot of black and Puerto Rican people. My sister and my brother are both married to black people and my nieces and nephews are half black. I never mention any of that on stage because I don't want *that* to be a reason I can say anything.

But the big problem in *our* business is that people who grew up in lily-white neighborhoods end up being TV executives who go, "That's offensive to black people." I go, "Shut your mouth and mind your business. If black America's proven anything, it's that they're very capable of speaking up for themselves when they're angry; don't worry about it."

But that's troublesome for people in the business; they're uncomfortable with that language. They had all these rules at college and political correctness is the only way they know to deal with any of it.

Tough Crowd was a great example. We were on literally two hours after *Chappelle's Show.* Now, you'd figure we're on later, we'd be able to get away with more, right? On *Chappelle's Show,* they'd say "nigger" thirty times a show. Our show? Black comedians would say "nigger" and they'd bleep them.

Because it's a "white" show. And that was white people making that decision. That's part of the disease.

PAUL PROVENZA: Is it because your audience was mostly white?

COLIN QUINN: Chappelle's audience was mostly white. And his show was huge, so if only *half* his audience was white, it's still more white people than my entire audience.

PAUL PROVENZA: You represent white America, Chappelle represents black America? I'm trying to posit a reason.

COLIN QUINN: It's because they just live in fear, and they make decisions that affect everybody.

PAUL PROVENZA: Do you think there's any validity to their decision?

COLIN QUINN: Nope. None. I'll debate anybody, anytime, anywhere about this shit; put me with Al fucking Sharpton right now. There's no validity to any of it, because what they're actually saying when they're doing this stuff is, "Don't get black people mad. You know how *they* are. They're a little *different*."

They think they're being sensitive, but they're actually holding black people to a lower standard.

And what it does is create illusions and fake realities. We're so enlightened and sensitive to never be using the word "nigger" or let anyone hear it, yet the underclass stays the same and there are more black people in jail now than ever, so how's this whole patronizing-every-one-and-trying-to-be-sensitive thing working out? Is it really working out societally? For black people, white people, or *anybody?*

Obviously, it's *not* working out at all—because it's bullshit. It's a lie. Truth is the only thing that works, and that kind of shit ain't it.

PAUL PROVENZA: Does any of your stuff ever get you into racial altercations?

COLIN QUINN: Minor ones. Most black people understand by my jokes where I'm coming from. And everything I say is based on shit that I've lived. It's about real situations and real people, so I don't really get much of that.

But I also don't just blurt shit out, I do my homework. I don't *assume* I can just get away with things, and I'm not just, "Fuck you, I say whatever I want to." I make sure what I'm saying is what I really believe, and I make sure the setup's clear so no one's wondering, "Where's he coming from with this?" and I make sure it's fucking *funny.*

If you're coming from an ugly place, or you're trying to be slick, or be a guy who says

"nigger" on stage so you can say you're a guy who says "nigger" on stage, then *fuck you*, you know?

PAUL PROVENZA: The audience can tell that, and they won't accept it.

COLIN QUINN: Exactly. You'd better know where you're coming from and you gotta be sure *they* know where you're coming from, and then it'll either be fine, or it won't. But if you've done all that work and it's *not* fine, *then* you can think, "Fuck you, audience." If it's not fine and you *haven't* done all that work first, you can only go, "Fuck you, *you.*"

But that's the beauty of comedy: there's no hiding. A lot of showbiz, all they do is talk about it, write it, research it, market it . . . *We* actually go out and live this shit every night. We can talk about it all we want, but ultimately when we live it, there's no more hiding.

Television, radio, movies—they have the courage of the knife, but not the fucking *blood*. We go out to a fucking club and deal with it face-to-face, and they're real people now. And that's the beauty of it.

PAUL PROVENZA: I think the difference between comedy on TV and doing live stand-up is like the difference between playng a war video game and being in a war.

COLIN QUINN: *Perfect* example! That's exactly it! People have *no* idea.

PAUL PROVENZA: I also think comedians treat audiences with more respect than television *ever* has.

COLIN QUINN: We have to! We *know* them. We *live* with them. We know them as people, not just as some demographics. We don't have the fucking luxury of *assuming* anything about them or second-guessing them. They'd be, "Motherfucker, I just paid twenty bucks, this is my one fucking night out this month, and you're treating me like I'm some idiot?"

If for nothing else, comedians treat the audience with respect because they gotta sell fucking CDs after the show and you just can't go, "Fuck you people!" and then stand by a folding table in the lobby going, "Uh . . . they're $10 each, two for fifteen."

PAUL PROVENZA: Network people just don't seem to get any of this.

COLIN QUINN: It makes me *crazy*. They go, "Well, the people in the Midwest . . ."

"I was in the Midwest three weeks last month, I was in Kentucky last week, I'm in Missouri next week. What are you *telling* me? They're the fucking same as me and you, stupid."

There is *no* finite difference in what people get or what offends them between anywhere else and New York and L.A. As if New York and L.A. are the *hotbeds* of intelligence? Get the fuck outta here. *Iowa* has the highest reading level in the nation.

It's not 1950. Everybody has the same cable, the same stores, the same fucking iPods, gets the same movies, the same news . . . Most of this country has pretty much the *same* fucking life now, more or less.

We're *all* the fucking *same*.

BILL BURR

SOME TIME AGO, white America withdrew itself from any substantive discussion on race, ceding the field to black artists and commentators, for fear of saying the wrong thing—or of genuinely lacking insight into it. Comedy is one of the few arenas where white people can speak freely and fearlessly on the volatile subject if they have the courage, the talent, and—most important—the heart to tackle it. Bill Burr does. Burr talks about the racial divide with intelligence, honesty, and such deep, intuitive understanding of the subject's complexities that people of every color laugh about its absurdities together. He approaches that risky subject as if it were no different from any other comedy fodder, and in his experience, it isn't. His observations are as profound as they are hilarious; as revealing as they are recognizable. He relates the personal experiences that shape his perspective, and what happens when he shares them in parts of our country where few have what it takes to do it more than just once.

BILL BURR: When I was eighteen, I saw Rodney Dangerfield live. A *master* comedian. Right after that, I saw Eddie Murphy—another monster performer. Back to back, Rodney then Eddie. At Rodney's show, everybody looked like me. But looking at Eddie's audience, I remember consciously thinking, "He's making *everybody* laugh."

Five years before I even started, I knew I wanted to do what Eddie did: make *everybody* laugh. Of course, in this country, "everybody" means black people and white people—I wasn't really thinking about Asians.

I'm joking about that, but really, no one ever *does* think of Asians with the same sensitivity as black/white stuff. I saw an Asian duo once, and one of them was rapping. He's already Asian, but he put on *extra-Asian-looking* glasses, and—literally—a big fortune cookie hanging off a gold chain. He absolutely destroyed—which I thought was so fucking funny 'cause you won't get some black guy up there eating watermelon and fried chicken, 'cause other black people wouldn't let him get away with it, but you get some Asian guy with a fucking *fortune cookie*. Granted, that was his choice, but still, it was one of the most cringe-worthy moments I ever saw. No Asian Al Sharpton is complaining about shit like that, so everyone laughs freely, but I was, just, "Christ, man! Have some fucking *respect* for yourself."

Here in L.A. some club has an Asian comedy night called "Slanted Comedy." It's insane! What's next, "Gock Gags"?

PAUL PROVENZA: Asian comedy shows almost *always* have awful, racist names! My pal Dan Pasternack says if they had an all-Asian show at the Aspen Comedy Festival, they would've called it "Hit the Slopes."

BILL BURR: Fucking *hilarious*! See, when something's offensive but really smart and funny like that, you can just take it at face value.

PAUL PROVENZA: It's surprising how people can be hypersensitive to offense at some things, yet such patently wrong things can go completely unremarked upon.

BILL BURR: It's weird. When I'm down South, I always ask, "Did you find *Dukes of Hazzard* offensive? A couple of rednecks driving an orange car through a barn, screaming, 'Yee-ha'?" Where was the Redneck NAACP on that one? That was the *Amos and Andy* of white Southern culture.

People never see redneck jokes as racist or offensive, because if you're a white, heterosexual male in America, you couldn't have been dealt a better hand, let's be honest, so you get less sympathy, that's all there is to it. But it's fucked up that, to the media, poor *white* people don't even *exist*. When media show poor people, they always go to the projects and pan across a bunch of black people. Poor white people are always some "Joe Dirt" character; like it's comedy. Poor whites are only there to be made fun of, it seems: mullets, guns, drinking, ignorance, racism . . . No one ever defends poor white people, not even other white people. Maybe because of the idea that if you're a white, heterosexual male and you fucked all that up, you *must* be a fuckin' idiot.

PAUL PROVENZA: Do you find it different playing all-white or all-black crowds versus mixed crowds?

BILL BURR: I started doing black rooms and did BET and The Apollo for the same reason I love doing stand-up in cities where you get those mixed crowds: what you're saying doesn't get lost. With an all-white crowd, the same joke can take on a whole different meaning, whether you want it to or not. Back in the day, I used to do a joke about kids acting like gangsta rappers. In New York, people were, "Oh yeah, I know guys like that. They're hilarious."

But in South Bend, Indiana, I go, "What's up with these white kids acting like gangsta rappers?"

And this angry white guy in the back goes, "YEAH!!"

I was, like, "Hey, easy, fella. I'm not going the Klan route with this, I'm just making *fun* of 'em." On the road, I always have to make sure what I was saying wasn't being twisted by the crowd to mean something I never intended.

But I find it interesting that people think we can't openly discuss race or gender or any of that, 'cause it's really not that big a deal. People say it's "taboo" or "edgy," but those walls were broken down long ago; people aren't nearly as shocked as we think they are. You can watch a guy get fucked to death by a horse on the Internet, so *nothing* we say onstage is gonna shock anyone.

I've maintained for the longest time that most people really don't give a shit about most

of these things. Like when Janet Jackson's titty pops out during the Super Bowl. Now they didn't get anywhere near this number, but even if they got *a million complaints*—well, there are *three hundred* million people in this country. Do the math. The amount of people who *didn't* give a fuck is *staggering*.

Obama's election should shed light on just how many white people couldn't give a fuck about skin color in this country, either. But during Barry Bonds's attempt at breaking the home-run record, ESPN did a study to find out if more blacks were rooting for Barry Bonds than whites! He got booed everywhere on the road, then comes home to a Giants game where about an 80 percent–white crowd gave him a standing ovation every time he went to bat. Plus, he was breaking a record held by another *black* guy! Now why would ESPN deliberately go out there with a study like that? They just tried to shoehorn some race bullshit in there. I don't want to watch the ignorant fucking moron who makes white people look like we have some problem with Barry Bonds when in reality it's, "We don't *give* a shit. It's *baseball*. It's *boring*. Hit a *million* home runs, Barry, nobody gives a *fuck*." I'm *for* steroids, myself. Score *more* runs; knock yourself out.

But the bottom line is that whenever a black guy's involved, any idiot can easily find racist shit to talk about. They need to shine some light on all the people who just don't give a shit about race.

PAUL PROVENZA: Do you think people find racism in *comedy* because they're looking for it more so than that it actually exists there?

BILL BURR: Context is everything—and that's the problem with the whole "politically correct" thing, too. Basically, "politically correct" is, "These words are good, these words are bad. The good words are *always* good, the bad words are *always* bad, and if you only use the good words, then you're a good person." Well, all *that* does is give psychotics a roadmap to navigate it. A complete psychopath can convey really fucked-up thoughts at any dinner party if he just doesn't use those bad words.

I saw some guy on TV after some school shooting, who said, "The Second Amendment has to be defended. If anything taught us that, it was Hurricane Katrina."

Then this *big* pause, and he covers his ass with, "You can't just have roving bands of . . . *violent people*."

He said "violent people" instead of what he really meant, which, you know, was "black people." So he never used any bad words, he just danced around it, and there's no way to call him on it.

People just don't own up to the fact that *everyone* has issues with race. We make judgments all the time, but silently, in our heads, so unless you have a meltdown that shows up on YouTube, you can pretend you're walking around with no issues whatsoever—but we *all* have issues.

Whenever anybody gets caught saying something fucked-up, white people with their white guilt go, "*That* guy's fucked up. He's the reason we get a bad rap; I'm not like *him*." Everybody really should admit, "I've thought that way myself at some point, but now I think this other way." But we can't, 'cause it's like we're not allowed to have evolved or learned something: you're either in the Klan if you admit you've been ignorant at some point, or you're some saint who's *never* been wrong about anything. It's complete bullshit.

I always make sure at least twice during a show to let people know the limited reading I've done in my life and how I don't really know what I'm talking about. Like them, most of my opinions are based on movies and shit I overhear in bars—and that's why *I* ask questions: "Am I weird because I think this?" Or, "I'm *asking* this, because I *know* I don't know anything and I'm *trying* to educate myself."

PAUL PROVENZA: Growing up in Boston was racially charged, wasn't it?

BILL BURR: I describe Boston as "a racist San Francisco." I lived the whole spectrum of it. Growing up, we were friends with only one other family—a black dude my father had been in the Navy with. So, early on, black/white was no big deal. But we moved to a very blue-collar town where I was surrounded by racist jokes at school, and I went through a period where I thought racial slurs made you sound tough. I told all the jokes and laughed at them all—but that frame of reference, growing up friends with this black family, was in my mind, too. Then you grow up, you go to big cities and meet a range of people: black people, gay people—even Asian people! That changes everything.

PAUL PROVENZA: Do you get flak from women for jokes like, "Of course men make more money for the same job. There's a dollar an hour surcharge for the fact that women get to get off the *Titanic* first"?

BILL BURR: One time I started going off about women, and this woman yelled out, "Watch it!"

And I said, "Or else *what*?"

You know what that's about to me? It's an over-correcting. There was a time when smacking a girl on the ass and having a bottle of booze in your desk like Lou Grant was considered acceptable. *We* came up during this *over*-correcting period, and we're all trying to find some balance.

But let's bring up whatever fucked-up ideas people have, instead of pretending they don't exist. If anybody watched a special of mine and demanded an apology, I'd say, "I'm sorry you thought you were watching the State of the Union Address. I'm a *comedian*. I'm *joking*. Don't take it seriously."

I hate when they make artists apologize. A lot get railroaded into it. When you apologize, on some level you're saying they're right, you *did* mean it, and now you're sorry you said it. That's why I never liked that expression, "getting away with" something. That implies you *meant* something malicious and just didn't get in trouble for it. You can't "get away" with anything; if you say something malicious, it comes across as malicious. I don't "get away" with anything, because I never mean anything malicious.

PAUL PROVENZA: I think one reason comedians may be misunderstood is because most audiences aren't very comedy-literate. They may not pick up nuances or a particular irony, or more subtle sarcasm in things. Most people only know the comedy equivalent of "Top 10" pop music.

BILL BURR: It's funny you put it that way, 'cause I view all this just like music: if you want pop-star status, you basically have to do Britney Spears tunes. If you don't do that, you can't get upset that you don't sell as many records as Britney.

But not knowing a lot about comedy doesn't mean people are dumb. Again, it's like me with music: I listened to hair metal in the eighties, so what the fuck do I know about music? It's not that I'm dumb, I just didn't listen to much else.

The comedians *I* like are ones who don't pander to the crowd, but it's hard to get your name out there in the business without being a cheese-ball about it. I'd love to fly in on my private jet to do one-nighters in theaters instead of being stuck in some strip-mall hole Wednesday through Saturday—who wouldn't? But I'm trying to get my name out there without tattooing 1-800-COME-SEE-ME on my forehead. You lose a little credibility that way.

Some guys will turn some joke into a hook, 'cause that's the quickest way to get out there if you haven't found a real voice. Suddenly you're "The Suitcase Guy" and everyone knows you. "There's this guy—he just talks about suitcases! It's unbelievable!" Then you're stuck just talking about suitcases.

I want a balance of personal stories, comments on stuff going on in the world . . . and then some shit jokes. I don't wanna put myself into some box, like, "the guy who talks about race," or "the guy who talks about M&Ms."

I had a bit where I imitate some girl at brunch going, "Is that *pesto*? Is that *pesto* in your omelet?" When I did my HBO special, a lot of people wanted me to do that joke and that voice. *Immediately,* I ran in the other direction. I don't want to suddenly be "the pesto guy."

I want to be "The Talks About Whatever He Wants To, However He Wants To Guy." But I could easily have been "The Pesto Guy."

PATRICE ONEAL

MOST CULT FIGURES wind up cult figures by accident, on their way to being something else. Not Patrice Oneal. Attaining some conventional success only to find it hollow and lacking, he ditched the tepid atmosphere of L.A. for the edgier comedy scene of London, where he honed an act and persona that revels in the shocking and profane as he thoughtfully tackles subjects social, political, and disturbingly personal and honest. He returned to the States a true artist and a "comedian's comedian," delivering three cable specials and filling a cultural niche as a thinker and sometimes pundit—occasionally on, of all places, Fox News. Here, he discusses his need for authenticity and personal truth, and why anything else is just a waste of time.

PATRICE ONEAL: I was "the *Web Junk* guy." I used to do *Web Junk* on VH1 and could've probably been a celebrity if I stayed there doing that, every day another video of some Chinese guy kicking another Chinese guy in the balls. But then I would've had eighteen-year-old girls at my live shows going, "This is not the *Web Junk* guy. This is *weird*. Why's he talking about fingers in girls' butts?"

And I'd be, like, "Why don't you just get the fuck outta here?" That's what would happen. I'm not dying to be a celebrity.

It's kinda like selling drugs: I could sell them to anybody, but I don't want everybody fucking up the neighborhood. I want *my* clientele. I'm happy being boutique. I want customers who want what *I'm* selling, and for anyone buying it to know what *my* deal is. If I have only a hundred thousand people in the entire world that love me, that's all I fucking need. I need *my* people, that's all.

I don't wanna set myself up for any kind of "fall from grace" like Pee-wee Herman, or Michael Richards, you know? Richards deserves what *he* got. I defend his right to say anything, but internally I go, "You got the fall, and you deserved it because you're a *phony*. You're a goddamn racist, you tricked us all for years, and you just got caught being who you are."

Same with Pee-wee Herman jerking off in public. That's who he always was, that's always been inside him, but he decided to be a *kids'* superstar. No one gave a shit when George Michael got caught giving a blow job, because they *know* George Michael gives blow jobs; he never tried to hide that.

I know I have a propensity to do crazy shit like jerk off in public. But unlike Pee-wee Herman, I'll have a hundred thousand fans that *know* the real me and would just go, "Patrice, you got caught jerking off in a theater?" And I'd go, "Yeah, motherfucker, I did. And I'm doing a show over here all week, two shows Saturday." And they'd go, "I'll be there."

I don't even bother to present myself in certain ways, because I know *my* inclinations. I have to be who I am 'cause I'd eventually just destroy anything else anyway. I just gotta be who I am and find out who the fuck's gonna ride with me.

PAUL PROVENZA: So you look at your fans almost like a group of personal friends?

PATRICE ONEAL: Yeah, man. They trust me; they know I won't betray them. Even when I do bad shit, they go, "Fuck it, go ahead, do some more. We know you're trying to get someplace with it and we wanna go there with you."

What keeps your integrity going is the journey to find *your* people. That'll keep you alive when you're dead in the business, man. I know one guy, whose name I won't mention, who got elevated to "genius" status. "You a genius! The greatest comic ever!" That's worse than people saying you suck, because this guy is now stuck right at that point where they said he was a genius. He's doing the exact same material he was doing then, and he's irrelevant now. He stopped growing, because the world stopped spinning soon as he said, "I want my due. I want what I'm *owed* for being the shit." That's what gets you fucked up in this game. And *depressed*.

I was very sad and frustrated that my HBO special didn't get the response I wanted in the business, you know? I was proud of it, but that makes you question what you do. But I realized I'd just be betraying myself, which is sacrilegious—because then you're betraying the people who love you, too. I would *hate* to have people who love me as a comic have to ask, "What *happened* to you, man?"

PAUL PROVENZA: Did you grow into that perspective? And do you feel your work has grown because of it?

PATRICE ONEAL: Yeah, of course. I never studied art, but I'm pretty sure Picasso's art was different when he first started. Van Gogh, Norman Rockwell, or whoever were probably painting a lot of horses before they went on to other shit.

Comics who don't elevate their comedy to where they've grown *suck,* man. I used to just talk about being fat, you know? But as I got on in life, I hate being fat now. Being fat bothers me now; I don't want to be fat. It's a struggle and it's a pain in my life. But when I was twenty-six, twenty-seven, it was, "Hey! This makes the crowd laugh!"

Just making the crowd laugh is not really doing things for me anymore. That's just knowing how to kill; I've learned how to kill. But I also learned when a crowd's laughter is *meaningful.*

I acknowledge the pain I went through trying to be part of the status quo, and I learned that the pain of doing that is *much* worse than not making all that money. I took a two-year retirement from creativity at that time. I was performing, but wasn't really creating. I just rode off of my backlog of shit I already had. Nothing I was saying was new or meant anything to me. There was nothing making me mad.

PAUL PROVENZA: And what's making you mad now?

PATRICE ONEAL: Right now, what's making me angry is that people don't get *context.* I'm tired of someone saying I'm anti-Semitic because I say something about Jews, or that I'm racist because I say something bad about black people, or I'm sexist because I say women sometimes do and say retarded shit. I'm none of those things. I just feel how I fucking *feel,* whatever it is.

Everybody tries to back you in a corner and make you defend what you *feel.* I'm not saying it's always right, it's just the truth of how I *feel.* Don't get mad at me for telling you instead of *hiding* the truth of what I feel. Let's *explore* it.

Like I'd prefer white people to not like me *openly,* so we both know where we stand: you don't fucking like me because I'm black. Got it. I'm still gonna force you to stop doing unlikable shit to me, but your sentiment will still exist, and we'll all know the truth.

Racism today is covert. I'm from Boston, and I'm lucky that I understand covert, snide racism. Racism so nasty you can't even be sure if it's racism or not. When motherfuckers in the South came at you with dogs and a hose, you knew, "Okay, that's some racist shit right there." But if I'm sitting here and don't understand what passive-aggressive is or can't recognize snide sarcasm, then white people's mouths have power to control how I live my life.

I'm a master at that shit 'cause I learned it from the best, from white people. I want black people to understand how that shit operates, like I do. If you're a black quarterback and white people go, "He only runs," why the *fuck* would you stop running?

So fucking *what* if Bill O'Reilly says, "I was surprised the blacks didn't order loudly and everyone wasn't eating fried chicken." Why do I give a fuck about what he said? To let his words affect me like that is to *allow* him to be superior to me. That disgusts me.

This racial shit's a pimp game, man. Any black person trying to be successful in this world's gotta deal with a fucking white person. This victim shit perpetuates a resentment now that's even more dangerous than where it came from. Black people have not closed the chapter; it still permeates. We haven't moved on.

People go, "It's been two hundred years, move on from slavery." But that's easy to say when you're not still under it. It's not about hanging from trees and getting beaten now, but instead there's this nasty film, this nasty undercurrent we feel—and white people feel, too. I believe black people have *got* to learn how to move on, we just don't know *how* to move on.

See, "white" is not a skin color now, it's an *idea*. Whiteness now is only a vague reminiscence. You're not a white guy; you're a symbol of what's oppressed us. "White" is like Hitler's moustache, that's all.

See, slavery is for black people like the Nazi Holocaust was for Jews, but the Nazis were labeled *criminals*. If you were a Nazi at that time, you're going to jail. To this day, you'll still be arrested if they find you. Hitler was the architect; Himmler, Goebbels, and all these people helped out. We know who's responsible, called them criminals, and make them pay for it whenever possible. So Jews can move on and don't have to hate *every* German forever.

When black people were freed, it was, just, "Oh, well. We just fucked you all over for four hundred years, you don't have any culture, don't have any shit except for what we gave you. Okay, so long; take care of yourselves." So it's, like, "I'm living next door to my fucking tormentor, and it's not even a *crime* what happened?"

I think right now we just enjoy hating each other; it's just a part of our culture. White people and black people are mortal enemies. But it would stop if we would just both be honest.

Black people are *not* being honest right now. We're phony right now. We're not honest and saying, "Here's the deal: we want a *double standard*. We wanna be able to say words that you can't. We were slaves here, okay? We should get to use words that you can't anymore. That's not asking too much."

"Hey, this guy said it, why didn't you try and fire *him*?"

"Because he was a black guy saying it, and we want double standards."

"Don't you think that's racist?"

"Yes. It is. He's black, and we're not gonna chase black guys, we're only gonna chase white people."

Just be honest about it. It was *white* Kramer. It was *white* Don Imus.

PAUL PROVENZA: Do black people in your audiences think you're selling them out with some of that kind of thinking?

PATRICE ONEAL: Yeah, I used to get in fights when I was younger. Because, for black people, the only real crime is not being black. When I was younger, I'd have this duality: I love black people, I love being black—I *love* it—but there needs to be a growth, you know? Where you free your mind. Some black people are just unreasonable—just like some Asians and some white people are, too—and those are not the people you need to reach. But the status quo *majority* of black people are unreasonable when it comes to race. If you're black and you confront that, you'll be called a sellout. They'll say, "This fucking guy takes white people's side!"

But I'm, like, "Man, I'm not on nobody's side, I'm on the side of *right*. I'm on the side of God."

See, as a white person, your particular pain and suffering is your particular pain and suffering; you don't have to suffer for your whole race. If you watch the news and see some white guy who eats ten hookers—he stabs them, chops them up, and eats their fingers—no one talks, like, "What is it with white people eating hooker fingers?" You don't have a white community to answer to; there *is* no "white community."

But for black people, for some reason, it becomes this *thing*. Like with Michael Vick, it was, "Why do *you people* fight dogs?"

And we can't just say, "Fuck Michael Vick for hanging and drowning dogs. Fuck him." We can't *do* that.

PAUL PROVENZA: If you don't back up *Michael Vick,* you're "selling out" your *whole race*?

PATRICE ONEAL: *Exactly.* Drowning dogs in a bucket was despicable shit, and black people are gonna associate ourselves with even *trying* to think of a way to defend that shit? I have to defend drowning dogs in a bucket? Are you out your goddamn mind? That's hard for me to fight. But I think sometimes we just gotta let *some* people go. For black people to rise up, man, some people have got to fall. We just gotta let Michael Vick go, because *nobody* should be defending that shit.

That's why you need thinkers, man. I get caught up trying to be black *and* have individual thoughts at the same time. I've got to be an individual *and* a part of the black community at the same time. That's why I'm afraid to say, "Fuck Al Sharpton"—because if a cop shoves a plunger in my ass, Al is the one who shows up, going, "Hey! Somebody stuck a plunger in this black guy's asshole!" So I *can't* just go, "Fuck Al Sharpton."

PAUL PROVENZA: Whenever I watch you work, you absolutely destroy. Big, huge, consistent laughs. You're one of those powerhouse comics—but those big, powerful laughs come from your ideas and points of view. They aren't jokes at all, they're actually the points you're making, just made *really* funny.

PATRICE ONEAL: It has to be organic; something of who you *are*. That's why when I talk to some comics, I don't respect them—because all they talk about after a show is how many T-shirts and CDs they sold. It disgusts me, because I know it's just about the money with them. Look, we're all in this game and we're not in it to *not* make money, but it's, just, "What are your goddamn *thoughts*, motherfucker? Do you have a life philosophy? Do you have *any* goddamn ethics, you piece of shit?"

If you don't, then just don't talk to me. I don't wanna talk to motherfuckers who don't think.

EDDIE BRILL

ALONG WITH A thriving, global stand-up career of his own, Eddie Brill also holds the rarefied position of stand-up comedy talent coordinator for *Late Show with David Letterman*. By choosing which comedians will appear on that show—still a major barometer of stand-up success—his conscientious judgment informs America's comedy scene. Giving seminars for stand-ups around the world, Eddie holds forth on how to succeed in the television talk show format, but he's not above learning a few things himself. His own artistic journey brought him to the realization that he'd been on cruise control for far too long, and he's finally taken over the wheel to discover more power under his hood than he'd ever thought possible.

EDDIE BRILL: I knew Bill Hicks really well, and he once said to me, "Eddie, when we have a conversation you're so funny and smart. Then you get onstage and just dance around going, 'La, la, la . . . Love me, love me, love me.'"

PAUL PROVENZA: Were you conscious of that at all?

EDDIE BRILL: Semiconscious. I just kept doing it because it was easy. I guess I'd call myself a panderer for many years. When I started, I was whatever vehicle I could drive around the stage. I started *wanting* to please the audience, and it was really fun and easy.

One cold, rainy night, I was *so* sick of my act and in such a gray mood, so I rented some Richard Pryor and Bill Hicks videos. I watched Pryor do a bit which just *killed*, but instead of basking in that huge laugh, he turns around and drinks some water, his back to the audience. He gave them their chance to laugh, but he didn't *need* their laughter; he *knew* it was funny. I watched how Hicks talked about what he *wanted* to talk about, not caring what the audience thought. I learned a *lot* that night.

What put me over the top was becoming close with George Carlin, who was my hero. You know how when we start out we're not really comedians yet, we *act* like a comedian? *I* acted like George Carlin.

George pointed out that he did the same thing I was doing; *he* pandered to the audience, and then grew into something else. He wasn't embarrassed by his work—he was funny, it was successful, clever, different—but then he saw Lenny Bruce and thought, "*This*

guy's telling the *truth*. That's what *I* want to do," and a light switch flipped on for him.

At *Late Show* I've given many comedians the advice I never took myself until now: tell the *truth*. Get out of your *head* and talk from your *soul*. Talking from the heart and soul is Ray Charles; from the head is Kenny G—and I'm feeling more and more like Ray Charles these days. Now it's not about trying to please them, it's about being funny, about being a shining light and, hopefully, inspiring a little. Corny as it sounds.

PAUL PROVENZA: That kind of paradigm shift fifteen, sixteen years into a career can be devastating.

EDDIE BRILL: Thankfully, a lot of comedians supported me in it. Like when you saw me in Sydney, you went, "Wow. Really cool, man." For an hour I was just ad-libbing things I was thinking about to an Aussie crowd who weren't gonna put up with the pandering that American crowds are used to.

I never realize how *much* we pander here until I worked in England the first time. I gave my credits to the emcee, the "compere" as they call it, and he looked at me, like, "What an asshole."

PAUL PROVENZA: Because the attitude over there is, "We don't give a shit what you've *done*. Are you funny right *now*?"

EDDIE BRILL: *Right now*. That was 1989, and I've worked all these countries since then—France, Hong Kong, Holland . . . That made me really think about what I'm doing—the same way talking with George did. At one point, a lightbulb suddenly went off for me and I just started talking about whatever I wanted. It felt like this weight was lifted. I've been telling the *truth* ever since then, and the material's flowing like never before.

I met with this "life coach" and asked, "How can you help me?"

She said, "The Michelangelo method. Someone asked Michelangelo, 'How'd you make this perfect statue out of a block of stone?' And Michelangelo said, 'It was in there the whole time. I just chipped away at the parts that weren't it.'"

So I started getting rid of all the crap. All the stuff I preached to younger comics for years, I'm finally actually doing on my own. Comedians who thought of me as "Eddie Brill, the *booker*—who happens to have a serviceable, professional act" are looking at me now, like, "Wow. Eddie's really got things to say." It feels *incredible*.

PAUL PROVENZA: Do you feel like an artist now? Or just a different *kind* of artist?

EDDIE BRILL: I always felt like an artist, but now I feel like a real, *true* artist. I'm not worried about people's acceptance. To be a big star or to be rich and famous? That's horseshit. That's not my goal, those are *by-products* of what you do. I can now live the rest of my life knowing I'm doing what I want to do and saying what I want to say.

Like I'm talking about how I feel about religion—and people might not agree with me but they respect that I've given it a lot of thought. The key, of course, is to get a laugh with it.

I played to a very conservative crowd in Boise, Idaho, and talked a *lot* about religion, and of course they're tightening up; they don't want to hear that stuff. I had a friend there, and she told me that in the ladies' room, all these old, conservative ladies were saying, "Well, we didn't agree with one word he said, but we respect him."

I thought, "That's the greatest compliment I could ever want."

PAUL PROVENZA: Did you get laid?

EDDIE BRILL: Not even a *little*, dammit.

PAUL PROVENZA: Do you now feel like you have an agenda up there, to change minds or anything?

EDDIE BRILL: I'm not trying to change the world; I'm being a comedian. I'm still just a jester with bells on, I'm just *also* now making a point. For example, when I heard they wanted a constitutional amendment to keep gays from getting married, my stomach went, "Aaargghh!" like someone punched me in the gut. I feel the same way when I think about how women couldn't vote or blacks had separate water fountains and all that shit. I *had* to write about it: "If you don't like gay people, get counseling, because gay people exist. They're not gonna go away just because you want them to. And I understand people can be uncomfortable about gay people, because we grew up in a small-minded world. I'll admit I don't want to see two gay guys making out. I don't wanna see two fat people fucking, either. But *I* have no choice."

It was a nice way to get the laugh, make a statement, personalize it, and show some vulnerability—which is something I've noticed about all the greatest comics: a thread of vulnerability.

PAUL PROVENZA: You're in an interesting position, being a "gatekeeper" for the Letterman show, a major platform for comedians. I know there's politics and network guidelines regarding how often you can have stand-ups on—which isn't as often as it used to or should be, in my opinion.

EDDIE BRILL: I agree.

PAUL PROVENZA: And with some exceptions, I don't see particularly politicized or confrontational comedians.

EDDIE BRILL: I disagree with part of that.

First of all, it's David Letterman's show and my job really is to make Dave laugh, and Dave likes smart/silly. But I've pushed the envelope a bit myself, talking about religion and politics on the show. I've also had Jim Norton and Nick DiPaolo on the show, Colin Quinn, Lewis Black . . .

After 9/11, Colin Quinn had a fantastic joke—it didn't make fun of 9/11, because there *was* nothing funny about 9/11—but it was a great joke about how New Yorkers *reacted* to 9/11. The producers were scared, obviously, so I went to Dave, because I really believed in this joke. Dave said, "It's really funny," so Colin was able to do it just a couple months after 9/11, and it was a very cathartic laugh that people really wanted to have.

Of course, it's network TV, so there are places we can't go, even in late-night. But we *have* pushed it, as much as we could. I really *want* that, but these shows are cookie-cutter shows: forty-four minutes of show, sixteen minutes of commercials. All network television is really advertising—with some TV show around it. That's the bottom line. Advertisers want a show to be a certain way so they can sell their product the way they want it to be sold. So are you looking for the greatest artists to come out there and do their edgiest, most provocative satirical piece? You and I are, but advertisers aren't. And, in a sense, it's really *their* show.

I understand how a network show has those parameters that keep people from doing what they really want to do, but that game is a given; that's why people watch HBO, that's why people go to live comedy shows—or if they don't, they should—because that's where the real meat is.

The six-minute sets that comics do on this show really are basically just little promos for "go see this person live." Just like with a band: here's one song from the album; if you like it, buy the rest of it. It's just a nice, crafted, six-minute promo to interest you in seeing more of what this person does without the limitations of television.

PAUL PROVENZA: Kinda like "First taste is free?"

EDDIE BRILL: That's *exactly* what it is.

PAUL PROVENZA: I know this is not in your purview on the show, but when I watched that "feud" Dave had with John McCain, and watching other politicians on the show, the way Dave humanizes them is entertaining and it's great to see them playing ball with Dave, but I also feel like it's somehow trivializing, playing into the dumbing down of politics, playing into a really big problem in the political process right now, which is that it's all become personality over substance or policy.

EDDIE BRILL: Dave doesn't like political people to campaign or do talking points. What he likes is to get them to just be a regular guy or a gal; just have a conversation, see what they're like as human beings. He has real questions he wants answered, so he does as much as he can to get people to really be truthful in doing that. Sometimes he'll get angry because someone's playing a game or some weird political card.

And as much as I agree with you, a lot of people wouldn't even come on if they had to defend themselves politically. People are so egotistical and have so much to cover and so much insecurity, why would they want to be on a show where they could be attacked?

RICHARD LEWIS

AT THE HEIGHT of the eighties' comedy boom, Richard Lewis's neurotic paranoia gave voice to the lingering fears of the Baby Boomer generation. His one-of-a-kind persona and performance style has been discovered by yet another wave of fans through his starring role on HBO's *Curb Your Enthusiasm,* enabling him to inflict his obsessive worries on a whole new generation. Having sobered up and matured. Lewis finds himself more politicized and emboldened than ever. He takes on a wide range of top cs—some of which he's made peace with, many of which he hasn't, and all of which drive him crazy.

RICHARD LEWIS: I didn't know *how* to be provocative at first. By my second or third decade, stuff started to come out naturally because I knew the *craft* so well and I had more confidence to say what I wanted to.

Growing up, I heard Lenny Bruce, saw Richard Pryor, Jonathan Winters, and others, and I realized the *risks* they took. It took me fifteen, twenty years to really say, "Wait a minute . . . I'm taking risks, but I'm not going all the way." I'd been unconsciously afraid to go to the depths of how I was really feeling.

But what's the point of being a comedian if you don't go all the way and risk people throwing you off stage or not hiring you anymore? Luckily, I found a knack to say what I want to and have people say, "Ooh!" but not have the owners say, "Don't come back."

PAUL PROVENZA: So what are the issues that are most important to you?

RICHARD LEWIS: Number one is separation of church and state. It's the most horrific abuse of the Constitution.

Bob Dylan had a line in "Time Out of Mind" that goes, "I was born here, and I will die here against my will." Now, whatever he meant by that only he would know and good luck finding out—but I use it onstage. I say, "I could have popped out with a turban on, been Chinese, African-American—you name it, but I'm not. I popped out a Jew, and I was whining and didn't like it 'cause there wasn't enough applesauce with the matzo brei—that's who *I* am. If you want to believe in Christ and the Bible or Koran or whatever, that's up to you."

I try to disarm an audience by saying, "Be-lieve whatever you want. If the Rapture exists and you want to leave me down here playing pool with a couple of Buddhists and cold pizza, fine. But how dare you? Christ was a Jew, by the way." I like to remind them.

If Jesus lived and he's the prince of peace, fine—but don't give me these evangelists in Armani suits and bad rugs with a hundred thousand people putting money in boxes held by beautiful women, and a guy limping out with no tongue and one foot, who gets a hand touching his forehead and suddenly he's opening for me in Tahoe doing a tap dance. It's such bullshit.

I'm spiritual in my own way. Spinoza, a Jewish philosopher, said, "God is everywhere," which is more of a nature sort of a thing and I'm not so far from believing that, but this country was based on *laws,* not on Moses or Christ or Mohammed or anyone else. So when you hear Mike Huckabee—wasn't he the gas station attendant on *Mayberry R.F.D.?*—not believing in evolution, it makes me sick to my stomach. I *know* I came from a monkey. I *am* a monkey. A monkey with a skull cap. And I think I have a little aardvark in my posture. One more bad disk, my nose hits the ground when I walk.

But look at how they handled Hurricane Katrina—would Jesus leave those people down there with no homes for all this time? I don't think so. But I haven't read much of the New Testament—just bored one night in a hotel. And why am I stuck with the New Testament there? Why they don't have a deli menu in the other bedside table? It's not fair. Ah, it's all about money; there's only 2.5 percent Jewish people left in America so they figure why print a deli menu?

But if Katrina happened on Rodeo Drive, I guarantee you things would've been fixed real fast. And that's just it, man, that's the dark side of capitalism.

If you really boil it down, it's all about the rich get richer and the poor get poorer.

I was broke for seventeen years, but I felt like a million bucks because I loved comedy. I loved hanging out with comedians, and was waiting for a break so I could pay the bills, live a little better, and help people I love. It took me a long time. Until I was in my late thirties I didn't have much money, and I didn't give a shit. I was lucky because I was passionate about what I wanted to do, and as this poor, talented guy I had the opportunity to go onstage and try to get a break.

Unfortunately, most of the country has no breaks; they live on, like, two dollars a year. The world is fucked. When you think about the billions of dollars we spend every day . . . Even with Democrats in power you still drive through the same slums: the South Bronx, South Central . . . How come things don't ever change much?

It takes a consciousness to be raised, and I'm not sure how that's done.

PAUL PROVENZA: Do you feel you help raise consciousness through your comedy?

RICHARD LEWIS: Live onstage, in a small way. On a network TV show in front of three or four million people, in a much larger way—but here's the deal: I don't *care* about raising consciousness; I just want to make people laugh. I do it for *me*.

I got onstage in 1971 just to get some kind of test with an audience, to see if I wasn't crazy—'cause I sort of felt like I was "gaslit" growing up. Growing up with my family problems, I didn't feel I was on steady ground, *ever*. I always felt whatever my point of view was, it was wrong. And I had a lot of emotional problems, which I somehow churned into stand-up.

I've always gone on stage just for me, because I got so little help from my immediate family—they have their own problems and I didn't really get much support—so what was most important to me was to make the audience laugh so I didn't feel so alone.

When I go onstage now, I hardly know what I'm going to say. I ad-lib half the show. Whatever happens when I'm watching the news, I'll talk about right when I go onstage so I don't forget it. If the audience doesn't like it, I'll move off it, because I'm getting paid to entertain, but if they're laughing I'll continue.

'Cause all that matters to the people who pay you is that everyone there is happy, but what makes *me* happiest is that I'm *expressing myself*. Of course I like it if they agree with me, because they're usually laughing then. I'll get a couple of walk-outs, or some "Hey, come on," but then I just deal with it when I have to. But I don't care what they *think,* I want them to *laugh*. If they don't laugh, I'll get off the subject, because then I'm not doing my job I'm getting paid to do.

PAUL PROVENZA: Are you writing edgier these days?

RICHARD LEWIS: Well, I've told my lawyer to burn my computer if anything ever happens to me, because I write all these character situations about race, and you always see guys on TV who maybe get a little drunk or something and even if they're not racist or anti-Semitic, something will pop out, something dark way down there, and their careers are over. And I happen to be a liberal and happen to be color-blind, but I'll *write* things I think a racist might say, to try to turn it into a joke *about* racism—but if someone just read it, they'd go, "Oh my God! Lewis is like some closet neo-Nazi!"

PAUL PROVENZA: Were you politicized at all in college in the sixties?

RICHARD LEWIS: I was sort of a *semi*-revolutionary. We were supposed to burn down a building once, and they knocked on my door with the gas masks, but I said, "I can't go. Jonathan Winters is on *Hollywood Squares* this week."

I felt bad, 'cause I knew a lot of the professors—and some of them were very liberal. We'd be marching through a building, "Burn it down! Burn it down!" But I'd probably pass my professor's office and go, "Burn it *down!* Burn it *down!* Fred, I'm *sorry!* It's not *you!* It's the *war!* Burn it *down! . . .*"

So I wasn't really a tremendous radical.

P. J. O'ROURKE

P. J. O'ROURKE entered the world of satire as a writer, then editor in chief, for *National Lampoon*, penning such classics as 'Foreigners Around the World" and, with the late Doug Kenney, the quintessential "1964 High School Yearbook Parody." Over the course of the 1980s, this former hard-drinking, hard-drugging hippie Communist transformed into a hard-drinking, hard-drugging Republican-cum-"Libertarian." As chief of the foreign affairs desk at *Rolling Stone* for nearly two decades, O'Rourke circled the globe, skewering third-world dictators and self-proclaimed do-gooders alike, publishing countless books along the way. Today, as the H. L. Mencken Fellow at the Cato Institute and with a regular perch at the *Atlantic Monthly*, O'Rourke continues to stick his poisonous pen in any target he damn well pleases.

P. J. O'ROURKE: I was a hippie, but I wasn't a very good hippie. I didn't have all the earnest peace-love flowers in my hair; they made me sneeze. I just wasn't getting it, in a way. I was just in it for the girls.

Nineteen sixty-five, first weekend of my freshman year in college at Miami of Ohio: I'm walking down this alleyway in Oxford, Ohio, and there were two bars: one had all these beautiful girls in it, but all sorority girls with little circle pins on their little nice, tight sweaters. But unlike me, all the guys there were these big jocks and were really well-dressed, so I thought, "Man, those girls are great looking, but it's probably not happening."

In the *other* bar there were all these chicks smoking Camels and strumming on guitars, wearing leotards and ballet shoes and peasant blouses without brassieres—and they were pretty cute, too. I thought, "I'll bet *they* do it."

And they did. That was how I wound up in the counterculture. It didn't have anything to do with anything else, really.

PAUL PROVENZA: I believe pussy is the reason most men do anything.

P. J. O'ROURKE: And dope. Don't forget dope. And there was beer, too. An oft-forgotten part of being a Left-wing lunatic was that there was ample beer *and* motorcycles—other things I liked.

I *was* against the Vietnam War, of course—I mean, they were trying to send me overseas to shoot people I'd never even met, and what's worse, they were going to shoot back! It wasn't so much that I was against shooting people;

I would've shot my stepfather, no problem. But nobody was going to draft me to shoot my stepfather.

But my girlfriend was in college at Kent State, and she was in that crowd where the kids got shot, and I was freaked out and wanted to make sure she was okay so I went out there to see her, and that's where I saw the first *National Lampoon.*

I immediately thought, "Oh, my God! This is *perfect!* This is wonderful, I love these guys!" And I was just getting out of graduate school, so I thought, "I'd love to work for *them*. This is really what I want to do with myself."

I even wrote them a letter. I don't think I got any response. But I decided that if I was going to write for a living, I had to go to New York. When I got there, a friend of a friend there knew someone at the *Lampoon* and we went up and pitched a story, and I wound up working there.

PAUL PROVENZA: *National Lampoon* was "it" for subversive, countercultural, iconoclastic humor when I was a kid. Was it those countercultural values that you responded to, despite your less-than-committed hippie experience?

P. J. O'ROURKE: I don't think it was because they had countercultural values, really. They actually had a kind of *cynicism* about that stuff that I responded to.

PAUL PROVENZA: I can't believe that you, of all people, in the heyday of the protest movement in the late sixties, weren't seriously politicized.

P. J. O'ROURKE: I think I was, but only in an inchoate *and* an incoherent way. I got all upset about stuff and I used to like to riot—that was fun, you know? Breaking windows and things . . . And, again, there were girls: "Come on back to the crash pad, Sunshine. Let's get this tear gas off us. We'd better double up in the shower to save earth's resources." But it was more of a lashing out than anything else, and *Lampoon* was a perfect place to lash out.

Which relates to the one thing *Lampoon* did in terms of changing American humor: Until the *Lampoon* came along, and *Saturday Night Live* and the various things that *Lampoon* influenced, humor was urban, kind of Jewish—it was kind of a shield against an outside world gone crazy. So the dominant form of American humor was somewhat defensive. But *Lampoon* was more WASP and Irish: Doug Kenney, Sean Kelly, Michael O'Donahue, Brian McConaughey . . . For the Irish, humor is not a defense, it's a *weapon*. It's what you do when you haven't got fists or a gun; the next best thing is to make fun of people. They say there's one of two kinds of Irish families: You either get a hitting family or you get a teasing family. If you're lucky, you get a teasing family. I have a teasing family; they make fun of each other all the time, which is better than hitting each other.

So in the *Lampoon* and various things it influenced or that spun off from it, you see a kind of more aggressive humor. Not that that wasn't *there*; I mean, Don Rickles is not a basket of warm puppies. Humor always has an aggressive side, but by and large, the Jewish strain of humor was, "Oy, gevalt! What a world." More "Seinfeld" than "O'Donahue."

PAUL PROVENZA: Flash-forward thirty-some-odd years and you're known as being a Right-wing satirist. What happened?

P. J. O'ROURKE: That's fair enough. I'm pretty conservative, but I probably lean more toward the libertarian side of things. My politics started getting more conservative as things got more destructive at the end of the sixties, beginning of the seventies. I wouldn't want to say it's something as simple as Altamont or Charlie Manson, but the Weather Underground—that was close to the knuckle. I began looking around then, thinking, "This has got a dark side. This isn't just sex and dope and rock 'n' roll." And going into the early seventies, that dark side began to get pronounced.

Some kids blew up this town house in Greenwich Village right around the corner from where I used to stay in New York.

I was editor of this little underground newspaper, this little hippie-dippy thing in Baltimore, and honest to Christ, a bunch of guys who called themselves "the Balto-Cong" invaded our office and said, "We're liberating your newspaper and taking it over for the people!" We said, "Well, our newspaper consists of this little row house and we're about six months behind on the rent and we have a couple of junky typewriters and about ten thousand dollars in debt, so . . . Go crazy, dudes. You are *welcome* to it."

So I began to think this stuff through a little bit more and realized that I wasn't really a Leftist. I really just wanted to be left alone and I was perfectly willing to leave other people alone. I was much more libertarian than Leftist. And I really thought about that whole "everything you know, you learned in kindergarten" thing: "Mind your own business, and keep your hands to yourself."

Regarding free market, libertarians fall to the Right so they generally get lumped in with conservatives, but libertarianism is just the idea that what you want is a form of government that respects the individual, that gives the individual the maximum amount of liberty possible and the maximum amount of personal responsibility. It treats the *individual* with dignity, so it's more of a measurement of whether individuals are being treated equally, whether they're being given the greatest latitude that's consistent with public order—there's a lot of debate about that—and are being given the maximum amount of responsibility for themselves, with less involvement from the state and other sources of collective power.

Libertarianism is very dubious about big corporations, especially when they collaborate with the state. Libertarians are very opposed to corporate wealth; the tendency of business is to create a playing field that tilts in their direction.

You can be a conservative *or* progressive and libertarian, too—libertarianism measures a different thing. I'm opposed to abortion on moral grounds—but I don't think it should be illegal. I prefer a personally conservative life—monogamous, married with children, go to church, all that shit, but I *do not* believe these things should be compelled by law.

Libertarian philosophy becomes more difficult when it comes to one's duties of compassion and charity. And it comes apart a bit with foreign policy. The Cato Institute, the preeminent libertarian think thank, agree about all sorts of regulatory things—drug legalization, personal choice, personal responsibility . . . but when it comes to foreign policy, they're all over the map.

But I've *never* thought I had any answer. But I think there are certain of our humorous colleagues, and I don't need to name any names, who sometimes get a little high on their own cooking and start thinking that not only are they good at asking the questions but that they might have the answers, too. I've *never* thought I had any answer.

That's the thing I've always loved about humor: that there's a strong element of irresponsibility to it. Our *job* is to be *irresponsible*. My job is to turn on the lights in the dirty kitchen and watch the roaches scurry, which is fun. It's not my job to step on them, it's not my job to put the Borax in the cupboards. I just turn on the lights and watch them scurry.

PAUL PROVENZA: I love this quote from you: "Some people are worried about the difference between right and wrong and some people are worried about the difference between wrong and fun."

P. J. O'ROURKE: A much more important question! I can tell *big* wrong from *big* right. Where I draw the line is in ever declaring that I have any special knowledge about something, that I'm anything more than an ordinary person looking at these things.

PAUL PROVENZA: When it gets down to the questionable areas, you're okay just going, "I don't fucking know."

P. J. O'ROURKE: Yeah, "I don't understand." Understanding's not my job. Like, generally speaking I'm against gun control, but when it comes right down to the specifics . . . Hell, my father-in-law is a career FBI agent. He covered New York City organized crime for twenty-five years in the Bureau; I certainly know the downside of crime. But when it comes to registering guns? In some ways, I don't like the intrusion of privacy; on the other hand, I don't mind people knowing I have a gun. So, "I just don't fucking know."

PAUL PROVENZA: So is there any point other than generating some laughs to what we do? Or do we ever have any effect on changing people's minds or the way they think?

P. J. O'ROURKE: I think that happens fairly often if we're good at what we do. If we set out to change people's minds it probably wouldn't work, but if we just go with our own thought process and try to be honest about it and funny about it. . .

George Carlin changed my attitudes about a bunch of stuff. As did Paul Krassner back in the sixties before he became a complete nut. And think about the great black comedians and the incredible good they did for race relations—those guys made a *lot* of people really *think*. And once you start laughing with people, it becomes hard to start regarding them as humanly different from you.

I've been talking more to my side of the aisle lately about why Republicans should just leave the fucking abortion argument alone. I said, "People are conflicted about it. Very few people who are what you'd call 'in favor of abortion' will go out and just have them at random. And sit an anti-abortion friend down, get him drunk to the truth-telling point and ask him about his fourteen-year-old daughter. What if it's rape? Ask them, 'Do you keep that baby?' There are people so principled that they *would*—but I don't think I'm one of 'em; I might kill that baby. And what are the circumstances if she's thirteen or fourteen and it ain't rape? I'd *definitely* kill the boy."

I can get those ideas across with that kind of stuff even to a very Right-wing, evangelical Christian audience and get a laugh. If I were to go in and say, "I think we oughta back off on abortion because I just don't think it's tactically good for reclaiming Congress," I'd be booed out of the room.

You're never going to do a show for the Black Panthers that gets them to kiss and make up with the Aryan Brotherhood; we're just comedians, we're not miracle workers. But it's not like we're *completely* fucking useless when it comes to decency or making people think about stuff.

THE KIDS IN THE HALL

IN THE EARLY 1990s, The Kids in the Hall stormed down from the comedy ghettos of Canada to take America by storm. A cult storm, anyway. As a group, Dave Foley, Kevin McDonald, Bruce McCulloch, Mark McKinney, and Scott Thompson explain the philosophy behind their often dark and twisted humor, and explain why you can make fun of anything, including cancer, homosexuality, and, yes, AIDS. It all depends on whether you've got the right point of view—and, if not, how funny the wrong point of view had better be.

SCOTT THOMPSON: We mock our society and poke fun at the foibles of human behavior, and that would be satire.

BRUCE McCULLOCH: I think we do a *little* satire. I think the only piece of really big social satire we did was *Brain Candy*, which was our cult—or *ill-fated;* whatever way you wanna say it—film. I think it was actually Lorne Michaels who said, "Americans don't like satire, they find it cold."

But maybe he's changed his mind.

DAVE FOLEY: Yeah, ever since that big Oscar Wilde comeback.

PAUL PROVENZA: When you guys write, do you have a sense of a bigger idea in what you're writing, other than the comic idea? That it resonates in some way or other than just being funny?

MARK McKINNEY: Hopefully only after the fact, because if you start with that, you're an asshole.

KEVIN McDONALD: It's usually bad if we think, "Oh, we wanna blow this up." But if we come up with an idea, and later someone tells us what we were blowing up, then we go, "Oh! I guess that's what it was!" But the comedy idea comes first.

SCOTT THOMPSON: Except when we wrote that scene about ripping the lid off the satire industry.

KEVIN McDONALD: We ripped the lid off that!

BRUCE McCULLOCH: It's a pretty small, boutique industry, as you well know.

DAVE FOLEY: I think that we mostly just follow whatever makes us laugh, but often the stuff that makes us laugh is subversive or horrible. Sometimes, we'll get in discussions after we write something, "Well, what the hell are we saying with this sketch?" But it's usually after we've already started working on it.

BRUCE McCULLOCH: There's also something else about satire, and that is your point of view. People have to understand your slightly odd point of view on what you're satirizing. We actually were trying to write a piece for a show at the Montreal Comedy Festival. It was the twenty-fifth anniversary of the festival, and, I don't know whose idea it was, but it was, "Well, AIDS is also twenty-five this year, so let's do a *Celebration of AIDS*!"

DAVE FOLEY: Happy twenty-fifth anniversary, AIDS!

BRUCE McCULLOCH: We ended up not doing it, I think, because the point of view was sort of off.

DAVE FOLEY: It wasn't that the content was wrong or anything, it was just that we couldn't make it hold together structurally. It was more we that couldn't make it hold together.

SCOTT THOMPSON: We just couldn't find anything to rhyme with it. That's the truth.

MARK McKINNEY: With something like that, you have to load it up with really superb laughs if you wanna get away with it. We found that out the hard way in New York in the eighties.

DAVE FOLEY: With "The AIDS Bucket."

MARK McKINNEY: We had an AIDS bucket with confetti that we flung into the audience.

KEVIN McDONALD: And I was the AIDS fairy! I spread AIDS dust all over the audience.

BRUCE McCULLOCH: He was heavier then.

KEVIN McDONALD: It was funnier when I was heavier.

MARK McKINNEY: It's a little out of context, but it's funny right *now*.

PAUL PROVENZA: Did you have a point of view on that then?

SCOTT THOMPSON: No, just a bucket.

MARK McKINNEY: It was a dad's nightmare of what his son is up to. The dad just found out the son is gay, and the dad imagines him just flinging AIDS dust everywhere.

SCOTT THOMPSON: What's amazing is that since that time people have found that AIDS is actually transmitted by confetti in a bucket.

DAVE FOLEY: And there *is* an AIDS fairy.

KEVIN McDONALD: There's a satire scene that Scott wrote—and it has AIDS again, too.

DAVE FOLEY: *All* of our satire's got AIDS in it.

KEVIN McDONALD: It was about an actor who was pretending not to be gay. He's dying of AIDS, but he doesn't want anyone to know. After he's dead, there are rumors that it was AIDS, but from inside the coffin you hear him say, "Cancer."

DAVE FOLEY: CBS refused to air that, right?

SCOTT THOMPSON: They did, yes.

DAVE FOLEY: Yeah. But mostly because our show was sponsored by cancer.

SCOTT THOMPSON: Right.

DAVE FOLEY: They didn't think our cancer sponsors would approve of an AIDS sketch.

SCOTT THOMPSON: But you know, AIDS itself is a satire of cancer.

KEVIN McDONALD: I'd say it's a parody.

SCOTT THOMPSON: A parody. You're right, it's more of a parody.

KEVIN McDONALD: AIDS is a parody of cancer.

PAUL PROVENZA: We should call the CDC and tell them to stop all their research; we've figured it out. So . . . Do you guys have any manifesto for what's right and what's not right for you?

KEVIN McDONALD: It's gut.

MARK McKINNEY: It's gut, and argument. And plates of food flying around everywhere.

DAVE FOLEY: But there are things that we definitely try to steer clear of.

SCOTT THOMPSON: Parody. No parody.

DAVE FOLEY: Well, we never did parody, because that was *SCTV*'s turf.

BRUCE McCULLOCH: And also because it's heartbreakingly *simple*.

KEVIN McDONALD: No political satire.

SCOTT THOMPSON: And no celebrity impersonation, either.

DAVE FOLEY: And we made sure all of our sketches had endings, because we didn't wanna seem like *Monty Python*. That was one of our rules.

SCOTT THOMPSON: And we wanted our hair and our wigs to look very good.

KEVIN McDONALD: That was the big one.

PAUL PROVENZA: How much stuff that you work on together goes by the wayside? What's your ratio on that kind of stuff?

SCOTT THOMPSON: A lot. About a quarter. I'd say there's about forty bad, dead sketches littering the way to this show we're doing now.

PAUL PROVENZA: Will those ever see the light of day again?

SCOTT THOMPSON: Some, I think so.

DAVE FOLEY: Because Scott will resubmit them all for the next read-through.

SCOTT THOMPSON: You bastard. You've always been a bastard, Foley. You've always been a bastard.

MARK McKINNEY: You don't like it? Satirize him.

SCOTT THOMPSON: He's lucky I didn't satirize him, I can tell you.

PAUL PROVENZA: Not only do you still have your original audience that came up with you guys, but now you've also got a whole new generation of fans that is almost *more* rabid about you than your original audience.

SCOTT THOMPSON: Well they have more energy, don't they?

KEVIN McDONALD: "I grew up on you" is a phrase we're hearing a lot.

DAVE FOLEY: A *lot*.

SCOTT THOMPSON: Occasionally, "I *threw* up on you."

KEVIN McDONALD: "My mum loved you."

DAVE FOLEY: "My mum loved you when she was at college." We don't do topical humor; I think that helps us a lot.

SCOTT THOMPSON: That's also part of our manifesto, definitely.

KEVIN McDONALD: That makes you more timeless.

PAUL PROVENZA: Given that you'd do *A Celebration of AIDS* if you could only have figured out the structure, what kind of stuff have you come up with that really makes you laugh but that you just can't *quite* bring yourselves to do?

MARK McKINNEY: A lot of dark jokes from the tour bus are in the writing. Some of them are just orphan jokes that you can't build the sketch around. They're little orphan laugh bombs that you can't really find a place for.

PAUL PROVENZA: What have you decided is too offensive or crosses one too many lines?

SCOTT THOMPSON: Nothing.

MARK McKINNEY: Pack it with enough funny, and if there's a good premise and it doesn't try to prove a point, then you have to put it out there.

DAVE FOLEY: But despite what a lot of people think about our stuff, our stuff is never mean. Things can be really dark and they can be brutal, but none of it, I don't think, is ever mean.

SCOTT THOMPSON: Even when we are really vicious, there's still an empathy for how tragic human beings can be.

DAVE FOLEY: We're never hateful of the characters we're playing.

KEVIN McDONALD: We're not nihilistic, and some comedy is.

PAUL PROVENZA: I think that's one of the reasons your stuff is so interesting. You create these situations where you can't really tell whom you're making fun of, but it's not because you're making fun of everybody, it's because you're actually not making fun of *anybody*.

THE KIDS IN THE HALL: Right, uh-huh.

BRUCE McCULLOCH: Hey, you should do a documentary; you seem to know a little bit about this stuff.

PAUL PROVENZA: Why do you think each of you guys have spent your lives doing this?

There are easier roads than the one you've taken. You could go out there and just please the audience without challenging them with such dark ideas.

DAVE FOLEY: Part of it is we don't know *how* to please an audience. *I* don't. We kind of just do the comedy we know how to do.

BRUCE McCULLOCH: And I think we're obsessed with weird ideas. Some of us more than others. I mean, Scott *definitely* needs to process his life through his work and by thinking up weird stuff, but I think that's kind of why we all do it, really.

AS A STAND-UP comedian and radio personality, Joy Behar is edgy, outspoken, and, by her own admission, sometimes downright vitriolic. On HLN's *The Joy Behar Show*, she heats up watercooler issues in prime-time, but as the Emmy-winning cohost of ABC's morning coffee klatch, *The View*, she holds a position in typically anodyne daytime television that demands diplomacy, deference, and tact— qualities lacking in most comedians, let alone those who speak their minds as freely as Joy Behar. She speaks candidly about the advantages and limitations of that position and how she walks the fine line between them, bringing subversive ideas to an audience rarely presented with fearless opinion and blunt honesty.

PAUL PROVENZA: Were you drawn to stand-up, or did you discover it looking for a way to say the stuff you had to say?

JOY BEHAR: Interesting question; which came first, the chicken or the egg?

In the beginning, I talked about my Italian-American background. One early piece of material was about these little WASP girls I was working with behind the scenes at *Good Morning America*. One said to the other, "Are you going to Southampton for Thanksgiving?"

"No, Mummy closed up the house."

I thought to myself, "The last time 'Mummy' closed up the house, they left Italy."

It was an early joke of mine that really had a social context; it says a lot of things. I think that that was the beginning for me. I wanted to address social inequities in some way, and did it by telling stories about my background. How my family used to take me to the cemetery for a vacation. About how I never went to camp: "My family didn't believe in camp. They believed in 'stoop.'" All of that was to say, "I'm going to tell you the truth."

I didn't come from an abusive background, nobody hit me or verbally abused me, no one told me to shut up; I was a little princess. It took me till I was older to be on the bottom, on the balls of my ass. I lost my job, my marriage, and had a near-death experience, and those three things catapulted me to finally do stand-up, and to be able to endure the abuse of being onstage. I was in my late thirties, had already been married and had a kid, and was practically a grown-up when I started stand-up.

My goal always was to have a party and have fun while I tell things to people. To have laughs, but also say something. You've got the microphone and the position, why *not* say something? If you bring humor to something, it's disarming, and you can say things that people would otherwise get into trouble for. If I set out *only* to make them laugh I might as well put an arrow through my head.

I come from the sixties and seventies, a generation of people who marched against the war in Vietnam. We hated Nixon, hated Johnson, hated the war, all of that, and we wanted to speak our minds. I lost a teaching job at one high school because I was telling the ninth-graders not to enlist and to make sure they didn't go to Vietnam. The school didn't like that, so I was out of there pretty fast. I was more blatant than subversive then.

PAUL PROVENZA: Are you aware when you're being confrontational on *The View*?

JOY BEHAR: Sure, but sometimes I *pretend* I'm not. It's a funny way to go, you know? Like if they react when I say something blue, I innocently go, "What?" My friend Angela said, "You don't even realize that you're saying things the average person doesn't say."

I asked my first manager, "Why do you want to manage me?"

He said, "Because you say 'fuck you' to people and they say 'thank you.'"

I don't know if that's exactly accurate, but I'm edgier than most people. For me, that's de rigueur; it's the normal way I talk to people.

PAUL PROVENZA: In daytime television we generally see mostly bland, vacuous people who play it safe rather than voice real opinions. You're confrontational, yet somehow you've avoided controversy.

JOY BEHAR: Yeah, thirteen years at *The View* without any real controversy. I've had minor skirmishes with Donald Trump, but that's about it. Oh—and some Christians. Somebody asked, "Are you glad your diet's done?"

And I said, "Thank you, Jesus."

I was *bleeped,* and ABC were mad at me for saying that. But interestingly, Jerry Falwell himself said on *Hannity and Colmes* that he was on my side because he thought that I was "testifying." Now *there's* an example of subversive behavior: I was *not* testifying, but he decided I was.

I seem to have an instinct about where the line is and I go right up to it without crossing too far over it, I guess. No one says "bitch" on the air more than I do, and they seem to be okay with it. I practically *defy* them to take that word out.

But my confrontations are about issues; I don't get into interpersonal fights. I don't say "You're an idiot" to one of my cohosts. If I don't like what they say, I'll go after that, not them personally. For example, we have Sherri Shepherd on the show, who is very religious, raised a Jehovah's Witness. A conversation came up when the governor of Georgia prayed for rain during a drought there, and she wants me to pray. She wants everybody should pray for rain. I took the position that I don't believe it does any good. Native Americans have been praying for rain for centuries; did it work? I want to see statistics.

PAUL PROVENZA: Critical thinking. Often a problem on television.

JOY BEHAR: Yeah. And Sherri's position, which is very religious and adorable, I thought, was, "Well, it couldn't hurt, why don't we all pray anyway?"

My answer to that is that it distracts you from science, *that's* why not. It makes people think *maybe* it's a solution, as if somebody's watching over you going, "Oh, Paul Provenza's praying for rain! Let's give him rain." It's very self-centered, when you think about it.

Religion is very narcissistic. How come at any given moment, thousands of people die in hurricanes or earthquakes somewhere? Because *those* people weren't praying? I don't get it. The whole thing is over my head.

But Sherri Shepherd, who believes all this, is a comic also, just with a whole different view of the world. The next day, very subversively, she brings some information and says on the air, "Look Joy! They got a half-inch of rain in Georgia."

I was now in the position of, "How shall I respond?" Instead of getting angry, I said, "You know what? I think I helped because I lit a scented candle last night."

I guess people could be mad at me for that, so I don't know how it works exactly.

PAUL PROVENZA: From the way I've heard network executives talk about mainstream audiences, you don't exactly fit their profile, do you?

JOY BEHAR: For a long time, in their eyes, I was in some category of New York/Jewish/ethnic/Italian-Jewish—whatever the hell they call it. I was considered a type the mainstream audience would not relate to. Thanks to Barbara Walters, who doesn't really buy into that, I got this job and—surprise! I appeal to the mainstream! Even though I come from New York, from a small ethnic group, and I'm a liberal Democrat, they find me "highly relatable." I think that's because I'm also a woman who's been married and divorced, has a child, went to school, and lives in the world. So obviously, network executives are just wrong about who's relatable and what mainstream America really likes. They're just *wrong*.

PAUL PROVENZA: Do you find your stand-up audience thinks they're going to get Joy Behar from *The View* and then have issues with Joy Behar the comedian?

JOY BEHAR: I think they do, actually. But in the first five minutes they get that I'm much more raunchy, more raucous, more edgy, and more pointed than on *The View*—more of everything television's always pushing away. But when people come to see you in person, they're paying actual money, so you want to give them something they can talk about, something different than what they get for free on television.

I don't think anyone is shocked by my language or anything like that, but sometimes they're shocked by my disdain for the Right wing. I have nothing but complete disdain and negative things to say about them. In fact, when I had surgery, one of the surgeons told me he had voted for Bush. I was beside myself. As I'm being gurneyed in, I made him swear that he would never, ever vote Republican

again. I wanted to stop the operation, but it was too late. I was already anesthetized and starting to go under.

PAUL PROVENZA: That's how Republicans operate. Anesthetize people before they can stop them.

JOY BEHAR: Pretty much! I'll run across audiences at Caroline's on Broadway or when I do benefits where they're not coming specifically to see me and I still tell them what I want to tell them. If they don't like it, I just have to bring them around. You have to work them a little. That's what being a pro is all about. Once I've got them, *then* my goal becomes not just for them to laugh with me, but to agree with me. I make them swear to me that they'll never vote Republican again, too.

PAUL PROVENZA: Do you think you have any influence, really, on people's politics?

JOY BEHAR: Well, I'll tell you this: I once met Joe Biden in Florida somewhere—and I like him, too, very much—and he told me that he was more scared to go on Jon Stewart's show than on *Meet the Press*. Why? Joe Biden is witty. He's very witty and could probably play around, but he knows comedians are subversive and could sabotage him in some way, or play a game with him that he's gonna get caught up in and lose. That's why he doesn't want to sit with Jon Stewart. That's the power of the comedian.

And there's a childlike quality to comedians, too, that's another part of this. You know how kids will just say things like, "You have funny hair," out of naiveté or innocence?

PAUL PROVENZA: A friend of my family got

a nose job, and he grew a moustache after the surgery, figuring that when people saw him looking so different, they'd think it must be the new moustache. He came over one night and out of nowhere my five-year-old cousin innocently and guilelessly said, "Hey Al, you know what? Your moustache makes your nose look smaller."

JOY BEHAR: That's what I mean. There's a *bit* more of an adult filter than your five-year-old cousin, of course, but we're always in touch with that kid in us, and we could just come out and ask, "Why'd you say that? What were you *thinking*?"

It's ingrained in our brains that we're still kids just having fun. That scares politicians. Republicans particularly do not want to come on *The View*. Almost every Democratic primary candidate came on the show, but where was Giuliani? Mitt Romney? Why wouldn't Mike Huckabee, who doesn't believe in evolution, sit and talk about that with *me*? What are they afraid of?

They're not afraid of Sherri, she's much more on their side. I don't think they're scared of Barbara Walters, she's a journalist, more *Meet the Press,* which they're used to. Are they scared of me and Whoopi? We're just *comedians,* right?

LEE CAMP

ASIDE FROM HIS opinionated stand-up, for which he was singled out as one of the best New Faces at the Montreal Just for Laughs Festival, Lee Camp ran for "president" on Comedy Central's "Fresh Debate '08," does frequent comedic commentary on E!, SpikeTV, MTV, and *Good Morning America,* is a regular contributor to *The Huffington Post,* contributes headlines to *The Onion,* has authored two books, and continues creating a prolific and varied body of satirical work on the Internet. Mistakenly invited to do commentary on Fox News, Lee provided catharsis for millions as a Left-wing Trojan horse confronting Fox in its own henhouse.

LEE CAMP: Fox News invited me on to do a few jokes commenting on the primaries. I don't even know how they found me, but my first thought was to say no, because I've watched this festering pile of propaganda wrapped in the American flag spew its poisonous eggs into the brains of average Americans for twelve years. Watching the flag flapping behind a Fox "news" program—*that's* desecration. But my *second* thought was, "Why not do it once and burn that bridge—just fucking set the thing on fire? *That* might be fun and interesting."

I figured I've got one shot, live on their own airwaves, to tell some truth. I didn't plan it word for word, but I had some ideas. I'd read an article about how woefully underreported civilian deaths in Iraq are and that it was probably closer to a million than anything they've told us, so I kept that in my head to keep my nerve and remind me why I was doing this.

So, live on air, after some lame jokes about Mike Huckabee, I just suddenly stopped being funny and said, "Excuse me—what *is* Fox News? It's just a parade of propaganda, isn't it? A festival of ignorance. A million people dead in Iraq, and what are you *doing* here? It's ridiculous. You people watching, go outside instead. Go hug your children, love your families, do something with your life." Then they cut to a commercial, I got up, took my microphone off, and walked silently back to the green room, itching to get the fuck out of that sixth circle of hell.

Back on air, Clayton Morris pretended he'd thrown me out of the building, saying something like, "I had to get rid of that guy!"

His cohost said, "Well, that proves that we show both sides of the issues here at Fox News." So, in a three-second span, they stated that they accept all viewpoints *and* that they physically throw opposing viewpoints out of the building.

The segment blew up online with about a million and a half hits, and I got interview requests from all these national radio shows. I had no idea people would get so excited about it, but apparently I struck a nerve.

I'm very happy with my decision. Too many people have died for me to just look the other way and tell asinine jokes on their couch. If there's anything else that disgusts me as much as Fox News, given the opportunity, I'll do the same.

Some people criticized me as being rude or disrespectful or lacking class. But in my view, knowing that nearly a million civilians have died in Iraq and reporting only eighty thousand is "lacking class." "Rude" is calling peace activists "anti-American." My view of "vulgar" is knowing that genocide goes on in Darfur but refusing to speak about it on-air because the people funding it are your corporate friends. "Disrespectful" is labeling the first African-American presidential candidate "Muslim," hoping to inspire enough racism to defeat him at the polls.

PAUL PROVENZA: How did it affect you professionally?

LEE CAMP: There are people now interested in me *because* I tore them apart live on TV, but—and I was prepared for it—it also hurt my career in many ways. I do a ton of colleges, and now some of them Google me and think I'm too far Left.

PAUL PROVENZA: There was a time when you'd have been inundated with offers to play to college crowds because you fought "the man."

LEE CAMP: Well, they've got their Student Activities Board, which I was on at my school, and it's five or ten kids who know their advisor's looking over their shoulder and who want to make everyone happy. So rather than get angry letters, they just won't book a comedian who might offend some people.

I definitely try and push their limits, though. Perhaps I don't have the balls to go so far out on a limb that people walk out by the tens and fifteens—I always bring it back to something most or all of us can laugh at—but I definitely have moments where I insult things they probably don't realize they're loving. Like I'll tear apart celebrity culture—and they won't admit it, but they're the ones who love that shit and follow everything Kim Kardashian does. So for at least that moment they're thinking, "Why *do* I give a shit about Kim Kardashian?" That's the nice thing about playing colleges—I feel like I open some kids' minds up. I like mentioning things *I* didn't know *anything* about in college. Like I'm doing something about how kids sit through whitewashed American history in third grade and if they can't sit through it well enough, we pump 'em full of Ritalin. We're fed lies, and then we take tests

on the lies: "Was Christopher Columbus a great man?"

And if you say, "Well . . . He did come and kill millions," they put you in a special class. *I* never saw it *that* way when I was in school.

I talk a lot about how we're getting dumber as a country, about standing up for things, and about having *opinions*. I take on issues like the death penalty that I think just don't get debated enough anywhere. I go after advertising and marketing, the death of media, how people don't get news, they get *entertainment* about what *used* to be news.

Maybe the underlying theme of everything I talk about is just "doubt." You're fed these things; don't just take them for face value, *doubt* them. I don't know that I ever say that specifically in my show, but that's the underlying theme: "Doubt *everything*." If you find it's true, *then* accept it as truth. It probably comes from my anger at not having "doubted" more back in college myself. I'm ashamed to say when I was in college, *I* never showed up to a protest.

PAUL PROVENZA: My theory is that most college students have already bought into the system. From the fifties on, kids have become a demographic and have been indoctrinated as good American consumers from a very young age. They don't want to question or subvert the system because they're already a *part* of it. Long before college, they're already dedicated to succeeding within the system; they're not interested in challenging it.

LEE CAMP: Marketing may have succeeded

in commodifying "cool," so big corporations are now what's cool. You'll wear a Nike swoosh or Abercrombie & Fitch logo—why? It doesn't say anything; it's meaningless. But that age thinks what's *cool* is whatever megacorporation brand name I have on my shirt. So if "cool" is considered "rebellion," and *that's* what's considered cool . . . Well, then there *is* no rebellion.

PAUL PROVENZA: The wars, the economy, the protests against the IMF and corporations . . . are they not politicizing college students again?

LEE CAMP: I don't really see it all that often in college-age kids. I think that's mostly post-college people. At twenty-five and twenty-six, you look back, as I did, and think, "What the hell is this *about*? Is this *really* what it's about?"

PAUL PROVENZA: Do you think you can make a difference?

LEE CAMP: I'd love to make a difference, but it doesn't have to all be onstage; I try in other ways as well, but comedy is one of the few places where you can really speak about things and people really come to sit and *listen*. It's such a rare opportunity we're given, so I don't want to waste it; I want to *use* it for something.

Comedy's great because people can disagree with everything I say but still enjoy themselves. You can't do that everywhere. No one's at a Klan rally, going, "I'm just here for the hoods. I only like the hoods."

PAUL PROVENZA: You do so many different kinds of pointed, issue-oriented comedy on the Internet. It seems as though TV is almost irrelevant in getting your work out there.

LEE CAMP: With some wonderful exceptions, like *The Daily Show* and Colbert, there's a lot of crap on TV that leads people to believe stand-up comedy is not supposed to ever say anything and should be this one, predictable thing. Certain comedy has always been viewed as dangerous by parts of society—like Carlin or Lenny Bruce—and slowly, eventually, it gets narrowed down. I suppose what's allowed on television is one way of narrowing it down to a little window of "acceptable." The Internet allows you to go places you couldn't before. You can take more risks, and people can get to know you without that filter of somebody deciding what's allowed and what's not.

PAUL PROVENZA: Do some people turn off to you as a performer as a result of your strong points of view?

LEE CAMP: When I have trouble with audiences, I think it's because they can't bring themselves to doubt the system they've been sold, even just for an hour to laugh at it. It's sold so deeply, it hurts them to think, "Maybe we *are* being manipulated."

Sometimes it's a matter of having come up with a great idea, but I just haven't made it funny enough yet and there's still work to do. I'm working out this idea about how we create all these ways for rich people to avoid anything bad that everyone else has to deal with: you get through airport security faster if you fly first class, there's now even "pay-to-stay" prisons in California, where if you pay $80 a day you can stay in a nicer prison . . . So I take that idea to the extreme: soon we'll have rich churches and poor churches. Rich people will pray to the *real* God, and poor people will pray to Earl, God's intern, because they don't *deserve* the real God.

It doesn't work very well yet, and it's possible I just haven't made it funny enough yet, but it's *also* possible that the idea puts people off. The idea that America's not *one* society, it's one society for the rich and one for the poor, is not what we want to believe of America.

GREG GIRALDO

STARTING OUT AT New York's Comedy Cellar in the early nineties, Greg Giraldo felt, like many of his generation, that the comedy world had become stale and inauthentic. Giraldo has since made his name as a frequent performer on *Tough Crowd with Colin Quinn,* and on Comedy Central's celebrity roasts, dishing out sharp savagery. Making his aggressive brand of comedy a standout in today's scene, Giraldo has carved out a style mixing raw, raucous laughs with tough, personal truths while still maintaining an everyman identity. After headlining the "Indecision '08 Tour" and appearing regularly on Lewis Black's *Root of All Evil,* he took some time out to deal with the conflict raging within him.

GREG GIRALDO: I want people laughing, not agreeing with me or cheering me on. When I hear someone clap 'cause they agree with a fucking joke, I wanna smash them in the head with a bat. So much of what passes for what everyone calls "political comedy" is just sort of pied-pipering.

My favorite jokes are always jokes that have some real insight into the human condition, in some way more so than about some specific current event, you know? There are things that have an impact that lingers, that stick with you for a while, and a lot of it's self-revelatory or shows a lot of honesty about yourself onstage. Like I used to do a joke—which got turned into this techno/dance song that became a bit of a hit by the guy from Aqua with his side project, Lazyboy—called "Underwear Goes Inside Your Pants." It was about this homeless guy who asked me for money and I was about to give it to him, but I stopped and thought, "But he's just going to use it on drugs or alcohol." And then I realized, "Wait a minute . . . That's what *I'm* gonna use it on!" You know, why should we judge this guy and do that "go and get a job" and all? The guy was wearing his underwear outside his pants, so I'm guessing his résumé ain't all up to date, you know? And that joke plays with the idea of sorta confessing your own weaknesses, but in the context of some broader social statement. And to have said it in the context of my own alcoholism and addiction problems makes it feel like maybe something even more substantial. That feels like a substantial piece of *something* to me.

You know, you can use comedy that highlights a broader, deeper issue that impacts society as a whole in what on the surface is just a funny little ballbag joke or something. And then it's not just "Agree with me," it's "This is me; this is how I perceive the world."

PAUL PROVENZA: That's one of those jokes where half the audience could think you're making fun of homeless people and half think you're making fun of yourself—and themselves, too.

GREG GIRALDO: That's kinda what I'm getting at about not preaching to the choir. But you know how much shit we have to write to get something to work? That's where I think the *lack* of commitment to some point of view hurts. You just have to write what *you* want, because when you're trying to get stuff that's gonna kill, that the crowd is going to love, while still tweaking certain elements of the crowd, you're trying to do a lot of things in very few words. When everyone agrees with your worldview it's a lot easier to do, so it doesn't feel like much of a challenge.

I always hear people say they started stand-up because they saw George Carlin or Richard Pryor, and, "I knew that I had to do what those guys were doing." To me, that is the most extreme arrogance. *I* realized I can *never* do that. But I watched *Evening at the Improv* and I thought I can definitely do *that*. I can definitely be funnier than those shittier comics—and they're on TV! They *must* be making money. I didn't really know what I wanted to do except that I wanted to be on stage. I know I wanna sleep all day, I wanna get laid a lot, and I wanna drink for free. These were the reasons; there was no big fucking "high art" going on at the beginning. I didn't come into it with any lofty ideas, I got into it to fucking have a weird, cool life. That was it.

What I found most appealing about stand-up at the beginning was the musicality of the words and rhythms and the performance. I used to love coming off stage with my neck hurting from talking so aggressively, that feeling of exhaustion after really rocking it. But it wasn't like I had something to say that I thought was so important. Over time, I guess what's happened is, as you know, you get respected by your peers, and you realize that you can do this for *real*. So I've started to care more about the insights of each joke, but I'm also at that crisis point of, like, "Fuck it. What am I afraid of? Why don't I just really commit to a satirical point of view, stop talking about my balls, and start focusing exclusively on headier shit?"

PAUL PROVENZA: Or at least focus on just *one* ball.

GREG GIRALDO: Yeah, on the one with the growth on it that I'm a little concerned about. But I'm told that's normal at my age.

But everyone acts like comedy is this purposeful, conscious, calculated artistic effort—but I'm just throwing shit up; I'm, just, "Go on stage and don't bomb." I'm not purposely doing anything. I guess a *real* artist would, but I'm just going on stage trying to be funny and making people laugh. I *do* appreciate the jokes I write that I think are smart and interesting and clever and satirical, but I don't sit down

and write anything. I write an idea, I go onstage and do it five, six, seven times in a row, and eventually it coalesces and becomes . . . something.

I was actually thinking about all this just yesterday, because I realized that I've *stopped* trying to kill in the way I used to. I used to wanna just pound, pound, pound, and just *crush* all the time, you know? But I've started doing a lot of stuff that doesn't feel like that rolling kind of killing all the time, and I realized that everyone's *listening* for long stretches now. And it's okay, because they're being entertained anyway, and I guess being challenged more in some ways, too, now.

PAUL PROVENZA: Is there a difference?

GREG GIRALDO: That's a fucking great question. God damn.

PAUL PROVENZA: Are you conflicted, being at a place where you can "do this for real," as you put it?

GREG GIRALDO: I feel conflicted about everything. I can barely function day to day. That's part of it.

PAUL PROVENZA: Is this conversation about more than just your comedy right now?

GREG GIRALDO: Yes, that's true for sure. I broke my hand one night at Gotham. I broke, like, four bones in my hand punching something.

I talked about some of my issues on a panel on *Conan* recently, and they were, like, "That was a little dark." I had done *Conan sixteen* times already, but they fucking freaked out. I was, like, "Really? That was dark? Talking about my addictions was dark? What the fuck?"

On *Root of All Evil,* I was on the "Viagra vs. Donald Trump" episode arguing that Viagra is the root of all evil, and I said the real problem is that people are starting to use Viagra with illegal drugs like cocaine and methamphetamine and that increases the use of illegal drugs, because that counteracts cocaine's built-in deterrent: you couldn't get erect. You'd look down and see your horribly shriveled coke dick and think, "Maybe coke's *not* so great." I said that I would end up spending the next four hours telling a stripper how misunderstood I've been as an artist. And I closed with, "I also have other arguments, which are not just painful personal memories."

And the producers freaked: "Are you really going on TV telling people that you couldn't get it up with a stripper?" And I was, like, "Well, if you had done a lot of blow you would understand the point. If you didn't, then it doesn't matter, you might think I'm kidding. It doesn't matter. You tell me." They were, like, "Do you not care that your *wife* hears this??" I go, "I don't know. I guess I care."

I thought that was actually the least of it, to tell you the truth. Let me put it this way: a week ago, my wife's shrink—who met with me just so he could tell her what to say to me—called me psychotic, violent, and suicidal. I'm telling you this on purpose, for dramatic effect, so you can just cut and paste this right into my obituary.

PAUL PROVENZA: Do you feel like you perform a little bit better when you're in turmoil?

GREG GIRALDO: I used to. But then I had a lot of months when I wasn't. When you start breaking your hand on things and smashing your face into things . . .

But you know what? It's a pussified piece-of-shit world nowadays. The reality is artists used to be cut slack for shit, but now you gotta be such a fucking tool. You ever hang out with young bands nowadays? They're all such fucking pussies with their MySpace and their street teams and their fucking merch tables.

To be famous and successful now you need to be a fucking torpedo. You need to know what your market is in today's world. You need to stay consistent. A consistent point of view, consistent voice, message, look, package. It all has to go driving forward like a shark in the water to make you successful, you know? If you have any qualms, soon as you start feeling successful and people start appreciating you on a certain level, if you're the kind of person who goes, "Fuck that, I'm going a different way," you're *fucked* in today's world.

Plus, stand-up comedy is the most extremely subjective art form I've ever seen. You're watching one person walk onstage and that person could remind you of someone that kicked you in the face when you were in third grade, or someone who fucked your girlfriend before you did, and all that affects how you judge that one individual. It's more subjective than anything else I've ever experienced. I've had people who were *exactly* my fucking demographic: my best friends, my brother, other comics I think are brilliant—and they don't like all the same comics I do. There are guys who all my friends think are hilarious that I find intolerable. I don't know why, I just know that's how I feel.

So yeah . . . I'm conflicted. I guess I've always been. But about everything, not just comedy. I was in rock bands in college and wanted to be a musician. Then I went to law school and that didn't work, so I thought fuck it, I'm *gonna* be a rock star, but of course, I couldn't be. So I didn't know what I wanted to do—

PAUL PROVENZA: But you actually practiced law?

GREG GIRALDO: I worked in a big law firm for a year. It was ridiculous. A nightmare. The whole thing was retarded. It takes me—I'm not exaggerating—an hour to leave my house some days because I can't tell which sneakers to put on. I can't even find my wallet, literally. I'm not kidding.

I know this is almost trendy now, but when they first started coming out with that ADHD stuff and they had those checklists, on every single one of them I was off the charts. How are you supposed to function as a lawyer with that? But I was so young, I thought, "Maybe I'll mature into it." I thought I'd *mature* into

wanting to be a lawyer! I don't know *what* I was thinking. My brain is so fucked up, and here I was trying to believe for a minute that I was going to be in charge of someone's serious legal issues? It was such a joke. I had to do all the legal work for this really huge deal to buy a jet for *Rolling Stone* magazine. I didn't file *any* of that shit. There are planes flying around out there completely undocumented; with fucking *nothing*! To this day, there are huge shopping malls and all kinds of shit out there with all the wrong paperwork filed on 'em.

I was clearly not cut out for it. Plus, I always see both sides to everything—and that's maybe what comes up in terms of "political" comedy for me now, too. As soon as I see one side of anything, I try to balance it with another side of it just to hit every angle. With law shit, especially these big corporate cases, both parties are usually fucked-up wrong, so I could never seriously advocate one side knowing full well there were all these other arguments to be had.

But really, quite honestly, most of it was just the practical day-to-day life of getting up, wearing a suit, and working hard, and who wants to do *that* shit?

WILL DURST AND GREG PROOPS

GREG PROOPS IS most recognizable as the scene-stealing improv master from *Whose Line Is It Anyway?* With his retro-hipster look, Proops has cultivated a persona as the sarcastic, nimble-minded know-it-all, dissecting politics and pop culture with uncensored gusto. Will Durst credits Mort Sahl and Will Rogers as inspirations, combining Rogers's penchant for wry observation with Sahl's biting political disenchantment. Having started in comedy during Watergate, Durst represents a generation of comics that had no choice but to be politically minded. Here, they compare and contrast what they've each learned over their respective multiple decades in comedy.

DAMON WAYANS

JOHN OLIVER

EDDIE IZZARD

TENACIOUS D

PAUL DINELLO, AMY SEDARIS, AND STEPHEN COLBERT

DAVE CHAPPELLE

SARAH SILVERMAN

IAN SHOALES

JIMMY TINGLE

MARIA BAMFORD

PAUL F. TOMPKINS

TIM MINCHIN

ANDY ZALTZMAN

GLENN WOOL

JIM JEFFERIES

SHERROD SMALL

PAUL PROVENZA: I don't think anyone can imagine how much hard work is involved in stand-up. I'm not talking about the business of it and all the challenges *that* entails, just the basic act of creating, writing, and performing comedy.

WILL DURST: I do research, I have to construct a script, I have to write everything down, go over it and over it—I'm really a plodder, you know? I work like a craftsman. Proops, here, goes onstage every night with stuff that's in the paper that day and just waxes on it to get the audience laughing.

He has the ability to do that—partly because of the character he's got onstage. His erudite language, the costume he wears . . . it all adds up. They get him, and just follow him.

Really, Proops, I don't even understand *why* they follow you because some of the words you use are so fucking arcane. I'm going to my *Webster's* half the time you're on. But you get Joe Six Pack to connect with you.

What's your favorite word you use in your act that flummoxes them?

PAUL PROVENZA: "Flummox" would probably flummox a few.

When I first moved to Los Angeles from New York, like anyone at that early a stage in their comedy development I fell prey to that obvious "L.A. versus NY" thing onstage. But after way too much hard-core L.A. bashing, I'd give a sucker-punch faux apology: "I'm not saying that people in Los Angeles are vapid. I wouldn't say *that* . . . because no one here knows what 'vapid' *means*."

GREG PROOPS: I used to talk ironically about Dick Cheney's personality: "It just lights up the night sky like the aurora borealis." It got a laugh the first time I did it, and then for the next year in the clubs, nothing. Then suddenly, out of nowhere one night, a *huge* laugh. And these two guys came up after and said, "That's the first time we've ever heard 'aurora borealis' in a joke."

But for a year I was just toiling in the vineyards of the Lord throwing it out there night after night, every night, and *nothing*. I've even done it way up North where they *have* the aurora borealis! They could walk outside after the show and see it *right there*! But, nope. Maybe there was fog that night.

I could've said "northern lights," but it's just not as funny. And I think you have to make the audience work a little. It's like football: You're throwing the pass, and you want the audience to run to get it. Of course, if you're throwing eighty-yard bombs all the time the audience will get tired, so you gotta throw a slant over the middle once in a while, but generally you want the audience to *reach* a little for the joke.

A lot of comics we have to follow sometimes, their comedy is just . . . *SMACK!* It's right there, just handed to the audience. Following them, after the audience has not been asked to make any intellectual leap whatsoever in twenty minutes is just . . . *ugh*. For me, it's awful.

WILL DURST: And you gotta be careful with irony, as anybody who's worked the Midwest can tell you. Or parts of the South where they like their humor: "Hold the hidden agenda, please."

GREG PROOPS: "Smart-ass" is okay, and sarcasm they get, but they're not as effective in some areas.

WILL DURST: But I kinda focus on politics of the day. Proops does *some* of that but he goes more into the social/political stuff. And then he mocks the audience.

GREG PROOPS: I denigrate them for not appreciating my jokes for the full worth of their brilliance. Someone once said, "You tell one joke, then for the next ten minutes tell the audience how stupid they are for not getting it."

When people disagree with me I'll go, "I'm here to make you laugh. And when you laugh at something you disagree with, that's called 'being hip and sophisticated.' As in, 'I disagree *utterly* with your West Coast point of view, but oh how cogent your remark on our vice president's mendacity was! Ha ha ha . . . '"

WILL DURST: *"Mendacity!"* See?

GREG PROOPS: But most crowds go with you if you couch it enough and make it *funny*.

Opening acts sometimes ask, "Do you want me to stay away from any topics?" I'll always say, "No," because someone doing the same topic before you just opens the floor for it; unless they're doing the exact same joke as something you have, it doesn't burn the premise to the ground. So I go, "Do anything you want—just *don't* do racist stuff." That's the hardest thing to follow.

Material *about* racism? Right on. But when it's, "The thing about Asians . . ." or "I don't like Arabs . . ." or whatever, the crowd goes to a weird place. The ability to even go for the joke is so removed then, because "knee-jerk" has come into play. "Knee-jerk" is the *worst* comedy reaction.

WILL DURST: Comics who do that identify themselves. That ugly little monster has come out through their mouth, and they can't pull it back. Then when you go up there and try to come from a place of, "Can't we all get along?" there's this real thing of, "No, actually, we *can't*," because that monster's been unleashed in the room.

There's so much we always have to consider and deal with in comedy. But it becomes such a mosaic of craft and technique and skill. We've all learned so many tricks over the years. And you *do* get better because you've learned so many tricks. You've learned the difference that one syllable can mean in a joke by taking it out or putting it in. You've learned how to deal with hecklers—whether to bring them *into* the act or if you need to ignore them and how to balance it . . . With enough years, you know so much about yourself and audience dynamics and all that.

You learn so much that you're able to put more and more depth and texture and different brushstrokes into the work.

And for me, after so many years I can now cannibalize my own act from, like, 1985. I can steal from myself, which is endless, because I don't get pissed off at me for it.

GREG PROOPS: There's nothing wrong with doing variations on a theme of your own, *working* a theme in a different way. I saw Ornette Coleman play recently—and if *he's* not allowed to do riffs he came up with forty years ago, then who is? That's what art is, you know? That's what *craft* is.

PAUL PROVENZA: Monet did over thirty distinct paintings of the Rouen Cathedral, all from the exact same viewpoint.

GREG PROOPS: Exactly. And Durst's stuff has so many levels to it anyway at this point. He had this off-the-hook-*hilarious* bit during the Bush years that was the most baroque, literate, colorful, labyrinthian . . . What was it, like, *two hundred* adjectives in a row?

WILL DURST: That was just a trick, really. It's that same thing you see some comics do at the end of their set that always makes us go, "Jesus Christ, what a cheap trick *that* is." You know, they'll do a rap or something just calculated to get *huge* applause at the end and we always *hate* following it. It's like following a guy on a unicycle juggling kittens on fire—which I actually had to do once.

The bit he's talking about is really just that same kind of "drum solo" thing—but it *is* truly *me*, though. It starts like an off-hand summation of my feelings about the whole Bush administration: "I *hate* these lyin', theivin', holier-than-thou . . ." and it goes on for 237 different adjectives like that. It's *really* fun to do, and it's a bit of an acting exercise, too.

GREG PROOPS: The audience is exhilarated at the end of it.

WILL DURST: But it's such a cheap trick. It's just an audience *"Wow!"*

GREG PROOPS: It is *not*! It's taking a point to a ridiculous, extreme level. It's satire!

WILL DURST: No, it's not satire. It's *pointillism* if it's anything. Just a big bunch of words that from a distance all add up to one big, obvious thing.

PAUL PROVENZA: What *isn't*?

GREG PROOPS: He likes to denigrate himself. He thinks it makes him more "populist."

PAUL PROVENZA: I've seen you do the bit, and executing it is a real feat. And at least *you* can say, "No kittens were harmed during the making of this joke."

WILL DURST: He only juggled *phony* kittens on fire. But that doesn't make any difference when you're following it.

GREG PROOPS: Interviewers always ask, "Are you nervous before you go on?" I always say, "No, and not because I think I'm so great—which I do—but because if we're nervous or shaky in any way, that'd be the worst comedy you'd ever see." The key element for any comedian is absolute *confidence* on stage. That's what enables you to handle whatever happens in the room, and the crowd won't freak out on you.

PAUL PROVENZA: They freak out when they think the ship has no captain.

GREG PROOPS: Right. So you can tell a joke that maybe only ten percent of the crowd gets because you've got the confidence that you can come right back after that. You *know* you've got a forehand and a strong backhand or whatever it may take.

WILL DURST: As you get longer into the business you also trust that voice you've come up with when writing your material more. I did *some* political stuff when I started, but it wasn't the bulk of my act. I had to learn the language of stand-up first and find a voice before I could write political jokes that fit me. Now if I write a joke that doesn't fit what I believe or isn't clearly in what I feel is *my* voice, I can't get behind it. I have to believe a joke is really me.

Lately there's more gray area coming into my act, though. A bit more middle-of-the-road stuff. I don't know if it's that I'm getting older, or if it's having a mortgage or what.

GREG PROOPS: How do you mean that?

WILL DURST: Well, part of my one-man show, *The All-American Sport of Bipartisan Bashing*, was me saying that I'm actually a moderate. I'm in the center—but the center's been kicked so far to the right that by just staying in the same place I'm suddenly a commie, pinko, yellow, red bastard. How the fuck did *that* happen? So I'm talking more about how twenty percent of America is far Left, twenty percent's far Right, and you never hear about the sixty percent of us in the middle.

It kinda feels more like my *real* voice now—good timing, right? I keep narrowing it down; becoming more centered.

Have you watched tapes of yourself from twenty years ago? Christ, what the fuck was I so angry about?

GREG PROOPS: That was *passion!* Look at Carlin. He got more and more vicious and morbid and dark . . . and it was so *exciting!*

He didn't care about the abyss at all anymore. He was just, "I hate God. I hate bullshit. I hate obfuscation . . ." When I saw him last, he *opened* with, "Fuck you!" Standing ova-

tion. Then he went, "I just thought I'd make you feel comfortable."

I hate seduction onstage. I do it, we *all* do it—but I loved his brand of *non*-seduction. Right up front: "Fuck *you!*"

I'd watch him on Maher or Colbert and he'd almost become like Pinter or Beckett. He was boiling things down to, like, *two sentences.* So sharp, so well thought out, so well written. It's startling how sometimes just a sentence can be so rich.

But Carlin sat down and wrote and rewrote, and crafted it, then memorized it and reworked it . . . That's how Durst works. I never work that way. I write an idea and then bang it around on stage.

WILL DURST: That's more exciting, though, because you never know *exactly* how it's going to come out. I *love* the comics who don't give a shit what the audience thinks.

GREG PROOPS: Well, you chose to be a political comic.

WILL DURST: Not a greased chute to the big time, is it?

GREG PROOPS: It was *not* a "Hey, everybody! *Like* me!" choice.

WILL DURST: Well, I was forged in the crucible of the Vietnam War era. I remember being in school and *everything* was about the war. Fucking math class would be like, "We've got six bombs. If we drop three . . ." The war was *everywhere.*

I started in '74 when Nixon, Watergate, Vietnam . . . it was all coming to a head. You couldn't *not* be political. And I had all *that* going into comedy.

If you think about it, there was almost no political comedy between Kennedy's assassination pretty much up until '73, '74 during Nixon. Look at all the comedy breaking through in that ten-year period: It was people like Cheech and Chong, Steve Martin . . . No political comedy to speak of, really.

GREG PROOPS: Political comedy's included in the discourse much more now. Maher, Stewart, and Colbert have important people on their shows—prime ministers, senators, people active in the system. When you do that, you become part of the discourse as opposed to being on the outside throwing darts at it. When people refuse to go on Colbert's show, that's a talking point; people talk about the fact that you won't go on.

WILL DURST: And that hasn't blunted their arrows at all. Mark Russell, on the other hand, is a Washington insider and his barbs always have that little rubber tip on the end.

GREG PROOPS: It's a little bit "lunch-y." He's too cozy with them: "We had lunch together yesterday, so I'm not really going to go after you."

PAUL PROVENZA: I don't think Mark Russell really does satire or political comedy—it's more "political cabaret."

WILL DURST: As do the Capitol Steps.

GREG PROOPS: But a satirist's business, according to Swift or Voltaire or whomever, is not to be a clown for your party, and you're supposed to take everybody out, right?

WILL DURST: You're the leech, bloodletting *all* the poison out of society.

GREG PROOPS: But I say if I'm doing too much on one side, tough shit; *that's* my point of view. I did a political panel once with Garry Trudeau, and when that came up, he said, "We have *no* responsibility to show both sides."

But I do also go after that whole NPR mindset of cozy, wine-drinking white people.

PAUL PROVENZA: "Limousine liberals"?

GREG PROOPS: I *have* to take *them* out just as much—but I don't think you have any *responsibility* to show both sides of anything. Others do. Journalism *should*, sort of.

WILL DURST: We're supposed to "afflict the comfortable and comfort the afflicted," right? I actually believe that has to be done—but you can't change anybody's mind in a comedy club. The Right-wing, Bush-supporting Ben Stein once even said to me, "Keep making Bush jokes because every time you do, it just humanizes him."

Your first responsibility is always to get the laugh—but if you can make a statement *with* the laugh, then you're doing something that at least *approaches* art.

And what we *can* do is plant seeds of doubt in the mortar of people's apathy or inattention to things. Little seeds that may grow and crack that mortar someday.

That's really the most we can aspire to.

ANDY BOROWITZ

AFTER FACING AN existential crisis in the repetitive, soul-numbing world of television sitcom writing, Andy Borowitz took advantage of that newfangled Internet to launch his own satirical news site, The Borowitz Report. He's since become a regular source of biting Left-wing (mostly) humor and commentary. We discuss satire's relationship to the truth, how it's sometimes indistinguishable, and how sometimes it may not be "true" at all.

ANDY BOROWITZ: The pretentious analogy I use is the solar eclipse: if you look directly into a solar eclipse, it'll burn your retina or cornea—or some part of your eye I didn't learn about in science class. But if you look at it through a pinhole, suddenly you can see this amazing phenomenon without getting hurt.

If you said, "Hey guess what, America? This country that you love tortures people, eavesdrops on you illegally, we're destroying the environment, our bridges are falling down, our banking system's collapsing . . ." you want to put a gun in your mouth after that litany. However, you can watch *The Daily Show,* or read my site, or *The Onion,* and you're really going to hear all those same tough realities, except you're *laughing.*

So you can either burn your eyes out, or you can observe a fantastic phenomenon—in this case, the truth—from a safe perspective. That's what satire does: it points you toward the truth in an oblique way, rather than making you want to throw yourself out a window.

PAUL PROVENZA: How'd you go from writing mainstream sitcoms to being a political commentator, quoted on op-ed pages and taken seriously as a pundit?

ANDY BOROWITZ: I don't know if I'm being taken seriously; that would probably be a bad thing in this line of work. But I got burned out producing and writing sitcoms for about fifteen years. It was very repetitious—which is the *goal* of sitcoms, but maybe that's more fun for the viewer than for the writer. So I moved to New York and didn't do anything but read and be a bum for a couple years, sort of like what people do in Los Angeles except *they* say they're writing a screenplay. I was *admitting* being a bum.

I was a latecomer to it, but around 'ninety-seven, I discovered the Internet. I realized you could do things like cut and paste Associated Press stories but change one word and make it absurd. It took me back to my college years on the *Harvard Lampoon,* where the most fun of everything we did were these dead-on parodies of the *Harvard Crimson,* the "legitimate" campus newspaper. On a day they weren't publishing, we'd publish a really absurd look-alike edition—with real mature stuff, like "Motherfucker Crimson Publishes Dirtiest Headline Ever."

For comedians or satirists there's something irresistible about making up news. In an early newspaper job, Mark Twain used to slug in fake headlines. It's a great target; it's a repository of people who take themselves very seriously—not only people *in* the news but newspapers themselves.

So I started cutting and pasting articles and sending them to friends, until someone said, "Instead of sending out articles, just have your own Web site." So I started The Borowitz Report. It was just a step-saving, lazy-man move on my part; I didn't predict that anyone besides my thirty or forty friends would be interested in it—but I now have about half a million daily subscribers.

It's free, because I believe if you can't charge for Mapquest, the most useful thing in the world, you *really* can't charge for a satirical news site, but satire's big business now. There've been waves in the past where satire exploded, like the early seventies Nixon years—times not dissimilar from the times we're in now, actually, with even some of the same characters: Donald Rumsfeld is one colossus that strides both eras; Dick Cheney's another. The Nixon era gave birth to *National Lampoon,* which came out of *Harvard Lampoon,* and from that came *Saturday Night Live,* and satire became big business.

Around the late nineties, Jon Stewart took over the *The Daily Show,* and his presence and the topical, political focus he brought to it took it through the roof. That spawned Lewis Black, who'd been around but really broke through there, and to Stephen Colbert and *The Colbert Report.*

The Onion cooked along in Madison, Wisconsin, with nothing happening for years besides making some people in Madison laugh, but they went online and suddenly were getting fan mail from around the world. That spawned their books, The Onion Radio News—and now *The Onion*'s become a "brand."

So the Bush years have been as kind to satire as the Nixon years were. It gave us what the Pentagon calls a "target-rich environment."

PAUL PROVENZA: So much news satire often ends up actually having been *prescient.*

ANDY BOROWITZ: I say it's not that we're doing *fake* news, we're just *early.* Sometimes it's shocking when that happens. But one reason the craziest fake headlines actually come to pass is because for any satire to work you have to write true to character—much like writing a sitcom: for nine years of *Seinfeld,*

Kramer always sounded like Kramer, Jerry sounded like Jerry, et cetera. The same's true writing satire with "characters" in the news—if you're true to character, odds are that some things you write will come true.

People say, "That's really funny, but there's *an element of truth to this.*"

Well, no shit. Maybe that's why you thought it was funny.

The truth can be hilarious. The funniest fake news story may be a press conference where somebody just says exactly what's on their mind instead of couching anything.

PAUL PROVENZA: *The Borowitz Report, The Onion, The Daily Show,* and *The Colbert Report* are also about the way we *get* our news as much as about news itself.

ANDY BOROWITZ: Along with the president, Congress, and all the traditional targets of authority, media have risen to the level of an appropriate target this time around. Slipshod, opinionated reporting, bias—especially on cable news—have become worthy of ridicule, sometimes more so than the news they report.

But we also have to be careful. *Saturday Night Live* did some very funny things during the 2008 election, but they also injected themselves into it in a partisan and not terribly funny way by basically just saying, "We like Hillary Clinton." You have to hand in your satire membership card when you do that.

People get accustomed to me taking whacks at Republicans, then, when I go after something stupid Democrats do, Democratic readers come out of the woodwork saying I've been a "traitor to the cause." I don't know why they ever assumed I signed onto "the cause"; my only agenda is to express *my* view of things. I'm not an expert, so that's all I've got. I'll make fun of either side that's being ridiculous enough that I see comedy in it.

PAUL PROVENZA: Do you think we make any difference?

ANDY BOROWITZ: It's that cliché of turning around a supertanker: it's such a huge undertaking, it takes forever. This is a big country with some awfully powerful people in charge of it. I'd like to think we bloggers *can* undermine the system, but it's going to take a lot more blogs to do it.

But having said that, you never know where revolutions are going to start from, you know? It was dockworkers in Poland who ultimately led to the total collapse of the Soviet Union. Maybe a really good joke on *The Colbert Report* will start some kind of a cascade, and we'll be able to trace it all back to one great punch line. But when I, or Jon Stewart and his writers, or anyone else sits down to do what we do, if we have any agenda or sense of self-importance, we're *fucked*. Because the only time anything really good happens is when you're not thinking about it too much. It's the people who always swing for the fences that usually wind up hitting foul balls. So, we'll just try, and see what will be.

It's gratifying to get e-mails like, "I'm Right-wing and vote Republican every election, *but I still think you're funny*." You can actually communicate to people on the other side of the aisle, if they're laughing, but they'll

tune out to preaching. It wasn't surprising when Obama said he never heard any of those things Reverend Wright said in church; he was probably asleep half the time. If you can make people laugh, you've gotten them in a visceral way. Even if they don't realize *why*, you've hit the bull's-eye.

I've said common-sense things about the war on terror that even Republicans find funny. Like how a "war on terror" is highly ambitious—we've declared war on a human emotion. If this works out, will we go after shyness? Maybe a "War on Malaise"?

PAUL PROVENZA: Is it enough to have someone laugh? Shouldn't we want to change their mind?

ANDY BOROWITZ: You're never going to reach some people. Dick Cheney was never going to pick up *The Onion* and think, "My God, I'm a horrible human being." But when our government comes up with a really bad idea—which it's been so great at, I think they have a Department of Bad Ideas—*sometimes* the cumulative effect of ridicule makes it hard to continue with certain things.

Katrina was an example where we certainly couldn't *do* anything about it, but we *could* point out horrible mistakes being made. Like how the people we needed to help us were all in Iraq—we *have* a National Guard, but they were *busy*. *The Onion* did a great piece where the National Guard gave residents of New Orleans emergency information over the phone from Baghdad. That *needed* pointing out.

That's all satirists can really do to help. We should be the annoying people who always point out how other people are screwing up. We're *not* part of the solution; that's not part of our job description. We don't *pretend* that we can fix things, but we *can* point out and explain how other people are fucking up. We do *that* better than anybody.

PAUL PROVENZA: Characterizing the Katrina shambles as mismanagement or incompetence may be part of the bigger problem: what if the shameful response in New Orleans and Mississippi is exactly how some powerful people wanted it to play out? Racial concentrations are permanently altered; gerrymandering and redistricting taking place as a result. As the brilliant comedian Matt Kirshen put it, "They should rename it like a laundry detergent: 'New *Improved* Orleans Ultra . . . Now whiter than ever!'"

A hugely profitable corporate agenda's fallen perfectly into place, with massive land grabs and private entities profiting from it in lieu of government addressing it in any meaningful way. What if, opportunistically, it went *exactly* according to a bigger-picture plan?

Now this is not some nut conspiracy theory, of which I am always skeptical. The commissions and agencies officially charged with rebuilding are all comprised of real estate moguls, hoteliers, multinational developers, construction companies . . . It's a variant of the military-industrial complex: the "tragedy-condominium-resort complex."

ANDY BOROWITZ: Yeah, the "Army Corps of Realtors" came to the rescue.

PAUL PROVENZA: Well, by satirizing the response to Katrina as some failure or mis-

management, aren't we just reinforcing the narrative the media *prefer* us to have, rather than seeking *other* possible narratives? Aren't we just giving further traction to that obvious narrative? If so, then we're part of the *distraction* from meaningful analysis and criticism.

ANDY BOROWITZ: In other words, we're unwittingly serving "the man" by making fun of the narrative they *want* us to make fun of, so we're just hapless tools in some bigger picture?

PAUL PROVENZA: I wonder.

ANDY BOROWITZ: Hmm . . . Well . . . I just want to kill myself now. Thanks.

PAUL PROVENZA: Welcome to my existential nightmare.

ANDY BOROWITZ: You know what? I don't totally buy that.

Both can be true. People say Bush couldn't be both an evil genius *and* an idiot—but I think you can have an evil agenda *and* still be incompetent. There've been some obvious nefarious agendas, but there's also no denying that it's been a pretty incompetent group of people running the show. Even if you had the most sinister objectives for Iraq, which I'm sure a lot of people did—blood for oil, enriching Halliburton, whatever—you still wouldn't have constructed the war they did. If you want to steal their oil, you don't want to get into the situation where insurgents are blowing up pipelines every two days.

PAUL PROVENZA: But huge corporations are paid handsomely to protect and rebuild those pipelines. The more "insurgency" the more private security and reconstruction firms hired, the longer Blackwater's contracts, the more KBR feeds and services them, the more no-bid, cost-plus, no-oversight contracts are handed out.

ANDY BOROWITZ: That's certainly true, too. Even chaos does work *for* them up to a point . . . Boy, you have an answer for everything, don't you?

PAUL PROVENZA: Sadly, no. Just questions and some jokes.

ANDY BOROWITZ: The problem is that you reach a point, especially with Iraq, where it gets *so* dark that even *my* audience, which has a taste for that sort of thing, doesn't want to hear it anymore. There's a tipping point where the sad truth overwhelms how funny it can be.

There've been moments in my life where I've felt democracy has broken down and I feel we *are* powerless. The Supreme Court decision during the 2000 election was truly dispiriting. Another moment, weirdly enough, was the O. J. Simpson verdict: a jury was told, "Ignore the facts, nullify everything, vote *this* way." That was another case where something we—or some of us—believed in, the justice system, seemed to break down. I'm a little bit less sanguine about it now.

PAUL PROVENZA: You're also white and privileged.

ANDY BOROWITZ: So the system *generally* works for people like me, true. But Iraq is another instance; everyone knew Bush wanted to invade Iraq and it seemed no one could do anything to stop it. Most of us knew it was a terrible idea and it felt like a runaway train. I suppose a lot of Americans put up with Iraq, thinking, "Oh, well. Let's just hope this works out." But the last straw, and another sign that perhaps we *are* powerless, was Katrina.

Domestically, there are things we always took for granted our government is capable of doing. You get the feeling that even Nixon—a crook, a lunatic, and who knows what else— would've at least gotten enough sandbags to New Orleans. There's a sense now of total incompetence on the part of the government, and that it's not really serving *us,* the people.

This is not a Republican/Democrat thing at all, but it does seem like large corporations are in the driver's seat, dictating a lot of what our government does. *And* they control the media.

PAUL PROVENZA: Remember the good old days when it was just the Jews controlling the media?

ANDY BOROWITZ: Yeah, can we go back to that?

TODD HANSON

FROM HUMBLE ORIGINS as a weekly free student paper in Madison, Wisconsin, *The Onion* has ridden the rise of the Internet to become one of the nation's preeminent satirical voices. For evidence, look no further than its lauded 9/11 issue, which was perhaps the first and still most incisive use of humor to understand the massive psychological blow of those attacks. Todd Hanson has been a writer for the paper since its earliest days, penning many of its most memorable stories. Here, he discusses how *The Onion*'s humor helped us cope after 9/11, and how humor helps him survive and make it—barely—from day to day.

TODD HANSON: I'm no businessman, and I'm certainly no expert in these matters, but I can tell you this for a fact: the only reason that *The Onion* is successful is because it is a voice that is outside of all those normal restrictions that apply to other comedy outlets. That is the reason it's different, and if it ever stopped being different, that would be a terrible mistake, because that is called killing the golden goose. The point is, if you want more eggs, you don't want to serve that goose for dinner. Then again, what do I care? I'm not making any money off it anyway.

But as far as satire in general, I'm not an expert. I don't even know the precise literary definition of the word, but here's what it means to me: it's not just that you ridicule things that are deserving of ridicule. It's broader than that.

I respond to the late work of Mark Twain, because he would be satirical and dark in his comedy. Early on, he would ridicule a specific institution or a specific action of the U.S military or a specific thing about religion, but eventually, in his later years, he was ridiculing the entirety of the human condition. The same thing happened with Jonathan Swift's four books of *Gulliver's Travels*. He started out with a narrower scope of what he was satirizing, specific local things about current and recent political history in England, then he expanded more to talk about intellectuals in general, but by the time he got to the part at the end about the Houyhnhnms, which literary people always talk about as "Oh, he went too far! At that point, it was just mis-

anthropy. It's the least effective part of his book." Well, that's my favorite part of the book, because in that part he's just ridiculing *everything* about humanity. The way I look at it, that's sort of the thesis behind satire in general, which is this: the human condition is inherently flawed, to the point that it is deserving of ridicule. No matter what you're talking about, if it involves the human condition, there's something in there that deserves to be ridiculed.

Some people would call that fatalistic, nihilistic, horribly negative, and maybe it is. I don't know, but there's got to be some sort of idealism behind that, saying, "Well, things should be better than they are, or you wouldn't be criticizing it." I'm a sad, miserable person. Like, it's kind of a miracle that I'm not crying right now. If there weren't some way of finding an outlet for these terribly bleak thoughts about the nature of this earth and our place in it, I don't know what I would do. For me, it's a survival mechanism.

There is a letter from Jonathan Swift's *Letters to Alexander Pope* from 1725, and he says, "The chief end I propose to myself of all my labors is to vex the world rather than divert it." In other words, rather than to entertain people with comedy, I'd rather point out things that make me angry, and in so doing, make them angry. That's kind of the idea of satire: to vex the world.

PAUL PROVENZA: Simply to vex it, not to improve it?

TODD HANSON: I don't think *The Onion*'s going to change the world. I don't think it's going to have any positive social effect on anybody.

PAUL PROVENZA: None?

TODD HANSON: I don't know, maybe it does. I remember one of the coolest things that ever happened to me was I got to meet one of my comedy heroes. It was Jim Abrams, one of the three guys who had written and directed *Airplane!* I met him at the Aspen Comedy Festival. He waved, came over, sat next to me for a little bit, and said, "I wanted to thank you guys."

He'd had a terrible battle with cancer—was, in fact, dying of cancer—but he had come through it. But he said while he was in the hospital dying of cancer, someone brought in *The Onion,* and it had the story about "Area Man Dies Following Long Cowardly Battle with Cancer." Every story like that is always "His Long *Brave* Battle with Cancer," so we had switched it to his "cowardly" battle with cancer, and it was all about how he showed no dignity whatsoever during the process of dying and he begged God to take his relatives and loved ones instead of him, like, "Why couldn't my wife have gotten it instead of me?"

Abrams said that that story made him laugh for the first time in weeks, that he loved it and that it gave him the courage to go on. He was saying all these things that are just blowing my mind. So that was very powerful. And, thing is, that is exactly the kind of story we would run and we'd get lots and lots of e-mails from people, saying, "This is inappropriate. This is not something to make light of. You cannot make light of this."

PAUL PROVENZA: Like the 9/11 issue?

TODD HANSON: Yeah, every single thing in there was all about 9/11; we never expected it to be that way, it just came out as we were trying to think about what we were going to do.

First thing we did after the Twin Towers fell was go dark for a week, because we live in New York and were flipping out. Then, when we started talking, we were, like, "I guess we should definitely not do anything about current events."

Everyone agreed. So we started to try and brainstorm other stuff, and the more we tried the more we realized, "Well, we've got to say *something* about it, because it's ridiculous to publish anything that says nothing about it." So, we thought we'd do one appropriate reference to it and then everything else will be something light and inoffensive. Then we thought, "Well, you can't put anything else *next* to that piece," so just in the process of deciding what to do, we ended up arriving at this decision to do the entire issue about what had happened.

If you read it, it's not making light of anything and it's not even funny ha-ha. There's humor that comes from rage. There's humor that comes from sadness, and there's a lot of cry-cry-type punch lines, as opposed to ha-ha punch lines. It was a rage-based outlet, and a lot of people responded to that.

I wrote a story on the front page: "Real Life Turns into Bad Jerry Bruckheimer Film," and it was just about the weird sense of unreality that everyone was feeling at that time, and also the fact that it was a scenario straight out of a really over-the-top action thriller, but there was nothing entertaining about it in real life. The main story I always get comments on wasn't on the front page, it was in the inside story, but people still talk about it to me. It was "God Angrily Re-clarifies Don't Kill Rule." I was feeling maudlin, and I was crying when I wrote it, so it wasn't, like, "Hey! We're gonna be wacky about the World Trade Center!"— you know? It was a genuinely heartbroken voice and we had no idea how people would react.

This was published before almost all the comedy came back. But, when we walked into the office the day it came out, there was a big letter in the fax machine, in really huge font, just saying "NOT FUNNY NOT FUNNY NOT FUNNY" over and over again. But during the course of the day, more and more e-mails piled in. There were hundreds and hundreds of them, and then there were thousands of them, and 90 percent of them were saying things like, "God bless you, thank you."

PAUL PROVENZA: Were you unified in your mind-set there, or were there stories submitted where you had to go, "No."

TODD HANSON: Tim Harrod, who was a guy who worked here for a long time, had a brilliant joke; it was a great joke, but we didn't run it because we decided the target was wrong. It was "America Stronger than Ever, Say Quadragon Officials," and it would have been very irreverent and funny, but we just felt it was the wrong target because the target was the fucking dead people at the Pentagon,

and we just didn't think that was right, so we ran something else.

Whenever anyone talks to us about *The Onion,* they always say, "Where do you draw the line?" It's like a form letter we get every week: "I have enjoyed your publication for many years, but the last thing you did about [insert specific subject] went over the line. My son or my grandmother or my child or my husband had [insert specific subject] and it is not funny."

So, we did a joke specifically about that. It was called "That's Not Funny; My Brother Died That Way." And there's this scene in *Police Academy* where the blustering authority-figure cop is driving a motorcycle and his motorcycle comes to a sudden stop and he flies forward into the back of a police horse and his head goes up the horse's asshole. So, we picked this incident and then had the author describe it in a totally straight voice about how that happened to his brother, and his brother died from having his head up a horse's ass and that *Police Academy* went way over the line and should not have included that scene because it is inappropriate. So, it really just comes down to your subjective experience.

PAUL PROVENZA: Well, that's fair. People always talk about "crossing the line," and I would say it's not a line. It's a point. If you get the point, you don't have to talk about lines.

TODD HANSON: Is the point you're making legitimate, or what? If it's illegitimate, then you have every right to be offended.

I don't think there's any subject that you can't do, but it just depends on the angle. So, anyway, point being, with 9/11 we were thinking really carefully about what the target was, but the 9/11 issue isn't really a good example if you want to talk about hard-edged satire, because it was almost very sentimental.

PAUL PROVENZA: Most of the comedy and satire I really like is unsentimental. To me, it comes down to the Mickey Mouse/Bugs Bunny dichotomy. Bugs Bunny was always funny and completely unsentimental, and whenever it did get sentimental, it was always just the set up for a punch line. Mickey Mouse and Disney were always sentimental.

TODD HANSON: Why does everyone act like Mickey Mouse is the icon of American humor or something? Mickey Mouse is lame. There's nothing really cool about Mickey Mouse. The only cool thing I can think about Mickey Mouse is the Mickey Mouse sequence in *Fantasia,* and the only reason that is awesome is because it is *fucking terrifying.* But Bugs Bunny, on the other hand, *always* ruled every time; Bugs Bunny is just the shit, man—he is the coolest.

PAUL PROVENZA: Mickey Mouse is just bland. You can't even define his character. Bugs Bunny is anarchy, chaos, and satire. Bugs Bunny is the antihero. He's the archetype of Arlecchino in Commedia del Arte; Scapin in Molière. He is the wise fool, the person who's

not supposed to be the one who knows everything, but for whom it's so clear that everything's absurd, and it's that awareness that allows him to always succeed. There's real character there.

TODD HANSON: It also gives an example of what we were talking about: the target. Because Bugs Bunny is the prey of the hunter, he's not the guy with the gun—he's the guy *without* the gun.

I don't know that much about the ancient Greek rules of theater, but I read something recently that really surprised me. It touches on what you said about the sentimental and unsentimental. It said that tragedy was the genre that was associated with emotion and comedy was associated with rationality. I always thought it would be the other way around. You would think having a strictly realistic view of life would be tragic, and having a more emotional, positive way of thinking would involve laughing. But that's not the way it was. Comedy comes from just looking at things rationally without sentimentality. It was counterintuitive, but then I was, like, "Okay, yeah." It's tragedy that's the emotional drama, making a big grandiose thing about it. And, looking at it that way, tragedy is actually less deep than comedy, and less true.

BOB ODENKIRK

BEST KNOWN AS half of HBO's *Mr. Show*, Bob Odenkirk is a big thinker when it comes to comedy. After getting his feet wet with improv and sketch comedy in Chicago—where he wrote Chris Farley's legendary "Motivational Speaker" sketch—Odenkirk went on to become a writer for *Saturday Night Live*, *Late Night*, *The Ben Stiller Show*, and countless other groundbreaking shows, including *Mr. Show*, the one in which he was taller than his partner, David Cross. Today, Odenkirk is producing and directing a wide range of television series and feature films, and he's taken time to sit with the author for one of his favorite pastimes: dissecting the minutiae and art and craft of comedy.

BOB ODENKIRK: I think about comedy all the time, all my life, for years. I watch it and think about it. I think about what's good and what people are doing and why. I can't help it; it's just what we do. I'm not really passionate about too much else.

PAUL PROVENZA: I think that's true for a lot of people in comedy—that it feels more like a "calling" than a job or a living. And I am always amazed, and sometimes impressed, by comedians who don't think about it as much as you and I seem to.

BOB ODENKIRK: There are some very smart guys in comedy who won't talk about it. There's an element of it being almost like a magician thing: "You don't tell people the trick." So they don't break down comedy. And then there's also an element of maybe thinking it's pompous and an element of "If you don't know, it doesn't matter how much you're told; you'll never really get it, so what's the point of talking about it?"

Me, I like to talk about comedy. I talk about it *too* much.

PAUL PROVENZA: So how did you start?

BOB ODENKIRK: I started doing sketch comedy because I always loved Monty Python. That's my biggest influence by far. I wrote sketches in junior high. I even wrote sketches for class. We'd get an assignment to write something about a foreign country or an event in history or something, and instead of a paper, I'd write a sketch about it and perform it in class. So I wrote first, and then I gravitated to doing improv. Obviously, improv is mostly really about sketch comedy. I grew up just outside of Chicago, so Second City was naturally the place I heard about. I went to Second City and was ecstatic about it, so I got into improv through that.

I think improv is really fun, but it's really just a bit of a parlor trick. Now, Del Close is a guy who influenced me in a huge way in my life choice to write comedy and to be in entertainment, but I completely disagree with him—respectfully—about improvisation being an art form or being a form of real entertainment. It's just a parlor trick that you can get really good at if you do it all the time. I've seen groups who are fucking *unbelievable*—who can do a forty-five-minute show, and then another one and another one after that, and they're great shows and they make sense and tie together, and they live on another plane of consciousness—but those are people who do it all the time. The only way you get that good is by just doing it so much, and *they* can only do it that much for like a year and a half.

PAUL PROVENZA: That's interesting you feel that way. With some groups it sure seems like a lot more than a parlor game; it really feels like pure verbal jazz. Isn't there something to be said for the tightrope-walking aspect of it?

BOB ODENKIRK: But the tightrope aspect is not good. It causes a lot of artificial reaction. Most everybody who is getting a laugh through improvisation is getting it because the tightrope is what's generating it. It's the fact that we're all in this room and we know you just got that suggestion and we know it's hard and we know you don't know where you're going and you're kicking up these little twists and turns and these funny little moments. Ultimately, that's all it will ever be. It's fun, but it's a little artificial in that the funny is bumped way up by that circumstance.

PAUL PROVENZA: I see where you're coming from. Most improv groups end up spinning off sketch shows based on things that come out of improv, so really their improv is just kind of writing in public.

BOB ODENKIRK: That's exactly what it is. When you sit at a desk and try to write something, you make shit up, come up with a scenario, make some more up, sometimes talk out loud and try out a line—you're improvising. And then you clear out all the crap, find the point, and go further.

PAUL PROVENZA: I once heard you define the difference between satire and parody. Can you do that in a nutshell?

BOB ODENKIRK: Well, look, this is all made up in my own mind. I didn't go to school for it, and I'm sure there is a clear definition of both satire and parody, but "satire" makes a point. It exaggerates to make a point or to illuminate something. And "parody" merely exaggerates—usually just a form—and it doesn't really have anything to say about it except to point to the building blocks of whatever form that is.

Generally, parody is considered kind of lesser, because it's easier to exaggerate and just leave it at that. *Mad* magazine exaggerates whatever it's making fun of that month. It just takes the formal aspects of something and blows it up. It doesn't have anything to

say about it. Parody is easy and satire is hard, that's the difference.

PAUL PROVENZA: Which do you consider most of your work?

BOB ODENKIRK: Satire, for sure. I don't care about parody. I've only participated in parody—I make it sound like an orgy, but I've only participated in a few parodies. I usually decline the invitation. I think on *The Ben Stiller Show* we did a lot of parody. I helped with a few of them that I liked, like the *Husbands and Wives* parody, which kind of had another level to it.

But I don't think much of parody, I really don't. It's easy to do. You know, if *Mad* magazine ever is satirical, it is in a very thin, obvious way: "We talk like *this,* with *these* catch phrases and in *this* tone of voice because *you* will buy anything if it sounds like it's coming from a *reporter.*" That's your point right there, and it's being stated right in the parody. It's not a very nuanced point, and there isn't anything more to it than that. And I am not putting down *Mad* magazine here at all, by the way. When I was between the ages of nine to about thirteen or fourteen, I would ride my bike to the store every month and buy it and read it cover to cover.

PAUL PROVENZA: We all did.

BOB ODENKIRK: Absolutely. Because it's at that first level of funny. It's basic. It's almost like a how-to manual for comedy. It shows you the directions you can head in to be funny.

PAUL PROVENZA: I think *Mr. Show* was predominantly satire rather than parody, but David Cross was hard-pressed to say that wholeheartedly, though, which surprised me. Why do you think somebody in comedy would prefer to champion that their work is *not* about content or making a meaningful point?

BOB ODENKIRK: Well, being in comedy is all about poking fun at and letting the air out of pompous people and pretension and all that, so the last thing you want is to appear to be pontificating or self-important. But on *Mr. Show,* we *always* had a point to make. We always asked ourselves, "What is the point of this sketch? Who is this going after? What are we saying here?"

All our stuff came from different places and directions: we made fun of politics, we made fun of standards, we made fun of assumptions people have about entertainment, and things like that. I would always ask myself, "What's the 'voice' of this piece? How does it work on a person?"

I was thinking about *All in the Family* recently, because I'm also working on a TV project that I think will be related to it, and I really feel that in *All in the Family,* every character had *dignity,* you know what I mean? Archie Bunker was hilarious and reacted in knee-jerk, thoughtless ways to everything, but he *loved* his family. And because he loved them, he looked at the world in the way he really thought was best for them, and all that gave him more depth than just his surface reactions to things. He was forced to grow a little and forced to find different shades of himself, which gave him dignity. He wasn't just funny because he had this conservative or bigoted attitude. That was a much more nu-

anced kind of satire. That was *great* satire.

PAUL PROVENZA: I agree. That show was really a bold, thoughtful, and very humanistic look at a type of person that all too often is written off as a cliché. Understanding the depth of people contributes so much to understanding why we look at the world in such awful ways. That show also brings up another thing that I think about a lot, which is that I don't think in today's PC climate you could get that show on the air, despite the fact that its values are all about ridiculing the ignorance of small-mindedness and bigotry.

BOB ODENKIRK: I don't know about that. I think you could. The fact is, it's hard to get *anything* on the air. It's just hard to get a project to go all the way to TV, and then to be supported enough to grow on TV to where it is all it can be. That's always been hard, and possibly it *is* harder now than it ever was. But, given that, if you had a good, satirical show that was very well-written, it would have a pretty good chance, I think.

PAUL PROVENZA: But the language on *All in the Family,* which was authentic and character-driven, would have to be watered down today. The ideas could still be expressed, but I think it would have to be done differently and not as viscerally and realistically with such blatant dialogue.

BOB ODENKIRK: I think network TV is really evolving into something different than what we grew up with; I think those days are long gone. Cable television is the real television now. Networks are kind of a way station for mainstream fare and special events. Network TV is soon gonna be just about event programming, I think: specials, big sporting events, high-budget mass-appeal events. Anything with a stronger voice, or any remotely pointed voice, is going to be on cable, and it's all the same to any kid watching TV.

PAUL PROVENZA: So network TV will be to broadcasting like Walmart is to retailing?

BOB ODENKIRK: And kind of is already.

PAUL PROVENZA: What comes to you first, the comic scenario or the idea behind it?

BOB ODENKIRK: It can come any way, really. A lot of the time, with David Cross, we would sit around and read the paper and go, "Did you read *this*?"

That's what happened with a piece for the live *Mr. Show,* which came right out of the paper, about this guy on death row who happened to be mentally retarded and there were all these legal issues around executing a mentally retarded guy. So we wrote this sketch where the state spent all this money to educate him so he would be at a level of intelligence where they could legally put him to death. That just came up reading some newspaper article.

PAUL PROVENZA: Well, that's a really good piece to deconstruct for a moment here. I get that the absurdity of that reality is just juicy with comic possibilities, but what would you say was the politics of it? What was the point you were trying to make in exaggerating that scenario?

BOB ODENKIRK: Well, it's all around the idea that we think it's more important to put people to death than it is to educate people; we'll educate people so that we can put them to death, and that's the best education this guy ever got. It's such a high priority for us to have a death penalty that we will go to great lengths for it. It's more important for us to build prisons than to take that money and invest it in helping people before they're so broken and damaged and committing crimes. Our valuing of punishment and revenge on wrongdoers is so great that we take it to ridiculous extremes.

And before you think that we're exaggerating, a few years after we wrote that scene, something almost exactly like it happened with a guy in Texas, who was mentally retarded and they did all kinds of things to help raise his IQ to execute him. Cross called me up, going, "Did you *see* this? Did you see it? It's our sketch!" It was our story almost exactly. They gave the guy all this therapy and tested him a number of times as they tried to find a doctor who would sign off on his being out of the range of "retarded" so they could execute him.

PAUL PROVENZA: Do you consider the points that you make in your writing or performing to be political?

BOB ODENKIRK: I think that political points are not really all that worthwhile. To say, "Our side is right, their side is wrong" is not really worth much. The real point is to try to get *behind* the story.

PAUL PROVENZA: Do you think anything anyone does in comedy makes any kind of difference?

BOB ODENKIRK: You know, it's disappointing for comedians as we go through all of this for our whole lives to accept that we're just entertainment. That people *entertain* themselves by going to see George Carlin's show. They laugh at the cranky hippie, and then they leave and get into their gas-guzzler and go to the country club and tell their friends, "I saw George Carlin. That guy was fuckin' hilarious," and it doesn't affect them at all. It's a shame to feel like some of us are being very conscious and trying hard to express something and thinking really hard about points we want to make, but that ultimately all it is is just a diversion for most people. And that's just true.

PAUL PROVENZA: When you think about comedy as much as you do, do you focus more on the art of it or the craft of it?

BOB ODENKIRK: First of all, "art" is a very weird word. It's hard to define "art." I probably talk about the art of it because the craft isn't that interesting to me. It's something to think about, and it's certainly there, but it's not really all that mysterious.

Aaron Freeman, a comedy writer and performer who came out of Second City, was fa-mously proud of having written a computer program that actually *wrote jokes*. They're not good, you know, but they are *technically* jokes. It's interesting, my son and my daughter both tell jokes, but my son makes more of a conscious effort to be funny. When he was seven or eight, he would do all these things that were *like* a joke but weren't really jokes. But he thought they *were,* because they were constructed like a joke. He would be laughing his ass off, and most of his buddies would be, too. They could *feel* it. They could sense, "That's like a joke, what you just did."

Of course, I'm sitting there thinking, "Oh my God, he doesn't actually think that's funny does he? Is he always gonna think *that's* funny? Uh-oh. I'm gonna have to put him into a 'special' class." Now that he's nine, the jokes are starting to make sense, and I'm really loving him. Wait a minute: I've always loved *him*. I mean, now I'm loving his sense of humor. No, I'll just say it: I'm loving him now that he's funny, dammit. Now that he's authentically funny, I can love him.

AUDIENCES GOT TO know David Cross as part of HBO's subversive sketch comedy series, *Mr. Show.* In the years following, on top of numerous television and film roles, Cross has staked his claim in stand-up comedy as one of the country's most outraged, outspoken, and funniest critics. But for someone who's spent his life speaking his own mind, he's adamant about how any one person's opinion is both inconsequential and important.

DAVID CROSS: People are just not that thoughtful about most things. It's not like people go, "I refuse to listen to politics or watch the news; I'm only going to watch *American Idol*." There've always been distractions; there will always be distractions. It's just now there's more stimulation, more media, more bombardment of the advertising culture we're in. I don't think it's a calculated, cynical ploy; it's just capitalism. It's giving people what they want and finding a way to make money out of it. Long before *American Idol* there was Zsa Zsa Gabor, or Ava Gardner and Frank Sinatra, or Montgomery Clift that everybody was talking about.

PAUL PROVENZA: It seems that people are checking out more than they ever have in my lifetime. I was a kid in the sixties, a teenager in the seventies, and there just seemed to be a greater political awareness.

DAVID CROSS: I think that might be a bit of solipsism. I have to check myself when I have those observations. Like, "Okay, this is what I'm observing, but . . . I *do* live in New York City." If I'm not in New York, I'm usually in L.A., and neither of those places represent what's going on in America. More people voted in the last election than in any other in the last forty-two or whatever years. That was the highest per capita vote we've had in a long time, so "checking out" doesn't really apply.

There's a great deal of misinformation and disinformation, and the effect of that is probably more the polarization of people than that they're checking out. You have a guy on the Left, say Michael Moore, well-meaning as he

may be, manipulates his films, in my opinion, but calls them documentaries and presents them as investigative truth. Then there's the ones on the Right, like Bill O'Reilly—and, honestly, I don't understand how he is legally able to, but he is consistently spouting blatant, wrong information on a daily basis, never correcting any of it. I don't understand why there's no recourse or penalty for that. If I was that wrong that often, I would be fired, and should be.

But those types all say, "I'm not a journalist. I'm just a guy expressing my opinion." That's their out.

PAUL PROVENZA: Which really is saying, "Hey, it's just show business."

DAVID CROSS: Of course, and I don't think he'd deny that. He knows. But it doesn't seem right, really.

The other thing is, this country has 300 million people in it, and on average about 2.8 million people tune into Bill O'Reilly every night. I'm just pulling these numbers out of my ass, but let's say they're accurate. So who actually gives a shit about Bill O'Reilly? He has no influence. Didn't he try and start like a couple of boycotts against Pepsi and against, like, France, I think? They were a joke. The man is a joke.

PAUL PROVENZA: If not influenced by that kind of rhetoric, how does half a nation consciously turn its back on war crimes, on violations of international law, on an illegal occupation of another nation? How does that happen?

DAVID CROSS: Well, you're presupposing

that everyone in America is magnanimous and ethical. I'd be hard pressed to find five people out on the street or that I know in my life that haven't stolen from the office or haven't lied when they've had something to gain.

PAUL PROVENZA: There's a big leap between that and war crimes.

DAVID CROSS: And that big leap is filled in with all those teeny, tiny leaps.

And America's number one in a lot of things in the world, and we're also number one in propaganda. We have the best, most finely tuned propaganda machine that works without you even realizing it. We honestly believe that we are a blessed country, the best, greatest country in the world, that we've done so much good stuff that we aren't capable of doing any evil, that the rest of the world are all just jealous 'cause we have the highest quality of life on the planet and we live in a true democracy, and that in America if you don't like something, you can always do something about it. You and I can sit here and know that's a crock of shit, but there are plenty of people who believe all of it. Whatever they are—Christian, Jew, Muslim, atheist, whatever—they believe it.

PAUL PROVENZA: Because the myth of all that's been ingrained in us from such a very early age.

DAVID CROSS: Right. I don't have that problem, because at a very early age I said, "Well, this doesn't sound right" a *lot*. There were always examples. The Vietnam War. Or like when I was a kid, the Union Carbide plant blew up in Bhopal, India, thousands of people

were killed and we did everything we could to *not* compensate the families of the people who died or were mutilated or crippled because of that negligence. I was really young but I remember going, "How could America call itself such a perfect place? This doesn't seem right." I didn't see everything through an American flag draped over my glasses.

PAUL PROVENZA: Do you think that comedy can serve to dispel those kinds of myths? I get a sense that it sometimes contributes to *creating* myths, as it seems as though John Kerry was, to a certain extent, brought down by a lot of jokes on late-night talk shows that reinforced a mythology and narrative that had been created about him. Al Gore was mythologized as being this robotic, uncharismatic character, and that, too, was reinforced again and again by a steady stream of jokes.

DAVID CROSS: I think there's an element to that. Like I was saying, one Bill O'Reilly doesn't matter, but two thousand Bill O'Reillys *do* matter. One joke doesn't matter, but two thousand late-night Jay Leno jokes? That starts to add to the cultural feeling.

PAUL PROVENZA: Does it speak to people actually "not checking out" that so many of the top comics in America right now—

DAVID CROSS: —Larry the Cable Guy, Dane Cook—

PAUL PROVENZA: Well, I'm not referring to them at the moment—

DAVID CROSS: Oh, I thought you were talking about the top comics in America right now.

PAUL PROVENZA: Okay . . . There will always

be monster truck shows, NASCAR, *and* the ballet and Chekhov, too, which is exactly as it should be. I don't expect subversive or political comics to reach *that* kind of level of popularity, for any number of good reasons, but it is notable to me that *The Daily Show*, Stephen Colbert, Lewis Black, Bill Maher are as huge as they are, and all simultaneously. Historically, that's a rare occurrence that I think describes some trend or cultural sway.

DAVID CROSS: But they're *not* huge. They're big, sure, but they're not huge. And I'm not denigrating him in any way by saying Bill Maher is not "huge"; I think he'd be the first person to tell you that. Those people you mentioned are all really successful—*in their niche.*

And to knock myself down a peg or two as well, I got a lot of credit for doing what I was doing when it was unpopular right after September 11. It might have been different if I didn't live in downtown New York and hadn't watched the towers fall with my own eyes, if I wasn't here when we had guys with hazmat outfits and those big, crazy-looking Humvee things that the military had down on Houston Street. I talk about what happened two days ago in the shower; I talk about all kinds of shit that occurs to me, whatever it may be. Since I witnessed all *that* and that's what was going on, that's what I talked about. And I think I got more credit than I deserved for being "courageous" for that, because I was doing it all in front of like-minded people. Sure, I am who I am, my act is my act, I would never change my set, I'm not going to alter it for anybody— But I wasn't out there picking

up the mic in front of a bunch of Sean Hannitys, you know?

There's nothing *wrong* with preaching to the choir—we need that—but it's in my nature to be contrary. I spent years and years where—and I don't, or *barely,* do this anymore—if I was having a good set, I would purposely tank it. I would just bury it. I would subvert a good set, 'cause there's that part of me that tries to push buttons and get a reaction from the audience that's not necessarily . . . "adulation," you know?

And I think more than any other subject you can mention from now until dawn—more than politics, race, class, culture—*religion* is the one that makes people sit up and really either voice their displeasure or get behind you. So I'm doing tons of stuff about religion, which is something I find at its best mildly annoying and at worst extremely dangerous.

I'm an atheist, and atheists are a *lot* less popular than either liberals or neocons are. An atheist is still looked upon with suspicion by all different kinds of people.

PAUL PROVENZA: I often get violent responses to my atheist opinions. One night in particular, I was by the door after my show and some guy actually spat on me as he walked out.

DAVID CROSS: No way.

PAUL PROVENZA: Spit a big, honking goober on me. On the other hand, I also find that a lot more people in the crowd actually feel the same way I do, but for whatever reason feel like they can't say it out loud to their families or in their workplaces.

DAVID CROSS: I don't understand that. That

is a form of self-preservation or cowardice that I cannot comprehend. It just doesn't compute with me. I mean, not saying you're gay is one thing, because you might get the shit kicked out of you in some places. But no one is going to beat the shit out of you for being an atheist.

PAUL PROVENZA: Like a lot of people, I was raised to believe one should *never* talk about politics or religion, so I guess it's just not that easy for everyone to go against that particular grain.

DAVID CROSS: I was raised a lot of ways, and I did stuff anyway. It's called being an individual. We're not talking about fucking barnyard animals, by which everybody would understandably be repulsed. It's about not believing in God. It's not that big a deal.

PAUL PROVENZA: Some people live in a world where not believing in God is about the same level of wrong as fucking barnyard animals.

DAVID CROSS: That's bullshit. That's hyperbole. It's just not true.

PAUL PROVENZA: Have you ever seen all those YouTube videos of kids coming out as atheists to their parents? The reactions are incredibly emotional. It means way more to some people than you may think it possibly could.

DAVID CROSS: I'm not talking about a fucking fifteen-year-old living at home with Mom and Dad who feed him. I'm talking the husband, the wife, the brother-in-law, the grandfather . . .

PAUL PROVENZA: Did you forget about that finely tuned propaganda machine in this country? Religion and theism have had that on their side for a long time. Why is it so hard to believe that some people genuinely fear being ostracized if they openly declare their atheism?

DAVID CROSS: That is like the most pussy, cowardly stance. Even if it means you're unpopular . . . Just what kind of person *are* you? It's borderline shameful that you'd live your life like that. I don't get it. I just don't get it.

PAUL PROVENZA: Well, maybe that's an example of where a comedian's jokes about something can be empowering. They can sit there, laugh, and know that they're not alone.

DAVID CROSS: Go on the fucking Internet! There's people everywhere! Read a fucking book!

PAUL PROVENZA: People work long hours, they come home and want to spend time with their families and don't—

DAVID CROSS: Blah, blah, blah; bullshit, bullshit, bullshit.

I just cannot comprehend having *any* belief, *any* conviction, and just swallowing it. That, to me, is like having one of those Oliver Sacks kind of maladies.

BILL MAHER

KICKING OFF HIS career as the emcee at New York's Catch a Rising Star, Bill Maher hammered out a clear, sharp, committed voice in his stand-up, ultimately forging it into the groundbreaking *Politically Incorrect* on Comedy Central. The unorthodox roundtable borrowed the format of the journalistic Sunday-morning talk show and mixed it with the wittiest entertainers and pop culture icons of the day. Maher was the bright sun at its center, and quickly gained a reputation as a comedian who would put the lie to any hypocrisy that crossed his path. The show moved to ABC, where Maher ran into presidential-sized controversy when his comments about the 9/11 hijackers were singled out by the White House as going too far. His show canceled in the controversy's wake, Maher quickly found a home at HBO, where *Real Time with Bill Maher* raised his own stakes with the most biting, incisive, no-holds-barred political commentary on television today.

BILL MAHER: I get a little flap going here or there; I had a dust-up with the Vatican when the pope was here. They claimed it was that I referred to him as a Nazi, but I think it was more about child-abuse jokes.

PAUL PROVENZA: One was quoted in the papers: "President Bush spoke at a Catholic prayer breakfast. It was early in the morning; he said, 'I'm dying for a little joe,' and they brought him an altar boy."

BILL MAHER: I also called the Catholic Church "the Bear Stearns of organized pedophilia: too big to fail."

That could've gone a different way if I was on any broadcast network, but there are no sponsors to write to on HBO. Some people say they'll cancel their subscriptions, but hopefully HBO feels more people will subscribe because I'm on than will leave because I said the pope wears funny hats or whatever nonsense upsets them.

But there's this misconception that I was shackled like Hannibal Lecter on ABC and when I went to HBO the shackles came off. I was hardly restrained at ABC. I talked about religion all the time there; they didn't care, as long as there was someone with an opposing viewpoint. I've *never* skirted around it; I always attacked religion as stupid and destructive. ABC was okay with that.

The one subject that freaked out ABC was marijuana. We wanted to do a "Harry Pothead" sketch, because Harry Potter's all about stuff you might imagine when high, you know? That was a huge *battle royale*—which I lost. That gives you an idea of the nineties

mind-set: THE verboten topic was drugs.

It seems odd that I could say anything I wanted to about religion but couldn't do "Harry Pothead." It's a few subway stops more innocuous to me.

PAUL PROVENZA: Your big controversy was taking issue with calling the 9/11 hijackers "cowards," saying, "*We* have been the cowards, lobbing cruise missiles from two thousand miles away. Staying in the airplane when it hits the building, say what you want about it, it's not cowardly." Was *that* innocuous, or did you intend to be provocative a week after 9/11?

BILL MAHER: *No one* saw it as provocative at the time. There was no reaction in the studio, none in the green room afterward, none the next day. Nothing happened until somebody made a point of saying everyone should be upset.

This disc jockey in Houston had been trying to get me off the air for years for saying things about religion and Ronald Reagan; he saw *this* as his opportunity and fanned the flames. And people are such sheep, all it takes is one person to say, "Aren't you mad about what he said?"

And it's, "Hey, we *are* mad! Thanks for reminding me; I almost forgot to be mad today."

It felt like the whole country had all this rage and no place to really put it and they turned it on *me* for a few weeks. It was the subject of White House press briefings for days; Ari Fleischer and officials at the highest levels commented on it . . . but within six months people were telling me, "You were right. They *weren't* cowards, were they? They stuck with a suicide mission."

By a year later, people were, "Didn't you say something a while ago that was some kind of a thing . . . ?" They had a vague notion of some brouhaha, but I could hardly find anybody who remembered what the fuck the whole thing was even about. The cycle was quick and complete, and I was back on TV within six months of leaving ABC. It's amazing.

I've seen that same scenario play out with the Dixie Chicks, Don Imus—so many people who've gotten in trouble for something they said—and in every case, a short while later there was a reversal of thinking on the initial rush to judgment. I'm not comparing Imus's comments to mine; he just made a silly, shock-jock insult whereas I made an adult comment about an adult subject—one also echoed by intellectuals like Susan Sontag, and not-so-intellectuals like Rush Limbaugh, too. *Dick Cheney* even said pretty much the same thing. But what *was* similar is that all those instances show over and over how this is a nation of *panickers*. It's so supersensitive. Anything upsets it, it panics right away. As we panicked about 9/11 and ended up invading Iraq. And always, a short time later the country goes, "Oh jeez . . . Maybe we overreacted. I guess Don Imus can have a job." Or Janet Jackson, another one where people flipped.

PAUL PROVENZA: The Janet Jackson furor was just a handful of organized people duping America into *believing* it was outraged. Most

Americans were outraged that anyone was outraged.

BILL MAHER: That's what happened with me. It was a handful of people whose opinion doesn't reflect "America" at all—it doesn't even reflect people *watching* the show, it reflects people who *heard* about it somewhere else. But it's amplified, because it's easy to send mass e-mails, so Sears or FedEx, who pulled their advertising, could easily believe an army of people is upset when it's really just a few people contacting other people going, "Can we put your name on this list?"

People go, "Sure! You *bet* I'm mad as hell about whoever on whatever show I've never seen because I go to bed at nine o'clock!"

It seems unfair that you don't actually have to *watch* a show to insist that it not be on.

PAUL PROVENZA: Then powerful people with their own agendas fan the panic flames.

BILL MAHER: Anytime people are in the dark they're susceptible to being frightened easily. When September 11 happened, we had no idea why, what to do, how to fix it, what caused it, or how to make sure it didn't happen again. It was just put forth that they're crazy, we're pure good, they're pure evil. To a nation of ignoramuses, that worked.

Using our army against an enemy with no army? That's *pure* panic. Al-Zawahiri's plan to take down the superpower never involved an army; he doesn't have one. But he knew he could draw us into a backbreaking conflict, economically, spiritually, and militarily, and he's done that. It reminds me of *Gulliver's*

Travels, where the Lilliputians tie down the giant. He used our own panic as the means to take us down.

Bush and his people were so naive as to think the little three-week war before occupation *was* the war. The Iraqis understood that was just the *trailer.* And now . . . your feature presentation.

Torture's another example of panic. We blundered into war, our guys were getting blown up instead of greeted with flowers, and, "We don't know why they're blowing us up! Let's get some people under a lightbulb and beat some information out of them!"

We've fought every other war we've ever waged without needing to go there. But the Bush/neocon crowd believed that whatever they do is justified, because the big picture is *keeping the right people in power in America.* Nothing is more central to their belief system than that Americans are always the good people: "All we gotta do is show up and spread some freedom dust and they'll all fall in line."

They believe we can do *anything*—torture people, create millions of refugees and send them back to countries where they'll be assassinated for collaborating with us, treat our own veterans horribly—because it's in the greater service of keeping them in power, and they view their staying in power as the lynchpin to maintaining this great American experiment. They think they're the only ones who can uphold what *they* see as America. But their knowledge of history is faulty and shal-

low: *their* idea of America is what we think of as Middle America—but America was founded by enlightened liberals from Boston and Philadelphia. *Their* path is the one that's diverged from the original intent and conception of this country.

PAUL PROVENZA: Some of their religious-Right power base see American Mid-East policy as a means to fulfill Biblical "rapture" prophecies, too.

BILL MAHER: That had a *lot* to do with Bush's policies, especially toward Israel—but this affection many on the religious Right claim to have for Israel is a cynical one; they don't love the Jew or Israel, it's just important that Israel not be wiped out or moved, because Israel *must* be in the hands of the Jews when Jesus returns. And what happens when Jesus returns? Jews either convert, or they're *killed.* That's the prophecy: 144,000 Jews are "raptured" up into heaven—I guess they're, like, "grandfathered" in, but aside from them, when Jesus comes back, *no more Jews.*

PAUL PROVENZA: It's hard to believe there's really all that much support for these ideas among people who call themselves Christian.

BILL MAHER: It's a smaller group than the power suggests, but it's considerable; I wouldn't call it "fringe." Their power's outsized to their numbers, because they're so well-organized and devoted. Smaller, more devoted groups always succeed over a larger, more apathetic group. And few things fire people up more than religion, because it's connected with the ultimate questions. And if you're crazy enough to think you know with utter certitude what happens after death, then you're crazy enough to do *anything*.

This is what *Religulous* is all about, and what I've been saying on TV about religion being so destructive. I've pretty much owned the subject on television for the last fifteen years.

I give great credit to George Carlin; he talked about it in stand-up *long* ago. I'm glad all the books by Richard Dawkins, Sam Harris, and Christopher Hitchens are on the scene, but Carlin and I were talking about this long before they came out.

My fervent hope for *Religulous* is that it helps give people permission to say, "We're *rationalists*."

PAUL PROVENZA: Yet you don't consider yourself atheist?

BILL MAHER: I wouldn't describe myself as a strict atheist, but even Richard Dawkins doesn't describe himself that way. In *The God Delusion,* he establishes a scale of one to seven: one being completely certain there's a God, seven being completely certain there *isn't*. Dawkins says he's only a 6.9, because you *just don't know*. You *can't*. So I say I'm a "rationalist."

I would like *Religulous* and this burgeoning movement to give the millions and millions in this country who think along those lines permission to say, "*We're* not the crazy ones; people who believe in talking snakes are the crazy ones. We believe in empirical proof, not in personal gods and prayers that obviously don't get answered and cosmic justice that obviously doesn't exist."

Sixteen percent of Americans say they're atheist or agnostic. That's a really sizeable minority—bigger than blacks, Jews, homosexuals, or NRA members. Any other minority that big would have tremendous political clout, but this is the one minority with *none*. Because, one, they're individualist—by very nature, they're not joiners. And, two, they're cowed to such a degree as to believe they should just go in the corner and shut the hell up. I'd like them to come out of the closet and assert themselves.

PAUL PROVENZA: Can you change minds through jokes?

BILL MAHER: I used to answer that with that textbook modest answer: "Oh, no. I'm just out to get laughs." Well, I'm out chiefly to get laughs, no doubt about that—if you *don't* get laughs you don't have a job, then you're not speaking to anybody about anything—but honestly, in the last few years too many people have said to me, "I've changed my mind. You convinced me."

So I have to say I guess I *do* change some minds. I think minds are more open than people realize, and that you *can* change them—it just can't be your *raison d'être,* or you get lost in your own causes rather than be a comedian. And that's self-defeating; that's the *least* effective way of changing anyone's mind. The most effective way is to make them laugh. Being an involuntary response, laughter lets people know there's some truth to what they're laughing at. When they *can't help* laughing, they kinda *have* to question it.

And one of the great things about being a comic and not a politician is that you're *allowed* to change your mind. If a politician changes their mind anytime after they're eighteen years old, they're "flip-flopping"; "inconsistent." But anyone else is just a human being who's learning—and we don't want *that* in a politician.

But changing people's minds is a far cry from changing government policy. I guess changing minds is a step toward changing government policy, but is it enough? I'm skeptical. Not long ago, 80 percent of the country thought we were on the wrong track, yet half of them were still willing to vote for the guy who's for a *more* wrong track, so . . . I never underestimate inertia in this country.

It's that "Who *are* these people?" factor: "Who *are* these people upholding such failed ways of thinking?" They're out there. There's obviously so many of them it's always an uphill battle for progressives.

PAUL PROVENZA: Like, if two-thirds of America believes marijuana should be decriminalized—another topic you feel strongly about—why is it still illegal? Individual states have decriminalized it, but the federal government won't allow them to listen to the will of their own people. "We the people" aren't controlling that issue at all.

BILL MAHER: Marijuana should be a no-brainer, why can't we move those goalposts? They haven't moved since I was a child, and before that. That's what I mean about inertia in this country. I think if you asked most people if marijuana should be a criminal offense, most people would say, "Not really," yet nothing changes.

A lot of it's because no politician wants to look weak or "soft on drugs." They're scared into backing off what they *know* is the right stand on this. I've talked to politicians privately about this; privately, they all concede that marijuana should not be criminalized, but publicly, they don't want an election fight where somebody runs an attack ad: "My opponent wants your child smoking marijuana! Marijuana leads to other drugs and your child will be blowing people behind a Dumpster for heroin money, so vote for me, the *other* guy."

Intelligent arguments only work for a politician if enough intelligent people who hear the bullshit smear campaign come back against it with, "Oh, please. *Stop* it. It's one of the more benign things around. Look in your medicine cabinet, it's all *worse* than marijuana."

You can't move the country past where people are willing to go, so if people are so easily panicked like that, so easily herded toward one dumb position after another, I don't know how we'll ever move forward.

PAUL PROVENZA: Let's not forget how much money is made in imprisoning people. The prison industry is big business. Building, operating, maintaining prisons—it's all outsourced to big corporations, and the more prisoners the bigger the contracts. America has the largest prison population in the world.

BILL MAHER: It's horrible—and *another* example of doing anything other than actually thinking about an issue. "Let's not think about it, just lock them up, throw away the key. Criminals are criminals." I did an essay once, comparing the word "criminal" with "terrorist."

It's a name to put on somebody so no matter what happens to them or what you do to them, it's okay; you don't have to think about it.

PAUL PROVENZA: Which is how you get compassionate, rational people to accept torture.

BILL MAHER: Right. "Terrorist" is a *magic* word: it makes *rights* disappear. No cruel and unusual punishment, no torture—*unless* it's a terrorist. No tapping phones, no search and seizure without a warrant——unless we think it's a terrorist.

I have a relatively clear idea of who the Taliban is: the people who harbored Al Qaeda, religious fanatics who make women wear beekeeper suits and cut people's heads off in soccer stadiums. I know who they are; I don't have a big problem going after them and killing them. But who are we fighting in Iraq? The media uses a variety of names, including, guess what? "Terrorists."

PAUL PROVENZA: In this country of 300 million, are there really not enough intelligent people to give traction to intelligent arguments about these things?

BILL MAHER: You know what it takes for a novel to make the bestseller list? Like, fifty thousand copies. In a country of 300 million. A *bestseller* means one in six thousand people has read it. A *million* people watching Stephen Colbert is one in three hundred. It gives one pause when you consider the numbers: how many people are really taking this in? How many are really involved in any issue? How many are really aware, or really knowledgeable? Well . . . Not *that* many.

I lay a lot of blame on the media, for many of the same reasons that our schools are failing. All too often the teachers are not that much brighter than the students. It's the same thing with news media. They're in the position of being our teachers. If they're not smart enough to tell us what's important or to understand things themselves, we're certainly not gonna get it.

That problem begins with the corporate takeover of news organizations. They *used* to be loss leaders. Networks didn't care about ratings when it came to news; news wasn't about that. News didn't *compete* with *The Beverly Hillbillies,* it was *subsidized* by it. Entertainment made money for CBS, and Walter Cronkite did his thing—he didn't have to contribute to the pot; it was *news.* That's *not* how it is anymore.

It's distressing to watch news channels geared supposedly to the "smarter" people. MSNBC dumbs down whenever Chris Matthews isn't on, and CNN—my hero Larry King, half the time he's interviewing Scott Peterson's lawyer or some other bullshit—and this is for the smart people! If what's put on the air for the smart, interested people who care more than most others is so terribly dumbed down, what hope is there for anyone else?

The Mike Judge movie *Idiocracy* really captures America to me. It satirizes the dumbness we live in every day; it's just brilliant. It takes place five hundred years in the future, but to me, it's not even five hundred *days* in the future.

I was just at an airport, trying to get a

ticket, in a scene I see every time: one person ahead of me, and it takes twenty minutes to process him. The airline person's looking puzzled at the computer, another one comes over and they look puzzled at the computer together . . . I'm, like, "What the *fuck* could be the problem? How many fucking passengers have you processed in the last fifty years, Delta?!? He's flying from Tampa to somewhere in the U.S., he's got a ticket and a bag—what could be so complicated here?"

They looked like the people in *Idiocracy*.

I swear, it seems like America can't do *anything* anymore. We can't give health care to our people, can't get cell phone service without cutting out—so many things people don't realize *other* countries have already figured out how to do. I did an editorial about this at the end of *Real Time* once and got some responses just so *insulted* that I would even *suggest* it. I said, for all of you out there waving that big foam "We're #1" finger, going, "We're the greatest country in the world!," I'm sorry, but they have actual statistics about this stuff—standard of living, where we place in education, the health care we provide our people—and we're nowhere *close* to #1.

And our shit is *dingy*. Our airports look dingy, bus stations, train stations—have you been to the original Disneyland lately? Doesn't it look like it hasn't had an upgrade since, like, the fifties?

PAUL PROVENZA: It's always looked Soviet to me.

BILL MAHER: Exactly! Our shit is becoming like Havana, behind the pace of the rest of the world in so many ways. We're coasting on this image of being number one that we've had in our minds, but it's not 1955 anymore.

I don't have confidence that this country can get anything done. I hope a new generation of inspired, hope-filled people come in and turn this country around, but I wouldn't bet the house on it.

The heart of the problem is the corporate takeover of government—otherwise known as *fascism*. Congress is just the leisure service of American corporations now. That's hard to defeat because people don't understand; they can't seem to see "the corporation" as *the* entity: they *work* for a corporation, they *love* Nabisco's cookies.

But we're so easily bought off. It's so easy to throw people a sop: "Look! You can transfer your old cell phone number to your new cell phone," and we're dancing in the streets. I once asked on my show, "If you could wipe out global warming tomorrow by giving up your TV remote, *would* you?"

I'm not sure even *I* would. Can you imagine having to get up every time you wanted to change the channel or volume?

PAUL PROVENZA: Hey, say what you want about Jesus, but don't fuck around with my BlackBerry.

BILL MAHER: Well, that's what "iconoclast" means, right? Destroying the icon.

HENRY ROLLINS

FEW PEOPLE ARE as outspoken as Henry Rollins. Former front man for the seminal punk band Black Flag, author of numerous books and spoken-word albums, and host of his own no-holds-barred talk show on IFC, Rollins is a first-rank polemicist possessed of keen intelligence and biting wit. While he's not a comedian per se, his spoken word bristles with searing humor, provoking the awed laughter that only comes from speaking truth. The most daring of comedians share the DNA of his punk sensibility, so it's no surprise that Rollins's innate sense of irony and hypersensitive bullshit detector churn out full-blown, genuine comedy. He speaks passionately on channeling the anger of his youth, and how today's generation needs to wake up and do the same.

HENRY ROLLINS: With Black Flag, people said I was angry. "Yeah, I'm *very* angry. And very lonely, very sad *and* very easy to please and wanting something different, and I'm getting it *all* out with this loud, angry music." I've written twenty books and people say, "The writing's dark and heavy." Because I'm in *pain,* man! Should I shoot someone or write a book instead?

For years, media rendered me as this angry guy with no brains. Sure, you see a shirtless, tattooed guy yelling and screaming, you'll think: "Angry psychopath! Hide your kids!" Truth is, kids *love* me. So I got a better press agent. And found out there's something else under the hood.

I started doing spoken word in 'eighty-three. A local promoter put on shows where, like, fifty poets, artists, whatever got seven minutes each. He said, "You've got a big mouth. Wanna do seven minutes next week?"

I said, "What am *I* gonna do?"

He said, "We pay $10."

I said, "See you there," 'cause I was broke.

And I really enjoyed that format; I liked telling stories. So I did another, and another . . . I'd read tour journals, tell stories from when I was eight years old, crazy Black Flag anecdotes. Related my life. By 'eighty-five, I'm in a van doing my own little tours to twelve, fifteen people a show. I *hoped* to break a hundred.

Now I do up to a hundred talking shows a year, everywhere from JP Morgan to Harvard to theaters; in Russia, Israel, Australia . . .

PAUL PROVENZA: All with an attitude similar to your music?

HENRY ROLLINS: All of it comes from an attitude of pushing back *against.*

My talking shows aren't "Daddy never held me" stuff. When you talk about being in third grade in 1968, where kids punch you in the mouth because "you killed Martin Luther King," and your mother says, "Honey, it's a tough time right now," then you hang out with your dad, who says, "Your mother's a good woman, but she's a nigger lover so don't listen to her too much," that's stuff that forms you. When I tell those stories, it's to say, "Here's where I'm from" and "Here's where *all* we Americans are from." You strike a chord.

I talked about a friend who got his brains blown out in front of me—the guy shot at me, missed, got my buddy, and *I* had to clean it up. I got so much mail like "My brother got shot in the face in a parking lot. Now I know I'm not alone." Talk about the most obscure minutiae of your life, and someone will be, "Dude! I thought you were talking about *me*!" And the more intense you get, the more people go, "Thanks, man!"

The older I get, the weirder my stories get. And the angrier *I'm* getting. I'm forty-eight, and angrier than at twenty-eight. Shouldn't I be getting fat and content? I'm getting leaner and meaner.

PAUL PROVENZA: Is it because your anger's expanded from the personal to a bigger consciousness?

HENRY ROLLINS: That's *exactly* it! When I was young, all I wanted was to be in a band, eat three times a day, and meet chicks. Women, glory, and music. And a van with five smelly guys and not enough gas to get to the next gig. The motivation was pure: "Play or die. Fuck it, I'll take either." I was on a tight, feral, Nietzschean leash.

But you get a little older, you can eat regularly, and . . . What's the anger about now? You start to look around, see the world for what it is.

When I was young, it was, all, "I can't meet a girl; my world sucks; me, me, me, me, me." As a nineteen-year-old is wont to be. My anger now comes from having more access to the world.

PAUL PROVENZA: Some people say entertainers should just entertain and shut the fuck up. Granted, as in all walks of life, *some* are misinformed, gullible, and trite, but some are intelligent, aware, and well-read with the luxury and ability to think about and process things. And, as performers, they travel *far* more than any businessman or politician, to a far greater variety of places, interacting with countless people around the globe on a regular, ongoing basis.

HENRY ROLLINS: Yeah, every armpit of the world, you do a gig in it. *Twenty-five* gigs! For over twenty-seven years, I've crisscrossed America and circled the world. And with travels, you learn.

You learn that a good part of the world is always hungry. Most of Africa is all food insecurity and poverty, which leads to everything bad. To a fifteen-year-old mother deciding, "Do I sell my body and feed my kids today, or *not* sell my body and *not* feed my kids today?" Guess what? They're the little girls with their

own kids at the AIDS clinic I visited in Cape Town—with a hundred fifty others just like them, out of two hundred people the one doctor and three nurses treated that day.

That gets me up in the morning. You see parts of the world where people are eating snow and making rock soup and you think, "Am I Nero? I can't sit and watch this or *I'm* part of the problem. To be a responsible person of the planet I've got to do *something*."

We who travel *do* get an understanding. It doesn't make us experts—believe me, I'm no scholar—but you can't tell me that after being to all these places I've been to, the tremendous access to all *kinds* of people I've had, that I don't know a thing or two. You get perspectives.

Day after September 11, I asked my manager, who's traveled so much he's sprouted wings, "Were you surprised?"

He went, "Nah. Were you?"

"Nah."

So many people said, "I can't *believe* they did that!" *Really?* I can't believe it didn't happen *sooner*. Don't they understand what we *do* in other parts of the world? I *beg* my fellow Americans to *think critically*. What might another country looking critically at America have seen recently? They'd see wonderful people oppressed by an imperialist leader, a government eroding the line between church and state, revoking civil liberties, and referring to the Geneva Conventions as "quaint" as they torture prisoners. They'd see the only country ever to use nuclear weapons with stockpiles of weapons of mass destruction, more conventional arms than all other countries *combined,* and military spending greater than any nation in history.

Maybe that country might go, "The American people need to be rescued." Let's say it's Belgium. They come over with Jean-Claude van Damme DVDs and hazelnut hair gel, going, "We're here to save you, with the best of intentions!"

What would Americans do? They'd go, "Thanks, but you got 'til this afternoon to get the fuck outta here before we kill you all." We'd throw everything we had at them, and blow ourselves up before we'd give up. Why should Iraq be any different?

Americans are aware of very few other countries: one to the north we've built a virtual fence against lest they attack us with gay rights and health care, and one down south where we're building a real fence to keep them out unless we need our hedges trimmed or our children cared for, and then it's, "Come on in! Shhh! . . . Ninety to a room."

All other countries just "hate our freedom." Never mind that we've been stirring their coffee with our dick since Truman. Or before.

I was detained at San Francisco Airport when they saw in my passport that I'd gone to Syria: "Why'd you go to Syria?"

"Curiosity. And that's a legal passport and visa, so why are we *really* here?"

"Were they nice to you?"

"Yeah, the people were wonderful to me. How do you like them apples?" I could tell that bugged him.

"Our government says it's dangerous."

What temerity! I said, "Sir, if you drive about eight exits to Oakland, you'll get shot in the face in a parking lot."

I was invited into people's homes in Iran. Hung out with cab drivers and their families in Lebanon. The women were beautiful, the food was great, everyone was friendly. Is it always that way? No, you can have a hard time anywhere there's humans, but in this country, we don't *want* to know what things are really like elsewhere.

PAUL PROVENZA: Your crowd mostly already agrees with your worldview. Do you care that you're preaching to the converted?

HENRY ROLLINS: With my crowd, it's "preaching to the *perverted.*" But remember, the already converted pass their books and CDs around and spread your stuff *for* you. I sign beaten-up copies of things and they'll say, "It cruised my whole dorm," or "It hit every bunk in the barracks."

But a lot of people who aren't my crowd bounce off me from TV, the Internet . . . I get hate mail, so I know for sure I'm reaching beyond my crowd. You know you're breaking through when you get that "Get out of my country!" stuff. That's a "Eureka! We've made contact! This one's got gills and a primordial tail!"

With some of those, you just have to accept there'll be intellectual casualties along the way. What you hope to do is make sure their *kids* get to hear P-Funk before it's all over for them. Try to bring their kids over to the bright side, where the Ramones are.

I'll get some kid, "I read your interview where you talked about Henry Miller so I read *Black Spring* that you said made you want to write books. That guy's amazing!"

And I'm, "Ahhh! We have a reader!"

"What else should I read?"

"Oh, we're cookin' now!"

PAUL PROVENZA: So you think you're making a difference?

HENRY ROLLINS: I *know* I'm making a difference. I get letters every day, "You helped me get off drugs." People on the street, "I thought I'd never vote, but after hearing you, I've *got* to."

Plus, my little record company has this "Talk Is Cheap" line of CDs, two for ten bucks, and a dollar from each goes to the Hollygrove Children's Services Center in my neighborhood. Another line, one dollar from each goes to the Southern Poverty Law Center, fighting hate groups. We did a benefit CD for the West Memphis Three, three kids serving life on charges a *lot* of people believe are false.

How much have we contributed? Who knows? Who cares? If I only paid for Christmas presents for the kids at Hollygrove, maybe one of 'em won't rob a liquor store because they've seen there is *some* good in the world.

You think we're pissing in the wind because the world's not changing? You don't change the world, you change *worlds*.

PAUL PROVENZA: You mentioned reaching the younger generation, but I find an overwhelming conservatism at colleges. There are exceptions, but in general I find them predict-able, consumerist, and resistant to counter-cultural or subversive ideas.

HENRY ROLLINS: Because those kids are going right into the Right-wing, corporate world and they train them all that way.

America's school system should be the envy of the world, but we're what, forty-sixth in literacy? Now what can't America do better than everyone else in the world if we cared to? But man, they don't *want* us thinking. That's why in the "halls of academia" they're just beer bonging and consumer-ing their lives away, texting themselves into oblivion.

It distresses me that young people don't see college for the opportunity it is. I run them down at universities: "If you privileged little bastards drop below a certain grade point average, I want you pulled from your seat, a kid from the ghetto put in it, and I want your parents to pay *their* tuition. You get to learn, drink coffee, and hang out with interested, interesting people all day—*and you're not even paying for it!* So many people *want* to go to college, but they're in Compton or the South Bronx. Working at McDonald's will be *their* best option. They want so much more; you *have* the opportunity and want so much *less?* It *hurts* me. You wound me when I get another of your typo-ridden letters."

It does hurt, 'cause I come from the high school education, $3.50 an hour minimum-wage world managing a Häagen-Dazs store, thinking, "Dead end ahead." I saw $3.50 an hour for the rest of my life. Black Flag came along; I told my supervisor I was leaving, and he said, "I'll make it $5 an hour."

I said, "It's not the money. It's the *shot*." We stay in touch to this day, by the way. He's so proud of me.

PAUL PROVENZA: Do you consider yourself brave?

HENRY ROLLINS: No. I'm not brave, I just don't have much fear. There's a huge difference. Bravery is one thing; I'm, just, "Ah, I don't give a fuck when I die."

I really don't, either. Don't get me wrong; I don't *want* to die. I'm not jumping in front of speeding cars; I see a gun, I'm running. But if it happens . . . Whatever. I'm not really all that taken by life. I don't wake up every morning going, "Yee-hah!" Maybe because I think too much, but I'm not really all that happy to be here.

In Iraq, I was in this building that was getting bombed, and this soldier rushed over, "Sir! You're in a fortified building! You're in *no* danger!"

I went, "Cool," and kept signing autographs and chatting.

"Sir? You're not scared?"

"Oh, I'm scared. I just don't really care when I die."

"Sir? . . . Uh . . . That's really fucked up."

"You have *no* idea."

JELLO BIAFRA

JELLO BIAFRA EMBODIES the political conscience and artistic integrity of the post-punk, hard-core movement of the Reagan era. Leader of the Dead Kennedys and founder of the independent record label Alternative Tentacles, Biafra found himself, his band, and his label singled out as guinea pigs for Tipper Gore's PMRC and its crusade against music they deemed too vulgar and explicit. Biafra won his case—but at the cost of his band and the exclusion of independent artists from mainstream distribution. As a successful spoken-word artist and active Green Party member, he's now one of the most recognized voices against censorship, organized religion, and corporate hegemony in America. Biafra displays his signature candor and sharp humor about the ordeal of his trial and tells us how he stays informed and fights back, and how being a punk taught him the DIY ethic.

JELLO BIAFRA: Let's rewind to the obscenity bust: even though the vigilantes, Tipper Gore's PMRC, had announced they were targeting the Dead Kennedys, I thought surely this country has grown up enough since the McCarthy era and Lenny Bruce that no one was going to waste public money trying to bust us on this. But lo and behold, on April 15, 1986, the LAPD flew officers to San Francisco, where, in conjunction with the SFPD, both showed up at my house, broke a window by the front door, walked on in, and trashed the place, claiming that they were looking for "harmful matter." They even looked in the cat box for "harmful matter."

All they wound up walking away with was my address book, some Alternative Tentacles Records stationery, copies of the *Frankenchrist* album, and H. R. Giger's poster. I suspect they were *hoping* to find drugs or guns.

Even my mother said she was relieved they didn't plant drugs on me during the raid. It's easier to laugh now, but at the time I was scared shitless. I knew what the LAPD were like; the Rodney King video was no surprise to me, 'cause I had seen them treat my fans that way with my own eyes in Wilmington, California, and in front of the Whisky a Go Go.

Then this cop walks in with his Eliot Ness trench coat, asking, "What are all those pictures of missing children doing on your kitchen wall? Do you know where they are?" One of my roommates had been collecting milk-carton kids and lining our kitchen walls with them. I was tempted to tell him they were all buried downstairs, but I was afraid they'd dig up the entire house and the landlady would get a little upset.

A few months later, me and four others in the record distribution chain were charged with one count each of distributing harmful matter to minors—a law they'd never used before. Then an attorney friend called and said I was charged in Los Angeles. I said, "Oh, *great*. What do we have to do? Pay a fine or something?"

He said, "No, you don't understand. CNN is calling. CBS is calling. They all want to talk to you."

I thought, "Oh my God, this is it. I'm Tipper's pigeon! We're going to have to fight this with everything we have."

Michael Guarino, the prosecutor assigned to the case, even said before they started looking for me, "We believe that this is a cost-effective way of sending a message."

In other words, "We picked a small, independent person to pick on in hopes that this artist will collapse, then we can use the guilty plea as a precedent to go after bigger fish."

He later admitted to an *LA Weekly* reporter that he had files on other musicians—they were looking at going after others after they convicted me.

Trouble is, they wound up not being able to convict me. The thing they used on me was that I was doing something that was harmful to children. The defense we used was "Look, if everything that might harm one child gets banned, all art, all media and literature will be dumbed down to the level of a first-grade reading book."

And I think that's a valid point. But I was shaking in my shoes. We sat for three weeks in Los Angeles as the *Frankenchrist* album got dragged over the coals. The prosecutor built up the offending H. R. Giger poster as being so shocking, so terrible, that this guy should be put away for it. My attorney opened his defense with handing out a copy of the Giger to the members of the jury, and I thought, "Oh shit, here it goes."

But I could see out of the corner of my eye that they were studying it up and down, and if you've seen this painting you'll know how funny that is. Then one or two of them realized they were looking at it upside down.

In the end, the jury deadlocked seven to five in favor of acquittal, at which point the judge dismissed the case. The prosecutor later admitted that as soon as the lyrics were allowed as evidence, he realized that they were probably going to lose the case. Not only would we be able to prove thematic content and why I wanted that visual art to be part of the album in the first place, but we could also then show that there was real value in the lyrics. They may be offensive, they may be shocking, but they're making a point.

Interestingly, the jurors who I thought would want to hang me, the older African-American parents, were the ones who were most hard-line for acquittal. They didn't like attacks on freedom of speech, because they'd seen those kinds of attacks used on other people they respected.

Unfortunately, the real impact was on the marketplace. Only after the charges were dismissed did all these chain stores kick out anything with the Dead Kennedys or the Alternative Tentacles label on it. So, in that sense, Tipper and her goons succeeded in damaging us in the marketplace and intimidating retailers into not stocking other things that might be controversial, out of fear that they might get busted.

PAUL PROVENZA: That's what happened to Lenny Bruce. Club owners were afraid they'd get shut down, so they stopped booking him.

JELLO BIAFRA: And most of those kinds of club owners never book me to this day. Plus I have a policy of avoiding—*like the plague*—Clear Channel, Live Nation, and other monopolies like that. Luckily, one of the important things that punk gave us, besides the music, was bringing back the old DIY ethic: do it yourself. If nobody will put your music out, put it out yourself. If nobody will publish what you write, publish it yourself. If nobody will bring the people you wanna see to your town, put the show on yourself.

PAUL PROVENZA: George Carlin. Lenny Bruce . . . You're one of the few artists who actually went head-to-head with the government in a First Amendment case.

JELLO BIAFRA: The prosecution was very openly trying to chop the First Amendment down. That's why they charged me not as a member of Dead Kennedys but as the owner of the label who put out the CDs, as a manufacturer. They were deliberately experimenting with the law to see who they could convict in order to scare the shit out of any other distributor who would attempt to even sell something like this to a store in the future.

Tipper Gore lied through her teeth all the time, saying she didn't want to get musicians busted and that they weren't against the First Amendment, but a year or two later, who'd they go after with an even bigger attack? Hip-hop artists, specifically the political ones. They went after Public Enemy, Ice-T, N.W.A. . . . "Oh my God, our sheltered middle-class teenagers aren't just listening to political music, but by *black* musicians! We can't have this."

PAUL PROVENZA: Having fought for your First Amendment rights, what's your reaction when people say, "America's not perfect, but it's still the freest place on earth."

JELLO BIAFRA: They haven't been to too many other countries, have they? Just cross the border into Canada and you'll see how even their avowedly more conservative newspapers have a lot more actual content in them than newspapers here. That kind of lack of content is censorship.

America has a far *less* free press than many other countries. You can write anything you want to, but who's going to publish it? Sure, you can put anything you want on the Internet until somebody complains and MySpace, Facebook, or Google take it down. You can say anything you want to—as long as nobody gets to read or hear it.

Even though you've reached adulthood, you're not really done with being spanked and sent to the principal's office.

PAUL PROVENZA: Are we actually involved in our political process or is it a machine that's too much bigger than us?

JELLO BIAFRA: It *is* a machine that's bigger than us, but that doesn't mean we can't sabotage it. It's like sticking a pin in the foot of an elephant or something. There's all kinds of ways to fight back. You can fight back through your words, through your art. You can fight back by refusing to give any of your money to chain stores or global corporate predators.

Nobody can be as pure as the driven snow about that unless they wanna go crazy in a cabin in the woods like the Unabomber did, but I tell people it's important to unplug from the corporate food chain, but don't become a fundamentalist about it. Fundamentalists turn people off to good ideas. Or they're the first to find they're making themselves miserable. They see things in such a humorless, black-and-white way that the only way they can see out is to go completely in the other direction. Like the singer of a militant anarchopunk hard-core band I knew, whom I hadn't run into for years; I asked him, "What've you been doing all these years?"

He said, "I'm a stockbroker." And he saw the look on my face and said, "Well . . . I just couldn't take it anymore."

It doesn't have to be that way. If you only go *this* far instead of *all the way* on the radical meter, sure some people will put you down for not doing enough, but you're much more likely to hang on to your ethics and ideals if you pick a moral, ethical code and lifestyle you can actually live with and live up to in the long term.

PAUL PROVENZA: Do you still speak about religion and the religious Right?

JELLO BIAFRA: Not in as much depth as I did when I was linking them to Tipper Gore and the real goals of all the people who want to censor our thoughts and sexual desires and start with music.

Allen Ginsberg made a good point to me once: "The reason they always go after sex and what's 'obscene' is because they know if they choke *that* off in you, even in your own mind, it'll make it easier for them to control the *rest* of your mind. That's what religion *is*."

People ask, "If America's really as insane as you think it is, why haven't you fled and live elsewhere?"

I say, "I like being in the belly of the beast."

I like living in a country where people are so off the wall that a preacher in Niles, Ohio, is arrested for burning an Easter Bunny in the public square because he thought it was a pagan god. Or a woman from the National Abstinence Clearing House in Sioux Falls, South Dakota, goes to public schools telling kids not to have sex, while wielding rubber snakes named Herbie Herpes, Albert AIDS, Poor Pregnant Peggy Sue, and Lucy Loss of Reputation.

There's just that twisted edge to America that fascinates me. "Home is where the disease is," that's what I say.

PAUL PROVENZA: In what ways can someone who can't be in their own Dead Kennedys,

can't go to court to defend their rights, put that pin in the elephant's foot?

JELLO BIAFRA: Just to keep doing what we're doing and not be afraid. It's not just about voting.

Whether we're musicians, stand-ups, spoken-word artists, painters, whatever—we're artists whose viewpoints people take seriously. More seriously than they take the views of corporate McNews, in fact, otherwise our corporate lords wouldn't be so afraid of us. That's the power *we* have: people *listen* to us.

Pinochet was so afraid of the power of artists that one of the first people he had executed—after our own Henry Kissinger helped him take over Chile—was a folk singer, Victor Jara. He was executed for the *words in his songs* and what he meant to people there. That's the power *we* have, and we'll always find new ways to use it. We'll always find new ways to sabotage what our corporate lords want everybody to accept as the only available entertainment or factual news.

We can't lose focus on the most important part of all—especially if we're working with humor: we *have* to be able to laugh. We have to be able to have *fun* with what we're doing, even if it's about a deadly serious subject. I know I've written a good song when I'm just laughing with glee at how proud I am of what I've just created. If it's something that really makes me laugh and feel evil again, I know I'm succeeding.

Supposedly, you've become more of an adult or more grown-up when you stop shooting spit wads at your teacher. Well, some of us never outgrow that and find new outlets for that part of our personalities, because that's the part of our personalities we liked in the first place. In some ways, I'm a very immature person—but that's also a good thing, because I've never become the kind of adult that I find colossally boring.

I've gone further out of my way than most of my peers to take on the industry itself and refuse to cooperate with it. The band's name was Dead Kennedys, thus ensuring no major-label contract for us. It's also given me the label "hard to work with" by some elements in Tinseltown, but that's exactly the *kind* of "hard to work with" that I think is important. No, you *can't* put my music in some stupid-ass Levi's commercial. No, I *won't* automatically agree to have one of my songs used in a rape scene in a Tarantino movie. It may give me a bad reputation in some circles, but it's exactly the kind of reputation enjoyed by the artists I respect the most.

CHEECH & CHONG

CHEECH & CHONG set the comedy world of the seventies ablaze with their unabashed celebration of the stoner counterculture. Wildly popular, they quickly made the leap to now-cult films like *Up in Smoke* and *Cheech & Chong's Next Movie*. Following a mutually acrimonious breakup, Cheech Marin shed his outlaw-stoner stage persona, going on to mainstream film and television success in movies like *Born in East L.A.* and *The Lion King*, and TV shows like *Nash Bridges* and *Lost*. Tommy Chong's outlaw stage persona ceased to be a persona when he was raided by federal officials in 2003, arrested, and charged with distributing drug paraphernalia, as part of a high-profile crackdown in the ongoing saga of America's "war on drugs." For disturbing reasons, Chong pleaded guilty, paid a $20,000 fine, and served nine months in prison—his conviction due in large part to their comedy from over thirty years ago. Since then, Cheech & Chong staged a reunion tour, are making a new film, and are helping a very uptight country learn once again to just . . . exhale.

TOMMY CHONG: We always thought of ourselves as a band, really. When we started, we actually used to refer to ourselves that way when we booked gigs, because we played places that would only book bands. So we'd say we were "a band."

CHEECH MARIN: When we got there they'd find out we were a band that did comedy.

TOMMY CHONG: We actually did have a band at first. We thought we'd do a little comedy, and we just never did get around to playing.

PAUL PROVENZA: You guys were one of the first and loudest voices of the counterculture in comedy at the time. Comedy was becoming more alternative, but you weren't *just* alternative comedians; you were something very particular *within* that. You helped define in stand-up the shift in culture in general—which didn't really exist in comedy yet as it had so strongly in music. Carlin, Pryor, Robert Klein, and you were *becoming* it.

CHEECH MARIN: We came at it from a kind of "foot soldier" point of view. We were the dog soldiers of the Cultural Revolution, the grunts in the trenches. But it was just our point of view, and we just did what we did from there.

TOMMY CHONG: We started out in a strip club so we could say or do anything we wanted to, 'cause it wasn't like we were gonna shock anyone. Plus . . . the *truth is the truth*, you know? So there were no repercussions.

When we got into playing different venues, especially in Los Angeles, political correctness maybe played a part. Cheech playing Pedro, the Chicano? I didn't know it at the time and

I don't think Cheech knew it at the time, but it upset a lot of, y'know . . . Chicanos.

CHEECH MARIN: Not a lot . . . Most Chicanos loved that. It was *their* character; they were being *represented*. They never were before.

PAUL PROVENZA: College audiences were your core crowd back then, but if you play colleges now, there's a laundry list of things that you're not supposed to talk about, and first on that list is anything glorifying drugs.

TOMMY CHONG: Back then, we were hired *because* of our drug point of view!

CHEECH MARIN: Maybe soon it'll turn around again and they'll start producing thinkers instead of engineers, which is what's happening right now. All the system seeks is engineers for the machine. It'll come around again, though. The pendulum is already starting to swing back, I think.

PAUL PROVENZA: And it's that current climate that really was behind your recent bust, Tommy, in that they reached back in time to all the glorifying of pot you both did thirty years ago, and busted you *now* essentially for *that*.

TOMMY CHONG: Yeah, totally. I had the audacity to still be doing what I did before and be non-repentive. I just carried on doing what I knew was right; that's really what I got busted for.

And the weird thing is, Cheech & Chong were one of the big reasons marijuana could *never* have gotten legalized back then. We became kinda like scapegoats for the anti-marijuana people, who would always point to us as representing what would happen if it *was* legal. Even though we were doing these extreme characters, not the "average" or typical pot smoker, they used what we were doing as those characters as an example of what would actually happen if you let people smoke pot.

So it really cracked me up that in the indictment they said that I'm a danger to society and they were putting me in jail because we made movies like *Up in Smoke* all those years ago.

PAUL PROVENZA: That irony aside, didn't that statement in the indictment make it a First Amendment case more than a contraband case? And you still chose *not* to fight it, even on that basis?

TOMMY CHONG: Totally. See, the thing is, if I had fought it, I would have won. I would have won *hands down*. I would have walked away. But they blackmailed me. They threatened my wife and they threatened my kids. This was the government saying, "If you don't give up and plead guilty to one count, we're going to go after your wife and kids and charge them, too, and we're going to make all your lives hell." So. . .

CHEECH MARIN: And he thought about that the whole time he was in prison. "Hmmm . . . Did I . . . ? You know, maybe . . . What if . . . ?"

PAUL PROVENZA: Given that we're still dealing with legal issues like that, when you're doing a lot of those original characters and bits now, does it feel like it's still relevant?

CHEECH MARIN: You know what? It feels like they're *classics*. Like we're going out and performing the Frank Sinatra Songbook. The

things we did really didn't have a time and a place; they're kind of evergreen. We updated some to what is going on right now, and Tommy does a lot of stand-up between the Cheech & Chong bits, so we stay somewhat current that way, but the bits that we do together kind of have that timeless quality about them.

TOMMY CHONG: And they've been polished and reworked and done for so many years, they're gems. It transcends the normal comedic thing, you know?

PAUL PROVENZA: Since not much has changed around marijuana since then, do you think performing that material now makes as much of a political statement today as it did back in the day?

TOMMY CHONG: Actually, if we start heading anywhere near *any* obvious political statement, we get shouted down by our own audience! We were Obama supporters in the last election—of course, who else were you going to support?—but the minute I'd start going in that direction, McCain supporters—which were *half* the crowd!—shouted me down. They loved Cheech & Chong, but they were McCain supporters, too. As well as Obama supporters, Ron Paul supporters . . .

CHEECH MARIN: The fact of the matter is that 80 percent of the audience who come to see us is between thirty and forty, which means they weren't even born yet the last time we were onstage. So they've known Cheech & Chong in the abstract, just from movies and TV and our records. They're not the same audience we had back then.

TOMMY CHONG: And back then, because of Vietnam and the draft, everybody was forced into taking a political stance, and pretty much the whole younger generation was forced into being against the war, which meant that everyone in our crowd was against Nixon. But there's no draft now, so we got McCain voters *and* Obama voters in our crowds now. You would've thought that if we mentioned Obama in the show during election time *everyone* would've gone, "Yeah!" But that wasn't the case at all. At *all*.

CHEECH MARIN: Cheech & Chong have become like butter. Everybody likes butter. There's no one type of person who likes butter. You don't have to have a political affiliation to like butter. And we transcend ethnic categories, socioeconomic, political persuasions . . . everything.

PAUL PROVENZA: Aren't we led to believe that those thirty- and forty-year-olds are a big part of those who vote against decriminalization? Who supposedly support keeping it criminalized?

CHEECH MARIN: Depends on who's writing the press, 'cause I find it just the opposite.

PAUL PROVENZA: Do you feel that most people believe the war on drugs in general, and marijuana specifically, is kind of ridiculous?

CHEECH MARIN: If they're smoking dope in our shows, yes.

TOMMY CHONG: You know, when I got busted, it was my experience that people only pay attention to what affects *them*. There are so many people that had no idea that I was busted, or *why* I went to jail, or what it means in the bigger picture in this country. Nowadays people only worry really about what affects them.

You'd be surprised how so many people are so uninformed, don't watch the news. I'm a news junkie and Cheech is a news junkie, so we stay up to date on everything—especially since we're in comedy, we have to be. But when you meet the average person, they don't have a clue about anything really, except what bothers them specifically, you know? What affects *them* directly.

Who's keeping it criminalized is the law enforcement officials—because it's their *gig*. Half the people in prison are in there for drugs. Locking people up is big business. I was part of the private prison industry—firsthand.

It's not only owned by private corporations, but the corporations change their names periodically to avoid lawsuits. When I was in jail, the corporation name went from Wackenhut to Geo.

CHEECH MARIN: Did you say "Whackin' It"?

PAUL PROVENZA: That would be a perfectly appropriate name for a prison.

TOMMY CHONG: And I was also in prison with a lot of people who are there because it's a financial thing, too—like for not paying taxes. I was there with tons of people who had said, "Hey, you don't have to pay taxes." And they're sitting there, rotting in jail forever.

Take forfeiture laws, for instance: millions of dollars that never get reported. Friends of mine got busted with millions of dollars of cash and weed, and all they did was take them to the station and put them in a room while they went and raided their houses. They grabbed all the cash and drugs, came back, and said, "Get out of here," and my friends just walked away. Nobody ever knew about the millions of dollars. No one knew about the pot, which the DEA and law enforcement themselves just went ahead and sold. They're one big criminal enterprise themselves. While I was in prison, this guy from Colombia told me about a "secret" airstrip there that the DEA flies out of *daily*. Now, who searches the DEA when *they* land a plane full of drugs in America?

PAUL PROVENZA: Which was the whole idea behind the Iran-Contra scandal back in the eighties.

TOMMY CHONG: Exactly. Did that go away? Uh-uh. Did that all of a sudden stop because people found out about it? Nope.

CHEECH MARIN: So there you go.

RANDY CREDICO

FROM A CROWD-PLEASING Las Vegas impressionist, Randy Credico evolved into a political satirist,
and then kept going—all the way to radical activist. Finding Reaganite eighties crowds too far Right,
he took an even sharper Left to Nicaragua, where
his comedy and activism merged. He's the subject
of the documentary *60 Spins Around the Sun* (pro-
duced by Jack Black), and is featured with Russell
Simmons in *Lockdown, USA,* a documentary about
New York's Rockefeller drug laws—the harshest in
America—against which Randy crusades tirelessly.
He is director of the William M. Kunstler Fund for
Racial Justice, a legal aid service founded by family
and friends of the radical lawyer/activist—Randy's
friend and hero. As of this writing, Randy just announced his candidacy in a primary challenge for
the U.S. Senate seat currently held by Sen. Charles
Schumer (D). On Wednesday and Thursday nights,
in New York, Randy's uncompromising political
commentary can be appreciated in a perfect trian-
gulation of his natural elements: he hosts The Lenny
Bruce Comedy Club, at the Yippie! Museum in
Greenwich Village.

RANDY CREDICO: I had just done an ounce of cocaine the previous week, and was watching something about drug laws on C-SPAN, and I see guys getting twelve to fifteen years in prison for the same thing I'd just done. So I started digging and saw how they're jailing people left and right for the war on drugs. But I used a *lot* of cocaine in my life and I didn't go to jail over it—because I'm a white, middle-class man.

We have *two million people* in prison—double what China or Russia has—and most are *political* prisoners; victims of a political decision to lock up unemployable, uneducated people, almost *all* of whom are black. It's a reinvention of the convict leasing of the 1890s.

Worse than Slavery, by David Oshinsky, about Parchman Farm in Mississippi, details the minor offenses that only applied to blacks then. You could *murder* someone and do less time than a black man stealing a chicken. Well, you can murder someone *now* and do five to fifteen, like Robert Chambers, or you can be Rufus Boyd getting twenty-five to life.

We went from slavery to Reconstruction, for the next sixty years had convict leasing and social control, then a whiff of change in the sixties with the Civil Rights movement, and we've now regressed to where we basically have slaves and social control again.

It's the biggest crisis in America, and no one gives a fuck. It's not part of the public debate. Do people care about the Sean Bell shooting or twenty other black kids shot in the back by police across the country? You hear about Virginia Tech, but you can't even compare it to the number of black people killed all the time in this country. There are absolutely *no* rights. It drives me crazy.

I'm working on a case now with a guy who's done *eighteen years* for two dime bags. It's not anecdotal; I've got files of cases like that. I know the pain and suffering a child endures when their mother's in prison. Elaine Bartlett was set up by a drug dealer who could get off if he brought people in, so Elaine, with five children and a mother dying of sickle cell anemia, was sentenced to twenty years. There are *so many* stories like that.

Someone once said, "You can judge a society by its prisons."

Well, ours *suck*. You don't need to go to Abu Ghraib; go to Sing Sing, Attica, Leavenworth—they're the same.

I'm not balanced about this—my father did eight years in prison. He was a model prisoner at Ohio State Penitentiary before I was born, and I was born to a guy who was *angry*.

PAUL PROVENZA: It's so far outside conventional discourse, how do you make it funny if people aren't even *aware* of the realities?

RANDY CREDICO: I don't *know* how to! It's funny, I suppose, comparing Bush's drug history or Rush Limbaugh's oxycontin addiction to these guys', or the time some Wall Streeter gets for stealing millions versus the petty crimes these guys get *life* for. But it's been morally and physically debilitating, being involved in this for the last ten years.

People just don't give a fuck—it's poor

black people. They're like Jews in Germany in 'thirty-three. *Five hundred thousand* black people were stopped and frisked without probable cause in New York City last year—more than were stopped in Berlin in 1933, okay?

PAUL PROVENZA: The private prison industry adds yet another layer that people don't really understand.

RANDY CREDICO: Right! Wackenhut, Correctional Corporation, Pricor, Cornell Companies . . . New York's got Corcraft, where prisoners make furniture for the state and eyeglasses for Medicaid/Medicare—which put people in that business out of work.

If you bring twenty thousand prisoners into your district, you've created an entire *county* big enough to qualify on the census, and you get more federal money. Factories have shut down, so legislators fight to get prisons instead.

It's big business for everyone: they get these guys and throw them into, say, 100 Centre Street in Manhattan, where in every courtroom you've got a black defendant, a white judge, a white jury, and three white cops just slamming these fuckers through the criminal justice system right into the prison system. There's five hundred DAs and assistant DAs, plus judges, lawyers, bail bondsmen, clerks, and all their entire staffs. You have buses going to Rikers, the vendors that sell everything to Rikers . . . it goes on and on.

Then they'll go to prison upstate—with staffs, buses, vendors, that whole system there, too. Then families who visit their sons or dads

need motel rooms, places to eat . . . A whole economy's tied in, so you *need* defendants—and they're using young, black eighteen-year-olds to feed this fucking *monster.*

And thanks to this drug war, hundreds of thousands of African-Americans are politically disenfranchised. Republicans have *banked* on that disenfranchisement! And Democrats are unknowing accomplices.

In Tulia, Texas, forty-six people—*13 percent of the black population*—were arrested in one fell swoop on trumped-up drug charges. No one knew about it, so I just parked myself down there and spent four years working their cases and doing benefits and stuff.

Arianna Huffington knew about Tulia; she helped me out there. But Bill O'Reilly *really* helped—*I* did *his* show, can you believe it? He said on air, "Senator Corona, you've *got* to reopen these cases."

The very next day they reopened them. Everything else about him sucks, but he did help there. I hate to say it, but Arianna Huffington and Amy Goodman aren't gonna influence the Texas criminal court of appeals—but a guy like O'Reilly *can.* He's got a lot of listeners there.

PAUL PROVENZA: So which came first for you, the comedy or the real, hands-on activism and involvement in the issues you care about?

RANDY CREDICO: I'm a product of the sixties. I did a lot of psychedelics, my cousin was a radical SDS speaker, and I got the politics of that era.

I do political impressions, so David Frye

was a big influence, but Mort Sahl—personally—inspired me to do political humor. In 'seventy-five, I was working a lounge in Vegas, and Sahl was playing at the Las Vegas Hilton. I'd watch him every night—very, *very* smart—and started hanging out with him. One day he said, "If you're doing impressions, make them political. Start reading the paper."

It kinda creeped in, but my act got more and more political—to the dismay of people there, who would plead, "You're such a gifted impressionist. Do Jimmy Stewart; do Bogart; do Archie Bunker . . ."

And I'd do those, but something inside me wanted to do political stuff. I'd do Humphrey Bogart—but I'd do him giving his speech against the death penalty from *Knock on Any Door. That* got me fired from the Sahara.

I worked a cruise ship and got kicked off because I just couldn't keep my mouth shut. They said it was a suicide streak, I'm my own worst enemy . . . But it was impossible to just do shit that didn't *mean* anything. I just couldn't get inspired to get up and do impressions of Redd Foxx talking to Lamont.

I remember the moment I really made the switch: November 1980, when Reagan won the election. The country was turning to the Right, and I kinda flipped and submerged myself in political humor from that point on.

But there wasn't much activism in Vegas. With all these police killings there, judges giving black kids *thirty years* for burglary . . . I'd go crazy reading the paper. And I'd be working in revues, doing Jack Nicholson impressions. I'd beg them to let me do the other stuff.

I was writing really Left-wing humor, and social/political humor had emerged again in New York in the late seventies after Watergate, and I thought that'd be a better place to do it. A lot of comics were just developing on that scene, and most of them weren't doing that kind of stuff. But I didn't do it to distinguish myself; I did it because I was an activist inside.

I wanted to use comedy as the vehicle *for* my activism. I was a political-activist satirist. There was zero objectivity in what I was saying up there. I definitely had an agenda. A hard-Left agenda.

PAUL PROVENZA: That was an uphill battle. Did you have anyone championing you, helping you get some breaks?

RANDY CREDICO: Some people in the business appreciated what I was doing. I got on a few television shows, thanks to yourself, Richard Belzer, the manager/producer David Steinberg, who put me on one of his shows . . . Jim McCawley, who booked *The Tonight Show,* appreciated it.

I did *The Tonight Show,* but only once, in 1984. I used it as a platform to slam Reagan and his policies in Central America and elsewhere. And I'm the only comic ever to do *The Tonight Show* whose price went *down* the next day. I got nothing out of it except a headache from the owner of Dangerfield's for not mentioning his club on the show.

At one point, Carson did one of those winces, you know? And up until a point I got a lot of applause—until I basically called then–UN ambassador Jeane Kirkpatrick a Nazi. I said, "If you look at her and analyze what she says, you gotta ask yourself, '*Did* Eva Braun die in that bunker in 1945?'"

It was very difficult to go after Reagan on TV at the time. Like how in 2002 it was suicidal to do anti-Bush stuff on television. *No one* was doing it. No one went against the grain. That's why we ended up in a war.

Everyone was afraid to challenge the Patriot Act; no one was challenging Ashcroft when some excessive shit started happening. Letterman fell into the fear; he had Ashcroft on his show being all friendly. Jon Stewart fell into the fear; he jumped on the patriotic bandwagon. It took six or seven years before people finally caught on.

Keith Olbermann was one of the guys who finally opened the door. But he doesn't have enough black people on his show. No one does. They all use Eugene Robinson from the *Washington Post* and shove him around from show to show so it looks like they're pluralistic. They're not.

The majority of people doing political comedy on TV are only riding the surf; I don't think they're deeply involved. It feels superficial. It's all just about Democrats or Republicans instead of the whole *spectrum* being delved into.

They're all just "headline-hunting." That's what Jay Leno does—but he admits he's not political. The others won't admit they're just headline-hunting. But what *can* a million people watching *all* identify with? Some verbal gaffe from the day before, Dick Cheney shooting someone . . .

But there's way more important things they should have gone after Cheney for. Like everybody went after Bush with "He's so dumb." Well, his policies weren't dumb to the people he was working for and with, and they were horrendous. People died, and a lot of people still suffer because of them. You have to go after that *real* stuff—and early. Way before it's safe.

Anyone who's not blind could see in 2001 what was going on with Bush. They should've been attacking him on the Patriot Act eight years ago, on Guantanamo seven years ago, on the Iraq war seven years ago. Mark Twain would have; he went against the Spanish-American War in 1898. Thomas Nast went against conventional wisdom to satirize supporters of slavery in his day.

But you're not gonna stay on television five days a week unless you're acceptable to powers that be. You can maybe tiptoe out there, that's all.

PAUL PROVENZA: Well, no one goes quite as far as you do. You weren't content just to do material about Nicaragua, you had to actually go and live there. How'd that come about?

RANDY CREDICO: I'd been talking on stage for a few years about Nicaragua and Reagan's Central America policy. So many people died there and the war was a complete lie—like the Iraq War now.

My uncle was a CIA operative in the fifties and was *banned* from Nicaragua. He'd say, "You think it's so great down there? *Go.*"

So I did. And I fell in love with it. It was like being in Mexico or Berlin in the twenties, where all these journalists and writers and cultural figures would hang out. They were all over Nicaragua. All these great writers and journalists . . . And Julie Christie—weird, right? There were people who'd been friends with Frida Kahlo and Diego Rivera . . . That was the kind of environment it was.

I became well known there. It was a great refuge for a comedian who didn't have any standing here anymore. It was my crowd down there. I'd do shows in front of the embassy Thursday mornings after drinking this rum they have there until three A.M. and trying to get up at six thirty to do a set when the sun came out.

I did shows for Manuel Ortega and the minister of interior at a couple of private parties. They loved it.

I really plunged into it. I started working for the Sandinista government raising money for the election in 1990.

And I took other comedians down there—Jimmy Tingle, Barry Crimmins—who is the finest political comic around; there's no one better. "Humorists Against War," or HAW, I called it. We toured the country; we'd perform for American volunteers picking coffee up in Esteli, Matagalpa. . .

It was weird, but those were the greatest moments of my life. Great crowds, great shows, and I was exposed to a *real* social and political revolution. A possible one, anyway, snuffed out eventually, like the Mexican revolution was. I look back wistfully that that kind of stuff might reappear.

I went about twenty-five times. I was so involved and obsessed with it. I'd come back and talk about it nonstop onstage and other comics would say, "What the fuck are you doing up there? No one cares about Nicaragua."

Now a lot of them wish they'd been talking about it back then, too, because if everyone was maybe things wouldn't have gotten so bad.

And I proved to be right about it, you know? Iran-Contra and all that . . . Between Nicaragua and El Salvador, about 150,000 people died—all to destroy a great experiment.

But . . . Whatever you could do, you know? One person can't change anything, you can just be part of change.

PAUL PROVENZA: Was Nicaragua about activism, or really more about just finding *your* audience?

RANDY CREDICO: Both. And it transformed me as a person to be able to blend political activism and comedy and feel like I was doing something.

I'd come back here and write about it, and perform at all these political events around the country before the 'eighty-six elections. They were my crowd. I had a nice run in these circles that stemmed from Nicaragua. It opened the door to a lot of performing opportunities I'd never have known. And I'd work comedy clubs a bit . . . but the Nicaragua experience gave me the sustenance to continue.

PAUL PROVENZA: You're so strident about satirists not being committed enough, being too soft, or taking the easy road—how did the hard-core, radical activist in you allow you to just "preach to the choir" like that?

RANDY CREDICO: A lot of it's the psychological reasons you get into comedy to begin with. You do it for acceptance, to say something, and because you like that applause—it's very addictive, that applause. So it's nice to get the kind of response Richard Jeni would *always* get in front of *any* crowd. He'd *always* kill. It's just really nice to get that once in a while.

Yes, a lot of it *was* preaching to the choir, but they'd tell others about me and expand my base a little. I'd also bring up stuff with "the choir" that even *they* might not have been familiar with.

And there are a lot of people who are not yet *in* the choir who might join. There are open-minded people out there and you can get to *them*. People who are aware and ready for something different are out there.

Yes, you really want to get to *other* people, and there *are* ways to do that. But "the choir" also needs to know there's some art out there, if you want to call it art, that reflects their views. Antiwar activists and liberals and Leftists need comedy, too, you know. *Everyone* needs something to laugh about and to inspire them. And to help *keep* them inspired.

MARGARET CHO

MARGARET CHO IS unusual, and not just because she's the first, and perhaps only, Asian-American comedian to find such high-profile success. After an ill-fated sitcom experience that tried to package her as something she wasn't, Cho tore up the package and set it on fire. In her stage show *Margaret Cho:* *Beautiful,* her stand-up framed a loving, inspirational sideshow burlesque of the beauty in all that is "perverted," wondrous and strange. Here, she explains why comedy means more to her as a celebration of good than as a confrontation against evil, and why it has given so many of her fans cause to rejoice.

PAUL PROVENZA: Do you care if all that you're doing is "preaching to the converted"?

MARGARET CHO: You're not preaching, you're *celebrating.* Celebrating what you feel, and what you think, and what *they* think. I think that's the nature of comedy; we laugh because we agree, and that is wonderful.

PAUL PROVENZA: *Margaret Cho: Beautiful* was an incredibly political show that said very little about actual politics, if at all. You presented all these burlesque dancers who do not fit conventional notions of "beautiful." You had a transvestite; you had Ian Harvie, a transgender comedian; and you had Dirty Martini, a big, female erotic dancer in a flag-themed G-string, pulling dollar bills out of her ass to Lee Greenwood's "God Bless the U.S.A."

These are things that are generally scorned in America, but you declared them "beautiful." Did you intend the show to be political or subversive or socially significant?

MARGARET CHO: I think of it as socially significant. This show can make people think about what they *feel* inside, whatever their frustration or alienation is, and feel good about that. I think it's really beautiful to be able to do that. It's kind of healing work; it helps me get through life. As opposed to feeling negative about things, why not feel beautiful? I think that's really a scary choice, but it's backed up by the fact that the show is funny and fun and it feels good. I want people to feel good about *themselves.* I feel this is possible.

I'm critical of society and the way it treats women and people who are different—not even different, people who are *normal,* actually. Being different *is* the norm, that's really the truth of it. The human experience is so varied. And if you are a woman, if you are a person of color, if you are gay, lesbian, bisexual, transgender, if you are a person of size, if you are a person of intelligence, if you are a person of integrity, then you are considered a minority in this world. It's really hard for us to find messages of self-love and support anywhere. If you don't have self-esteem, you will hesitate to do anything in your life. You will hesitate to report a rape, to vote, to defend yourself when you are discriminated against. You will hesitate to *dream.*

For us to have self-esteem is truly an act of revolution, and our revolution is long overdue.

PAUL PROVENZA: I think your line "People say, 'Don't go there.' I *live* there!" sums up what you're doing with your comedy.

MARGARET CHO: I think when you just say, "Okay, this is who I am, this is what I'm doing, this is what my journey is," that's really exciting. You let go of pretense and of trying to act cool and you're just admitting to everything— and I'm guilty of *everything.*

PAUL PROVENZA: You "live there."

MARGARET CHO: I live there. I'm constantly there.

PAUL PROVENZA: Have you always owned that and tried to express that, or have you evolved into it?

MARGARET CHO: I think it's just getting older and wanting to mother people; wanting to mother myself and parent myself. I hope that when I'm long gone people will look back at what I've done, and they'll be fond of it, love it, that they'll remember me with great . . . affection.

I just want to love everyone. Really.

PAUL PROVENZA: Even those who oppose you?

MARGARET CHO: Yes, absolutely! That's my favorite kind of person to love. I love to turn the other cheek. I'm so Christian sometimes.

PAUL PROVENZA: So how did you come to comedy as your creative voice?

MARGARET CHO: I did comedy because I didn't know what else to do. I was a dropout at school. I was a terrible student. I was fucking up. I didn't know what to do, and this was *real*. This was totally the right thing, and it totally made me feel good and I was so excited.

I remember when I started I was so scared of doing it that every time I had to do a show, I would question myself up and down, like "Why am I doing this to myself? I'm so fucking scared!" I was afraid of people and what they thought. I'm still afraid of it.

I'm still afraid when I get a really good run where people are really laughing and I'm just riffing. I don't even know what I'm gonna say next, but I'm just riffing and going and they're really laughing and laughing . . . That's a really scary place to be in, because you have to keep topping yourself and keep it moving higher and higher, you know? It's really terrifying. You have to hold that energy up there like it's a big piece of fabric you're trying to keep in the air. It's a very weird experience.

PAUL PROVENZA: You want to empower people through your comedy and encourage possibilities for them, and I've seen people in your audience really touched by that. I would imagine they get very personal, sharing pretty intimate things with you when you talk to them.

MARGARET CHO: People are really beautiful. One woman wrote to me saying that her father had just recently died of AIDS. She had never really gotten to know him, because he had abandoned her for many years and she was alienated by him because he was gay. He really loved my comedy, so she would talk to him about me, and he was excited to talk to her about me. By the time he died, she had been able to reconnect with him through my film. That was such a beautiful moment for me. I'm really proud to be able to give that to people.

When you laugh at something, you can alleviate yourself of the pain of that situation. So humor is healing that way. Something that's horrible, something that's humiliating, can somehow have a kind of redemption in the telling. I want people to feel brave, that their opinions about things are being validated, that they're being accepted. I hope I'm making a difference. I really feel I make a difference for myself. I'm really enjoying the ride; I just love it.

PAUL PROVENZA: Your portrayal of your Old World, traditional mother in your act has been a source of some conflict for you, with some Asian-Americans declaring it a racist portrayal. That must have shocked you, of all people, to be accused of that.

MARGARET CHO: Well, that's my *truth*. It's really who she is, those are the things she says, that's the way she says them, and to me it's always been funny.

I think to some people it sounds racist because we don't really see that truth very often. We don't see Asian people talking about anything, ever. It's a very rare thing to hear us talking about our lives, or who we are, or what our families are like. It's racist if you view it through white eyes, because you don't know that experience.

PAUL PROVENZA: Weren't there some Asian groups that called you out on that?

MARGARET CHO: Because it's unflattering, maybe. It's an unflattering view, but it's real.

PAUL PROVENZA: Do you ever find yourself on the other side of that when you watch something and think it's racist or it's homophobic?

MARGARET CHO: Oh, yeah. I definitely am critical of people and of things I find racist. Like the Jena Six— just a terrible injustice and a sickness in our nation. That's where I get puritanical on race stuff. It's very convoluted. It's a very complicated issue, racism.

PAUL PROVENZA: So, if I lived next door to your mother and knew her and *I* got up onstage and did the same impression of her as you do, would that be racist?

MARGARET CHO: I don't think it would be racist, but it may be racist to *somebody*. But is it preferable for characters who have an accent to be completely invisible? Should foreign characters not be seen then? If somebody says it's racist, it's because they don't want to know what's real. They'd rather maintain this idea

of invisible people. Basically, that's what that statement is.

PAUL PROVENZA: But saying that you should portray them in a positive light is not the same as preferring them to be invisible, is it?

MARGARET CHO: It *is* a positive light. I think it *is* positive. I think I'm very positive.

PAUL PROVENZA: When you got these criticisms of racism on your part, which is the antithesis of what you're all about, what went through your head and your heart?

MARGARET CHO: Oh, it just shows me that there is racism there, too, *within* the Asian community. They don't want to see that, because they're afraid of themselves. That conservatism is very Old World; it's from another generation. The people who accuse me of certain things are generally of that generation. The younger generation loves me so much. They're grateful, because they grew up with me. And that's beautiful. But because I'm a woman, and Asian culture is generally very sexist, when I "talk out of school" or whatever, *that's* a problem for the older generation. It's a weird situation.

For my parents, after all that I've accomplished in my life, all that I've done, their proudest moment was when I got married. That's all they cared about. They were so happy that I chose a man to be with, that I settled down with a man, that a man would *have* me.

They don't know how to handle the idea that I'm actually successful, so they don't celebrate it, really; they don't know how to. It's very painful for me, because they just don't get it. And it's because of the way that Asian culture is for them.

PAUL PROVENZA: And you've endeared yourself to the queer community. You can do a "fag" joke, and they understand it's just like them at a diner at three in the morning making fag jokes.

MARGARET CHO: Yeah, it's *us*. It's *me*. It's because *I'm* a big fag.

PAUL PROVENZA: Why do you think it is that so many comedians get misinterpreted when they try to get into nuances of things like race and sexuality and gender, much like what happened to you around how you portray your mother? Lately I've seen really fine, thoughtful comedians try to talk about Israel and its military activities, for example, and immediately they're accused of being anti-Semitic. Yet, the whole point of exploring the subject is to try to figure out how we can all just *get along* better.

MARGARET CHO: Well, the misinterpretation has to do with the fact that sometimes people are so used to being invisible that when they're seen they don't know what to do. They automatically freak out. So in the rare instances when it *is* talked about—like when I talk about Korean culture—it has to be hotly argued. Just the introduction of it is so bizarre and out of the mainstream that it shocks people. It shocks them into disagreement, into just being disgruntled.

PAUL PROVENZA: So they impose their own narrative on it, because it's all they *can* do?

MARGARET CHO: Exactly.

PAUL PROVENZA: One of the things I love about the art form of comedy is that we have the freedom to say what other people can't. I feel like if you don't take advantage of that and confront people and say all the shit you're not supposed to, then you're wasting your time.

MARGARET CHO: Yeah! I think it's great to provoke people, to make them think. I think it's beautiful. I think what's beautiful is Dirty Martini pulling chewed-up, digested dollar bills out of her ass—out of her beautiful, beautiful ass. It makes me want to cry.

PAUL PROVENZA: Isn't it a strange world where if you just embrace what you believe and how you want to be, it takes you out of the mainstream? The truth is that despite this mythology of "normal, middle-class Americans," a whole lot more people are buying fetish gear, gay porn, and hookers than most would think. So while a lot of stuff you're doing is celebratory for you and your audience, it must cause some inner conflict or turmoil for people who aren't able to admit to themselves who they really are. People who are in denial of things they feel but would rather *not* be feeling must get their worlds rocked to see it celebrated.

MARGARET CHO: Yeah, well, I *hope* so! It is strange that when you delve into the personal it becomes political, but the whole existence of it is political. It's very strange. I'm Asian-American, I'm a woman, I'm queer, I'm so many different things that we don't hear in comedy. So I feel like I'm doing something revolutionary just by *existing*.

PAUL PROVENZA: I think what you do is actually kind of *backwards* satire. Stephen Colbert, for example, embraces the point of view he wants to criticize, and, by committing to that point of view so completely, ends up mocking it. You, on the other hand, fully embrace what you really *do* believe, become an example of the joy in looking at the world the way you do. That, by extension, becomes a criticism of the status quo. Colbert mocks the opposing point of view; you never even engage it but instead present an alternative. That joyful, inclusive alternative mocks the opposing viewpoint by contrast rather than in conflict.

MARGARET CHO: Yes. You know what? It's *sincere.*

I'm sincere. And sincerity is the new black.

RICK OVERTON

AS A DYSLEXIC kid, to avoid getting in trouble, Rick Overton cultivated his ability to make authority figures laugh. That ability grew into a truly original stand-up voice and a stunning, unique performance style—winning him an Emmy, countless film and television roles, and the respect and admiration of just about everyone in comedy. His quick, keen intelligence and fearlessness have even made him one of Robin Willams's favorite improv partners. Having lived his life as a spiritual journey, Overton believes comedy is a way to teach some of what he's learned—but that doesn't mean he's above a good boner joke, either. A self-described "imperfectionist," Overton celebrates nonconformity, denounces the status quo, and warns us of the normal guy who mows his lawn and hides bodies in the basement.

RICK OVERTON: I consider myself to be a parody of a satirist. I think satirists take themselves way too seriously; I'm *pretending* to take myself seriously. I'm really very hip to myself. I'm on to me.

PAUL PROVENZA: The thing that's always struck me about your work, and continues to, is that there are real substantive points of view and ideas in your work, but it's also surreal, absurdist, silly, and even embraces brilliant physical comedy, too.

RICK OVERTON: And my raging boner. I try to put a boner in there for the folks that *just* want boner jokes, because they're the ones that *need* the other satire. Rather than just give satire to people who want satire, you *sneak* it into the worlds of the people who don't with things based more "lower chakra," if you will—and I'm *one* of 'em. There are times I don't want the huffy-puffy, hoity-toity stuff either, I just want a good, dirty joke.

The hardest challenge—but also the coolest thing—is to get satire to the folks that weren't expecting it, as opposed to the ones who are.

PAUL PROVENZA: Do you get tough responses?

RICK OVERTON: Sometimes it's *real* tough. Sometimes things get rough because of how *good* it went. When you're challenging authority, eventually authority finds out. Not only are you challenging authority and rattling *that* cage, but peers will tell you you're paranoid for pointing things out about it. So you'll have like a double-layer thing going on: a big shark's coming and you're trying to pull your friend ashore, but your friend's fighting you as

you're trying to get him ashore from the shark trying to get you *and* your friend.

PAUL PROVENZA: Janeane Garofalo talks about how the role of pundit was sort of thrust upon her—they kept calling to have her come in and do the wacky liberal viewpoint, and she said that she feels like they wanted her because she's not a threat. Whereas if you bring on Noam Chomsky, you've got trouble on your hands.

RICK OVERTON: Yeah, and . . . Oops!—she *still* became a threat. Evil people are clever, but no evil person is intelligent. They're just the height of cleverness. Because clever is bite to bite, moment to moment, grab to grab—not "overall picture." You can't afford to look at the overall picture when you're evil, because you'll see how fucked you are and what you've done. You're just really good at grabbing, biting, running, hiding.

As a little kid, all through school I was in a special class, which is why I tell jokes now to "Jedi" my way out of trouble. I'm dyslexic, and of course ADD. I couldn't read a book, so instead I'd read people.

To a soul, comics are all misfits. Where we didn't fit in for reason A, we'll *make* you love us for reason B. We learn people skills that no one else gets.

PAUL PROVENZA: Do you get accused of being elitist in a way? That you're basically saying, "You're all stupid"?

RICK OVERTON: I'm *facing* elitism this way. I think out of the box because I was never invited *in* the box, so outside the box is the only territory I know. I say, "a 'misfit' is a part made *better* than the machine it's installed in," because that's how it appears to me. To me, this isn't elitism.

Who is it thinking me elitist? One of the guys I've bagged on? Of course *they'll* say I'm elitist; they don't want to hear any truth in what I've said about them. They'll go to great lengths to put it back on me.

Hey, not all the turtles make it to the ocean. A lot of 'em just push sand, or birds get 'em or whatever. I don't wanna *sound elitist,* but . . . someone will call you elitist whenever you tell the truth, and otherwise I'm sitting here with, "Should I say that? Wait, am I afraid of being called elitist?" We're out of fuckin' time. Just say it. Everyone just start saying what you mean. Back and forth, faster, faster! Let's get going!

PAUL PROVENZA: Do you feel like you have a *mission* to communicate these things, or is it just that you want to?

RICK OVERTON: I *want* to say it, and if people learn, that's good. And if people have things to teach *me,* great! I'll shut up and listen. My manhood isn't based on, "I have to be right about everything I say over you." I don't need that; it means nothing to me. I *love* not knowing stuff and then learning it.

PAUL PROVENZA: What do you think of all these issues about language?

RICK OVERTON: The new C-word is "Constitution." Look, there's the upper level of politically correct and the lower level of politically correct. Racists have picked up the trick now of using "Hey, you're censoring me," when they do things that are actually harmful. They just imitate, because they *learned* to imitate. And now they go, "Hey don't censor me, man! I want to say 'nigger,' 'kike,' and 'spic.' Why don't I get to say that?" Well, there's a different history to you. It means something different when you do it.

PAUL PROVENZA: Since the Michael Richards thing, a good half of any audience understands the irony of saying the word on a nightclub stage now. And it's a really interesting dynamic.

RICK OVERTON: Right. Sometimes it takes some gigantic horrible event, and Michael's not a racist as much as he is a rage-ist. If it was an Asian guy or a Hispanic up there, it'd be a whole different bit. He was just trying to push boundaries, but he didn't get that we're not in Andy Kaufman mode anymore and we don't have Irony 8.6 installed. We don't hear whole sentences, and we assemble our own sentences with three or four words out of the entire paragraph that you said and we make something we can be mad at out of it.

PAUL PROVENZA: How do you share that with an audience so they receive it the right way?

RICK OVERTON: I'm not trying to preach it. I just try to sneak it in with my act. I try to have a joke ratio that's more about the joke than anything else. I love jokes. And I love jokes that have nothing to do with anything. I need that, too. But we're in a crisis time, and I think it's negligent not to put stuff like that in.

PAUL PROVENZA: Have we ever not been in a crisis time?

RICK OVERTON: This is worse. I think it's not accurate to say it's like the other times. How are you gonna feel if you didn't say anything? Whatever punishment you're taking now for being called Chicken Little, well, the sky is actually falling this time.

PAUL PROVENZA: One of the things that frustrates me is that a lot of mainstream comedy is very much status quo. The person who gets targeted is the one who's different. It makes me crazy when people get picked on in an audience by a comic for having a weird hair color or dressing differently.

RICK OVERTON: I don't do that. I honor those people.

PAUL PROVENZA: Yeah, me too! I celebrate them.

RICK OVERTON: You know what? The normal guy mowing that lawn is always the one with the stinky basement that the dog whines about.

PAUL PROVENZA: With the bodies in it?

RICK OVERTON: A collection of hands in a jar. Human teeth in the fridge. That's always the guy, and that's why you've got to put on your "look how normal I am" uniform all day. There's nothing in my apartment I'm ashamed of except the porn collection and, you know, it depends on who you are for me to be ashamed. Otherwise, I don't have any reason to hide it, so I get to be me all the time.

PAUL PROVENZA: Why do you think some comedians just pander to the status quo but others choose to be more of who they are and remain unique?

RICK OVERTON: I hate to tell you, they're *all* being who they are. And I pander, too, sometimes, when I have to. I mix it. But it's fly fishing. Cast far, reel near. And they're doing what they're meant to do. Not everyone's supposed to do the same thing. I'm not judging that part. Good for them. Get your laugh any way you can.

PAUL PROVENZA: If you had to give yourself a theme or something, what's the takeaway that you love an audience to pick up and go home with?

RICK OVERTON: Misfit's rights.

PAUL PROVENZA: Misfit's rights.

RICK OVERTON: That's right. You have the right to be here, and not everyone that judged you was authentically good at their job of judging you. And almost everyone, to a soul, if you boiled them down or gave them sodium pentothal, they feel like a misfit. Almost everyone does. But mostly it's "difference is better than sameness." And not just arbitrary, but conscientious difference.

PAUL PROVENZA: Owning it.

RICK OVERTON: Conscientiously. That is, you know, some guys go, "Hey I'm a man, I feed my family."

Hey, a squirrel can feed its fucking family. I see them do it up the trees all day. They're bringing nuts up to their family, that's nothing. That's not what made you a man. Being a man is how you can protect people you've never met. Sometimes they need a spank to hear it, because they don't like hearing it—because they spent most of their life not doing it.

PAUL PROVENZA: A spank is the language they know.

RICK OVERTON: Yeah, and they respect big tough guys. I don't do it a lot. I try to be playful, but I let them know I'm playing.

The thing I strive for is "keep your kid alive." But there's two kids—childlike and childish. One makes, the other destroys. I'd rather you walked out with a childlike kid inside you more than the childish one.

The only way we ever get out of problems is by being inventive. Being repetitive does not solve problems. Every culture is defined by its innovators, its artists.

PAUL PROVENZA: I think people have kind of been shamed out of passion in life, too.

RICK OVERTON: Absolutely, shamed out of passion. Because passion makes you do what's next, rather than what was, and it makes you disobedient.

PAUL PROVENZA: It makes you follow something other than just rules.

RICK OVERTON: And fear cancels passion. And I'm not saying I'm not afraid. I try to remember that I'm afraid, and have passion override it.

PAUL PROVENZA: So how do we as artists or performers, and as human beings, spread non-fear?

RICK OVERTON: Try to be brave, so there's an example somewhere. So someone can imitate you, and get it even better than you. And don't be freaked when they beat you at it. As a teacher, teachers hate it when a student beats them, but fuck that. That's one of your fears.

People are scared of change, because they're afraid that if they're not evolving at the right rate, they'll disappear. "Oh shit, you're replacing me. Everything was great until the next thing showed up. I'll be replaced. Food supply cut off. Mammal scared."

PAUL PROVENZA: This is an odd little paradox: That the two things that remain from all rich cultures are warfare and art.

RICK OVERTON: That's it. And art's more important than warfare, because everyone copies the weapons until they spread. So everyone's got the exact same weapon but they don't get the exact same art.

The only actual "authority" can come from an author; everything else is fake. There's a lot of frauds, a lot of book bullies, a lot of pseudo-intellectuals. They quiz you on everyone else's book. It's despicable. "Oh, really? You didn't read that book? I thought you would've."

Hey, don't start getting tough until it's *your* book. "Stop being so brave with everybody else's hard fucking work, you coward. I want *your* opinion. You only remotely become interesting at that point. And by the way, I don't hate you. You just had it coming. You needed a good spank. We're both 98 cents worth of minerals and salt water with a meat battery on top. You get to do that, and I get to do this back. We're exactly equal. You had it fucking coming. And I'd rather see you as my friend next week because you came around, which is not the result you were looking for with me."

PAUL PROVENZA: Or you at least respect that I gave you what you had coming.

RICK OVERTON: You should respect when someone takes you at your own horseshit game, if you're any kind of man or any kind of woman. And I'm not here to babysit you, though it ends up being that sometimes. And I've *been* babysat and I've had this handed down to me, so I know it works. I came around.

GEORGE CARLIN

GEORGE CARLIN WAS well on his way to main-stream stand-up success when Lenny Bruce unlocked a door hiding hitherto unknown depth and meaning in the art of stand-up. Inspired by the possibilities Lenny revealed, Carlin veered sharply off his care-fully planned, Danny Kaye–wannabe course to crash through the door with a comedic force that splintered it to oblivion.

Doing original, cleverly inventive, lighthearted comedy had launched Carlin on a people-pleasing comedian's dream trajectory to Las Vegas hotels and prime-time television variety shows, satisfying his childhood dream of becoming an all-around showbiz personality and feeding his self-aware need for attention and recognition. But the trouble-maker inside him—the thirteen-year-old pot smoker and unruly school cutup—was growing stronger and demanding attention, too As the late sixties' popular disillusionment with the cultural and politi-cal status quo grew more urgent, so did that rogue voice within him, becoming too disruptive to be ig-nored.

His straitlaced, conventional appearance steadily began to transform: his hair grew longer and a beard materialized in sharp contrast to the customary jacket and tie, which soon gave way to a T-shirt and jeans. Material began to come more from the obstreperous anti-authoritarian in him than his crowd-pleasing urges could keep at bay, and he began pushing language and subject matter past the narrow boundary lines that mainstream Vegas and television had known him to stay eagerly com-fortable within. More and more rebellious onstage, he was fired from a lucrative Vegas contract for breaking the sacrosanct rule against uttering the word "shit" onstage, and he found himself at the crossroads he'd consciously and unconsciously been heading for.

Turning to the "underground" of coffeehouses and college crowds, Carlin began developing a new comic voice before a new audience steeped in political and cultural turmoil and yearning for a subversion of the status quo. With Lenny's example fueling his new artistic journey, Carlin emerged a timely comic voice, now speaking uncensored, un-compromisingly irreverent truth to power along with his long-honed playful insights, silly characters, and childlike glee.

With sharp, biting wit and a clear point of view, Carlin revelled in taboos. His subject matter steadily spread across the spectrum of politics, religion, sex-uality, media, consumerism, corporate control, the hypocrisies of American culture, and all of life—and death—itself. But with new audiences growing and appreciative, and with the timely arrival of cable television to give his new voice widening access, the crowd-pleaser remained satisfied as the trouble-maker thrived.

Lenny's accomplishments proved only a starting point for George Carlin. His characteristic love for language and a focus on its absurdities led to his becoming a First Amendment advocate after a 1972 arrest on, like Lenny before him, obscenity charges. A Pacifica network public radio station broadcast his now classic "Seven Words You Can Never Say on Television" and thrust him to the center of a land-mark Supreme Court free speech case. He was quickly embodying the very ideals that drove him.

Carlin spent the next four decades exploring comedy through his own, singular voice, inspir-ing generations of comedians to follow and never slowing down enough for anyone to catch up. He continued not only being creative but also *relevant*. At seventy-one he was still being enthusiastically discovered by fifteen- and sixteen-year-olds—not as some past-his-prime classic; they were falling in love with what he had just done. I defy you to find an-other seventy-year-old comedian with people in his audience who've been fans for twice as long as the teenagers sitting next to them have been alive, and all of them laughing just as hard.

To talk of Carlin "in his prime" is pointless; his "prime" lasted forty years. His career had phases and passages, but distinctions such as those between the vim and vigor of his youth and the piss and vinegar of his later years are irrelevant: His targets and values never changed, his barbs never dulled, and his passion for his work never diminished. He created enough first-rate stand-up for ten outstanding careers, but never once looked back, and never rehashed or rested upon any of it. He kept raising the creative, artistic, and humanistic bar for himself, and well beyond the reach of others.

Crafting fresh, bold, challenging, and fearless work until the day he died, he left new fans the Sisyphean task of exploring a daunting oeuvre created with a prolificness never before seen in the art of stand-up. With a stunning clarity of purpose, his brilliant talents, resolute work ethic, and unwavering honesty resulted in a body of work and a cultural impact that profoundly and permanently altered the comedy landscape.

Right up through his last performance, to see George Carlin work was to see an artist still discovering, still growing, still digging deeper into his and our psyches, still delighted with language, and still refusing to stop bothering. His legacy will long remain a paragon of innovation, artistry, creativity, craftsmanship, irreverence, reason, truth, and above all, laughter.

Here, from what sadly turned out to be his last videotaped interview before "he upped and fuckin' died," he unabashedly reveals some of the paradoxes and passions that are George Carlin.

GEORGE CARLIN: When you're born in the world, you're given a ticket to the freak show. When you're born in America, it's a front-row seat. And some of us in the front row, like me

and you, Paul, bring our notebooks. We make notes about the freak show and report it to others. That's the role I found myself in, and I really don't care about any "issues."

When I'm one-on-one with someone, I'm empathetic and sympathetic; if you need help and I can, I will. I'll help a *person*, but I will not help a group of people a hundred or ten thousand miles away. Fuck them. I don't see them, I don't feel them, they're not part of me.

I'm here with you, part of you, we're us, here together for the moment, and my empathy opens. You, I feel. I have a brother, a daughter, a wife—they're close to me. But you start to talk about people somewhere down in Ridgefield, Something? I don't give a fuck. I really don't.

PAUL PROVENZA: Do you not care about human suffering in Darfur?

GEORGE CARLIN: Intellectually, I care. Intellectually, I see the problem.

PAUL PROVENZA: But not emotionally?

GEORGE CARLIN: Nope.

Here's the thing: human beings have made all the wrong choices. They turned everything over to the traders and the high priests a long, long time ago. It's all superstition and materialism. And I understand there's not a whole lot of other ways to run this thing, but that's for other people to worry about. I'm just criticizing what is; I don't have answers or a nice alternative, and I don't pretend to. But we humans were given great gifts: binocular vision, a great big forebrain, walking erect, opposable thumbs, being able to objectify: "That's an object, I'm a subject," being able to make these wonderful distinctions, to think of the word "zero." We've squandered the wonderful gifts we were given in the interests of a superstitious god and mammon.

And America was given great gifts as the first real, working, self-governing democracy— of course it was an Iroquois concept that we stole from the Indians, but it works. But again, we gave ourselves over to superstitious shit: "In God We Trust" on our fucking money? We open Congress with a prayer to an invisible man?

PAUL PROVENZA: And we pledge allegiance to a flag? If we pledge allegiance to anything, it should be the Constitution. Cut out the middleman.

GEORGE CARLIN: Exactly! See, I can't identify with *any* of these systems. If someone says, "Darfur this," "Myanmar that," or "tsunami this," I say, "Yeah, interesting. The numbers keep going up."

That's what I do: I root for big numbers. For nature against man. Because man is part of nature, but he doesn't acknowledge that, he thinks of himself as separate. "I'm going on a nature walk . . . Nature's out in the country, I'm a person." They don't realize they're part of nature, and they deserve whatever they get. Humans deserve whatever the fuck they get, and they usually get what they deserve in the long run. I have no use for them, to tell you the truth. One on one, they're brilliant and bright— I see people, I look in their eyes, and I can see the *universe*. Every human's like a hologram of all the potential we had but will never realize because we made all the wrong choices.

And we're pulled along by it. That's why I swim *against* the tide: I really don't care for the way the tide goes.

By the way, before 9/11, I'd originally planned to call my HBO special scheduled to air that October, "I Kinda Like It When a Lot of People Die." Hadda change that.

PAUL PROVENZA: Do you consider yourself a nihilist?

GEORGE CARLIN: "Nihilist" is definitely an identity, and I shy away from identities.

PAUL PROVENZA: Some might describe your worldview as cynical or dispassionate.

GEORGE CARLIN: If an outsider wants to say that, fine, but I don't think of myself as cynical. To me, "cynical" is when Ford refused to retool gas tanks that were exploding and killing people. It cost more to retool than it did to pay the widows, so they chose to just continue paying widows. *That's* cynicism.

I understand that a person who doesn't believe in a lot is *called* a cynic—but I think of myself as a skeptic and a realist. I look at things and say, "Wait a minute . . . I don't fuckin' buy that." I have a realistic, skeptical viewpoint; if someone thinks it's "cynical," fine. But they say if you scratch a cynic, you'll find a disappointed idealist, and I'd have to cop to that. It's just who I am.

I think it's 'cause you don't wanna be disappointed, so you lower your expectations, that's all. But you find when you look at the world this way there's a great deal to enjoy about it. The spectacle of it all, the way they just march off the edge of the cliff like the rest of the lemmings . . . It's a circus.

I'm in the midst of writing something called "The Great American Cattle Drive," about *people* being led to market—but not to be sold, to do the buying. They're all branded—they've branded *themselves* with "Nike" across their chests, a Gucci hat, all that shit. At least calves struggle when you try to brand them; we brand ourselves *willingly*: "Ooh, a hat that says 'Tennessee's a great vacation place!' I gotta have *that*." It's just pathetic. Pathetic, pathetic, *pathetic*. All the life has been squeezed out of humans by commerce.

PAUL PROVENZA: Is your worldview the result of so many years on this planet, or did it crystallize earlier?

GEORGE CARLIN: It happened a while after I went through my period of change around 1970. From then on I was a bit different, and acknowledged more of myself as being real rather than something I needed to overlook. The realization I'm talking about now happened in the late eighties/early nineties.

My 1992 concert, *Jammin' in New York,* was the first time those values in me really showed, in a piece I called "The Planet Is Fine, the People Are Fucked." I didn't notice it until afterward, when I thought, "Hmmm. This is *different*." In fact, several comedians, names you and I know and most people recognize, went to the trouble of telling me that that particular show was important. No one's ever done that before or since, with any other show I've done.

That show was a life-changer for me. It made me realize I was more of an artist than a performer; that I was performing my *art* rather than just writing stuff and putting it on stage.

PAUL PROVENZA: What clarified that distinction for you?

GEORGE CARLIN: For many years, in interviews, I used to proudly say, "I write my own material," because I knew a lot of comedians didn't, and I was proud of that. It made me feel different. A writer is an artist by definition, because he creates from pure observation and impressions he gets from observation. I realized I was kind of in that special category as well as being a performer.

PAUL PROVENZA: As a comedian, I find something about the way you build a set that is rare: most comedians get a flow going, as if they're chatting with the audience, and it's conversational. But you will craft certain pieces and present them as crafted pieces, like a singer about to do another song. A piece like "Modern Man," for instance.

GEORGE CARLIN: Yeah, I think of it as the way a poet would say, "And now I'd like to read this from my early period . . ." Or I compare it to like being a sculptor, too: "Here's a nice finished piece. Look at this, I worked all summer on this . . ." I like presenting that sort of thing now and then. I never cared much for the rambling sort of "Now we're on the wife, now we're on the kids, now we're on shopping . . ." thing.

And you know what? It's a little bit of an ego thing, too. I never like to sound like anybody else if I can help it. I kinda hate to be part of the pack, even if it's just someone's perception of how I walk or anything, I just like to feel, "Hey, I'm a little bit apart from this." Not better—just a little apart. I've kinda just constructed an act that suits me.

PAUL PROVENZA: While the landscape has certainly changed for language in comedy, there are still people who believe that using profanity or any of those "Seven Words You Can't Say on Television," if you will, somehow says less of a comedian.

GEORGE CARLIN: Yeah, that "You don't need to; you're a funny man, you don't *need* that stuff" thing. Well, my argument is that you don't *need* paprika or oregano or a few other things to make a stew, technically, either—but you make a better stew. If you're inclined to make a stew of that type, "seasoning" helps.

I know from Bill Cosby's work, he clearly feels that way, and I've always felt that by taking that stand and developing a body of work that didn't include it, Cosby can *never* now choose to use that language. I, however, can choose either.

I can do six minutes on *The Tonight Show* with none of that in it—I can use other parts of my tool kit that work for me; I'm good at them, too, and can do that no problem—but I can also be more of my street-corner self elsewhere, with language of the street if I want to do that, too.

Why should I deprive myself of a small but important part of language that my fellow humans have developed? Why not use *all* of what we've developed to communicate with?

Sometimes I overdo it intentionally, because it has an effect of its own. I think there are a lot of sentences where the adjective "fucking"—I guess it's a gerund, isn't it?—sometimes just makes the joke work *better*. And not because they're laughing at the word "fuck" but because including that word may make the language of a sentence more powerful, and it just gets *in there* better. It just gets in that channel you've got open with a harder punch, you know? That's why people use it in life—because it makes something they're trying to say stronger; it gives it a particular effect.

I think the folks who choose to deny that part of our language have limited themselves. And that's fine; that's good. Good choice over there . . . but I'm just fine over here.

PAUL PROVENZA: I'll be using that argument myself, thanks. As far as content, is there any subject that's taboo for you? If not, should there be?

GEORGE CARLIN: I'm a great believer in context. I say you can joke about anything. Baby rape is a very difficult subject to do three or four minutes on, but if you created a context—and that includes not only the context you've created for the jokes but your bigger context, too; your act, the persona they know when they buy a ticket—if all that's in place, you can . . . let's call it "get by" with it. You're still gonna turn off some people, but they'll be right back for the next piece of material. I believe you can joke about *anything*.

PAUL PROVENZA: With thirteen HBO specials, twenty-three albums, five books, and who knows how much else over your career, you're one of the most prolific stand-ups ever to have worked a stage. Is there something systematic to how you create, or any process you can identify?

GEORGE CARLIN: I've identified three wells I've almost always drawn from for material. One is language and purely analytical humor; how we speak to one another, the words and phrases we use. Sometimes they're only analytical, with just a little humor to them, and sometimes they have a lot of jokes in them.

Another is the universal world of everyday experience we all know: driving, what's in the refrigerator, picking that thing off your leg, whatever—things we all know, with the frame of reference already in place and you can just go right into it.

Then there are the "issues," as I call them, for want of a better word. The things that will never change: life, death, cruelty, inhumanity, hatred, love, the abortion issue . . . all those things that have real social and political overtones to them.

I've always drawn from these three things, especially since the changes I went through, and I've always kind of kept a balance of those three overall things without consciously trying to.

PAUL PROVENZA: Do you care about educating or opening people's eyes to make a *difference*?

GEORGE CARLIN: No. Not really at all. This is really a selfish show-off's job. It's the job I had in fifth grade that I didn't get paid for: making fart sounds in class, or twisting my face into some grotesque look to make Heeney laugh during a history test. That's showing off, and I'm a show-off. When people ask me, "Do you

try to make people think?" I say, "That would really be the kiss of death." What I do is try to let people know that *I'm* thinking. I'm showing off.

When you have a pretty good mind but quit school in ninth grade, there's a lifelong feeling that "I've gotta prove that I'm smarter than they would think I am if they knew I quit school in ninth grade." I know I didn't finish school, and I know what they *think* of people who don't finish school. I'll show them that I'm not one of those people; I'll show them I'm as smart as they are. That's what I do this for. I do this for ego gratification, a good income, and it's wonderful that at this point there's practically no city or state I go to where someone isn't gonna say, "Hey aren't you that guy? My sister and I saw you in Milwaukee in 'seventy-one."

I have this kind of extended family, which makes me feel great. Every time someone says something like "My daughter's in college now, she went to see you," I just *love* it. I didn't have much family life, but now I have this really big, extended family.

PAUL PROVENZA: Do you think any comedian can affect anyone's worldview?

GEORGE CARLIN: Yes, because people tell me so. Meeting people in the street, at the airport, restaurants, hotel lobbies . . . people say—and I've been in this long enough that there've been a *lot* of them, "You really changed my point of view about things," or, "Boy, you turned me around with what you did on the show."

Lots of variations of that, from people of

all ages. Kids have said, "My father and I were at odds until we laughed at one of your HBO shows together. It started us talking more . . ."

Parents say, "My kid saw that show, et cetera . . . and his grades in school got better." If not "changed my life," though some people *have* said that, a lot of people say, at least, "changed my point of view" on some thing or things. I swear I hear this kind of shit from so many people *all* the time—and even if you eliminate half of them to offset exaggeration and bullshit, there's still half left. And there's that old rule of thumb that one fan letter represents a thousand people that didn't bother to write, so I figure for everyone who's said something like that there were a lot of other people who feel the same.

And that has given me such *power*—not power to *use,* but power to *have.* It's given me such a feeling of "Yeah, man! I'm okay. I'm fuckin' *okay.*"

PAUL PROVENZA: But you wouldn't care if no one ever said those things to you?

GEORGE CARLIN: Nope. See, that's the nice thing I learned with my change in attitude: if you follow your heart, if you do the right thing for you, if you listen to what's on your mind and in your heart and in your brain . . . good things will happen from it. Good things *will* come.

By changing who I was, and following my heart instead, I suddenly had a record contract, HBO specials, and just spiraled upward. By doing just what pleased *me* in my shows, I've had an effect on some people—the kind of effect I can't have on the people in Darfur. If I send money or all my old sweaters to Darfur, I will not have the effect on them that I may have on one person sitting and listening to something when he's twelve years old.

All I do this for is for *me.* The fact that it involves other people is great. That it amuses them and gives me an income is great. But I do this just to have a chance to *sing my song.*

Sometimes I will self-consciously use notes in a performance and I'll come right out and tell the audience, "I'm using these notes now, but I want you to know I'm not 'trying' this on you. I don't 'try' things; I figure them out and then do them. But I'm *learning* this one, okay?" Because the audience doesn't really figure in my equation.

The way I put it is, "*You're* here for me, *I'm* here for me, and no one's here for *you.*" And they *love* that! They just eat that up; it's a big laugh. And then I go ahead and do it for *me.*

I *always* do it for *me.*

ACKNOWLEDGMENTS

The authors would like to gratefully acknowledge the following:

All the comedians, performers, and writers who sat for portraits and/or gave interviews.

The people who had interviews and/or photos cut for unavoidable reasons regarding space, design, and the impossibility of a seven-hundred-page full-color book: Maria Bamford, Drew Carey, Troy Conrad, Tom Dreesen, Merle Kessler, Tim Minchin, Taylor Negron, John Oliver, the *Onion* editorial staff, Tim Reid, Mo Rocca, Sherrod Small, Paul F. Tompkins, Damon Wayans, Fred Willard, and Andy Zaltzman.

The managers, agents, publicists and assistants who helped hook a lot of it up: Glenn Alai, Geoff Barnett, Dave Becky, Michael Berkowitz, Wendy Blair, J.P. Buck, Cindy Carrasquilla, George Chen, Janice Frey, Traci Gilland, David Himelfarb, Lori Kaplan, Cathy Kerr, Marc Leipis, Mark Loewinger, T.J. Markwalter, Tina O'Rourke, Helga Pollock, Eve Sadof, Estee Seward, Helene Shaw, Bruce Smith, Ed Smith, Marcy Smothers, Rebecca Erwin Spencer, David Steinberg (MBST Management), Heather Taekman, Melanie Truhett, Christie Ward, and Krista Williams.

Industry bigs for throwing their weight behind us: Estee Adorim and Ava Harel of The Comedy Cellar, Louis Faranda and Caroline Hirsch of the NY Comedy Festival and Caroline's on Broadway, Bruce Hills and Jodi Lieberman of Just for Laughs, Karen Koren of the Gilded Balloon in Edinburgh, Jamie Masada of The Laugh Factory, Reeta Piazza of the Hollywood Improv, Mareen Taran, and Lou Wallach.

The staffs of these clubs for throwing their doors (and taps) open for us: Cobb's Comedy Club, The Fillmore, Gotham Comedy Club, The Purple Onion, SF Punch Line, Upright Citizens Brigade Theater, and The Warfield.

Other locations that generously obliged us: Amante and O'Reilly's in North Beach, Karma Hookah Lounge in NYC, The New York Cook Shop, and The Lakeshore Theater in Chicago.

All the transcribers who had no idea what the hell they were getting themselves into: Jonathan Brown, Keith Buzzard, Matthew Dominick, Jesse Irwin, Richard Lang, Meredith Merchant, Nicole Millikien, Marc Morgan, Carrie Shemanski, Elke Sniderman, and Meagan Stewart.

Contributors in myriad ways: Rohan Acharya (ITV-London), Tiffany Almudarris, Len Austrevich, Tracey Baird, Rocky Benloulou-Dubin, Doug Berman ("Wait, Wait . . . Don't Tell Me!"/NPR), Jack Boulware (Litquake), Neil Campbell, Wyatt Cenac, Jeremy Cesarec, Will Davis, Jessica Delfino, Nick Doody, Jordan Ellner, Emery Emery, Varsh Farazdel, Hank Gallo, Paul Gilmartin, Hannah Gordon, Jackie Green, Matt Greenberg, Cash Hartzell, Matt Harvey (Phil McIntyre Entertainment), Penn Jillette, William Keeler, Matt Kirshen, Kambri Krews, Lance Midkiff, Troy Miller, Dan Pasternack, Mary Pelloni, Tristan Prescott, Chris Ritter, Abbey Robertson, Vanessa Schneider, Jennifer Schulkind, Nell Scovell, Sarah Silverman, Pasquale Tropea (Cineprise-Montreal), Tona Williams, and Bret Witter.

Additional thanks from Dan: Rick Bates, Judi Brown-Marmel, Francy Caprino, Seth Cohen, Jim Cornett, David Fahey, the Forrester family, Budd Friedman, Robert Hartmann, Tony Liano, Don Lokke, Harrah Lord, David Owen, Morgan Pitman, Joel Selvin, George Shapiro, Ollie Simon, Frank Weimann, and Kurt Weitzmann. Immense gratitude to and admiration of photographers Jonathan Becker, Mike Carano, Susan Felter, Laura Hannifin, Steve Jennings, Pat Johnson, Jim Karageorge, Michael Kohl, Michael Light, Jock McDonald, Kandace Millhouse, Anthony Pidgeon, Michael Rauner, Michael Read, Bill Reitzel, Martha Jane Stanton, and the Swartz family. Special thanks to Tim Bedore and Alex Bennett from KQAK, Will and Debi Durst, JoAnn Grigioni, Martin Higgins, Jeremy Kramer, Tom Sawyer, and Molly Schminke. Two in the comedy industry giving unlimited support—Chris Mazzilli and Geof Wills. Two in photography who lifted me up—Dan Oshima and Jim Marshall. Much love for the Dion family, Parker and Roman, and mad love for my wife, Lisa.

¡Satiristas! was especially supported through the tireless efforts of Tanner Colby, Mauro DiPreta, Dave Rath, Barbara Romen, Alice Sinclair, and Kara Welker. Peter McGuigan and Foundry Media made sure it happened.